Liberal Child Welfare Policy and its Destruction of Black Lives

How can we end the inter-generational cycle of poverty and dysfunction in the US's urban ghettos?

This ground-breaking and controversial book is the first to provide a child-centered perspective on the subject by combining a wealth of social science information with sophisticated normative analysis to support novel reforms—to child protection law and practice, family law, and zoning—that would quickly end that cycle.

The rub is that the reforms needed would entail further suffering and loss of liberty for adults in these communities, and liberal advocacy organizations and academics are so adult-centered in their sympathies and thinking that they reflexively oppose any such measures. Liberals have instead promoted one ineffectual parent-focused program after another, in an ideologically-driven quest for the magic pill that can save both adults and children in these communities at the same time.

This 'insider critique' of liberal child welfare policy reveals a dilemma that liberals have yet to face squarely: there is an ineradicable conflict of interests between many young children and their parents, especially in areas of concentrated poverty, and one must choose sides.

It is a must read for legal academics, political scientists, urban policy experts, as well as professionals working in social work, law, education, urban planning, legislative offices, and administrative agencies.

James G. Dwyer is the Arthur B. Hanson Professor of Law at William & Mary School of Law, USA, where he teaches Youth Law, Family Law, and Law & Social Justice. He has previously served as Guardian ad Litem for children in the Albany, NY area; on the Virginia Governor's Task Force on Expediting Adoptions; and on the Virginia Bar Association Family Law Legislation Committee. He authored the book *The Relationship Rights of Children*, as well as books on regulation and financing of schools and on children's moral status, in addition to dozens of articles on child welfare law.

Liberal Child Welfare Policy and its Destruction of Black Lives

James G. Dwyer

Routledge
Taylor & Francis Group

LONDON AND NEW YORK

First published 2018
by Routledge
2 Park Square, Milton Park, Abingdon, Oxon OX14 4RN

and by Routledge
711 Third Avenue, New York, NY 10017

Routledge is an imprint of the Taylor & Francis Group, an informa business

British Library Cataloguing-in-Publication Data
A catalogue record for this book is available from the British Library

Library of Congress Cataloging-in-Publication Data
Names: Dwyer, James G., 1961– author.
Title: Liberal child welfare policy and its destruction of black lives / James G. Dwyer.
Description: Abingdon, Oxon ; New York, NY : Routledge, 2018. | Includes bibliographical references and index.
Identifiers: LCCN 2018003148 | ISBN 9780815363262 (hardback : alk. paper) | ISBN 9780815363279 (pbk. : alk. paper) | ISBN 9781351109994 (ebook : alk. paper)
Subjects: LCSH: Poor African Americans–Social conditions. | African American children–Social conditions. | African American families–Social conditions. | Child welfare–United states. | Children–Legal status, laws, etc.– United States.
Classification: LCC E185.86 .D899 2018 | DDC 305.5/6908996073–dc23
LC record available at https://lccn.loc.gov/2018003148

ISBN: 978-0-8153-6326-2 (hbk)
ISBN: 978-0-8153-6327-9 (pbk)
ISBN: 978-1-351-10999-4 (ebk)

Typeset in Bembo
by Wearset Ltd, Boldon, Tyne and Wear

Katya, thank you

Contents

Acknowledgments

Elizabeth Bartholet has for many years given me inspiration, insight, encouragement, and opportunities for interactions with experts in other disciplines. Her own work in the child welfare field—as scholar, teacher, organizer, and advocate for children—has been uniquely and profoundly important. I add my name to an endless list of those in her debt. I have also learned much from the people to whom she introduced me: Richard Barth, Jill Duerr Berrick, Richard Gelles, Daniel Heimpel, Emily Putnam-Hornstein, Cassie Statuto Bevan, and Frank E. Vandervort. I greatly appreciate others who graciously traveled to Williamsburg to discuss these issues: Karen Czapanskiy, Nancy E. Dowd, David D. Meyer, Jane Murphy, Eric Reynolds, David Stoesz, John Stogner, Bruce Thyer, Betty Wade Coyle, W. Bradford Wilcox, Robin Fretwell Wilson, and Jo Ann Wilson-Harfst. Thanks also to my former mentor Michael Wald for his challenging feedback, and to my former students Briordy Meyers, Julie Silverbrook, and Kerrin Wolf for letting me bounce ideas off them.

Joseph J. Plumeri II is a rare friend to William & Mary, not only generously supporting his alma mater as an institution but also reaching out directly to the College's faculty, to let them know they are valued, as mentors to today's students and as scholars. I have been fortunate to receive three times the Plumeri Award for Faculty Excellence, which provided both financial and moral support for the extensive research and writing—and rewriting—which this book required. The research enlisted innumerable William & Mary students, as research assistants and/or students in my classes, law students and undergraduates. They enlightened and challenged me, and I was able to give them a vehicle for pursuing their passion for child advocacy. Passionate pursuit of greater understanding of our world, undertaken together by professors and students, continues at William & Mary with Joe's support. On behalf of all the William & Mary faculty, I thank him.

Certain student assistants stand out for the extensive and high-quality work they did for this book. I will be ever grateful to Siyu Gui, Claire Hunter, Aliye Kidwell, Lily Saffer, Katie Sheldon, and Abby Snider. You built the foundation for this project.

Introduction

Hopes for true racial equality and inter-racial harmony rose high with the election of a black President in 2008. They faded quickly. In his book *The End of Anger: A New Generation's Take on Race and Rage*, soon after Barack Obama's election, journalist Ellis Cose reported strong support among members of the black middle and upper classes for the view that American society had become a place of equal opportunity for all. But as Obama's second term drew to a close, after a rash of police shootings of black men and the retaliatory killing of five Dallas police officers, the *New York Times* reported that seven in ten Americans believed race relations were generally bad and six in ten said things were getting worse.[1] Underlying the protests over shootings by police was an intense frustration that everyday life had not improved as expected; said one black small-business owner in Milwaukee: "We went to the beach. And then eight years happened."[2] Many African-Americans now view their situation as dire, believing "black citizens … are experiencing a defining moment of racial terror in the United States in the twenty-first century."[3] The Trump election seemed to confirm the worst, and ensuing events cemented a fatalistic outlook.

Indeed, many facts about everyday life for black Americans today belie the optimism of the early Obama years.[4] Not just episodic police violence against black individuals, and not just violent rampages by racist organizations, but also the persistence of gross economic disparity across races, intensified residential and educational segregation, and rampant crime among residents of black communities themselves, fuel the anger and despair.[5] Both the violence and the despair are worst in urban areas of concentrated poverty overwhelmingly populated by black Americans, areas that saw little or no improvement during Obama's eight years in office and are likely to see intensified misery in coming years, as any gains are rolled back and anti-poverty programs are defunded at federal and state levels.[6]

Black Americans span the socio-economic range, of course, and how they fare under conservative economic and social-control policies differs to some degree based on current social position. In addition to those stuck in deep and entrenched poverty, there are affluent professionals, businesspersons, and performers; a substantial black middle class; and millions of strong working-class African-American families in which parents provide care and order in children's lives and instill in them good work habits and values, self-esteem, and ambition. For most black children, their neighborhoods are safe and their community cohesive. Most attend adequate, if not the best, schools. The greatest number, in working-class families, might not enjoy all the preparation, resources, and opportunities wealthy white families have, but most have sufficient health, safety, care, supervision, stimulation, instruction, and motivation to lead good and happy lives. If early difficulties hamper their achievement somewhat, they are likely to find college admissions officers eager to welcome them.

For wealthy, middle-class, and working-class black Americans, we might say there is at least formal equality of rights and opportunities and significant public and private efforts to ensure substantive equality, as well as special benefits we might collect under the heading of affirmative action. Liberals can plausibly claim the lion's share of credit for any gains made in opportunity for American blacks in the past half century.[7] There is, however, a large group of black Americans for whom formal equality of opportunity and efforts made at substantive equality are unavailing. These are people born into barely-functioning or dysfunctional families in areas of concentrated poverty. The police shootings created a rare occasion when their life circumstances were on display to the rest of the nation.[8] Their homes are characterized not only by very low income but also by more serious deprivations resulting from their parents' absence or struggles with substance abuse, mental illness or disability, violence, criminal records, family members' incarceration, and unemployment. Many are born with some brain damage from maternal substance abuse, and many incur damage from abuse or neglect in the crucial first years of life. Their neighborhoods are plagued by routine outbreaks of violence—a "constant crackle of gunfire"—and resulting deaths, sirens waking children in the night;[9] addicts and other adults who engage in erratic and predatory behavior; forces pulling them toward the illegal drug trade; lack of positive role models and lawful work opportunities, decrepit and toxic housing; and schools populated by unqualified, burnt-out teachers and students unprepared to learn. This is the population stuck in what some call "the inter-generational cycle of dysfunction" and others refer to as the "cradle-to-prison pipeline."

A great deal has been written about this phenomenon from a macro perspective. The macro-level diagnoses explain how economic policies and trends, governmental and private discrimination in many important areas of life, and mass incarceration have increased poverty among blacks, concentrated them in unhealthy urban areas, and produced high-rates of personal dysfunctions among them. The many macro-level solutions on offer propose legal and structural reforms and major new public investments aimed at improving statistics for urban blacks on measures of substance abuse, mental illness, incarceration, school dropout, uninhabitable buildings, teen pregnancy, and the like. A recent book on the pathologies afflicting urban housing projects is representative, extolling

> the need for a meaningful investment in the kinds of wrap-around supports that can help stabilize families and communities and help children to achieve their full potential … [T]here are no simple solutions and none that are inexpensive, but without a large and sustained investment effort on the part of the federal government in concert with local partners, we risk trapping yet another generation of children in deep poverty.[10]

Peter Edelman recommends, even less realistically, a full social-transformation package: change attitudes, reduce the number of guns, raise wages, facilitate unionizing, transfer enormous amounts of public money to programs of subsidized health care, housing, child care, preschool, and college, eliminate racism, reform prisons, and elect people who care.[11]

This book focuses on the micro story that nearly all observers and reformers miss, yet that best explains the intractability of deep poverty and dysfunction in urban black communities and best illuminates what is actually needed today to stop it. It directs attention to how individual children born into these communities are irremediably damaged in the first few years of life and, as a more or less inevitable consequence, become dysfunctional adolescents and adults whom we cannot fix no matter how much we spend, and who in turn damage the next generation. And it shows that this happens now because of laws and policies that liberals promote and defend.

The book's solutions rest not on an over-arching social-welfare policy or theory of racial justice, but rather on an account of the rights of individual children born to people who live in these communities—rights that 'we the people' routinely violate through our agent, the state, in its application of core family-law rules governing parentage, parental power, and reaction to child maltreatment. This perspective, focusing on the role played by state laws governing children's lives, promoted and defended by liberals, in destroying black lives, has been missing from the scholarship and public debate over inner-city poverty and the attendant inter-generational cycle of dysfunction.

The path of destruction

Judges, lawyers, and social workers who have worked in urban family courts for many years are all too familiar with the micro story. They have seen the inter-generational cycle play out over and over first hand, overwhelmingly in families of minority race. Children are born, often with special needs stemming from in utero exposure to illegal drugs, alcohol, or tobacco, to parents whose struggle with addiction, disease, criminal involvement, domestic violence, and/or the stress of living in an unsafe neighborhood undermines their ability to care for their children. As a result, the children suffer neglect in the form of malnutrition, emotional deprivation, and lack of protection from harm by persons other than their caretaker. Some suffer abuse at the hands of their caretaker or other household member, in the form of shakings, beatings, witnessing violence, and sexual victimization. This is when African-Americans who will later struggle to function adequately and lawfully typically make their first appearance in court, when they are children who have incurred abuse, neglect, or abandonment and the local Child Protection Services agency (hereafter CPS) must bring maltreatment proceedings against their parents or other adult household members. These children suffer lasting physical, developmental, neurological, and psychological harm.[12] A high percentage have problems with "attachment," a crucial developmental need and, as a result, have difficulty trusting anyone or viewing the world as a safe and positive place. Many end up in the foster care system or kin care, in the custody of persons not committed to caring for them permanently, and too often a succession of such persons, as one stranger or relative after another tires of trying to care for them.

Most children in black ghettos start school without the early preparation they should have had, preparation that only parents in a healthy environment—not any government program[13]—can provide, and the chaos and dangers of their home and neighborhood weigh on their minds and bodies, interfering with their concentration in the classroom and causing illnesses that keep them out of the classroom. All around them in school are other children suffering from "toxic stress" as a result of similar deprivations and traumas. They know of neighborhood friends or family members killed by gun fire, as participants or bystanders, and live with the persistent anxiety of wondering whether they will be next. They know others who have died of drug addiction, partner violence, or AIDS. They have seen parents, siblings, or other relatives taken away by police. This knowledge and awareness generate deep and debilitating anxiety and undermine hope. Moreover, they absorb, beginning when they first comprehend language and human attitudes and emotions, "an oppositional culture that devalues work, schooling, and marriage and that stresses attitudes and behaviors that are antithetical and often hostile to success in the larger economy."[14]

Few good teachers want to work in their blighted neighborhoods or deal with such high-need, unprepared, unmotivated students, so their school experience does little to restore hope or help them escape this environment.[15] For many, the emotional damage of early childhood abuse or neglect or simply the stress of living in a threatening environment—what Ta-Nehisi Coates calls "the killing fields of Chicago, of Baltimore, of Detroit," and of other American cities[16]—is manifest in acting out, or in hair-trigger self-defensive reactions to others' behavior. Then they might make their second appearance in court if the schools, in this era of "zero tolerance," initiate Child in Need of Services proceedings. They might also or instead be suspended or shunted off to "alternative education," a well-worn pathway to delinquency and substance abuse.[17] Many inner-city youths, because they do poorly in school, find more gratification in hanging out with peers and begin regularly to skip school. Or they stay home instead of going to school because they are pressed into a parental role themselves in relation to younger siblings, or into a breadwinner role in the underground economy. Still many others stay away from home for days at a time, their whereabouts unknown to parents, because their own home is a site of conflict or danger. Those children are likely to return to court as subjects of a Child in Need of Supervision proceeding.

When they reach early adolescence, girls lacking self-esteem or hope for anything else in life get pregnant while still children themselves, giving them another reason to end their schooling prematurely. Many are pressed into sex work or the drug trade by family members, boyfriends, or pimps who take them in when they run away.[18] Boys come to believe their only chance for what is viewed as success in their community— or even for survival—is to join a gang, sell drugs, or otherwise engage in criminal activity that will bring them money and esteem among their peers but also, inevitably, either a prison sentence or an early death. Boys and girls hurting from the emotional deprivations they have suffered throughout childhood see drugs and alcohol as an escape. Soon, a large percentage of youth who were once children in the child protection system are in the juvenile delinquency system, or on the other side of the child protective system as immature parents, or simply gone. Judges and CPS workers might feel sympathy for damaged youths in the system, having watched them "grow up" in it, but there is little they can do to help, having a responsibility to try to protect the community and the next generation of children. Social service providers and detention facilities have little success at this point in trying to change the course of these young people's lives, and instead the problems escalate. Juvenile detention facilities themselves watch youths "grow up," because many return repeatedly after a first commitment as early as age seven, and a substantial portion of inner-city black youth spend a substantial portion of their teen years behind bars.

By adulthood, a great number of African-Americans shaped by a childhood in dysfunctional families and dysfunctional neighborhoods (i.e., those characterized by concentrated poverty, low social cohesion, inadequate resources, bad schools, and pervasive disorder, violence, substance abuse, unemployment, and housing instability) are already involved in substance abuse and serious crimes or suffering from debilitating mental illness. If not yet, they are likely soon to fall into dysfunction because of "the terrible plight faced by uneducated, unskilled, unemployed, impoverished, traumatized blacks consigned to dangerous, isolated, neglected areas like Ferguson and West Baltimore."[19] A shockingly high proportion of inner-city black adult males end up incarcerated, many for life after doing what they had to in a 'kill or be killed' climate, most for one or more shorter stints.[20] Many inner-city black females end up substance-abusing. And they have children, at a high rate, in a chaotic regime of constantly changing relationship configurations that is bewildering for children.[21] Thus, the cycle repeats and expands. Another generation is trapped in an environment hostile to positive human development, very likely to follow the same life course as their parents.

The people caught in this inter-generational cycle constitute the Black America liberals have been unable substantially to help. In important ways, the situation for Blacks in poverty is worse than it was a half century ago—in particular, because the poorest communities today lack cohesion and are rife with violence and drugs. We liberals have great concern for this population. (I do not mean to suggest here or elsewhere that non-liberals lack this concern; it is just that this book's focus is on how liberals respond to this population's predicament.) Liberal scholars and policy makers are constantly trying to find new ways to help this population rise out of poverty and achieve health, and constantly urging government to spend more money on anti-poverty and early-intervention programs. So how could liberals bear any responsibility for the fate that children born in these communities face? And why the focus on race, given that this is just a subset of the black population in the United States and that there are also many white children born into poverty and dysfunctional families?

Mine is not one of the familiar criticisms of liberal social welfare policies—that they foster dependency, a victim mindset, harmful stigmatization, and white resentment.[22] Those criticisms focus on the experience and behavior of adults, and their validity is simply not my concern. Mine is, rather, that liberals are focusing their efforts and ideas too much (exclusively, in the case of most liberals) on adults, and that they are irrationally attached to false beliefs that (a) most deeply-damaged parents can be fixed and successfully raise the next generation, if we could just find the right "intervention," the magic pill to cure them, and (b) if they keep insisting, America will devote vastly greater public funds to trying to fix dysfunctional people and communities. They are so sympathetic toward adults, so "adult-centric," that they refuse to accept the hard-nosed, child-focused, reality-based legal measures necessary to stop the cycle, because those measures would entail greater suffering and restrictions on the liberty of many current adults who are poor, and therefore disproportionately of minority race.

What I have discovered in a quarter-century of studying child welfare law, policy, and practice, is this pattern: Across a range of legal and policy issues to which the poverty-related inter-generational cycle gives rise, the vast majority of liberal academics, advocacy organizations, child welfare professionals, and politicians implicitly gives categorical priority to protecting dysfunctional adults from losing "their children" and from incursions on their "autonomy," and to protecting dysfunctional communities against further erosion, at the (unintended, but nevertheless real) cost of children's life prospects. And their underlying motivation emanates as much from ideology as from empathy.

Introducing the Liberati

In his book, *Quixote's Ghost*, David Stoesz coins the term 'Liberati' to signify post-modernist liberals in the social work profession obsessed with perceived 'neo–colonial exploitation,' 'cultural imperialism,' and machinations of the 'prison–industrial complex.' They are hyper-sensitive to any policy measures they can construe as privileged whites' attempting further to exploit, suppress, or regulate the lives of persons who are poor and of minority race. Their social policy proposals and criticisms arise from this knee-jerk ideology rather than scientific evidence.[23] Nothing makes the Liberati's knee jerk more quickly than policies aimed at protecting children from dysfunctional adults, because those policies disparately impact the poor and, therefore, historically-subordinated minority-race groups. The Liberati immediately insert every such policy into an historical narrative about a monolithic white oppressor, the telling of which is intended to paralyze faint-hearted advocates for children ("First THEY enslaved, then THEY segregated and lynched, then THEY incarcerated, and now THEY are trying to take away black people's babies..."). [24] Never mind that you are trying to spare black children from being killed, this is nothing short of GENOCIDE! [25] A combination of anti-colonialist ideology, adult-centeredness, and denigration of children produces a tendency on the Left to view children as an ethnic group's "resource." Faculty in most schools of social work, says Stoesz, impress this ideology on students, who then go on to staff the child welfare system.[26] My experience is consistent with this diagnosis; child protection agency directors and line workers are, ironically, some of the staunchest defenders of parents' rights and community "autonomy"—regardless of the cost for children—I have ever encountered.

The Liberati are, however, not confined to the social work profession. Liberals who approach child welfare issues in a poverty context from within an adult-centered anti-subordination ideology also dominate the social sciences, the fields of family law and child law in the legal academy, and advocacy organizations lobbying for the poor and historically-subordinated groups.[27] In law journals, one finds countless articles demanding greater protection of the parental interests of mothers who are incarcerated, mentally ill, incapacitated by domestic violence, or drug addicted, and to a lesser extent the parental rights of criminally-involved fathers, while paying no serious or objective attention to the scientific literature on children's developmental needs or the normative literature on children's rights. The authors' adult-centric outlook is evident, for example, from their uniform failure to acknowledge and address relevant differences among children based on age and nature of existing relationships. Indeed, they manifest no interest in developing a more nuanced understanding even of parental interests, one that might take into account the tendency of parents after-the-fact to regret having mal-treated or killed their children. Because benevolent paternalism toward dysfunctional (and sometimes arguably non-autonomous) parents could never have a place in their ideological narrative of oppression, even the voices of those they purport to care about cannot shake their policy convictions.[28] Efforts to reduce the number of substance-abusing women who conceive children amount to "killing the black body."[29] Testing newborns for drug exposure, even when its only purpose is to identify special medical needs and prevent future maltreatment, is "a witch hunt" and "criminalizing pregnancy."[30] Separating a child from abusive parents equals "violence on families."[31] Transferring custody of a child from a mother to any other caregiver—even the child's father or grandmother—because the child has repeatedly witnessed the mother being beaten by men other than the child's father, is "punishing the victim."[32] Urging a policy focus on relocating people out of urban ghettos, say liberals who don't live in them, is offensively stigmatizing; it must rest on "caricatures of black social disorganization and family pathology,"[33] because the "downward gaze" could not possibly accurately perceive any part of the reality in the ghetto.[34] Across numerous child-welfare policy contexts and many academic departments, there is, if I were to express it in Liberati-speak, a concerted attempt at 'erasure of the black child as subject and subjectivity,' because acknowledging harm to black children from black adults might 'disrupt narratives' and lead to 'blaming the victim.'

In politics, the poverty-law lobby is the first to oppose the most effective measures for sparing today's newborn children from ending up in poverty or prison—for example, use of predictive tools to identify and assess high-risk parents and on that basis intervene *before* they abuse or neglect a newborn, or use of "fast-track" termination-of-parental-rights (TPR) rules with regards to parents with horrible records of abusing other children, so their newborn children can have permanency before the critical attachment stage of development begins. This is because the "client" they have in mind is the poor adult who might under such measures lose custody of a child or some freedom of choice (e.g., as to where and with whom they live) or some supposed dignitary harm. They complain that such measures would invade privacy and disproportionately burden and stigmatize people who are poor and of minority-race (overlooking that the proposals would disproportionately *benefit* poor and minority-race children, out of respect for their equal human worth). They obfuscate—for example, by pointing to the large foster-care population and asserting there is no one to adopt children following proactive, fast-track TPRs, when the plain reality is that unsatisfied "demand" for adoption of newborns and infants (as opposed to the older children in foster care who are available for adoption only after years of adversity) is enormous—according to one recent estimate, by a ratio of 36 applicant-couples to every 1 available baby.[35]

Liberals have also resisted efforts to facilitate adoption of children across races, ethnicities, and national boundaries, because their primary concern is the impact on 'subordinated groups' (i.e., adults in non-white communities or nations who don't themselves want to adopt the children but who might feel "denigrated" by the implication that they cannot 'take care of their own') rather than the life prospects of individual children, or because they do not like the "optics" of relatively affluent white people taking children from poor non-white people and developing countries ("NEO-COLONIAL EXPLOITATION!").[36] Research demonstrating positive outcomes for adopted children—the more positive the earlier the adoption—makes no dent in their ironclad views.[37] I delve, in the chapters that follow, into these and other child welfare legal measures, and into the flawed but politically-successful arguments liberals make to oppose them. In doing so, I will use the more muted term "adult-centered liberals" ("ACLs" for short), rather than the sinister-sounding "Liberati," to refer to those who predominate in the academic departments, government agencies, and advocacy organizations that have shaped child welfare policy. But there is more to the mindset I will challenge than just being adult-centered; I believe Stoesz accurately characterized the ideological dimension of the Left's resistance to stronger child protection measures, the disregard for or misuse of social science, and the tendency to post-modernist "argument by depiction" or "denunciation by labeling."[38]

Most often, when pressed to acknowledge that there is in fact a conflict of interest between adults and children in many families and communities, and to acknowledge that children themselves must have some rights to protection of their interests, ACLs retreat to what I call "The Better World Fallacy." They insist on their avowed first-best alternative—namely, massive increases in public spending on income support, housing, job training, therapeutic services, inner-city schools, free preschool, etc.—and assert that if child-protection Policy X would be unnecessary in a better world then it is wrong to adopt Policy X in the actual world.[39] Why, they ask, does America not fund top-quality drug and alcohol rehabilitation, instead of removing children from the custody of chronically substance-abusing parents? Why doesn't America eliminate poverty instead of incarcerating so many African-American parents who turn to crime after growing up in impoverished circumstances? The implicit suggestion is that children should bear the cost of life's having been unfair to their parents. In contrast, ACLs would never adopt such a posture in discussing state response to battering of women ('Why doesn't America provide more job training and opportunities and mental health services for these men instead of charging them with assault and restricting their liberty with stay-away orders?').

This liberal refusal to accept any child-welfare reforms that appear to entail increased suffering or loss of liberty for poor and minority-race adults, combined with (a) the pre-vailing and strong opposition in this country to increased wealth transfers, which has only grown in recent years;[40] (b) conservatives' tendency to focus on criminal law reactions to dysfunction rather than prevention; and (c) the reality that our best programs for "rehabilitating" deeply-dysfunctional individuals and communities rarely work and never work quickly enough from a newborn child's standpoint, means that no effective personal or community reformation occurs in time to avoid damage to children. ACLs have a ready list of parent-friendly programs they believe would eliminate dysfunction if only America would fully fund them, but their belief rests on either ignoring the scientific literature on the (in)effectiveness of these programs or grasping at any positive signs in any studies, no matter how poorly constructed their favorite studies are.[41] And so, one generation after another of black children born into areas of concentrated poverty is imprisoned in a world of deprivation, maltreatment, school failure, pervasive danger, unemployment, substance abuse, and hopelessness. They must wait until they are damaged adults before ACLs will put their interests (as ACLs see them) first. The black ghetto is, in large measure, a monument to the Left's post-modern sensitivities.

Not just the ghetto

My assessment of why there is a permanent black underclass thus focuses on the experience of children who enter the world in areas of concentrated poverty. Its central claim is that liberal opposition to doing what is really necessary for children—black children in particular—conceived by people who are damaged and/or living in toxic communities, so that the children do not become damaged themselves, is a large part of the explanation for why the cycle continues.

This book, though, also has something to say about race hierarchy and race relations more broadly. The effects of the toxic environment in which we force a large percentage of black children to grow up are not limited to those children and the adults they will become (if they survive). The cycle of dysfunction in America's worst urban areas continually reinforces the insidious stereotypes of black Americans that adversely impact all of them, regardless of what they accomplish, where they live, or who they know. Sociologist Elijah Anderson writes regarding urban black males:

Living in areas of concentrated ghetto poverty ..., too many young black men are trapped in a horrific cycle that includes active discrimination, unemployment, poverty, crime, prison, and early death. When they act out violently, or are involved in dramatic crimes that make the news, the repercussions for the general image of the young black male can be far-reaching. Strongly identified with violent criminality by skin color alone, the anonymous young black male in public is often viewed first and foremost with fear and suspicion ...[42] People—black as well as white—necessarily avoid him, and through their avoidance behavior teach him that he is an outsider in his own society. His image as bad and potentially dangerous is so powerful that it spreads to anyone who resembles him. This stereotype has implications for black males more generally, even those who are upper- or middle-class in education, achievement, and social standing.[43] ... Every black male is approached as though he has a deficit; he has a hole to climb out of before he can be trusted as an ordinary law-abiding persons. Every newspaper or television story that associates a young black man with a violent crime sends a message to everyone that reinforces the stereotype: the dark-skinned inner-city male who is to be closely watched, feared, not trusted, and employed only as a last resort.[44]

The stereotype is embedded in the minds of blacks as well whites: Consider the oft-quoted statement of Reverend Jesse Jackson: "There is nothing more painful for me at this stage in my life than to walk down the street and hear footsteps and start to think about robbery and then look around and see it's somebody white and feel relieved." A stereotype of the ghetto black woman, though somewhat different, also includes traits (criminality, laziness, dishonesty, animality) that trigger aversion, denigration, and mistreatment, and it likewise taints all black women regardless of their actual character and accomplishments.[45]

Thus, every black American has to worry, when stopped by police, that he or she will be presumed to be a lawless thug or crazed addict and will therefore be at risk of police brutality, because all Americans' view of black Americans is infected with a sinister image of "The Ghetto," the black urban gangster, the crackhead. All the more so as the Department of Justice in the Trump Administration scales back federal civil-rights oversight of local police departments. On Christmas Day 2017, a Chicago woman published an Op-Ed in the *New York Times* entitled "To the Chicago Police, Any Black Kid Is in a Gang," predicting that her well-behaved, studious teenage son would get erroneously entered in the city police's enormous gang database, with all the trouble that can bring, just because he is black.

To walk alone in some white neighborhoods would also put any black person in danger of unprovoked private violence; he is seen as menacing just because of his skin color. The stereotypes also handicap any black person when he or she interviews for a job, applies for a loan or apartment rental, tries to fit in with a mostly-white community or organization, or goes shopping. At the level of social policymaking, underlying the widespread public opposition or indifference to public spending on anti-poverty programs is a mental association of poverty with urban blacks,[46] coupled with what political scientist Juliet Hooker calls "the radical disregard for and antipathy to black life revealed by negative responses to the Black Lives Matter protests."[47] In sum, as Sheryll Cashin expresses it: "Black folks live with a constant awareness of the myriad ways in which race can obstruct, interfere, or in nightmarish, Trayvon-esque scenarios, ruin one's life."[48] Or as Ta-Nehisi Coates writes to his infant son: "You have been cast into a race in which the wind is always at your face and the hounds are always at your heels."[49] If there is any possibility of genuine substantive social equality across races in America, the reality sustaining the sinister image (and the popular entertainment that exploits and intensifies it) must be eliminated.

Liberals need a plan B

But how? As noted above, liberals' answer to that question has consistently been massive wealth redistribution, including greatly-increased public spending on cash assistance, services, and structural reforms they unrealistically hope will transform damaged individuals and dysfunctional neighborhoods. That is their Plan A. Most refuse to accept that this is simply not going to happen and would not work anyway, and that they need a Plan B—even though they have been making the same futile plea for decades. Richard Gelles, Dean of the School of Social Policy and Practice at the University of Pennsylvania, writes:

> I am convinced that we must stop believing that social and economic problems can be solved by creating new residual social policies [i.e., programs reacting to personal dysfunction after it arises or damage to children after it occurs] or piling money onto existing programs that do not work. To this day, when I attend academic conferences and think tank meetings, the bottom line of nearly every report, discussion, or white paper is that the government should spend more money. The calls for more money and more residual programs are naïve. First and last, *there is no more money*.... The obvious second point needs little repeating—*there is no evidence that more money for residual programs will work*.[50]

America has moved steadily away from genuine commitment to anti-poverty programs since Ronald Reagan declared that poverty had won the War on Poverty,[51] scaling back New Deal and Great Society programs for the poor. As Obama expressed it well before becoming President, "white guilt has exhausted itself in America."[52] This recognition seemed to foster a sense of hopelessness in him as well. As President, Obama's proposals for reducing poverty mostly addressed marginal working families, not those mired in deep dysfunction, and he had little success securing funding for any anti-poverty programs.[53] In fact, during his tenure, a Republican Congress substantially reduced funding for important programs, such as food stamps. Most states, too, cut their budgets for programs and institutions serving the poor, including public schools. After Obama's tenure, with conservatives holding both the presidency and a majority in both houses of Congress, the slashing intensified.[54] And it is far from clear that a Hillary Clinton presidency would have altered the trend. Concern for the middle class, not the poor, dominated the Democratic presidential nomination debates in 2016, even as blacks in blighted urban areas, in front of news cameras after police shootings of black men, protested their living conditions as well as racism. During the general presidential election campaign, when a debate moderator put directly to Hillary Clinton the question what she would do about disorder in inner-city neighborhoods, her vapid answer was designed to avoid worrying middle- and upper-income taxpayers: "We will build on the communities' strengths and improve communication with their leaders."[55] Truly progressive economic policies aimed at the worst off today have purchase, at most, in a few heavily liberal localities. There is also little public discussion of desegregation today,[56] even though residential and school segregation constitute a great obstacle to equal opportunity—the primary, core obstacle in the view of the Kerner Commission in 1968 and of many contemporary observers[57]—and have been getting worse rather than better in recent years.[58] As Erwin Chemerinsky noted in 2015: "No president since the 1960s has devoted any attention to decreasing segregation…"[59]

One aspect of Liberals' failing black Americans, therefore, is Liberals living in denial that not nearly enough non-poor Americans care enough about the plight of poor Americans—in particular, poor black Americans—to give up anything significant to improve the latter's situation. If liberal Democrats in Congress or in a state legislature were to put forward a Make Life Fair Act, entailing a great increase in taxes on wealthier families like mine to pay for such an extraordinary investment—that is, to try to raise everyone out of poverty, make the best substance abuse and mental health treatment available to all, ensure opportunity and order everywhere children live, change bad schools to good schools, and so on—I would support it. I believe some other moderately wealthy liberals would as well. We would rather end our lives in a just, harmonious society than in a big house with a high fence around it. But only a small percentage of all Americans would support it. Some commentators have remarked that even most wealthy liberals are not willing to give up much of their own wealth for the sake of social equality.[60] That is why talk of poverty had no purchase in the 2016 presidential election campaigns.

In addition, there is another, less well-known obstacle to stopping the intergenerational cycle in areas of concentrated dysfunction: We simply do not know how to fix deeply-damaged adults, nor how to improve horrible residential spaces other than by moving their occupants out to a different location. Adult-focused policies are not going to end the cycle, no matter how much money we put behind them. But the vast majority of liberals are fixated on the adults, feeling tremendous and understandable sympathy for them; and their living in denial about the poor rates of success with the various programs ostensibly devised to fix deeply-damaged adults, which I will document in later chapters of the book, is the other major aspect of their responsibility for the destruction of black lives.

Because what has to be done to prevent the many children those adults have from becoming deeply damaged as well, the only way to stop the cycle and improve life substantially for black Americans in general, is to focus on the children being born today to the adolescents and adults who are already victims of the cycle, and to make sure, by whatever means necessary, that we do not consign those newborn children to the same childhood experience. They simply must not begin life legally tethered to or in the custody of dysfunctional people living in horrible neighborhoods. That must become the fundamental and overriding aim of child welfare policy, and be seen as every child's right.

This is the truth of the Parable of the River Babies, familiar to many who work in the social work field. There are many variants of the Parable. Here is how I would tell it:

> A villager is working beside a river when she spies a baby floating down it, arms flailing, all but certain to drown or go over the waterfall downstream and be smashed on the rocks below. The villager jumps in the river and struggles against the current to reach the baby so she can pull it out. But then she spies another baby, this one floating lifeless, and another—too many for her to reach. She calls

out for help, and other villagers come running. They jump in also and try to fight the waters propelling the babies toward destruction. But there are too many babies and the current is too strong to save more than a few. As they work they shout out ideas for helping more babies. Some suggest taking all the village's wood and building a structure to divert the river into small streams that will make it easier to catch the babies and give them treatment. Others suggest sending all the village's healers to the base of the waterfall to bandage the babies after they fall onto the rocks. Still others suggest all the village's teachers stand on the banks shouting out instructions on how to swim. But one villager suddenly gets out of the river and begins hastily walking away from the rescue scene. Others cry out "What are you doing? We need everyone here, building the diverters and pulling out, bandaging, or teaching the babies in the raging river!" The departing villager pauses only a moment to shout back: "I am going upstream to stop whoever is throwing the babies in the river!"

We all bear responsibility

A third obstacle to ending the inter-generational cycle in the worst-off black communities is failure to recognize that *we* are throwing the babies in the river. Liberals, along with nearly all other Americans, fail to recognize the role that the state, which is an agent of the people, representing *us*, enacting and enforcing laws that at least a majority of *us* presumably support, plays in forcing children to enter the cycle. Liberals understand and rightly decry the state's undeniable role, historically, in getting the cycle started, in creating a ghetto, in digging the channel for the metaphorical river. But they fail to see that the state is also continually putting new children into the river, by virtue of laws we collectively have created that determine who will be each newborn child's legal parents and what powers those legal parents will have. It is only because the state decides, as to a black child born today of dysfunctional biological parents living in a hellish neighborhood, that those biological parents will be the child's legal parents and will have rights and powers that result in the child's living either in a destructive home and neighborhood environment with the biological parents, or in destructive foster care, that the child becomes a damaged human being. Most liberals do not want to acknowledge that it is the state (us) doing this, because then they would have to consider whether *those* laws are just. And if they considered it, objectively, they might have to concede that they are *not* just, that they are in fact a gross violation of the child's human rights, just as it would be if the state forced *you* to live in such an environment, directly or indirectly (i.e., by giving some other private individual power to make you live there). And if they conceded that, they might have to endorse changes in the law to stop this practice of forcing children to endure the same fate as their biological parents, even though those changes likely would cause further suffering to the biological parents. But their sympathy for and identification with the parents prevents them from even contemplating this possibility.

So this is the problem with liberal child welfare policy in a nutshell: The river exists. Money could not make the river go away, and anyway there is precious little money available for dealing with the river. The village has lost interest. Once the babies are in the river, few can be spared from lifelong damage or death. Those not spared become part of the river, part of the current that pulls along succeeding cohorts of babies thrown into it. This is what is now happening; this is reality. But most liberals are not willing to face this reality and do what is necessary for US to stop throwing babies in the river, even though (or because?) most of the babies are black.

In the chapters to follow, I explain this basic idea in detail. I first describe how the cycle works. Then I lay out the set of policies and legal reforms needed to stop it, taking into account the crucial points made above that: (1) There is no more money. (2) Regardless, we do not know how to fix deeply-dysfunctional adults or communities. (3) *We* are choosing to put newborn black children into life-destroying environments. I also explain why children are entitled to these reforms. Lastly, I explain why the vast majority of liberals nevertheless oppose them. In short, there is a tragic conflict of interests between many newborn children and their parents, in terms of what decisions the state makes about parentage and custody at the children's birth, what power the state confers on parents to determine a child's living environment, and what should be done later when parents abuse, neglect, or abandon children, and liberals do not want to make an explicit choice between them. So they deny that the conflict exists, unconsciously choose to prioritize the interests of adults, and then construct implausible arguments as to why their preferred approach—futilely demanding more money and experimenting with one ineffective and impermanence-prolonging parental-rehabilitation strategy after another—is actually the best that can be done for the children as well.

Conservatives, meanwhile, appear content to let the cycle go on, so long as the dysfunction remains contained in the impoverished communities. But whereas conservatives are generally unreceptive to liberals' pleas for more spending on anti-poverty programs, they might embrace the child-welfare-focused reforms I propose, because conservatives are generally less sympathetic to dysfunctional adults, because my proposals could be enacted without new funding and would produce substantial short- and long-term cost savings, and because I focus attention on young children, to whom no blame can be attached and whose plight most clearly belies conservatives' insistence that equal opportunity already exists.[61]

Specifically, I argue that the state must adopt policies and laws aimed at (1) reducing the rate at which people unable to care for a child nevertheless conceive them, (2) reducing pre-natal exposure to alcohol and drugs, (3) no longer forcing children to be raised by or legally tethered to grossly unfit biological parents, and (4) focusing what little money there is for preventive and rehabilitative services on parents who are marginal (i.e., struggling but capable with help) rather than deeply-dysfunctional, while at the same time giving parents less power to dictate where a child must live. Doing those four things would largely end the cycle, and incidentally reduce public expenditures on residual programs. But merely suggesting these things makes ACLs apoplectic. My hope is that by calling attention to what liberals are doing in the realm of child welfare and why it is wrong and part of the problem, they might become more self-conscious of their adult-protective tendencies and overcome them sufficiently at least to get out of the way, if not fully support these reforms.

Instructions for use

Before proceeding, an unusual number of preliminary cautionary notes is necessary. The subject of race equality in America is complex and sensitive to the extreme. An Introduction cannot address all questions and objections likely to arise nor present every point that is part of the analysis underlying my proposals. One must read the rest of the book to understand properly what I have said thus far and respond to it constructively. I hope thus far to have simply piqued interest and perhaps persuaded you that this book offers a new, nuanced, and non-ideological perspective on one of our greatest and most intractable societal problems. I will, though, add here a few clarifying points.

First, most people living in poverty in the US are white. So why emphasize race rather than just discussing poor people generically? Some of what I write is relevant to poverty's effects more generally, but poverty alone does not create the same kind of danger to children as does concentrated poverty in densely-populated areas, and the people who live in our worst urban environments are predominantly of minority race, and especially black. In addition, growing up in poverty *and being black* undermine a child's prospects in life to a greater degree than does growing up in poverty alone. There are also predominantly white communities marked by an inter-generational cycle of dysfunction, but these are mostly rural or small-town rather than urban, so the community dynamic is different and calls for a somewhat different analysis.[62] (This is true also of Native American communities, though in many other respects what I say about liberal policies pertains also to children the law labels as Native American.)

Another important reason why I focus on African-Americans is that dysfunctional white communities do not substantially affect the perception of white people that Americans generally have. In other words, there is no spillover effect on white people who do not live in such communities. This appears true of Hispanic poor people as well, even though some of the nation's worst urban environments are predominantly Hispanic. In contrast, as explained above, perceptions of crime-ridden black urban neighborhoods bolster the racial stereotypes and racist dehumanizing that adversely affect all African-Americans.[63] The inter-generational cycle among the worst-off African-Americans harms all African-Americans in innumerable ways, from the merely annoying to the financially harmful to the tragic.[64] It does not follow from this that disrupting the cycle, reducing dramatically the number of black Americans who incur early damage, and thereby eliminating communities of pervasive dysfunction, will eliminate racism. But eradicating the perceived reality undergirding the insidious stereotypes and stigma that make discriminatory treatment all but inevitable today should mitigate racism significantly and go a long way toward creating substantive equality of opportunity for all black Americans.

A final reason why I focus on race is that I believe when liberal or conservative academics and policy makers contemplate policies aimed at protecting children from the effects of concentrated poverty, they mostly have black communities in mind, and their feelings about racial equality influence their positions. The prevailing liberal resistance to more rigorous child-protecting measures often appears to arise from sensitivity to race, which means progress for at-risk white children might also not be possible until we directly address liberals' race-based perceptions. A common refrain in liberal objections to specific proposals I and other child-centered academics and advocates have made in publications and draft legislation is that they would have a disproportionately adverse impact on black families. Many among ACLs explicitly invoke America's ugly history of breaking up slave families and more generally denying black Americans the freedom and opportunities wealthy white people take for granted. And a question I will raise (but not presume to answer) is whether it is easier for white liberals to oppose child-protective measures that would disproportionately benefit black children, because the children are black. In other words, is the broader phenomenon of adult-centeredness in America (the only country in the world not to have ratified the UN

Convention on the Rights of the Child) more pronounced when white people think about minority-race populations than when they think about white people, perhaps because we white adults more readily empathize with any other adults or with white children than we do with non-white children? There might be an "intersectional" phenomenon where two categories of subordination—race and childhood—come together, a phenomenon infecting the thought process of liberals as much as that of most other people. This might explain why ACLs often seem to treat black children as things to be given to black adults to compensate the latter for their suffering, or as a community resource, rather than as persons whom we must respect.

All that being said, readers should not mistake my focus on poor African-American communities as implying parental unfitness and community dysfunction exist only among black Americans. Though the *rate* of poverty and its destructive effects is higher among blacks than among whites, there are a greater *number* of unfit parents in the white population. And, *of course*, the child-protection rules I advocate should apply to all persons regardless of race. Still, the emphasis on race might create an impression of unfairly denigrating black families and communities. Undoubtedly some will accuse me of being racist, or at least indifferent to people who have suffered injustice and a history of race-based subordination.

This charge of indifference (or worse), though, and this sense of unfairness to black people in singling out black communities for this discussion of child welfare policy, *reflect the very adult-centered perspective that is at the root of the problem*, the ultimate obstacle to achieving truly equal opportunity for all black Americans. If you look at the reforms I will describe from an adult-centered view, you will see an attack on poor adults, a population disproportionately of minority race. But I see child welfare issues from a child-centered perspective, and that is what explains my divergence (along with a small number of other liberal scholars) from predominant liberal views on many child welfare issues. I think first and foremost about what children need and are entitled to. I explain in Part II why that is *the* morally appropriate way to think about state decision-making concerning children's family life, and why it is unjustifiable to compromise children's basic welfare in order to mitigate adults' suffering. But even if one cannot accept that position, one should concede that *someone* ought to be advocating exclusively for these children, and that an exclusively child-focused view should have *some* place in policy debates and receive full consideration. This book presents such a view.

From that child-focused view, the reforms I propose should be seen as reflecting special and *positive* concern for people of minority race—namely, black children. When I write, I picture in my mind a newborn black child, entering a world that should be full of care, nurture, devotion, protection, safety, stability, and opportunity, but whom the law says belongs to biological parents who are not in control of their own lives, and perhaps not even physically present, let alone able to provide these things for a baby. I think about the tragedy that likely awaits that baby, because existing legal rules and state practices tie her fate to unfit or absent parents and a toxic social and physical environment. And then I think about the children she will have after she, too, becomes a deeply-damaged adolescent and adult. My aim is to provoke a new way of thinking about how to prevent injustice and subordination from destroying the life of any black child born today. Every real liberal should welcome that.

Second, I do not blame the adults I discuss for their deficiencies and struggles. I see them as victims also, as most liberals do. We caused them to be damaged during their childhood, and we should blame ourselves. A liberal law professor essentially accused me of lying about this, when I presented my ideas to a gathering of students and faculty at her university, smugly insisting I must be imputing blame to adults because of their substance abuse, mental illness, or involvement in crime. This is another symptom of adult-centered thinking; if one's primary focus is on the plight of dysfunctional adults, it is difficult to understand any proposals that would further increase their suffering except as based on a condemnation of them for being the way they are. It is also an instance of a general tendency among ideologues, left and right, to shut down conversations that make them feel uncomfortable by "shooting the messenger," and the form this frequently takes among The Left is to accuse people of "blaming the victim." I do not know how one could ever convince such a person that one does not in fact harbor the imputed thoughts. There will always be people who refuse to listen to anything you have to say if they do not like what they think are your "real thoughts" or your "real motivation" or simply fear the implications. Such is life. But perhaps the Left has learned a lesson from its club-fisted reaction to the Moynihan Report in the late 1960s, a reaction that "shut down public discussion of the family for a generation" and thereby contributed to a steady worsening during the post-industrial era of the conditions in which too many African American children have been forced to grow up. [65] As William Julius Wilson has observed, "Moynihan's predictions about the fragmentation of the African American family and its connection to inner-city poverty were largely borne out," but for decades the Left shouted down anyone who tried to talk about or research this connection and develop a policy response based on it, charging them with racism, because such talk was stigmatizing and inconsonant with the new ideology of racial pride.[66]

I am optimistic that enough people can be convinced to try on child-centered lenses and give serious consideration to the reforms truly needed to give as many children as possible what they deserve—a real chance for a happy and fulfilling life. When I look through those lenses, blameworthiness of parents or other adults in poor communities is utterly irrelevant. If there is any blame in this book, it is just for liberals who fail fully to respect children's equal personhood and rights.

The roadmap

Chapter 1 paints a picture of life in the US for African-American children, compiling statistics on indicators of wellbeing for different groups and places, and in particular for areas of concentrated poverty. It is worse than most people think. Chapter 2 describes the current legal environment that consigns a substantial portion of black children to the custody of unfit parents and to lives in dangerous and unhealthy homes and neighborhoods, or else to the limbo of foster or kin care, and as a consequence all but destroys for many their prospects for a happy and fulfilling life. It shows that the law and the child welfare system, principally embodying ACLs' family-policy preferences, remain so deferential to biological parents' supposed entitlement to possess their offspring that states and social workers go to extreme lengths to protect the most unfit parents, despite federal legislative efforts to push them in a more child-protective direction. An example of "family-preservation" extremism that presents an apt metaphor (along with the river) for the phenomenon I address, is the growing real-world phenomenon of placing newborn babies, disproportionately black, in prison, to live for months or years with incarcerated mothers. We are imprisoning black children literally as well as figuratively.

Chapters 3 to 5 then speak from a child-centered perspective about what must be done going forward. They present proposals for reform of law and government practices that could dramatically improve life prospects for a great number of children, enough so to stop the cycle, to eliminate in perhaps a generation, if fully implemented, areas of entrenched and concentrated poverty and dysfunction. These chapters also describe the dominant liberal reaction to these or similar reforms, which in each case has amounted to categorically rejecting the proposals because of their expected impact on adults. Chapter 3 addresses procreation and pregnancy. Chapter 4 discusses parentage decision-making and state response to parental unfitness. Chapter 5 presents novel ideas for sparing children from having to grow up in dangerous and diseased communities.

In Chapter 6, I describe the succession of ACLs' "new approaches" to ending the inter-generational cycle of dysfunction—including "Intensive Family Preservations Services," Family Drug Courts, race-sensitivity training for (mostly black) social workers as a means of addressing "Race Disproportionality" in the foster care system, and "Differential Response" (putting most maltreatment cases on a soft-touch, non-coercive track), as well as prison nurseries. These approaches all share a primary focus on protecting parents and communities from further suffering, combined with a hope that this will trickle down to benefit children and an unfounded faith that if only the state would spend more money on addressing the cycle it would disappear.

Finally, in Chapter 7, I seek a deeper understanding of this prevailing liberal mentality, drawing on political science scholarship. Some insight is gained by contrast with liberals' reaction to religion-related dysfunction in families and communities (e.g., polygamist "cults"), which is vastly different from their reaction to poverty-related dysfunction, even though the harms to children seem more numerous and destructive in the latter context. I offer thoughts about how liberals might be persuaded to become as accepting of strong and effective child welfare measures in the poverty realm as they are in the realm of religion-related abuse. I also suggest here reasons why conservatives might be more receptive than liberals to some of the child-welfare-promoting reforms I advance in the book.

In a Conclusion, I share some reflections on the nature and quality of discourse about family policy in the academy, in government, and among the public. Perhaps we owe it to children, to all children, to raise our standards in this regard as well.

Notes

1 Russonello (2016).
2 Tavernise (2016).
3 Hooker (2016, 448–69, 449).
4 I use the terms "Black" and "African American" interchangeably, even though they do not mean exactly the same thing. Studies and government data reports generally treat the terms as synonyms, and alternating avoids having to choose sides in the debate over which is more respectful (or less disrespectful). Referring to people as a color is odd, but it is common even in self-description for African Americans and Caucasian Americans. When I use "white," I refer to people who identify as "non-Hispanic white or Caucasian."
5 Sugrue (2010, 101); Thompson (2013).
6 Obama's Office of Urban Affairs is widely regarded as having been ineffectual. See, for example, Holywell (2013). See also Riley (2014, 10, 15, 21–2, 32) (discussing disappointment with Obama's inattention to poor African Americans).
7 I do appreciate, however, concerns that some efforts to help—in particular, affirmative

action—have been counter-productive. See, for example, Sleeper (2002) (contending race-focused policies such as affirmative action and race-matching in foster care and adoption reinforce racial division and deny persons of minority race opportunities for important experiences such as a sense of personal accomplishment and stable life in a family).

8 See Cashin (2014, xiv–xv) ("While non-blacks see real and virtual examples of black success every day, they don't see black poverty, because they are removed from the deprivations of ghetto neighborhoods.... Watching Obama on TV and the race pride that engenders does not make up for twice the unemployment, nearly three times the poverty, and six times the incarceration that white people endure").

9 Reyes (2017); McDaniels (2014).

10 Popkin (2016, 19).

11 Edelman (2008, 256–66).

12 See, for example, Mariani (2017).

13 Gelles (2011).

14 Massey and Denton (2003, 8). See also Riley (2014, 41–5).

15 Cf. Alonso (2009).

16 Coates (2015).

17 Weissman (2015).

18 Williams (2017) (interviewing an 18-year-old who "has been sold for sex" since she was 14, now forced onto the street by government targeting of online prostitution ads, and complaining: "It's harder to catch a date now. Now everybody's daddy puts them out on the street.... Now, I'm one of the older ones"); Stolberg (2017).

19 Kennedy (2015, 91).

20 Goldberg (2015) (relating a tour of Angola prison with the mayor of New Orleans and discussions with inmates).

21 See, for example, Nicholson, Biebel and Katz-Leavy (2004).

22 See, for example, Riley (2014); Thernstrom and Thernstrom (1999).

23 Cf. Kahan (2017, 78) ("In an environment in which positions on particular policy-relevant facts become widely understood as symbols of people's membership in and loyalty to opposing cultural groups, it will promote people's individual interests to attend to evidence about those facts in a manner that reliably conforms their beliefs to the ones that predominate in the groups they are members of. Indeed, the tendency to process information in this fashion will be strongest among individuals who display the reasoning capacities most strongly associated with science comprehension").

24 See, for example, Goodwin (2008), 1666 (explaining that her analysis of fetal-drug-exposure laws "illumes the darker side of reproductive policing advanced during slavery and the eugenics laws of the twentieth century").

25 See, for example, Perry (1994, 72–3) ("cultural genocide may also refer to the effect of depriving individuals of the experience of their own culture. Transracial adoption clearly poses that threat to the Black children transracially adopted"); National Association of Black Social Workers (1972) (condemning trans-racial adoption as "cultural genocide").

26 See also Thyer (2010, 262–3) (citing publications documenting discrimination by social-work school faculty against conservative students, students' being forced to lobby for liberal political causes, and a student's being threatened with expulsion if she did not "lessen the gap" between her beliefs and those of the department).

27 See generally Gross (2013); idem, 160–1 (discussing complaints from conservative grad students in social science departments).

28 See, for example, Wilson (2015) (recounting interview with Jennifer Frazier, a Florida woman who mistakenly gave her baby girl methadone and is now serving a 15-year prison sentence for aggravated manslaughter, who told the reporter "I wish social services had been at my home investigating, talking to me, checking on Jacey. I didn't just slip through the cracks in the system; I fell through the canyon into hell.... If I was that social worker, I'd be knocking the door down, because I see what can happen. They need to find us, and they need to help."); Wilson and Shiffman (2015) (quoting Courtney Howell, a Utah woman discharged from a birthing facility with her child, and never reported to CPS, even though she was homeless and obviously substance abusing, who received a 30-year sentence for manslaughter after twice mixing methadone with her baby's Tylenol, thinking that would

improve her sleeping, as saying she wishes the hospital had reported her situation to CPS: "I would have welcomed the help, and it would have changed my life."), *idem* (recording statement of Angelica McKenney, who suffocated her baby girl after falling asleep high: "I think if I had been under the microscope, so to speak, I think things would have been a lot different with somebody coming in and looking at me. That probably would've changed everything"), *idem* (discussing Tory Schlier, a Pennsylvania mother who also suffocated her baby, who wrote from prison that she wished the birthing hospital had notified CPS, to have "someone check in at our home daily to see how things were going. I was an addict, and it was well known to everyone, but no one seemed to care."); Anonymous (2014) (account of CPS worker: "One time I took a baby away from his mother after he was born and I went to the car and cried and cried, I felt so awful. But many months later, that mum came to me and thanked me for taking her child. She had every problem in the book and she knew it was the right thing to do. And since then she's cleaned herself up, is attending all the appointments she's supposed to attend, getting all the help she needs to turn her life around and provide a good home for that baby").

29 Roberts (1998).

30 Lollar (2017, 947); Boyd (2015). See also Goodwin (2007).

31 Federle (2014), 703.

32 The "Failure to Protect" Working Group (2000), 850. Cf. Patterson (2006) (op–ed by renowned Harvard sociologist stating: "the pervasive idea that cultural explanations inherently blame the victim; that they focus on internal behavioral factors and, as such, hold people responsible for their poverty, rather than putting the onus on their deprived environment.... is utterly bogus").

33 Gregory (2003) (citing in support James Baldwin's "slogan 'Urban Renewal Is Negro Removal'" rather than any social science).

34 See Murray (2016, 421) ("The downward gaze looks 'down' on poor communities and sees them as contagious monsters"). See also *idem*, 398 (asserting that blight condemnations amount to "violent, racist, and colonial conquests").

35 Rinehart (2016) ("Nearly two million infertile couples in the United States are actively trying to adopt a child.... For every eligible baby, an invisible queue of 36 couples waits for the chance to take that baby home."); Jones (2008, 12, 22, 16) ("[I]n 2002 ... the domestic supply of infants relinquished at birth or within the first month of life and available to be adopted had become virtually nonexistent."), 23 table 5 (showing that 2.643 million women aged 18–44 had taken steps toward adopting a child, and 18.465 million had considered adopting), 25 table 7 (showing 228,000 black women and 195,000 Hispanic women currently seeking to adopt, most of them married); 33 table 15 (showing that over half of women seeking to adopt express indifference about the race of the child, only one-fifth of white women seeking to adopt express a preference for a white child, half express a preference for a child less than two–years old, and 89 percent would accept a child with a mild disability); 30 table 12 (showing that one fourth of women currently seeking to adopt are African-American), 33 table 15 (showing only 20 percent of women seeking to adopt an unrelated child express a preference for a white child, half express a preference for a child less than two–years old, and 89 percent would accept a child with a mild disability).

36 See, for example, Hawkins-Leon (1998) (urging adoption of a law like ICWA for black Americans, to give "the community" control over children removed from parental custody, in order to guard against "cultural genocide").

37 See, for example, Barth and Lloyd (2010, 58–9) (findings from longitudinal study of children taken into CPS custody in infancy as a result of maltreatment that those adopted (presumably because CPS judged return home unsafe) did as well as or better than those returned home (presumably because CPS judge return home to be safe) on a range of developmental measures, and far better than children who remained in foster care long-term); Vinnerljung (2010, 63) (citing studies in Sweden and France that found children adopted in infancy did as well as children in the population generally on measures of problem behaviors and school performance, whereas results for children who grew up in foster care were "dismal"); Ji (2010, 433) (describing research demonstrating better outcomes for adopted children the younger they are when adopted); Vandivere (2009, 7) (stating that most children privately adopted were under one month of age at time of placement); *idem* at 21–35 (providing comparative statistics

for all children in the United States versus privately adopted children with respect to physical health, social and emotional well-being, and relationship with parents); Bartholet (2012, 1326) (noting that "the adoptive parent maltreatment rate is lower than the norm for the general population").

38 See, for example, Murray (2016, 398) ("this apprehension depends on official and judicial gazes, which I call acts of peering").

39 See, for example, Roberts (2012) (arguing that instead of removing abused and neglected children from parents' custody, the government should "tackle poverty's societal roots"); Kennedy (2011) (arguing that imprisoning infants would not be necessary if our criminal laws were more rational and if the state instead built nice group homes in the community for pregnant convicts and their children and provided all the best professional assistance during convicts' stay there and after); Huntington (2006, 666–70) ("the state should address the deep-seated problems associated with poverty, rather than 'assisting' poor parents by removing their children").

40 See generally Gelles (2011).

41 On the prevalence of bad child-welfare research and its misuse, see Gelles (2011, Ch. 7).

42 Anderson (2008, 3).

43 Anderson (2008, 6).

44 Anderson (2008, 19).

45 Omolade (1995, 279).

46 Gelles (2011, 66–7) ("Many people still endorse the unsubstantiated belief that poor parents will use the money intended to help their children to buy drugs or fancy cars…").

47 Hooker (2016, 450).

48 Cashin (2014, xv).

49 Coates (2015).

50 Gelles (2011, 127, emphasis in original).

51 Porter (2013) (reporting contemporary poverty rate quite similar to that of 1964). Some liberal defenders of the Great Society accurately point out that government anti–poverty programs have helped millions of people and have prevented poverty rates from getting much worse than they currently are. Reasonable people can disagree on what it means to win or lose a war, but in the context of a military war, failing after decades of effort to achieve one's objective (e.g., reclaiming seized territory) is generally characterized as losing; merely having prevented things from getting worse (e.g., losing even more territory) is insufficient to fend off admission of defeat.

52 Obama (2007).

53 One limited exception was his School Improvement Grants program, which channeled $7 billion to poor urban schools—not an especially large investment and, sadly, largely wasted. See The Times Editorial Board (2017).

54 Paletta and Mufson (2017); Crookston (2017).

55 Cf. Smith and Fong (2004, 216–17) (explaining why "self-help strategies" for transforming dysfunctional communities have not worked and calling for "investment from the outside"). Clinton's platform did include a $125 billion Economic Revitalization Initiative that would partly address transportation and water systems in poor urban areas but would mostly support entrepreneurs in "underserved communities," which would likely not have produced any significant increase in jobs in the worst neighborhoods, where no significant start-up would want to start up. Obama's programs for job creation mostly supported "shovel ready" construction projects led and labored on by white men. Sugrue (2010, 131).

56 Hartman and Squires (2010, 1–8).

57 Anderson (2010).

58 Donnor and Dixson (2013, 244); Mickelson, Smith and Nelson (2015).

59 Chemerinsky (2015, 249).

60 See, for example, Sleeper (1997, 12–13) ("[S]ome liberals support racial remedies as sops to their own consciences, perhaps because they are complicit in a flawed liberal capitalism which they do not actually oppose yet cannot quite bring themselves to defend. They support such remedies because they have no serious intention of redressing deeper inequities that divide not only whites from blacks but also white from whites (and, increasingly, blacks from blacks).") See also Cohen (2001).

61 Although President Trump's choice to head the Administration for Children, Youth and Families sounded family-preservation themes, Trump's first budget proposal called for cuts to parent supports such as before- and after-school programs and for substantial new funding of foster care and adoption. See Heimpel (2017); Kelly (2017).

62 Gabriel (2014) (describing causes of poverty and rampant drug abuse in West Virginia's poorest county).

63 Lenhardt (2004, 825).

64 Ghandnoosh (2014); Feagin, Early and McKinney (2001, 1313).

65 Carbone and Cahn (2014, 28). *Idem* at 25 ("Today, scholars are more inclined to say that Moynihan was right"), 26 ("His description, with light of hindsight, reads as a roadmap for what would later happen to the country as a whole as the widespread loss of reliable jobs transformed gender expectations"). See also Wilson (2009, 96) (criticizing liberals who "believed that Moynihan's cultural arguments amounted to blaming African Americans for their own misfortune" and "ignored Moynihan's careful attention to structure causes of inequality, and [thereby] created a backlash against the report that essentially shut down meaningful conversation about the role of culture in shaping racial outcomes"); Bartholet (2009, 871, 876) ("Daniel P. Moynihan was accused of attacking the black family when he noted problems in the black community 'that amplified the effects of other social problems' and helped perpetuate 'black poverty over time and across the generations.' Recent commentary has tended to vindicate Moynihan, pointing out that he clearly targeted historic and ongoing discrimination as responsible for the plight of the black family, and he argued for significant social reforms which, had they been implemented, would have done much to empower the black community").

66 See Wilson (2009, 96–9).

Bibliography

Alonso, Gaston, Noel Anderson, Celina Su, and Jeanne Theoharis. *Our Schools Suck: Students Talk Back to a Segregated Nation on the Failures of Urban Education.* New York and London: New York University Press, 2009.

Anderson, Elijah. *Against the Wall: Poor, Young, Black, and Male.* Philadelphia, PA: University of Pennsylvania Press, 2008.

Anderson, Elizabeth S. *The Imperative of Integration.* Princeton, NJ: Princeton University Press, 2010.

Anonymous. "IT HAPPENED TO ME: I Worked In Child Protective Services." xojane.com, July 9, 2014.

Barth, Richard P. and Christopher Lloyd. "Five-Year Developmental Outcomes for Young Children Remaining in Foster Care, Returned Home, Or Adopted." In *How does Foster Care Work?: International Evidence on Outcomes,* edited by Fernandez, Elizabeth and Richard P. Barth, 58–9. London and Philadelphia: Jessica Kingsley Publishers, 2010.

Bartholet, Elizabeth. "The Racial Disproportionality Movement in Child Welfare: False Facts and Dangerous Directions," *Arizona Law Review* 51 (2009): 871–6.

Bartholet, Elizabeth. "Creating a Child-Friendly Child Welfare System: Effective Early Intervention to Prevent Maltreatment and Protect Victimized Children," *Buffalo Law Review* 60 (2012): 1323–6.

Boyd, Susan C. *From Witches to Crack Moms: Women, Drug Law, and Policy.* Durham, NC: Carolina Academic Press, 2015.

Carbone, June and Naomi Cahn. *Marriage Markets: How Inequality is Remaking the American Family.* New York: Oxford University Press, 2014.

Cashin, Sheryll. "Introduction," in *Place, Not Race: A New Vision of Opportunity in America,* xiv–xv. Boston, Massachusetts: Beacon Press, 2014.

Chemerinsky, Erwin. "Remedying Separate and Unequal: Is it Possible to Create Equal Educational Opportunity," in *The Enduring Legacy of "Rodriguez": Creating New Pathways to Equal Educational Opportunity,* edited by Ogletree, Charles J. and Kimberly J. Robinson, 249–62. Cambridge, MA: Harvard Education Press, 2015.

Coates, Ta-Nehisi. *Between the World and Me*. New York: Spiegel & Grau, 2015.

Cohen, G.A. *If You're an Egalitarian, how Come You're so Rich?* Cambridge, MA: Harvard University Press, 2001.

Crookston, Paul. "Trump Proposes $9 Billion in Education Cuts but Increased Funding for School Choice," *National Review*, March 16, 2017.

Donnor, Jamel K. and Adrienne Dixson. *The Resegregation of Schools: Education and Race in the Twenty-First Century*. 1st ed. New York: Routledge, 2013.

Edelman, Peter, "What Do We Do Now? Toward a Brighter Future for Young African American Men." In *Against the Wall: Poor, Young, Black, and Male*, edited by Elijah Anderson, 252–67. Philadelphia, PA: University of Pennsylvania Press, 2008.

"Failure to Protect" Working Group. "Charging Battered Mothers with 'Failure to Protect': Still Blaming the Victim," *Fordham Urban Law Journal* 27(3) (2000): 849–50.

Feagin, Joe R., Kevin E. Early, and Karyn D. McKinney. "The Many Costs of Discrimination: The Case of Middle-Class African Americans," *Indiana Law Review* 34 (2001): 1313–59.

Federle, Katherine Hunt. "The Violence of Paternalism," *Wake Forest Law Review* 49 (2014): 703–12.

Fernandez, Elizabeth and Richard P. Barth. *How does Foster Care Work?: International Evidence on Outcomes*, edited by Fernandez, Elizabeth, Richard P. Barth. London and Philadelphia: Jessica Kingsley Publishers, 2010.

Gabriel, Trip. "50 Years into the War on Poverty, Hardship Hits Back," *New York Times*, April 20, 2014.

Gelles, Richard. *The Third Lie: Why Government Programs Don't Work—And a Blueprint for Change*. Walnut Creek, CA: Left Coast Press, 2011.

Ghandnoosh, Nazgol. *Race and Punishment: Racial Perceptions of Crime and Support for Punitive Policies*. Washington, DC: The Sentencing Project, 2014.

Goldberg, Jeffrey. "A Matter of Black Lives," *The Atlantic* (September 2015).

Goodwin, Michele. "Prosecuting the Womb," *The George Washington Law Review* 76 (2008): 1657–746.

Gregory, Steven. "If Baldwin Could Speak." In *A Way Out: America's Ghettos and the Legacy of Racism*, edited by Joshua Cohen *et al*. Princeton, NJ: Princeton University Press, 2003.

Gross, Neil. *Why are Professors Liberal and why do Conservatives Care?* Cambridge, MA: Harvard University Press, 2013.

Hartman, Chester and Gregory D. Squires. "Integration Exhaustion, Race Fatigue, and the American Dream." In *The Integration Debate: Competing Futures for American Cities*, edited by C. Hartman and G.D. Squires, 1–8. New York: Routledge, 2010.

Hawkins-Leon, Cynthia G. "The Indian Child Welfare Act and the African American Tribe: Facing the Adoption Crisis," *Brandeis Journal of Family Law* 36 (1998): 201–18.

Heimpel, Daniel. "Trump's Top Child Welfare Official Speaks," *The Chronicle of Social Change*, November 6, 2017.

Holywell, Ryan. "Whatever Happened to the Office of Urban Affairs?" Governing the States and the Localities. March 29, 2013.

Hooker, Juliet. "Black Lives Matter and the Paradoxes of U.S. Black Politics: From Democratic Sacrifice to Democratic Repair," *Political Theory* 44(4) (2016): 448–69, 449.

Hungtington, Claire. "Rights Myopia in Child Welfare," *UCLA Law Review* 53 (2006): 637–99.

Ji, Juye, Devon Brooks, Richard P. Barth, and Hansung Kim. "Beyond Preadoptive Risk: The Impact of Adoptive Family Environment on Adopted Youth's Psychosocial Adjustment," *American Journal Orthopsychiatry* 80(3) (2010): 432–3.

Jones, Jo. "Adoption Experiences of Women and Men and Demand for Children to Adopt by Women 18–44 Years of Age in the United States, 2002," *Vital and Health Statistics* 23(27) (2008).

Kahan, Dan M., Ellen Peters, Erica Cantrell Dawson, and Paul Slovic. "Motivated numeracy and enlightened self-government," *Behavioural Public Policy* 1(1) (2017): 54–86.

Kelly, John. "Amid Cuts to Youth Services, Trump Includes Big Increase to Child Welfare Entitlement," *The Chronicle of Social Change*, May 26, 2017.

Kennedy, Deseriee A. "The Good Mother: Mothering, Feminism, and Incarceration," *William & Mary Journal. Women & Law* 18 (2011): 161–200.

Kennedy, Randall. "A Caricature of Black Reality," *The American Prospect*, November 2015, 87–91.

Lenhardt, Robin A. "Understanding the Mark: Race, Stigma, and Equality in Context," *New York University Law Review* 79(3) (2004): 803–25.

Lollar, Cortney E. "Criminalizing Pregnancy," *Indiana Law Journal* 92 (2017): 947–1005.

Mariani, Mike. "The Neuroscience of Inequality: Does Poverty show up in Children's Brains?" *Guardian*, July 13, 2017.

Massey, Douglas S. and Nancy A. Denton. *American Apartheid: Segregation and the Making of the Underclass*. Cambridge, MA: Harvard University Press, 1993.

McDaniels, Andrea K. "Collateral Damage: Advocates Aim to Save Baltimore Children from Impact of Violence," *The Baltimore Sun*, December 13, 2014.

Mickelson, Rosyln A., Stephen S. Smith, and Amy H. Nelson. *Yesterday, Today, and Tomorrow: School Desegregation and Resegregation in Charlotte*, edited by Mickelson, Roslyn A., Stephen S. Smith and Amy H. Nelson. Cambridge, MA: Harvard Education Press, 2015.

Murray, Yxta Maya. "Detroit Looks toward a Massive, Unconstitutional Blight Condemnation: The Optics of Eminent Domain in Motor City," *Georgetown Journal on Poverty Law and Policy* 23(3) (2016): 395–461.

National Association of Black Social Workers, "Position Statement on Trans-Racial Adoption," September 1972.

Nicholson, Joanne, Kathleen Biebel, and Judith Katz-Leavy. "Prevalence of Parenthood in Adults with Mental Illness: Implications for State and Federal Policy, Programs, and Providers," In *Mental Health, United States, 2002*, edited by R.W. Manderscheid and M.J. Henderson, Ch. 10, 120. Washington, DC: US Department of Human Services and Health, 2004.

Obama, Barack. *The Audacity of Hope: Thoughts on Reclaiming the American Dream*. London: Canongate Books, 2007.

Omolade, Barbara. "'Making Sense': Notes for Studying Black Teen Mothers," *Mothers in Law: Feminist Theory and the Legal Regulation of Motherhood*, edited by Martha Albertson Fineman and Isabel Karpin, 270–85. New York: Columbia University Press, 1995.

Paletta, D. and S. Mufson. "Trump Federal Budget 2018: Massive Cuts to the Arts, Science and the Poor," *Washington Post*, March 16, 2017.

Patterson, Orlando. "A Poverty of the Mind," *New York Times*, March 26, 2006.

Perry, Twila L. "The Transracial Adoption Controversy: An Analysis of Discourse and Subordination," *NYU Review of Law & Social Change* 21 (1994): 33–108.

Popkin, Susan J. *No Simple Solutions: Transforming Public Housing in Chicago*. Lanham, MD: Rowman & Littlefield, 2016.

Porter, Eduardo. "In the War on Poverty, a Dogged Adversary," *New York Times*, December 17, 2013.

Reyes, Jessica Masulli, Brittany Horn, Esteban Parra, and Christina Jedra. "CDC plan Lacks Political Will: Tynesia Cephas was 16 Years Old when she was Gunned Down on Wilmington's East Side," *News Journal* (Wilmington, Del.), October 9, 2017.

Riley, Jason L. *Please Stop Helping Us: How Liberals Make it Harder for Blacks to Succeed*. New York: Encounter Books, 2014.

Rinehart, Paula. "Why so Many Families Who Want to Adopt Can't," *The Federalist*, August 18, 2016.

Roberts, Dorothy E. *Killing the Black Body: Race, Reproduction, and the Meaning of Liberty*. New York: Vintage Books, 1998.

Roberts, Dorothy E. "Prison, Foster Care, and the Systemic Punishment of Black Mothers," *UCLA Law Review* 59 (2012): 1474–86.

Russonello, Giovanni. "Race Relations are at Lowest Point in Obama Presidency, Poll Finds," *New York Times*, July 13, 2016.

Schlanger, Danielle. "Obama's Urban Affairs Office Brings Hope but Not Much Change," *Huffington Post*, July 26, 2013.

Sleeper, Jim. *Liberal Racism: How Fixating on Race Subverts the American Dream*. New York: Viking/Penguin, 1997 and 1998.

Sleeper, Jim. *Liberal Racism: How Fixating on Race Subverts the American Dream*. 2nd ed. Lanham, MD: Rowman & Littlefield Publishers, 2002.

Smith, Margaret G. and Rowena Fong. *Children of Neglect: When no One Cares*. New York: Brunner-Routledge, 2004.

Stolberg, Sheryl Gay "Missing Girls in Washington, D.C. Widen City's Racial Divide," *New York Times*, March 31, 2017.

Sugrue, Thomas J. *Not Even Past: Barack Obama and the Burden of Race*. Princeton, PA: Princeton University Press, 2010.

Tavernise, Sabrina. "Many in Milwaukee Neighborhood Didn't Vote—and Don't Regret It." *New York Times*, December 20, 2016.

The Times Editorial Board, "The School Improvement Grants that didn't Improve Schools," *Los Angeles Times*, January 27, 2017.

Thernstrom, Stephan and Abigail Thernstrom. *America in Black and White: One Nation, Indivisible*. New York: Touchstone, 1999.

Thompson, Derek. "Your Brain on Poverty: Why Poor People Seem to Make Bad Decisions," *The Atlantic*, November 22, 2013.

Thyer, Bruce. "Social justice: a conservative perspective," *Journal of Comparative Social Welfare* 26(2–3) (2010): 261–74.

Vandivere, Sharon, Karin Malm, Child Trends, and Laura Radel. *Adoption USA: A Chartbook Based on the 2007 National Survey of Adoptive Parents*. Office of The Assistant Secretary for Planning and Evaluation: US Department of Health & Human Services, 2009.

Vinnerljung, Bo. "Commentary," in *Evidence on Outcomes*, edited by Fernandez, Elizabeth and Richard P. Barth (63). London: Jessica Kingsley Publishers, 2010.

Weissman, Marsha. *Prelude to Prison: Student Perspectives on School Suspension*. Syracuse, NY: Syracuse University Press, 2015.

Williams, Timothy. "Backpage's Sex Ads Are Gone. Child Trafficking? Hardly," *New York Times*, March 11, 2017.

Wilson, Duff. "As Social Services Stand Back, Mother and Baby Fall 'Into Hell'," *Reuters*, December 7, 2015.

Wilson, Duff and John Shiffman. "Newborns Die after being sent Home with Drug-dependent Mothers," *Reuters*, December 7, 2015.

Wilson, William Julius. *More than just Race: Being Black and Poor in the Inner City*. New York: W.W. Norton, 2009.

Part I

The cycle

Whether race is even a sensible basis for categorizing human beings is contested. Assuming it is, the ever-increasing commonness of inter-racial intimate relationships has blurred the boundaries and complicated the categories. Nevertheless, government agencies and social scientists continue to identify people by race, reflecting the continued tendency of the American people to attribute to everyone a racial identity, and these agencies and scientists compile demographic data on the basis of race. Using that data, we can draw a rough picture of life for children identified as black, and we can compare it with the circumstances of children identified as white. The differences help us understand why black Americans appear to occupy what some call a "permanent underclass."

Some differences across races in the aggregate are quite familiar to those immersed in social policy and to the public. Just how bad things are for people living in urban ghettos is less well known to people not living in them, so the principal aim of this part is to illustrate what future faces a child born today whom we consign to growing up in one of these ghettos.

Chapter 1

The world black children enter

A basic truth of human existence is that one's chances for a healthy and fulfilling life depend largely on two interrelated factors: The quality of parenting one receives and the character of the community into which one is born. This chapter describes geographical and economic circumstances into which black children in general in America today are born, then narrows focus to the bleak circumstances of children born into inner-city areas of concentrated poverty. There, a high rate of parental dysfunction combines with pervasively adverse social circumstances to perpetuate an intergenerational cycle of thwarted lives.

Black America

Over 40 million Americans identify as African–American, making up 13 percent of the US population. They live disproportionately in urban areas; over 40 percent live in inner cities.[1] Regardless of population density, the places where blacks live are predominantly black; in inner cities, rural areas, suburbs, and small towns alike, blacks mostly live in black neighborhoods and most black children attend predominantly-black schools.[2] Some scholars refer to this spatial separation as "hyper-segregation," others as "American Apartheid."[3] Black children mostly attend black schools; public schools in America have undergone a substantial re-segregation in the past 20 years, as court supervision of school districting has ended and white people who place little value on diversity of background in a student body (let alone feel a commitment to equal opportunity for all) highjack redistricting processes.[4]

The high rate of residential segregation partly reflects many white people's aversion to living in racially mixed neighborhoods coupled with government policies and real estate industry practices aimed at fulfilling whites' preferences.[5] It partly reflects economic disparity, especially in urban areas where gentrification drives up housing costs and quickly turns mixed-race neighborhoods into white ones.[6] In addition, many black Americans today prefer to live in all- or mostly-black neighborhoods, so they do not have to deal with racial hostility and discriminatory practices in their home environment.[7] An initially toothless Fair Housing Act was given anti-discrimination bite by amendments enacted in 1989, but by then the process of confining non-rural blacks to urban ghettos was largely complete and has never been undone. Thus, today one can plausibly speak of a White America and a Black America.

The basic economic picture for Black America over the past half century is that a substantial middle- and upper-income segment emerged (today 36 percent of all black households have income over $50,000),[8] but for the rest the economic situation did not improve appreciably and in some ways became worse. Most troubling has been the development of numerous large urban areas of predominantly-Black concentrated poverty, places from which whites fled in the 1960s and 1970s after industry moved out (leaving huge numbers of poorly-educated black people unemployed), schools were desegregated, and race riots erupted.[9] This section presents some data. Researchers are not consistent in what they include as income (e.g., whether they include government assistance and, if so, only cash or also in-kind benefits such as food stamps or housing vouchers). And official figures of poverty and unemployment typically do not include incarcerated persons, so they underestimate the rate at which these things afflict black Americans. But precision is not important, nor does it matter whether the current trend is positive or negative; the basic point is that there are an awful lot of black Americans in dire economic circumstances, and current policies in effect are not going to change that.

The percentage of black people below the poverty line is at least twice that of whites, comprising (depending on how measured) 8 to 11 million African Americans.[10] The official dividing line between "poverty" and "low income" is, in the view of many social scientists, actually about half what a family requires to meet basic needs, so people counted as "in poverty" are truly struggling. Further, by some accounts nearly half of black families living in poverty are chronically in "extreme" or "deep" poverty—with less than half of poverty-threshold income.[11] Kathryn Edin and Luke Shaefer's book *$2.00 a Day: Living on Almost Nothing in America* is eye-opening. Moreover, roughly one in five blacks are not only poor themselves but also living in neighborhoods where they are surrounded by other poor people.[12] This 20 percent of black Americans is the principal focus of this book. Half of the Americans who live in deep poverty are white, and many of them live in urban areas, but they are much more likely to live in mixed-income neighborhoods with safer streets, better schools, more jobs, and more enrichment programs for children.[13]

Poverty rates for black *children* are even worse: 42 percent of black infants and toddlers, compared with 14 percent for white infants and toddlers.[14] Even the *number* of black children (all ages) in poverty now exceeds that of white children.[15] Another 27 percent of black infants and toddlers are in "low-income" families—between the poverty line and twice the poverty line,[16] so seven in ten black children start life at or near the bottom of the economic ladder. Among the two-thirds of black children living with only one parent,[17] the poverty rate is around 60 percent.[18] Most likely the rate for black *infants* living with only one parent is around 70 percent. In the nation's capital, nine-tenths of black children live in a single-parent household, and nine-tenths of infants and toddlers in DC's 7th and 8th wards live in concentrated poverty.[19] These figures suggest that pretty much all black children living in poverty have only one of their parents in their home for most of their childhood, whereas only a small percentage of those living with both parents are in poverty.

Also important to avoiding material hardship is ownership of assets and freedom from excessive debt. Between 2000 and 2011, median net household worth plummeted by 37 percent for blacks.[20] Blacks collectively lost nearly $100 billion in housing wealth during the subprime mortgage debacle.[21] Even well-educated blacks have struggled to build equity. According to one source: "From 1992 to 2013, the median net worth of blacks who finished college dropped 56%," whereas median net worth for "whites with college degrees rose about 86% over the same period."[22]

One concrete manifestation of this gross disparity in income and net worth is that, in 2014, Black children under five years of age were 29 times more likely than White children to be in an emergency homeless shelter.[23] In addition to disorientation and danger, homelessness wreaks havoc on children's education.[24] Even if they have a home, children in poverty in urban areas relocate frequently, which also disrupts schooling; over 60 percent of low-income renting families change homes in a typical year.[25] These and other figures relating to poverty are probably worse than studies show; the poorest of the poor are likely to be missed by data collectors, because of residential transience or homelessness, parental incarceration, or inability to respond to surveys owing to substance abuse or mental illness.[26]

The higher poverty rate among black Americans primarily reflects high rates of unemployment and unwed parenthood. The official unemployment rate for blacks, which omits incarcerated persons, is twice that for whites.[27] Among the unemployed, more than a quarter are such because of mental illness or disability. Among Americans who are employed, blacks are much more likely to be in low-wage jobs without non-income benefits rather than managerial, professional, or scientific positions,[28] and they are likely to be the sole breadwinner in their household.[29] Only 20 percent of black women and 15 percent of black men obtain a bachelor's degree.[30] Working single black mothers on average have income less than $25,000 per year.[31] The greater economic hit Black Americans incurred in the recent recession (black household income declined by 10.1 percent between 2007 and 2010, white households 5.4 percent)[32] tracks a greater increase in unemployment among blacks in those years and reflects the greater tenuousness of employment for blacks who have it.[33]

The extraordinary rate of unwed parenthood among blacks translates to greater likelihood of households with only one income or no income. Blacks have a far lower marriage rate and much higher divorce rate than whites.[34] Married couples with children in the US have average income of $80,000, single mothers $24,000.[35] Unwed motherhood in poor urban areas does not equate to "single motherhood" in the sense of being a mother permanently parenting alone; most unwed black mothers in those areas are "together" with the biological father when a child is born, nearly half living with that man. But the relationships rarely last past the child's infancy, so the mothers moves on to a relationship with another man, with whom they have another child; Edin and Kefales observe that "relationship churning is more the rule than the exception among unmarried mothers with children" in the poor urban neighborhoods they observed.[36] The fathers also move on, to relationships with other females, with whom they have another child, and so on.[37] So what a child in this world typically experiences growing up is (a) a succession of men in the household or at least in a relationship with the mother, most of whom are not the child's father, and who provide little financial support; (b) no memory of ever living with his or her father and likely having little or no contact with the father; and (c) extraordinarily complex family relationships. Any given child is likely eventually to live in the mother's household with numerous half-siblings whose fathers also have children by other women, as well as half-siblings—through their biological father—who are living with their mothers along with several half-siblings of their own.[38] Paradoxically, black single mothers tend to have more children than black mothers cohabiting with a man, meaning whatever resources they have are spread even thinner.[39]

In addition to dealing with this household-composition chaos, more than a third of black children, as a result of household poverty, live in "food-insecure households," where there is often insufficient food to feed all members.[40] Mothers might have to choose each month between buying food and keeping the electricity on or paying medical bills. Welfare benefits for unemployed single parents declined by a third as a result of Clinton Administration welfare reforms.[41] A huge number of black families depend on Temporary Assistance for Needy Family (TANF) and Women, Infants, and Children (WIC) program benefits and food stamps.[42] Other forms of material hardship single mothers chronically living in poverty incur, which have manifestly negative psycho-emotional consequences for children,[43] include evictions, having to live temporarily in shelters or with a series of family members or friends, utility cut-offs, and not receiving preventive or remedial health care.[44] Children crave security, and seeing the panic in a mother's eyes when she receives an eviction notice and has no idea where to go, nor transportation to get her there, teaches a child that there is no security, no solid 'home base' to which he or she can always return.

One bright spot in recent years is that the Affordable Care Act extended insurance to millions of previously uninsured people and increased benefits for children under the Children's Health Insurance Program. Today only 5 percent of children in the US are without health insurance.[45] But most black households have only public coverage, with much more limited benefits and access compared with the private insurance most white children have.[46] Whether black children will have even public coverage at the end of the Trump Administration remains to be seen.

Inner-city impoverished neighborhoods

Poverty is experienced differently in different types of residential settings. Concentrated poverty in densely-populated areas creates a pathology pervading the community, and there is an adverse "neighborhood effect" separate from, but also intensifying, the impact an individual family's poverty and parental struggles directly have on children. Children living in poor single-parent families in general are likely to live in the most dangerous neighborhoods, and though rates of violent crime nationally have fallen dramatically in the past three decades, there are still places rife with it. A quarter of all children in single-mother or poor households live in neighborhoods categorized as "never safe or only sometimes safe."[47] Sixty-nine percent of black children live in the poorest 20 percent of neighborhoods,[48] 45 percent in areas of "concentrated poverty"—a locality where 40 percent or more of inhabitants are below the poverty line.[49] And because of the association between concentrated poverty and violent crime, 23 percent of black children live in neighborhoods categorized as "never safe or only sometimes safe."[50]

Importantly, the great majority of parents in unsafe neighborhoods (76 percent) say neighbors do not help each other, and that they feel socially isolated, so families or unsupervised children are on their own in trying to avoid the dangers present in their buildings and on the streets.[51] Struggling parents find little assistance or support within the community, because everyone else is also struggling to survive, and there is also little help from outsiders.[52] Youths cannot trust peers, even those that have been friends, once they reach an age when gang affiliation dictates behavior.[53] Edin and Kefalas observe: "Trust among residents of poor communities is astonishingly low—so low that most mothers we spoke with said they have no close friends and many even distrust close kin."[54] Edin and Shaefer write that "kin pull them down as often as they lift them up"[55] and generally cannot serve as a resource because "poverty is too often passed from one generation to the next" and dysfunction pervades extended families.[56] The romantic liberal idea of strong social networks among the urban poor, the whole village raising the child, is mythical.

These impoverished neighborhoods are full of dilapidated housing, much of it with lead paint, and lacking in quality day care, medical facilities, schools, parks, and grocery stores.[57] The violent crime statistics are horrific. Chicago 2016: 324 child victims of gun shootings, 36 of whom died.[58] Headlines such as "Chicago Reels as 3 Children are Gunned Down in 4 Days" have become commonplace.[59] Takiya Homes (11) was killed by a stray bullet while sitting in a van in a parking lot, Kanari Bowers (12) while outside playing, Lavontay White (2) while sitting in a car with a gangbanger on someone's hit list. Their lives over in a second. In a four-day period, in one part of one American city. Similarly grim figures, with a similar list of African-American names, exist for many other American cities with large black populations—Detroit, Flint, Milwaukee, Gary, Cleveland, Indianapolis, St. Louis, East St. Louis, Washington, DC, Baltimore, Syracuse, Hartford, Newark, Camden, Philadelphia, Wilmington, Atlanta, Jacksonville, Memphis, Kansas City, New Orleans, Oakland, Stockton, etc., etc. Life expectancy in black ghettos in these cities is similar to that in Rwanda.[60] The statistics include children targeted for murder as well as unintentional killings. A few more headlines: May 7, 2017: "Three teens shot after wave of violence across Indy." June 25, 2017: "Two Decatur teens gunned down in Tennessee drug deal." August 7, 2017: "Teens Drew Vaughn, Adarius Barber shot to death in Kansas City." October 25, 2017: "Community Mourns After 2 Teens Gunned Down In South Philadelphia." November 17, 2017: "3 teens shot—2 fatally—during Austin robbery." November 25, 2017: "12-year-old boy shot to death in Cleveland, 5 teens wounded." Children who avoid getting killed are highly unlikely to get needed mental health services to deal with the trauma they experience from events in their homes and neighborhood, with the hopelessness and societal denigration that pervades poor urban areas, or with parental incarceration.[61] For some, lack of health insurance is part of the problem, for many it is a combination of logistical and attitudinal obstacles, including a general parental inattentiveness to children's needs.[62]

Physical health problems resulting from toxins in the environment are also pervasive. Second-hand smoke exposure is detectable in the blood of seven in ten black children.[63] This can cause ear infections, asthma attacks, coughing, sneezing, shortness of breath, respiratory infections (bronchitis and pneumonia), and heightened risk for sudden infant death syndrome. Unsafe lead levels in blood have declined for children generally in recent decades, but remain three times as high for black children as for white.[64] Lead comes not just from paint but also second-hand smoke. Some poor black communities have to contend with a contaminated water supply, as in Flint, Michigan. Poor black inner-city children are likely to live near a carbon monoxide channeling highway or hazardous waste facility,[65] or in a flood plain.[66] Children carry all the trauma, exhaustion, illness, anxiety, and hunger into school, which makes it extremely difficult for them to control their behavior, let alone learn.[67] Observers describe inner city middle and high schools as chaotic and dangerous.[68]

Parental dysfunction

The underlying causes of parental unfitness are also present to a disproportionate rate among black parents living in urban areas of concentrated poverty.

Substance abuse and mental illness

For the African–American population as a whole, rates of alcohol abuse and illicit drug use are comparable to those for people of other races.[69] Black Americans on the whole have a lower than average rate of reported mental illness. However, they are only half as likely as whites to receive treatment for it, and blacks report significantly higher rates for negative feelings that do not rise to the level of mental illness, such as serious psychological distress, hopelessness, worthlessness, mental fatigue, and restlessness.[70]

If one looks specifically at blacks living in impoverished inner-city neighborhoods, the addiction and mental illness picture is much worse, and far above the average rate for Americans.[71] Most large cities in the US have witnessed an epidemic of heroin addiction in their poorest neighborhoods in recent years, along with suburbs and rural areas, and a substantial portion of heroin users are black.[72] Abuse of prescription opioids was initially mostly a white phenomenon but eventually spread to the urban black population. Cocaine use has declined since the 1980s but is still common and is the third leading cause of addiction-related hospitalization in the northeast. Most widespread in black urban areas today, especially among younger addicts, is abuse of marijuana and alcohol. Substance abuse in general is most prevalent among those in the prime reproduction age range (16 to 24) for people in impoverished areas.[73] Unsurprisingly, at least half of substance abusers have a co-occurring mental illness—severe and chronic depression, PTSD, bipolar disorder, etc.[74] Ironically, persons afflicted with substance abuse and mental illness, and therefore least capable of caring for a child, procreate at higher than average rates. A study published in 2014 found a birth rate for teenage girls diagnosed with a major mental illness at three times that for other teenage girls.[75] Even if they are not substance abusers and not "mentally ill," residents of neighborhoods marked by deep disorder are almost inevitably going to have mental health problems, particularly chronic anxiety and depression.[76]

These personal struggles, insofar as they afflict parents or other adults in a child's household, are at the root of most maltreatment and adverse childhood experiences. It starts before birth for some. Drug and alcohol abuse by pregnant women can have severe physical consequences for babies, as discussed further in Chapter 2.[77] When parents are absent or incapacitated or unable to pay for food or utilities because of substance abuse or mental illness, or are manufacturing drugs themselves, children are in danger at home and are likely to be pushed into a caregiving role for themselves, younger siblings, and even the parent. They are also more likely to exit the home and incur harm in the streets or get drawn into illegal activity, and more likely to run away and thereby become attractive targets for sex traffickers and other exploiters.[78] These children are also likely to become biological parents themselves at a very early age, and with a mental health problem.[79]

Violence within households

Black men are no more likely than white men of the same socio-economic status to engage in domestic violence, but partner-abuse rates, like child-abuse rates, are higher in low-income and impoverished households and neighborhoods (and twice as high in households below the poverty line as in low-income households).[80] This is what one should expect, given the stress and negative emotions that financial strain creates. The high poverty rate among blacks thus translates to a higher overall domestic violence rate.[81] A recent study found 45 percent of black women and 57 percent of multi-racial women are at some point victims of "contact sexual violence, physical violence, and/or stalking by an intimate partner."[82] In any given year, one in ten fall victim to partner violence.[83] The National Association of Black Social Workers has called domestic violence "the number one public health issue for women of African ancestry" and has identified reasons why Black women are especially unlikely to receive assistance in stopping violence against them in their home—namely, fear of police brutality against their partners, fear the police will arrest them also, a norm within the black community that makes reporting crimes by black men a "betrayal of the race," and the inadequacy of shelters and services available to them.[84]

The higher rate of domestic violence in black households is significant in several ways. First, liberals' reaction to it provides a telling contrast to their reaction to poverty-related child abuse; they manifest vastly different attitudes and recommend quite different state responses toward the abusers in the two situations. When poor adults abuse a partner, liberals manifest no concern whatsoever for the abusers' interest in continuing the relationship with the victim, whereas when poor adults abuse a child, liberals are sympathetic, to the extreme, of the abusers' interest in continuing the relationship with the victim. I will invoke this contrast later in the book. Second, the higher rate of domestic violence reinforces a point I will make in Chapter 2 about the racism fallacy in connection with foster-care race disproportionality; clear empirical evidence shows children in foster care are disproportionately black because maltreatment rates are higher for black children, not because of bias; family abuse in general is correlated with poverty and therefore occurs at a higher rate in black families.[85] This is well established. Yet liberals have not called for race-sensitivity training for police who respond to domestic violence calls, in the way they have done with respect to child protection workers, to make sure they do not intervene too hastily to break up families when abuse allegations are lodged against black adults.

Third, intimate-partner violence is another phenomenon that can make a home unsuitable for a child or render a parent incapable of providing proper care to a child. Inter-partner violence directly harms children in several ways.[86] When it occurs in the presence of children and is directed against their primary caretaker, it is likely to traumatize them, causing various adverse psychological and social effects with long-term implications. Further, it normalizes dysfunctional relationships for children and thus makes it more likely boys will commit acts of violence as adults and girls will become domestic-violence victims as adults. In addition, children present when inter-partner violence occurs are at high risk of incurring physical violence themselves, as a result of spillover intentional abuse or simply being physically in between perpetrator and victim. Domestic violence also harms children indirectly, by debilitating or necessitating separation from their caregivers. Finally, domestic violence victims, as well as perpetrators, abuse children at a much higher rate than parents in general.

Overlapping to some extent with domestic violence, but also encompassing sexual violence by persons who are not partners, are much higher rates of reported rape and other forms of sexual violence among African-Americans than among whites.[87]

Diseases and early death

Rates of disease and early death among different groups are relevant both for what effect they have on parenting and substitute kin care (e.g., grandparent custody) within a group and for what additional struggles they portend for current children in the group. Greater poverty and lesser education among black Americans translates into higher rates of disease and shorter average life span. The AIDS epidemic, generally in retreat in the US, remains a major concern for blacks, whose HIV infection rate is ten times that for whites and for whom the AIDS mortality rate is seven times higher.[88] Six percent of black men and 3 percent of black women, mostly in inner cities, are diagnosed with HIV at some point.[89] Other STDs also disproportionately afflict black Americans,[90] reflecting both a greater average number of partners and lower rate of condom use. Poverty and its other dysfunctions make pregnancy early and outside a committed relationship appear the best or only way to achieve esteem and gratification, or simply not much of a disruption in one's life (because one feels little hope for higher education, career, traditional family, etc.).[91] Accordingly, 61 percent of black high school students report having had intercourse.[92] Among adults, because of the gender imbalance that high rates of incarceration and early death among African-American males have created in inner-city neighborhoods, non-incarcerated black males are less inclined to monogamy and black women are less demanding of self-protective contraceptives.[93]

Other disparities relating to life expectancy: Blacks have the highest death rates and shortest survival times for most cancers and for heart disease among all racial groups, because they lack access to high-quality medical care.[94] Forty-four percent of black women have high blood pressure, because of stress and poor diet.[95] Black adults are 60 percent more likely to have a stroke than white adults,[96] and black men are 60 percent more likely to die after suffering a stroke than white men.[97] Blacks are twice as likely as whites to be diagnosed with diabetes and much more likely to suffer complications and death from it.[98] And blacks are four times more likely than whites to suffer kidney failure,[99] yet far less likely than whites to receive a kidney donation.[100] Related to the blood pressure, diabetes, and kidney problems is a very high rate of obesity among black women.[101] Blacks also disproportionately suffer from Tuberculosis and Hepatitis B.[102] The one group that has not benefited from the national decline in rates of violent-crime victimization since the 1990s is black teens, and for blacks as a whole the homicide rate remains eight times greater than the national average.[103]

Incarceration and its precursors

Despite substantial improvement in this measure in recent years, black Americans make up around four tenths of the prison population.[104] Over one third of black men will be incarcerated at some point in their lives, and at any given time nearly 10 percent of all black men are incarcerated.[105] Among young black males who drop out of high school, the percentage incarcerated on any given day is nearly 40 percent.[106] These males are overwhelmingly from high-poverty neighborhoods.

There is dispute as to whether this massively disproportionate imprisonment of black Americans reflects racial bias in law enforcement, substantive criminal law, quality of legal representation and sentencing,[107] or instead tracks actual rates of serious crime among different racial groups. In poor urban black neighborhoods, police indifference and a local culture that distrusts the legal system and severely punishes "snitches" provide some reason to believe arrest and conviction rates are low relative to actual crime.[108] But for child-welfare decision-making purposes, it does not really matter. What matters is the reality that, in the world many black children enter, a tremendous number of adolescent and adult males originally from their neighborhoods—including a substantial percentage of the children's biological fathers, as well as a significant portion of females in the neighborhood—are locked up in state custody or at high risk of soon being so. This contributes to the problem of fatherlessness discussed below, as well as to a high rate of mother–child separation, and in other ways (stigma, fear, neglect, etc.) seriously adversely impacts children psychologically, socially and educationally, and increases the likelihood of their being incarcerated themselves as adults.[109] Moreover, the impact of criminal conviction and incarceration lasts long after a person leaves prison; it severely hampers a person's ability to secure housing and lawful employment.[110]

Fatherlessness

Corresponding to the extremely high rate of non-marital births and single-mother households, father absence is more common than father presence for black children in poor urban communities. The phenomenon is far worse today than when Daniel Moynihan, as Assistant Secretary of Labor under President Lyndon Johnson, tried to warn policy makers about it and what effect it would have.[111] Yale sociologist Elijah Anderson writes regarding the impact on black boys:

> An important element that limits and destroys the lives of young black men growing up in concentrated poverty, especially the violence and social disconnection ghetto youths experience, is that adult men are basically absent. Fathers are rarely present, and many of those who are around are ineffectual. There is a fundamental disconnect between fathers and their sons and daughters.... The boys' mothers may be engaged in their lives, but they can only do so much. The culture is quite prepared to place a woman in a weak position, even as a supplicant. So young boys turn to peer groups to raise them. This dynamic generates profoundly ineffective parenting for young men and, in turn, makes those young men unable to parent their own children.[112]

Despite the commonness of fatherlessness in these neighborhoods, adolescent and young adult males voice an "aching sense of abandonment" that never leaves them.[113] The absence of fathers also makes girls more likely to be sexually abused as a child by other males, become pregnant in early adolescence, drop out of school, and end up doing illegal sex work—voluntarily or involuntarily. Many additional, indirect, effects for children result from lack of a second wage earner in the household, worsening the family's financial situation, with all the deprivations and stress that causes.

Why are fathers absent? The primary explanation is that they are not in a fully-developed relationship with the mother when procreation happens and they are immature and/or unable to provide, so after the initial thrill of fatherhood wears off or is overtaken by shame or attraction to another female, they leave.[114] One of the most striking figures one encounters in studies of family structure is that "the non-marital birth rate for African Americans without a high school degree is 96 percent."[115] An important, related explanation is incarceration. Forty percent of these biological fathers have been in jail or prison already before their offspring is born.[116] A substantial percentage will go to prison after the child is born. Twenty-five percent of all black children (50 percent of those whose father dropped out of school) experience paternal imprisonment before they reach age 14, and the rates are certainly far higher in inner-city neighborhoods.[117] The norm for children in black urban ghettos is to grow up with "prison Polaroids" on display in the home.[118] As noted, mass incarceration also skews gender ratios in inner cities, so the men remaining in the community can pair with many and commit to none.[119] From another perspective, when a child's father is in prison, his or her mother is likely to make herself available to another boy or man. A third explanation might be that people tend to imitate their same-sex parent, even in behaviors or choices they resent the parent having made; in other words, today's biological parents did not grow up with a model of a father participating in child rearing.

Anderson emphasizes unemployment, as did Moynihan and the Kerner Commission in the late 1960s, and as do many other sociologists today. The dynamic has not changed. Lack of stable income makes young men "unmarriageable" and unable to support children they participate in creating. Unlike Moynihan, Anderson points to peer pressure rather than a supposed emasculation of black men by black women as the connection between financial means and occupying a paternal role; other males look down on a boy or man who attempts to play the role of provider and fails, which is especially likely with immature fathers. Anderson notes also the "peer group's unflattering view of women" and the cultural norm of complete freedom, which together make it unacceptable to appear dependent on a woman. Yet, "[g]iven the longstanding social and political marginalization of black men in America, for many, it has become extremely important to play this role [family man, head of household] well—or not at all."[120]

Ethnographer Kathryn Edin makes a similar observation; the expectations for fatherhood are too great for young men in urban ghettos, so it seems to them better not to even try being a head of household.[121] Instead, they walk away with a 'no strings on me' bravado, ready for a fresh start, hopeful that things will work out better with the next girl. Edin also explains fathers' absence in terms of how relationships between boys and girls form; typically, pregnancy is part of the dating process, what they do when one or both decide to go beyond a casual encounter to being a couple, what used to be signaled by a boy giving a girl his varsity sweater or a necklace. With little self-serving reason to postpone parenthood, girls signal their immature devotion by letting him do it without a condom. Boyfriends show great enthusiasm from pregnancy announcement until shortly after birth, and then normalcy and their inadequacy gradually extinguish this enthusiasm.[122] Edin also heard males voice negative attitudes toward mothers—that they are mercenary, valuing biological fathers only for material goods, just as the legal system does.[123] Once detached from family, these fathers are even more likely to commit crimes and less inclined to seek work, so one cause of father absence leads to another.

Thus, by the time a child is four or five, the great majority of mothers have moved on to other relationships, with men unlikely to act as long-term substitute fathers.[124] Others prefer remaining single even after having children; contra Moynihan, many feel fairly powerless in relationships, and vulnerable to physical abuse and infidelity, because of the skewed gender ratio and the particular culture of masculinity in the inner city (Moynihan wrote at a time when incarceration rates were far lower).[125] But even though they know a baby's father is unlikely to stay, or might not even want a baby's father to stay, inner-city girls want babies. Motherhood seems the only lasting source of meaning, identity, and esteem available to them.[126] Girls do dream of marriage, but as something one does after having a baby with a man, and they know the dream is exceedingly unlikely to come true. In the short-term, extreme loneliness, struggles with family and peers, school failure, poor self-image, lack of hope for ever being in better circumstances, and a general sense that life is out of control lead them to get pregnant, in the expectation a baby will give them someone to be loved by forever and "the purpose, the validation, the companionship, and the order" they crave.[127] They might also get pregnant to thank a boyfriend for his attentions, seal a romance, show sympathy for a man who doesn't see his other children, steal a man from another girl, trap a man, or simply get the inevitable over with early.[128] Once they have had one, they feel they must give the child siblings.[129]

High rates of incarceration, unemployment, and teen pregnancy—prime factors underlying father absence—are in large part a result of inner-city black children not receiving preparation for productive involvement in the modern, post-industrial economy. Thus, the poor educational performance and outcomes for the current generation, which primarily reflect parental struggles and community disorder, later harm the next generation, because the parents of the future are not on a path to the stable employment and mature decision-making they would need to procreate responsibly and act as successful co-parents for children they produce. Consider the 96 percent non-marital birth rate for black high school dropouts in light of statistics for high school graduation rates; in 2008, "the average high school graduation rate in the nation's 50 largest cities was 53 percent," with some cities having shockingly low rates, such as 41 percent for Baltimore and 38 percent for Cleveland.[130] Those who do graduate are predominantly female.[131] The graduation rate for black males in many of the country's big-city school districts is less than one third.[132] And among black males who do not finish high school, 60 to 70 percent will be incarcerated by the time they are 30 years old.[133] Thus, if you think of all the black baby boys being born today, nearly half of those who go on to live in an impoverished urban neighborhood will one day be in prison. You could walk down the hall of the maternity ward of an inner-city hospital and know that every other black baby boy you see is a future prison inmate. Boys grow up knowing this, mothers know this, we know this.

Despite awareness of their inability to provide, their likelihood of incarceration, and their negative attitude toward women, young black males in poor communities also feel driven not just to have sex but to produce children. This is in part because of the status it brings among peers to display one's virility and ability to claim a woman.[134] But it is also because, like the rest of us, they seek gratification from participating in something profound that elevates their spirits, a gratification perhaps both more intense and less enduring because of the depressing and stressful circumstances of their lives.[135] A young man wants some semblance of family, and something permanent in his life, and he believes his offspring "can't deny me."[136] His spirit returns to the gritty reality of his life not long after the birth, as the mother devotes her attention to the baby instead of him and everyone becomes more conscious of his inability to provide steady financial support, so then he fades out of the quasi-family picture. For the girl's part, even if she dreams of a traditional family life with a provider-husband, simply having a baby offers social and spiritual rewards, at least for a while.[137]

Thus, a very high percentage of children born to mothers living in impoverished inner-city neighborhoods grow up without a father consistently present in the home, and in any event the presence of their biological fathers would not necessarily be on the whole good for them, because so many of the fathers are immature, averse to commitment, inclined to abuse the mother, substance abusing, or involved in criminal activity. Reducing the number of black men in prison or jail per se is therefore not necessarily going to improve children's welfare in the aggregate, though undoubtedly some of the men who end up in prison would have been good and consistent parents if not incarcerated.

All of these dysfunctions among black Americans are heavily concentrated in impoverished urban areas.[138] As explained in the next section, the overall consequence is greater than the sum of individual struggles; the concentration of many individuals suffering from addiction, disease, violence, and involvement with the criminal justice system creates an overall environment in a community of helplessness, despair, destitution, disengagement, and danger. Interviews with residents of such neighborhoods are sprinkled with statements such as "I'm just tired of people getting killed this summer," "You just don't get too attached to people,"[139] "everybody we know either dead or in jail," "asking me how many murders I've seen is like asking me how many red cars I saw this week,"[140] and "It's like death don't have an age right now."[141] This environment adversely impacts children even if they happen to have caregivers who are healthy, employed, law-abiding, and relatively well-off economically.

Community dysfunction

If there were a hell on earth for children, it might look something like this: They live in small, rat- and cockroach-infested apartments in crumbling buildings with utilities in disrepair. With few jobs in the neighborhood to provide income for inhabitants, apartments are overcrowded with siblings, half-siblings, cousins, various adult family members, and a constantly changing cast of non-family members, some of whom fill the air with cigarette and marijuana smoke. Their homes never feel safe because the dysfunctions of the outside world enter on a regular basis. The adults bring in drugs, weapons, prostitution, gambling, and a predilection to sexually exploit children, some using drugs to make the children submit quietly. Gunshot sounds—and sometimes bullets—come through windows. Severe stress weighs on everyone's mind and emotions, leading to violent outbursts and sexual abuse. The children are effectively trapped in this environment because the world outside is menacing. AIDS-infected drug addicts lie in a stupor in building hallways. On the streets, drug dealers stand on corners around the clock and lure children into the trade. Prostitutes stand on other corners, child sex predators look out of the windows of nearby buildings, and members of rival gangs cruise the streets intimidating residents and firing weapons at the least provocation. Gangs pressure boys to join in various criminal activities and pressure girls into sex service. The children's walk to school, past boarded-up buildings inhabited by drug manufacturers, dealers, and users, is harrowing. On the walk home they often see adults under the influence of drugs and hear gunfire break out. It hardly seems worth the risk, because the school suffers from dilapidation, burnt-out teachers, and frequent violence between students, and children are afraid to carry books that would weigh them down if they are attacked. Fatalism pervades the community, and children learn in early elementary school that being studious leads to getting beat up. There are no outdoor spaces safe for play, so children whose parents are sufficiently engaged are in "lock down" in their apartments except when they go to school.[142] Simply breathing anywhere in their world poses a threat; the air is clogged with pollutants from nearby factories, highways, and hazardous waste sites.

This depiction resembles many actual residential environments in America today, places where children—mostly black children—are now living, and where many are dying early.[143] This is not the judgment of a privileged outsider; the residents themselves attest to the hopelessness and horror of life in these neighborhoods and give the neighbor-hoods names like "The D.U.B." (Deadly Upon Birth) and "Murderville."[144] A represent-ative comment from one who managed to escape a horrific neighborhood in New Orleans is: "Dead bodies all the time. People being kidnapped and raped and killed and murdered. Who wants to be around that? I'm seeing crackheads walking around the street, homeless, poverty. I hated it."[145] Ethnographers and news reporters document the dangers and despair, in books and articles whose titles use evocative metaphors such as "Against the Wall" and "The Long Shadow" or blunter terms such as "Our America: Life and Death on the South Side of Chicago" and "Neighbourhoods that can kill." In the midst of turmoil over police killings of black individuals in recent years, a spotlight shone briefly on some of these neighborhoods and the desperation residents feel about their con-ditions, but without generating sustained attention to anything other than policing practices.

A very large literature on urban blight describes the causes, effects, and attempts at solving the problem. Its destructive impact on children is well-documented. Large American cities on the whole are safer and more vibrant today than they were a quarter century ago,[146] but that is largely because of downtown reclamation projects that either relocated or ignored the most impoverished communities in the inner city.[147] There remain a great many urban neighborhoods that pose grave threats to children's welfare. At the negative extreme, a neighborhood can pose threats to health and safety far exceeding those present within the home in typical cases of child protection removal. Violent crime and drugs are rampant in many places where black children live,[148] and these children receive little help in dealing with the psychological disturbance that causes.[149]

In addition to posing direct threats to children's physical and psychological welfare, the worst neighborhoods adversely affect children indirectly by imposing stressors on parents that undermine their ability to care for and protect children. As Gabardino *et al.* explain:

> These parents tend to deny or misinterpret their children's signals and needs, and thus are emotionally unavailable to their children. When parents begin to deteriorate or panic in response to stress and community violence, children suffer, as parents who are traumatized seldom offer their children what they need to cope successfully with these experiences. Without effective intervention or adaptation, day-to-day care breaks down and the risk of infant mortality, exploitation, or vic-timization increases.[150]

Infant mortality is, in fact, much more common among black Americans, occurring at twice the national average rate.[151] And the difference is more pronounced in urban areas; in Pittsburg, for example, black babies in 2011 were five times more likely than white babies to die by age one.[152]

To a large degree, community problems reflect an aggregation of individual prob-lems in a large portion of the population. For communities to function well and to be attractive to businesses and service-providers, they must have a critical mass of healthy, educated, gainfully employed, and law-abiding citizens. Conversely, when a high per-centage of residents in a highly-concentrated population area are chronically unem-ployed, uneducated, substance abusing, and/or engaged in criminal activity, the neighborhood is likely to be unsafe, demoralizing, unattractive to outsiders as a place to work or operate a business, and lacking in supportive social networks, and so everyone suffers.[153] Pervasive crime and substance abuse, in particular, frighten away potential employers and service providers, which limits opportunities for parents and youth, in addition to creating physical risks to children.[154]

Given that a relatively high percentage of adults who live in the worst neighborhoods are marginal to begin with, in terms of their inherent capacities for giving care and providing a safe and healthy living environment (their residing there "speaks for itself" on that score), the additional threats present in the larger residential environment push the experience of most children in such neighborhoods below what most people—including those who live in the neighborhoods—would regard as a minimally acceptable quality of life. Such neighborhoods are also likely to have inadequate—even dangerous—schools and few positive role models or mentors. When youth do not see many adults holding, enjoying, and benefiting from steady employment, they fail to form the aspiration and the knowledge necessary to obtain such employment themselves.[155] When they instead see their neighborhood ruled by criminally-involved school dropouts, their status among peers is likely to depend on affirmatively rejecting academics and lawful career ambitions. The poverty and racial uniformity of these areas makes them relatively powerless politically and therefore unlikely to receive sufficient government attention to infrastructure and basic services, such as clean water.[156] In fact, they are constantly vulnerable to policy decisions that make their communities even more unhealthy or dangerous—for example, siting of highways and polluting factories.[157] Thus, a constellation of pathologies in such neighborhoods severely diminishes the life prospects of children forced to grow up in them.

Nearly every large city in America has at least one such area of deep, multifaceted dysfunction, and many medium-sized cities do as well. Many of the largest cities have several (Indianapolis had three in the top 25 most dangerous nationally in 2017). The population of most of these neighborhoods is almost entirely minority race, and principally black. Indeed, four predominantly-black American cities are perennially in the top 40 most dangerous cities *globally*—St. Louis (repeatedly in the top 15), Baltimore, Detroit, and New Orleans, in a list otherwise full of Latin American cities that are drug-war battlefields. Telling indicators of dysfunction, in addition to crime, are rates of single motherhood, child poverty, unemployment, college completion, building vacancies, home ownership, residence change, and median house price.

Consider Detroit: It has on the whole a child–poverty rate close to 60 percent[158] and it contains three neighborhoods where each year a resident has over a 12 percent chance of becoming a victim of murder, forcible rape, armed robbery, or aggravated assault.[159] The West Chicago Street/Livernois Avenue neighborhood of Detroit, rated the worst neighborhood in America in 2013, is almost 90 percent black. In that neighborhood, only 1 percent of the adult population has a college degree, 80 percent of families are "economically disadvantaged," and the median house price is $50,000. Half the children live below the poverty line. The violent crime rate in this neighborhood was a whopping 150 per 1000 residents in 2013, compared with a national median of less than 4 per 1000. In the Broadstreet Ave/Cortland Street neighborhood of Detroit, the median residential real estate price is $31K, the vacancy rate 47 percent.

The Washington Heights neighborhood of Spartanburg, South Carolina, is more mixed racially but still majority black (55 percent). It has an extraordinarily high rate of single-motherhood, only 2.5 percent of adults have a college degree, and 40 percent of households do not have a car. Eighty-two percent of the children live in poverty, and residents stand a nearly one in ten chance each year of being a victim of violent crime. The Sunnyside neighborhood of Houston, predominantly black but with a substantial Hispanic population as well, also has an extremely high percentage of single-mother households, and less than 4 percent of homes are owner-occupied. Only 1 percent of adults have a college degree, and 60 percent of children are in poverty. City Center–East St. Louis captured the title of America's worst neighborhood in 2014. Seventy-five percent of children are in poverty, the vast majority in households headed by single mothers; only 8 percent of adults there are married. Every year 10 percent of residents are victims of violent crime.

Even higher child-poverty rates can be found—88 percent in the Chelsea Ave/N Claybrook Street neighborhood of Memphis, 80 percent in the East E.H. Crump/South 4th St area of Memphis (2017's winner of the 'most dangerous neighborhood in America' distinction), 92 percent in the McDaniel & Mary Streets neighborhood of Atlanta (where, in addition, 27 percent of people change residence each year and nearly 40 percent of residential real estate sits vacant).

Baltimore also has several toxic neighborhoods. They include America's very worst in 2015—the West Mulberry Street/North Fremont Avenue area, with a 73 percent child poverty rate, 38 percent single-mother households, less than 2 percent of adult residents holding a college degree, less than 10 percent owning their home, less than half of households having a car, and 9.4 percent of inhabitants reported as victims of a violent crime each year. In the Sandtown neighborhood of Baltimore, where Freddie Gray was killed by police, the population has dropped nearly 60 percent since the 1970s, manifest in a vacancy rate over one third.[160] In the East Oliver/North Broadway neighborhood of Baltimore, only 1 percent of adults have a four-year college degree, unemployment is the norm, and the residential vacancy rate is a whopping 58 percent.

The high number of moves residents in such places make, what some sociologists call "hypermobility," which is usually to escape something in an existing residence, creates chaos for children's schooling, as their parents are preoccupied with the search for housing, dealing with the practicalities of moving, and frequently changing school zones.[161] In a high percentage of cases, mothers with children change residence by moving in with a succession of relatives or boyfriends, which tends to result in overcrowding, conflict, children's exposure to unrelated adults, and constant vulnerability to eviction.[162]

The most extreme consequence of such pervasively-dysfunctional environments for children is, of course, death. In 2014, 15 children were murdered in Baltimore. In Chicago in 2016, 36 children were killed by shootings, nine murdered in other ways. Detroit averages 50 murders of children per year. Short of death, there are innumerable forms of injury, trauma, and threats to health. Assaults are common in schools.[163] Hundreds of adults are murdered each year in many large cities, many outside in daylight for children to see and have nightmares about. The rate of post-traumatic stress disorder among delinquent youth is astronomical compared with that in the general population.[164] Depression, attention deficit, and substance abuse by minors are also consequences of children's witnessing the horrors of the street, and these consequences are in turn contributing factors in anti-social behavior among youth.[165] A 2011 FBI report estimated there are 33,000 gangs in the US, most of which recruit boys early on for drug-trade work and violence, and "many gangs are using 'prostitution,' including 'child prostitution,' as a 'major source of income.'"[166]

At home, Black children are disproportionately subject to maltreatment, and as a result much more likely to be removed from parental custody and placed in foster care.[167] Black children manifest much higher rates of obesity, because of poor diet and unnatural (but necessary) confinement to home, and asthma.[168] Most "failing" schools in America have mostly black students.[169] The academic achievement gap between black and white children has narrowed but remains substantial across all income levels.[170] At middle and upper levels of income, sociologists attribute the gap in part to an oppositional culture among American blacks imitative of that in black urban ghettos, an observation consistent with the greater academic achievement of African immigrants.[171] Among the distressing figures: A 2010 study found only 12 percent of black fourth grade boys were proficient in reading, and 12 percent in math.[172]

The academic achievement gap continues in later years, especially among males. A far lower percentage of black students than white students ever reaches ACT college readiness benchmarks. In 2010, black male SAT critical reasoning scores were an average of 104 points lower than white male scores.[173] Most black males from poor urban areas never get to college; as noted, two thirds do not finish high school.[174] Those who grow up in impoverished urban areas and manage to complete high school, if they do attend college will most likely attend a two-year community college rather than a four-year college or university, half of them will need remedial courses,[175] and they are much less likely than whites to complete any degree program.[176]

Those who drop out of school, especially boys, end up in the juvenile delinquency system at a very high rate, reflecting the pull into the drug trade, gang violence, and other illegal activities as well as simply the high degree of conflict that exists in an environment where the stress of daily living is intense and displaying toughness is essential to survival.[177] Between 2005 and 2009, police in West Baltimore arrested one quarter of all children between the ages of 10 and 17.[178] Most of those regularly committing crimes are, as a result, also targets for crimes, because of the natural human tendency toward, and ghetto-code mandating, retaliation. And what was settled with fists or wrestling a half century ago is now settled with guns. Thus, the vast majority of those murdered or crippled by violent assaults in blighted inner-city areas are young people who have been on the same life trajectory as the perpetrators.[179] Conversely, even young people who have been on a positive path get turned into criminals when they are victimized or someone they care about is victimized—which is pretty much inevitable in American's worst neighborhoods—and so they then seek to retaliate.[180] Then they are also likely to drop out of school. Hence there is a complex and strong relation between crime and dropping out of school in these neighborhoods.

Girls in these neighborhoods whose education is truncated might also get involved in criminal activity, there being no opportunities for positive employment, or become immature parents, perhaps both. As Kathryn Edin has observed after living in such neighborhoods to study the dynamics of parenthood: "There's either guns or babies … If they have nothing to give them meaning in life and then we try to tell them they shouldn't have a child either, we're asking the impossible of them."[181] The teen pregnancy rate has declined considerably nationwide in the past 20 years but remains twice as high for black adolescents as for white,[182] and it is especially high among black girls in poor urban neighborhoods, where young people inhale daily a "despair over the prospect of a better future."[183] And so the cycle churns on.

In sum, poverty is both a symptom and a cause of problems for individuals and communities, in a circular fashion. People typically live in poverty because they do not have well-paying jobs, which is because of deficiencies in education, mental and physical health problems, criminal history, and/or substance abuse, which in turn are likely the result of growing up in poverty, trying to cope with the stress of being poor and living in an unsafe neighborhood, and having parents who lack education and the financial and personal resources needed to promote healthy development in children. In turn, being forced to live in a neighborhood full of such adults inflicts physical and psychological damage, by creating a constantly high level of stress.[184] Recall a moment in your life when you felt your life was in danger, then imagine that feeling persisting relentlessly for years and how that would impact you. Or imagine living in the worst neighborhood of Cali, Columbia, which has a lower murder rate than St. Louis. Children born to parents who live in an impoverished, crime-ridden, decrepit urban ghetto might be able to survive and have a decent life, but to accomplish even that modest aim they would need healthy, highly-capable, highly-motivated parents and/or strong community support, and both are in short supply in those neighborhoods. Children born into poverty whose parents are unfit, absent, immature, or only barely coping with life's challenges, and who in addition live in a neighborhood rife with crime and substance abuse and lacking adequate schools, health care, supportive social networks, and services for parents, have little chance of escaping this cycle of dysfunction and enjoying a healthy life in which they can realize their potential.

Notes

1 Housing Assistance Council (2012, 9). Most white Americans live in suburban residential communities. *Idem*.
2 Orfield (2015); Hannah-Jones (2014); Kucsera (2014); Plumer (2013) (showing that American schools are more segregated today than in 1980, with three-quarters of black children in segregated schools (majority of students of minority-race) and nearly 40 percent of black children in "intensely segregated" schools (over 90 percent nonwhite)).
3 See, for example, Lenhardt (2011); Massey and Denton (1998).
4 See, for example, Yow (2017); Siegel-Hawley (2015).
5 See also Sack and Thee-Brenan (2015) ("Most whites say they do not live (79 percent), work (81 percent), or come in regular contact (68 percent) with more than a few blacks").
6 Li (2016).
7 Hartman and Squires (2010). But see Massey and Denton (1998, 11) ("racially mixed neighborhoods are strongly desired by blacks").
8 DeNavas-Walt and Proctor (2015, 26). In contrast, 56 percent of white households enjoy annual income over $50,000. *Idem*, 24.
9 Edin and Nelson (2013, 12); See Edin and Kefalas (2005, 18–19).
10 Edin and Kefalas (2005, 13); Sherman and Trisi (2015).
11 Cuddy, Venator and Reeves (2015).
12 Jonsson (2016) ("1 percent of young white adults in the US are both individually poor and live in a neighborhood with more than 30 percent poverty. For blacks, that number is closer to 20 percent").
13 Edin and Nelson (2013), 14; Edin and Kefalas (2005, 14); Drake and Rank (2009).
14 Jiang *et al.* (2017). Another source puts the rate for black children ages 0–5 in 2016 at 38 percent, down from 43 percent just two years earlier, a significant positive sign. See Kids Count Date Center (2017).
15 Patten and Krogstad (2015).
16 Jiang *et al.* (2017).
17 Kids Count Data Center (2016).
18 The National Association of Child Care Resources & Referral Agencies, *Temporary Assistance for Needy Families and Children in Poverty* (2012, 160) (showing a rate of 61 percent).
19 Kids Count Data Center. Some poor rural areas in the south have similar statistics; over 80 percent of children are living without fathers in parts of Arkansas, Mississippi, and Louisiana that are primarily rural, black, and poor. Rosiak (2012); Murphey and Cooper (2015, 11).

20 It increased slightly (3.5 percent) for Whites, so the White–Black ratio is over 17 to 1. See Vornovitsky, Gottschalck and Smith (2011).
21 Lipsitz and Oliver (2010, 159–61).
22 Cohen (2015b).
23 Bassuk *et al.* (2014, 77).
24 Aviles de Bradley (2015).
25 Jiang *et al.* (2017, 6).
26 See, for example, Wakefield and Wildeman (2014, 17) ("The large prison population also gives the impression that racial disparities are improving when they are actually at best staying the same."); Mencimer (2014) (reporting empirical research of Kathryn Edin, who stated that "the people they're finding in Cleveland and other study sites 'aren't in the census.' Even she has trouble keeping track of her subjects. 'They can just fall right off the map,' she says."); US Census Bureau (2012).
27 US Bureau of Labor Statistics (2017) (showing 7.1 percent unemployment rate for blacks, 3.4 percent for whites as of November 2017).
28 Landivar (2013, 2); Jones (2007, 17).
29 Putnam (2016, 69–72).
30 More than 30 percent of white women and white men do. Office of Minority Health (2017b).
31 *Idem*, at 6.
32 DeNavas-Walt, Proctor and Smith (2011, 8).
33 Wakefield and Wildeman (2014, 27). Median income for black households is now under $40,000, versus $65,000 for white households.
34 Banks (2011).
35 Banks (2011); Kirby (1995).
36 Edin and Kefales (2005, viii).
37 See Edin and Nelson (2013, 32, 43).
38 See generally Edin and Kefalas (2005).
39 Edin and Kefalas (2005); Edin and Nelson (2013, 226).
40 Wallman (2016, 13).
41 Cohen (2015a).
42 Office of Family Assistance (2016); US Department of Agriculture, Food and Nutrition Service (2015).
43 Zilanawala and Pilkauskas (2012).
44 Bendheim-Thoman Center for Research on Child Wellbeing and Social Indicators Survey Center (2008).
45 Barnett and Berchick (2017).
46 FIFCFS (2017, 16).
47 Child Trends Data Bank (2013, 3, 6).
48 Fifteen percent of all other children live in those neighborhoods. Burns (2011).
49 Only 12 percent of white children do. Plumer (2013).
50 Seven percent of white children do. See Child Trends Data Bank (2013, 3).
51 Child Trends Data Bank (2013, 5); Alexander, Entwisle, and Olson (2014, 60–4); Smith and Fong (2004, 57ff, 214–18).
52 Gunn (2008).
53 Putnam (2015, 150).
54 Edin and Kefalas (2005, 34).
55 Edin and Shaefer (2015, 60).
56 Edin and Shaefer (2015, 78–80).
57 Plumer (2013).
58 Bordens and Epton (2016).
59 Hauser (2017).
60 Irwin and Bui (2016).
61 Stagman and Cooper (2010) (stating that 80percent of children in need of mental health services do not receive them); Samuels (2014); Foster and Hagan (2013) (reporting on study finding maternal incarceration induces depression and paternal incarceration leads to substance abuse when children transition to adulthood, and citing the literature on other

adverse results of parental incarceration); Dallaire *et al.* (2008) (citing research suggesting that community violence and poverty "undermine the child's sense of safety" and "significantly predicted symptoms of depression, even after accounting for demographic, familial, and personal protective factors"); Wagmiller (2007, 164).

62 Santiago, Kaltman, and Miranda (2013); Holm-Hansen (2006, 5–8).

63 Less than 40 percent for white children. Homa *et al.* (2015).

64 Schumaker and Scheller (2017).

65 Lenhardt (2011, 1558).

66 Struck (2012).

67 See, for example, Crouch and Moskop (2014).

68 Edin and. Nelson (2013, 34).

69 SAMHSA (2016) (showing 12.4 percent rate of illegal drug use for blacks, versus 10.2 percent national average).

70 Office of Minority Health (2016c).

71 Hughes, Sathe and Spagnola (2008, 2) (showing highest rate of cocaine use in Washington, DC, more than three times the rate in North Dakota); SAMHSA (2008), § C (showing significant variation in rates of illicit drug use among regions within states and among wards within the District of Columbia).

72 Williams (2016) (noting that "nearly all of the shooting victims and suspects in St. Louis this year have been African-American men and boys" and referring also to heroin-related spikes in homicides in Chicago, Baltimore, Milwaukee, and Philadelphia).

73 SAMHSA (2015).

74 National Alliance on Mental Illness (2017).

75 Vigod *et al.* (2014).

76 Anakwenze and Zuberi (2013).

77 See, for example, ABA Center on Children and the Law (2015), 79; Gnau (2015).

78 Smith (2014, 54–6); Ross (2015, 88–9).

79 Cooklin (2010) (stating that a child with an affectively ill parent has a 40 percent chance of developing an affective disorder by age 20).

80 Harrell *et al.* (2014); Renzetti (2009).

81 Mersky and Janczewski (2018, 481); Breiding *et al.* (2011) (41.2 percent victimization for black women, 30.2 percent for white women; 36.3 percent for black men, 26.6 percent for white men).

82 Smith *et al.* (2011, 121). Rates of sexual violence among black women are actually less than among white women, *idem*, 218, suggesting an extraordinarily high rate of non-sexual violence against black women.

83 Smith *et al.* (2011, 121). The lifetime rate for white women is also horrible, but significantly lower—37 percent.

84 National Association of Black Social Workers (NABSW) (2002).

85 See, for example, Janczewski and Mersky (2016, 123–32, 124, 130) (summarizing past studies showing actual maltreatment rates differ and presenting new evidence confirming absence of bias in state decision-making).

86 Dwyer and Bryant (2014, 55–8).

87 Breiding *et al.* (2011).

88 Centers for Disease Control and Prevention (CDC) (2015, 6–7, 67).

89 CDC (2017).

90 CDC (2014) (gonorrhea rate 19 times as high as for whites; chlamydia rate nine times as high; syphilis rate eight times as high).

91 Hartnett (2012) (quoting Harvard sociologist Kathryn Edin as saying "Both women and men at the bottom of the socioeconomic ladder see having kids as the ultimate form of fulfillment ... Early childbearing is highly selective of girls [who] have already diminished their life chances so much that an early birth does little to reduce them further" and concluding that "given their bleak economic prospects and minimal hope of upward mobility, being a parent is one of the few positive identities available to them").

92 FIFCFS (2017), 29.

93 Banks (2011).

94 American Cancer Society (2011); Office of Minority Health (2016b).

95 Office of Minority Health (2016b).
96 Office of Minority Health (2016d).
97 Office of Minority Health (2016d).
98 Office of Minority Health (2016a).
99 US Department HSS (2010).
100 Bardis (2012).
101 Office of Minority Health (2017a).
102 CDC (2014).
103 Patterson (2015).
104 Austin *et al.* (2001); Carson and Sabol (2012). Rates of incarceration are three times greater for black women as for white women, and six times greater for black men as for white men. NAACP (2017); Goode (2013).
105 Pettit (2012).
106 Pettit (2012). Black males aged 18–19 are imprisoned at more than nine times the rate for white males the same age. Carson and Sabol (2012, 7).
107 See Carson and Sabol (2012) at 9; Guzzardi (2011) (describing a 2011 study in Cook County, Illinois, showing that when convicted of a low-level drug offense, a black convict is eight times more likely than a white convict to serve prison time for it); NAACP (2017).
108 See, for example, Anderson (2008, 18); Gunn (2008); Thernstrom and Thernstrom (1999, 515–17) (pointing to racial solidarity as a motivation for not cooperating with prosecution of black defendants, including "jury nullification"); Urbina and Maag (2009) (reporting residents' view in poor black neighborhoods that police are apathetic about complaints of missing persons, sexual assaults, and other crimes they assume are simply a natural by-product of drug addiction).
109 Foster and Hagan (2012); Huebner and Gustafson (2007, 283–96).
110 Dwyer (2014, 465–541, 498–505); Potts (2014).
111 Carbone and Cahn (2014, 26) (noting that the non-marital birthrate among African Americans grew from 17 to 24 percent between 1940 and 1964, when Moynihan issued his Report, and then after 1964 it grew to over 70 percent).
112 Anderson (2008, 22).
113 Edin and Nelson (2013, 21, 224).
114 Edin and Nelson (2013, 208) (many fathers "withdraw from shame" because their behaviors prevent them from providing).
115 Carbone and Cahn (2014, 18). See also *idem*, 16–19 (describing the impact of educational attainment on relationship stability between intimate partners).
116 See Edin and Kefalas (2005, 2).
117 Only 3.6 percent of white children will experience this. Wakefield and Wildeman (2014, 33–7).
118 See Edin and Kefalas (2005, 23).
119 Carbone and Cahn (2014, 72–3).
120 Anderson (2008, 23).
121 Edin and Nelson (2013, 205).
122 Edin and Nelson (2013, 17, 24, 32, 205, 208–12).
123 Edin and Nelson (2013, 204, 215).
124 Carbone and Cahn (2014, 73–4).
125 Carbone and Cahn (2014, 73–4).
126 Eden and Nelson (2013, 211).
127 Eden and Nelson (2013, 10, 33).
128 Edin and Kefalas (2005, 35).
129 Edin and Kefalas (2005, 36).
130 Dillon (2009).
131 Greene and Winters (2006, 14–15).
132 Schott Foundation for Public Education (2008, 6, 8).
133 Wakefield and Wildeman (2014, 15).
134 See Anderson (2008, 22).
135 Anderson (2008, 22–3).
136 Edin and Nelson (2013, 212).

137 Edin and Nelson (2013, 22–4).
138 See, for example, Kneebone and Raphael (2011, 5, 9–10); US Department of Justice (2008) (showing rate of violent crime in metropolitan areas more than two and a half times as high as in non-metropolitan areas).
139 Gregory (2012).
140 Potts (2014, 18, 27).
141 Reyes *et al.* (2017).
142 Alexander, Entwisle, and Olseon (2014, 61).
143 Some excellent ethnographic work documents conditions in some of these places. See, for example, Venkatesh (2008) (Robert Taylor Homes housing project in Chicago); Venkatesh (2006) (the Marquis Park neighborhood of Chicago). There has also been a great number of investigative reports of the toxic living conditions for children in impoverished urban areas. See, for example, Hauser (2017); Fukada (2015) (Bedford-Stuyvesant neighborhood, Brooklyn); Goldberg (2015); Lah (2014); Bouffard (2014); Zeltner (2015) (listing asthma, diabetes, behavioral problems, truancy, and failure in school among the maladies afflicting children as a result of "toxic stress" in impoverished neighborhoods dominated by Blacks); Aldhous (2010); Dolnick (2010)l; Mack, Banchero, and Sweeney (2009) (melees between factions of students at Chicago's Fenger High School). For accounts of life for homeless children, see, for example, Elliott (2013) (five-part series documenting life of a homeless girl).
144 Eligon (2013).
145 Putnam (2015, 103).
146 Kneebone and Raphael (2011, 14).
147 See, for example, O'Connell (2016); Li (2016, 1197–200).
148 See Oppel (2015) (55 murders in one part of the city in six weeks, including some young children); Anderson (2008, 25) ("Neighborhoods of concentrated poverty in Philadelphia and other economically distressed cities are pervaded by high levels of crime, mayhem, and murder.... The urban environment continues to decline economically, socially, and physically."); Onishi (2013); Gregory (2012); Beatty (2013, 76–8).
149 Cambria (2016).
150 Garbarino, Bradshaw, and Kostelny (2009, 302). See also Dallaire *et al.* (2008, 831) (citing research support for the observation that neighborhood violence and poverty "decrease a parent's likelihood of engaging in warm, consistent, responsive and authoritative parenting behaviors" and thereby "significantly impact the development of children's competencies in negative ways").
151 MacDorman and Matthews (2011).
152 Williams (2011); MacDorman and Mathews (2011).
153 Gager (2007, 119) (explaining why pervasive adult unemployment inhibits the transition of youth in poor neighborhoods from dependency to self-sufficiency); Smith and Fong (2004, 57ff, 214–18) (discussing the critical need to improve social networks in impoverished neighborhoods).
154 Anderson (2008, 12, 15).
155 Darling-Hammond (2007) (discussing the persistent achievement gap between black and white students, the deterioration of many urban schools in the 1990s, the dim prospects for the many black students who drop out of school, the hiring of unqualified teachers for inner-city schools because qualified teachers were not applying, and emphasis on rote learning and lack of advanced courses in predominantly-black schools); Gager *et al.* (2007, 118–19) (noting "the social deterrents of employment resulting from social isolation of minorities in urban areas due to a lack of exposure to regularly employed middle class role models and/or social networks that lead to knowledge of and access to job opportunities" and that "growing up in a poor neighborhood during adolescence can lead to lifetime labor market disadvantage").
156 See, for example, Eligon (2016); Gross (2012). On the connection between racial composition of and government solicitude for a neighborhood, see Turner, Popkin, and Rawlings (2009).
157 See, for example, Katz (2012); Gammon (2012); Kay and Katz (2012).
158 National Center for Children in Poverty (2014).

159 NeighborhoodScout (2017).
160 Ashkenas *et al.* (2015).
161 Crouch and Moskop (2014) (stating that in St. Louis in 2013 "nineteen schools had mobility rates [number of transfers in or out divided by total enrollment] that exceeded 100 percent"); Skobba and Goetz (2013, 161); Jonsson (2016) (stating: "Some Atlanta elementary schools … see as much as 40 percent of the school population churn each year as parents struggle to find and retain housing … As with other factors in poor America, a sense of constant dislocation makes it more difficult for students to succeed").
162 Edin and Shaefer (2015, 73); Skobba and Goetz (2013, 157) (finding stress and strained relationships); Leopold (2012) (finding that 40 percent of very low-income households on waiting lists for housing assistance were living "doubled up" with family or non-relatives); Clampet-Lundquist (2003).
163 Smith and Smith (2006).
164 Haegerich and Tolan (2012, 129–30).
165 Haegerich and Tolan (2012, 126–32).
166 Smith (2014, 55).
167 See discussion of race disproportionality in Chapter 6.
168 Skinner and Skelton (2014).
169 St. John *et al.* (2015).
170 FIFCFS (2017, 34–5); Gabriel (2010); in math, black children of both genders are consistently and significantly below both white and Hispanic children of both genders. Anderson (2008, 44). A study of math performance in 2003–2009 among fourth graders found black boys' scores were 35–40 points lower than those of white boys' regardless of household income. *Idem*, 28. Another study found that in both fourth and eighth grade, black boys are behind white boys by at least 30 points in math. Gabriel (2010).
171 See, for example, Anderson (2008, 17–18).
172 Rates for white boys were 38 percent for reading, 44 percent for math Anderson (2008, 17–18).
173 Gabriel (2010).
174 Even if one looks at data for black males across all socioeconomic levels, the percentage of those not in school is a distressing 20 percent. See Pettit (2012).
175 Institute for Higher Education Policy (2010).
176 See Institute for Higher Education Policy (2010, 2); Zohang, Musu-Gillette, and Oudekerk (2016).
177 See generally Ross (2015, 95). *Idem* at 156 (suggesting that racial discrimination might also play a role: "If formally adjudicated, African American girls are three times more likely to be placed outside of the home as compared to their white counterparts").
178 Oppel (2015).
179 Schreck and Steward (2012, 47–69).
180 Schreck and Steward (2012, 52–3).
181 Hartnett (2012).
182 FIFCFS (2017, 7).
183 Beatty (2013, 76).
184 See generally Anakwenze and Zuberi (2013, 147–57). See also *idem*, 148 ("neighborhood disorder is a powerful chronic stressor").

Bibliography

ABA Center on Children and the Law. "Functional Brain Organization of Newborns Altered by Prenatal Cocaine Exposure," *Child Law Practice* 34(5) (2015), 79.

Aldhous, Peter. "Poor Neighbourhoods Can Kill." *New Scientist*, January 13, 2010, 2010, Special Report, sec. Health.

Alexander, Karl, Entwisle, Doris, and Olson, Linda. *The Long Shadow: Family Background, Disadvantaged Urban Youth, and the Transition to Adulthood.* New York: Russell Sage, 2014.

American Bar Association Group. "Functional Brain Organization of Newborns Altered by Prenatal Cocaine Exposure," *Child Law Practice* 34(5) (2015).

American Cancer Society. *Cancer Facts & Figures for African Americans 2011–2012*. Atlanta, GA: American Cancer Society, 2011.

Anakwenze, Ujunwa, and Daniyal Zuberi. "Mental Health and Poverty in the Inner City." *Health & Social Work* 38(3) (2013): 147–57.

Anderson, Elijah. *Against the Wall: Poor, Young, Black, and Male*. Philadelphia, PA: University of Pennsylvania Press, 2008.

Ashkenas, Jeremy, Larry Buchanan, Alicia Desantis, Park Haeyoun, and Derek Watkins. "A Portrait of the Sandtown Neighborhood in Baltimore." *New York Times*, May 3, 2015.

Austin, James, Marino A. Bruce, Leo Carroll, Patricia L. McCall, and Steven C. Richards. *The Use of Incarceration in the United States*. Columbus, OH: American Society of Criminology National Policy Committee, 2001.

Aviles de Bradley, Ann M. *From Charity to Equity: Race, Homelessness, & Urban Schools*. New York: Teachers College Press, 2015.

Banks, Ralph Richard. *Is Marriage for White People?: How the African American Marriage Decline Affects Everyone*. 1st ed. New York: Plume, 2011.

Bardis, Olympia. *African-Americans Less Likely to Receive Kidney Donation, Study shows*. US ed. Cable News Network. Turner Broadcasting System, Inc.: CNN, 2012.

Barnett, Jessica C. and Edward R. Berchick. *Health Insurance Coverage in the United States: 2016*. US Government Printing Office, Washington DC: US Census Bureau, 2017.

Bassuk, Ellen L., Carmela J. DeCandia, Corey Anne Beach, and Fred Berman. *America's Youngest Outcasts: A Report on Child Homelessness*. Waltham, MA: American Institutes for Research, 2014.

Beatty, Anne. "Survival Skills at a School in LA: Street Killings of Students are so Familiar in South Central that Kids Practice their Own Grim Rituals (Winter 2013)," *American Scholar* 81(1) (January 2013): 68–78.

Bendheim-Thoman Center for Research on Child Wellbeing and Social Indicators Survey Center. *Mothers' and Children's Poverty and Material Hardship in the Years Following a Non-Marital Birth*. Woodrow Wilson School of Public and International Affairs at Princeton University, 2008.

Bordens, Alex and Abraham Epton. "Young Victims of Violence in Chicago." *Chicago Tribune*, 2016.

Bouffard, Karen. "Detroit is Deadliest City for Children due to Prematurity, Violence." *The Detroit News*, January 31, 2014.

Breiding, Matthew J., Sharon G. Smith, Kathleen C. Basile, Mikel L. Walters, Jieru Chen, and Melissa T. Merrick. *Prevalence and Characteristics of Sexual Violence, Stalking, and Intimate Partner Violence Victimization — National Intimate Partner and Sexual Violence Survey, United States, 2011*. Atlanta, GA: Centers for Disease Control and Prevention, 2011.

Burns, Melinda. "Poor Neighborhoods Mean Fewer High School Grads." *Pacific Standard*. October 20, 2011, sec. Education.

Cambria, Nancy. "The Crisis Within: How Toxic Stress and Trauma Endanger our Children." *St. Louis Post-Dispatch*, February 21, 2016, sec. The Crisis.

Carbone, June and Naomi Cahn. *Marriage Markets: How Inequality is Remaking the American Family*. United States of America: Oxford University Press, 2014.

Carson, Ann E. and William J. Sabol. *Prisoners in 2011*. US Department of Justice, 2012.

Centers for Disease Control and Prevention (CDC), U.S. Department of Health and Human Services. *Health Disparities in HIV/AIDS, Viral Hepatitis, STDs, and TB*, 2014.

Centers for Disease Control and Prevention (CDC), U.S. Department of Health and Human Services. *Diagnoses of HIV Infection in the United States and Dependent Areas*, 2015.

Centers for Disease Control and Prevention (CDC), U.S. Department of Health and Human Services. *Factsheet: HIV among African Americans*, 2017.

Child Trends Data Bank. *Neighborhood Safety: Indicators of Child and Youth Well-Being*. May, 2013.

Clampet-Lundquist, Susan. "Finding and Keeping Affordable Housing: Analyzing the Experiences of Single-Mother Families in North Philadelphia," *The Journal of Sociology and Social Welfare* 30(4) (December 2003): 123–40.

Cohen, Patricia. "Aid to Needy often Excludes the Poorest in America." *New York Times*, February 16, 2015. 2015a.

Cohen, Patricia. "Racial Wealth Gap Persists Despite Degree, Study Says." *New York Times*, August 16, 2015. 2015b, sec. Economy.

Cooklin, Alan. "'Living Upside Down': Being a Young Carer of a Parent with Mental Illness," *Advances in Psychiatric Treatment* 16(2) (2010): 141–6.

Crouch, Elisa and Walker Moskop. "Poverty and Academic Struggle Go Hand-in-Hand." *St. Louis Post-Dispatch*, May 17, 2014, 2014, sec. Education.

Cuddy, Emily, Joanna Venator, and Richard V. Reeves. *In a Land of Dollars: Deep Poverty and its Consequences*. Washington, DC: Brookings Institute, 2015.

Dallaire, Danielle H., David A. Cole, Thomas M. Smith, Jeffrey A. Ciesla, Beth LaGrange, Farrah M. Jacquez, Ashley Q. Pineda, Alanna E. Truss, and Amy S. Folmer. "Predicting Children's Depressive Symptoms from Community and Individual Risk Factors," *Journal of Youth and Adolescence* 37(7) (August 2008): 830–46.

Darling-Hammond, Linda. "Educational Quality and Equality: What it Will Take to Leave no Child Behind." In *All Things being Equal: Instigating Opportunity in an Inequitable Time*, edited by Brian D. Smedley and Alan Jenkins. New York: The New Press, 2007.

DeNavas-Walt, Carmen and Bernadette D. Proctor. *Income and Poverty in the United States: 2014*. US Government Printing Office, Washington DC: US Census Bureau, 2015.

DeNavas-Walt, Carmen, Bernadette D. Proctor, and Jessica C. Smith. *Income, Poverty, and Health Insurance Coverage in the United States: 2010*. Washington, DC: US Census Bureau, 2011.

Dillon, Sam. "Large Urban-Suburban Gap Seen in Graduation Rates." *New York Times*, April 22, 2009, sec. Education.

Dolnick, Sam. "Problems Mount at a Bronx Building Bought in a Bubble." *New York Times*, January 19, 2010, sec. NY/Region.

Drake, Brett and Mark R. Rank, "The Racial Divide among American Children in Poverty: Reassessing the Importance of Neighborhood," *Children and Youth Services Review* 31(12) (2009): 1264–71.

Dwyer, James G. "Jailing Black Babies." *Utah Law Review* 3 (2014): 465–541.

Dwyer, James G. and Linda L. Bryant. "Promising Protection: 911 Call Records as Foundation for Family Violence Intervention," *Kentucky Law Journal* 102(1) (May 28, 2014): 49–101.

Edin, Kathryn and Timothy J. Nelson. *Doing the Best I Can: Fatherhood in the Inner City*. Berkeley, CA: University of California Press, 2013.

Edin, Kathryn and Maria Kefalas. *Promises I Can Keep: Why Poor Women Put Motherhood before Marriage*. Berkeley, CA: University of California Press, 2005.

Edin, Kathryn J. and H. Luke Shaefer. *$2.00 a Day: Living on Almost Nothing in America*. New York: Houghton Mifflin Harcourt, 2015.

Eligon, John. "In Places Like North St. Louis, Gunfire Still Rules the Night." *New York Times*, November 19, 2013, sec. US.

Eligon, John. "A Question of Environmental Racism in Flint," *New York Times*, January 21, 2016, sec. US.

Elliott, Andrea. "Invisible Child." *New York Times*, December 9, 2013.

Federal Interagency Forum on Child and Family Statistics (FIFCFS). *America's Children: Key National Indicators of Well-Being*, FIFCFS, 2017.

Foster, Holly and John Hagan. "Maternal and Paternal Imprisonment in the Stress Process." *Social Science Research* 42(3) (May 2013): 650–69.

Foster, Holly and John Hagan. "Intergenerational Educational Effects of Mass Imprisonment in America," *Sociology of Education* 85(3) (January 5, 2012): 259–86.

Fukada, Shiho. "Stray Bullets." *New York Times*, October 7, 2015, sec. Opinion.

Gabriel, Trip. "*Proficiency of Black Students is Found to be Far Lower than Expected.*" *New York Times*, November 9, 2010, sec. Education.

Gager, Constance To, Jacqueline C. Pflieger, and Jennifer Hickes Lundquist. "To Work or Not to Work? The Role of Poverty, Race/Ethnicity, and Regional Location in Youth Employment." In *The Promise of Education*, edited by Barbara A. Arrighi and David J. Maume. Vol. 3, 119. Santa Barbara, CA: Praeger, 2007.

Garbarino, James, Catherine P. Bradshaw, and Kathleen Kostelny. "Neighborhood and Community Influences on Parenting." In *Parenting an Ecological Perspective*, Tom Luster and Lynn Okagaki. 2nd ed. New York: Routledge, 2009.

Gnau, Thomas. "Abandoned by Parents for Heroin." *My Dayton Daily News*, November 7, 2015, sec. Local.

Goldberg, Jeffrey. "A Matter of Black Lives." *The Atlantic*, September 2015.

Goode, Erica. "Incarceration Rates for Blacks have Fallen Sharply, Report Shows." *New York Times*, February 27, 2013, sec. US.

Greene, Jay P. and Marcus A. Winters. *Leaving Boys Behind: Public High School Graduation Rates*. New York: Manhattan Institute, 2006.

Gregory, Kia. "On a Corner Plagued by Violence, Rallying to Say Enough is Enough." *New York Times*, August 19, 2012, sec. NY/Region.

Gross, Liza. "Pollution, Poverty, People of Color: Don't Drink the Water." *Environmental Health News*, June 12, 2012.

Gunn, Raymond. "David's Story: From Promise to Despair." In *Against the Wall: Poor, Young, Black, and Male*, edited by Elijah Anderson. Philadelphia, PA: University of Pennsylvania Press, 2008.

Guzzardi, Will. *Blacks Far More Likely than Whites to be Jailed for Low-Level Drug Crimes*. Huffingtonpost.com: HuffPost, 2011.

Haegerich, Tamar M. and Patrick H. Tolan. "Delinquency and Comorbid Conditions." In *The Oxford Handbook of Juvenile Crime and Juvenile Justice*, edited by Barry C. Feld and Donna M. Bishop, 129–30. OxfordHandbooks.com: Oxford Handbooks Online, September 2012.

Hannah-Jones, Nikole. "Segregation Now: Sixty Years after Brown v. Board of Education, the Schools in Tuscaloosa, Alabama, show how Separate and Unequal Education is Coming Back." *The Atlantic* (May 2014).

Harrell, Erika, Lynn Langton, Marcus Berzofsky, and Hope Smiley-McDonald. *Household Poverty and Nonfatal Violent Victimization, 2008–2012*. US Department of Justice: Bureau of Justice Statistics, 2014.

Hartman, Chester and Gregory D. Squires. "Integration Exhaustion, Race Fatigue, and the American Dream." In *The Integration Debate: Competing Futures for American Cities*, edited by C. Hartman and G.D. Squires, 1–8. New York: Routledge, 2010.

Hartnett, Kevin. "When Having Babies Beats Marriage." *Harvard Magazine*, July–August 2012.

Hauser, Christine. "Chicago Reels as 3 Children are Gunned Down in 4 Days." *New York Times*, February 15, 2017, sec. US.

Holm-Hansen, Cheryl. "Racial and Ethnic Disparities in Children's Mental Health." *Wilder Research*, 2006.

Homa, David M., Linda J. Neff, Brian A. King, Ralph S. Caraballo, Rebecca E. Bunnell, Stephen D. Babb, Bridgette E. Garrett, Connie S. Sosnoff, Lanqing Wang, and Centers for Disease Control and Prevention (CDC). "Vital Signs: Disparities in Nonsmokers' Exposure to Secondhand Smoke—United States, 1999–2012," *Morbidity and Mortality Weekly Report* 64(4) (2015): 103–8.

Housing Assistance Council. "Race & Ethnicity in Rural America." *Rural Research Brief*. April, 2012.

Huebner, Beth M. and Regan Gustafson. "The Effect of Maternal Incarceration on Adult Offspring Involvement in the Criminal Justice System," *Journal of Criminal Justice* 35(3) (May–June 2007): 283–96.

Hughes, Arthur, Neeraja Sathe, and Kathryn Spagnola. *State Estimates of Substance use from the 2005–06 National Surveys on Drug use and Health*. Rockville, MD: Substance Abuse and Mental Health Services Administration, 2008.

Institute for Higher Education Policy. *Mini Brief: A Snapshot of African Americans in Higher Education*, February, 2010.

Irwin, Neil and Quoctrung Bui. "The Rich Live Longer Everywhere. For the Poor, Geography Matters." *New York Times*, April 11, 2016, sec. The Upshot.

Janczewski, Colleen E. and Joshua P. Mersky. "What's so Different about Differential Response? A Multilevel and Longitudinal Analysis of Child Neglect Investigations," *Children and Youth Services Review* 67 (2016): 123–32.

Jiang, Yang, Mercedes Ekono, and Curtis Skinner. *Basic Facts about Low-Income Children: Children Under 3 Years, 2015*. New York: National Center for Children in Poverty, 2017.

Jones, Nicholas A. *The American Community—Blacks: 2004*. Washington, DC: US Department of Commerce, US Census Bureau, 2007.

Jonsson, Patrik. "In Poor Neighborhoods, is it Better to Fix Up or Move Out?" *The Christian Science Monitor*, April 4, 2016.

Katz, Cheryl. "People in Poor Neighborhoods Breathe More Hazardous Particles," ScientificAmerican.org (November 1, 2012).

Kay, Jane and Cheryl Katz. "Pollution, Poverty, People of Color: The Factory on the Hill." *Environmental Health News*, June 4, 2012.

Kids Count Data Center. *Children in Single-Parent Families by Race*, 2016.

Kids Count Data Center. *Children in Poverty by Age Group*, 2017.

Kirby, Jacqueline. *Single-Parent Families in Poverty*. Akron: The University of Akron, 1995.

Kneebone, Elizabeth and Steven Raphael. *City and Suburban Crime Trends in Metropolitan America*. Washington DC: Brookings Institute, 2011.

Kucsera, John. *New York State's Extreme School Segregation: Inequality, Inaction and a Damaged Future*. The Civil Rights Project, March 26, 2014.

Lah, Kyung. *Mother Loses both Children in Same Month*. US ed. Cable News Network. Turner Broadcasting System, Inc.: CNN, 2014.

Landivar, Liana Christin. *Disparities in STEM Employment by Sex, Race, Hispanic Origin*. Washington, DC: US Census Bureau, 2013.

Lenhardt, Robin A. "Race Audits," *Hastings Law Journal* 62 (2011): 1527–77.

Leopold, Josh "The Housing Needs of Rental Assistance Applicants," *Cityscape: A Journal of Policy Development and Research* 14(2) (2012): 275–98.

Li, Bethany. "Now is the Time! Challenging Resegregation and Displacement in the Age of Hypergentrification." *Fordham Law Review* 85(3) (2016): 1189–93.

Lipsitz, George, and Melvin L. Oliver. "Integration, Segregation, and the Racial Wealth Gap," *The Integration Debate: Competing Futures for American Cities* (2010): 153–67.

MacDorman, M.F. and T.J. Matthews. *Understanding Racial and Ethnic Disparities in U.S. Infant Mortality Rates*. Hyattsville, MD: National Center for Health Statistics, 2011.

Mack, Kristen, Stephanie Banchero, and Annie Sweeney. "Fear, Frustration Come to Campus: Days After an Honor Student was Slain, Kids List the Perils of Walking to School, while Parents Demand a Halt to Violence." *Chicago Tribune*, September 29, 2009.

Massey, Douglas S. and Nancy A. Denton. *American Apartheid: Segregation and the Making of the Underclass*. Cambridge, MA: Harvard University Press, 1998.

Mersky, Joshua P. and Colleen E. Janczewski. "Racial and Ethnic Differences in the Prevalence of Adverse Childhood Experiences: Findings from a Low-income Sample of US Women." *Child Abuse & Neglect* 76 (2018): 480–7.

Mencimer, Stephanie. "What if Everything You Knew about Poverty was Wrong?" *Mother Jones*. March/April (2014).

Murphey, David and P. Mae Cooper. *Infants and Toddlers in the District of Columbia: A Statistical Look at Needs and Disparities*. Bethesda, MD: Child Trends, 2015.

National Alliance on Mental Illness. *Mental Health by the Numbers*, 2017.

National Association for the Advancement of Colored People (NAACP). *Criminal Justice Fact Sheet*, 2017.

National Association of Black Social Workers (NABSW). *Domestic Violence in the African American Community*, 2002.

National Center for Children in Poverty. *Child Poverty Pervasive in Large American Cities*, 2014.

NeighborhoodScout. *Crime Rates Top List*. NeighborhoodScout's Most Dangerous Neighborhoods—2017: Top 25 Most Dangerous Neighborhoods in America, 2017.

O'Connell, Jonathan. "Can D.C. Build a $45 Million Park for Anacostia without Pushing People Out?" *Washington Post*, January 21, 2016.

Office of Family Assistance, US Department of Health and Human Services. *Characteristics and Financial Circumstances of TANF Recipients, Fiscal Year 2015*. Washington, DC: Administration for Families and Children, 2016.

Office of Minority Health, US Department of Health and Human Services. *Diabetes and African Americans*, 2016a.

Office of Minority Health, US Department of Health and Human Services. *Heart Disease and African Americans*, 2016b.

Office of Minority Health, US Department of Health and Human Services. *Mental Health and African Americans*, 2016c.

Office of Minority Health, US Department of Health and Human Services. *Stroke and African Americans*, 2016d.

Office of Minority Health, US Department of Health and Human Services. *Obesity and African Americans*, 2017a.

Office of Minority Health, US Department of Health and Human Services. *Profile: Black/African American*, 2017b.

Onishi, Norimitsu. "Overrun by Crime, Oakland Looks to make Allies in Community." *New York Times*, March 10, 2013, sec. US.

Oppel, Jr, Richard A. "West Baltimore's Police Presence Drops, and Murders Soar." *New York Times*, June 12, 2015, sec. US.

Orfield, Gary. "Education and Civil Rights: Lessons of Six Decades and Challenges of a Changed Society." In *The Pursuit of Racial and Ethnic Equality in American Public Schools: Mendez, Brown, and Beyond*, edited by Kristi L. Bowman, 405–30. East Lansing, Michigan: Michigan State University Press, 2015.

Patten, Eileen and Jens Manuel Krogstad. *Black Child Poverty Rate Holds Steady, Even as Other Groups See Declines*. Washington, DC: Pew Research Center, 2015.

Patterson, Orlando. "The Real Problem with America's Inner Cities." *New York Times*, May 9, 2015.

Pettit, Becky. "Black Progress? Not When You Include the Incarcerated." *Washington Post*, November 13, 2012, sec. Local.

Plumer, Brad. "These Ten Charts Show the Black-White Economic Gap hasn't Budged in 50 Years." *Washington Post*, August 28, 2013, sec. Wonkblog.

Potts, Monica. "Is There Hope for the Survivors of the Drug Wars?" *The American Prospect* 25(2) (March 24, 2014).

Putnam, Robert D. *Our Kids: The American Dream in Crisis*. New York: Simon & Schuster, 2015.

Renzetti, Claire M. *Economic Stress and Domestic Violence*. National Online Resource Center on Violence against Women: National Resource Center on Domestic Violence, 2009.

Reyes, Jessica Masulli, Brittany Horn, Esteban Parra, and Christina Jedra. "CDC Plan Lacks Political Will: Tynesia Cephas Was 16 Years Old When She Was Gunned Down on Wilmington's East Side." *News Journal* (Wilmington, DE), October 9, 2017.

Rosiak, Luke. "Fathers Disappear from Households Across America." *The Washington Times*, December 25, 2012, sec. National.

Ross, Richard. *Girls in Justice*. 1st ed. Santa Barbara, CA: The Image of Justice, 2015.

Sack, Kevin and Megan Thee-Brenan. "Poll Finds most in U.S. Hold Dim View of Race Relations." *New York Times*, July 23, 2015, sec. US.

Salzwedel, Andrew P., Karen M. Grewen, Clement Vachet, Guido Gerig, Weili Lin, and Wei Gao. "Prenatal Drug Exposure Affects Neonatal Brain Functional Connectivity." *Journal of Neuroscience* 35(14) (April 8, 2015): 5860–9.

Samuels, Robert. "Mental Health Services for Washington's Poorest Kids is Lacking, Study Says." *Washington Post*, May 6, 2014, sec. Local.

Santiago, Catherine DeCarlo, Stacey Kaltman, and Jeanne Miranda. "Poverty and Mental Health: How Do Low-Income Adults and Children Fare in Psychotherapy?" *Journal of Clinical Psychology* 69(2) (2013): 115–26.

Schreck, Christopher J. and Eric A. Steward. "The Victim-Offender Overlap and its Implications for Juvenile Justice." In *The Oxford Handbook of Juvenile Crime and Juvenile Justice*, edited by Barry C. Feld and Donna M. Bishop, 47–69. OxfordHandbooks.com: Oxford Handbooks Online, September 2012.

Schumaker, Erin and Alissa Scheller. "Lead Poisoning is Still a Public Health Crisis for African-Americans." *HuffPost*, December 6, 2017.

Schott Foundation for Public Education. *Given Half a Chance: The Schott 50 State Report on Public Education and Black Males*. Cambridge, MA: Schott Foundation for Public Education, 2008.

Sherman, Arloc and Danilo Trisi. *Safety Net More Effective against Poverty than Previously Thought: Correcting for Underreporting of Benefits Reveals Stronger Reductions in Poverty and Deep Poverty in all States*. Washington, DC: Center on Budget and Policy Priorities, 2015.

Siegel-Hawley, Genevieve. "Tearing Down Fences: School Boundary Lines and Equal Educational Opportunity in the Twenty-First Century." In *The Enduring Legacy of Rodriguez: Creating New Pathways to Equal Educational Opportunity*, edited by Charles J. Ogletree and Kimberly J. Robinson, 183–99. Cambridge, MA: Harvard Education Press, 2015.

Skinner, A.C. and J. Skelton. "Prevalence and Trends in Obesity and Severe Obesity among Children in the United States, 1999-2012," *JAMA Pediatrics*, doi:10.1001/jamapediatrics. 2014.21, 2014.

Skobba, Kimberly and Edward Goetz. "Mobility Decisions of very Law-Income Households," *Cityscape: A Journal of Policy Development and Research* 15(2) (2013): 155–61.

Smith, Deborah and Brian Smith. "Perceptions of Violence: The Views of Teachers Who Left Urban Schools," *High School Journal* 89(3) (Feb–March, 2006): 34–42.

Smith, Holly Austin. *Walking Prey: How America's Youth are Vulnerable to Sex Slavery*. New York: St. Martin's Press, 2014.

Smith, Margaret G. and Rowena Fong. In *The Children of Neglect: When no One Cares*, 216–17. New York: Brunner-Routledge, 2004.

Smith, Sharon G. *et al*. *The National Intimate Partner and Sexual Violence Survey: 2010-2012 State Report*. Atlanta, GA: National Center for Injury Prevention and Control and Centers for Disease Control and Prevention, 2017.

Substance Abuse and Mental Health Services Administration (SAMHSA), Department of Health and Human Services. *Substate Estimates from the 2004–06 National Surveys on Drug use and Health*. Rockville, MD: Office of Applied Studies, 2008.

Substance Abuse and Mental Health Services Administration (SAMHSA), Department of Health and Human Services. "Race/Ethnicity and Treatment for Substance use and Depression." *SAMHSA News* 17(5) (September/October, 2009).

Substance Abuse and Mental Health Services Administration (SAMHSA), Department of Health and Human Services. *Key Substance Use and Mental Health Indicators in the United States: Results from the 2015 National Survey on Drug Use and Health*. 2015.

Substance Abuse and Mental Health Services Administration (SAMHSA), Department of Health and Human Services. *Racial and Ethnic Minority Populations*, 2016.

St. John, Edward P., Victoria J. Milazzo Bigelow, Kim Callahan Lijana, and Johanna C. Massé. *Left Behind: Urban High Schools and the Failure of Market Reform*. Baltimore, MD: John Hopkins University Press, 2015.

Stagman, Shannon and Janice L. Cooper. "Children's Mental Health: What Every Policymaker Should Know." National Center for Children and Poverty, 2010.

Struck, Doug. "Pollution, Poverty, People of Color: Falling into the 'Climate Gap'." *Environmental Health News*, June 19, 2012.

The National Association of Child Care Resources & Referral Agencies. *Temporary Assistance for Needy Families and Children in Poverty*, 2012.

Thernstrom, Stephan and Abigail Thernstrom. *America in Black and White: One Nation, Indivisible*. New York: Touchstone, 1999.

Turner, Margery Austin, Susan J. Popkin and Lynette Rawlings, *Public Housing and the Legacy of Segregation*. Washington, DC: The Urban Institute Press, 2009.

US Bureau of Labor Statistics. "Employment status of the civilian population by race, sex, and age." Economic News Release, Employment Situation Table A-2, 2017.

US Census Bureau. *Census Bureau Releases Estimates of Undercount and Overcount in the 2010 Census*, 2012.

US Department HSS. Office on Women's Health, *Kidney Disease, Minority Women's Health* (May 18, 2010).

US Department of Agriculture, Food and Nutrition Service. *WIC Racial-Ethnic Group Enrollment Data 2010*, 2015.

US Department of Justice, Federal Bureau of Investigation: Criminal Justice Information Services Division. *2007 Crime in the United States*, 2008.

Urbina, Ian and Christopher Maag. "After Gruesome Find, Anger at Cleveland Police." *New York Times*, November 5, 2009, sec. US.

Venkatesh, Sudhir Alladi. *Off the Books: The Underground Economy of the Working Poor*. Cambridge, MA: Harvard University Press, 2006.

Venkatesh, Sudhir Alladi. *Gang Leader for a Day: A Rogue Sociologist Takes to the Streets*. London: Penguin Group, 2008.

Vornovitsky, Marina, Alfred Gottschalck, and Adam Smith. *Distribution of Household Wealth in the U.S.: 2000 to 2011*. United States Census Bureau, 2011.

Vigod, Simone N., Cindy Lee Dennis, Paul A. Kurdyak, John Cairney, Astrid Guttmann, and Valerie H. Taylor. "Fertility Rate Trends among Adolescent Girls with Major Mental Illness: A Population-based Study," *Pediatrics* 133(3) (2014): e585–91.

Wagmiller, Robert L. "Children and the Changing Social Ecology of Economic Disadvantage in Urban America." In *Child Poverty in America Today: Families and Children, Volume 1*, edited by Barbara A. Arrighi and David J. Maume. Vol. 1, 163–4. Westport, CT: Greenwood Publishing Group, 2007.

Wakefield, Sara and Christopher Wildeman. *Children of the Prison Boom: Mass Incarceration and the Future of American Inequality (Studies in Crime and Public Policy)*. New York: Oxford University Press, 2014.

Wallman, Katherine K. *America's Children in Brief: Key National Indicators of Well-being, 2016*. Washington, DC: US Government Printing Office: Federal Interagency Forum on Child and Family Statistics, 2016.

Williams, Timothy. "Tackling Infant Mortality Rates among Blacks." *New York Times*, October 14, 2011, sec. US.

Williams, Timothy. "Crime Spike in St. Louis Traced to Cheap Heroin and Mexican Cartels." *New York Times*, April 2, 2016, sec. US.

Yow, Ruth Carbonette. *Students of the Dream: Resegregation in a Southern City*. Cambridge, MA: Harvard University Press, 2017.

Zeltner, Brie. "More than Half of Cleveland Kids Live in Poverty, and It's Making them Sick." *Cleveland.com*, June 15, 2015.

Zilanawala, Afshin and Natasha V. Pilkauskas. "Material Hardship and Child Socioemotional Behaviors: Differences by Types of Hardship, Timing, and Duration." *Child and Youth Services Review* 34(4) (April 2012): 814–25.

Zohang, Anlan, Lauren Musu-Gillette, and Barbara Oudekerk. *Indicators of School Crime and Safety: 2015*. US Department of Education, and Bureau of Justice Statistics, Office of Justice Programs, US Department of Justice, Washington, DC: National Center for Education Statistics, Institute of Education Sciences, 2016.

Chapter 2

How *we* perpetuate the cycle

This chapter describes from a child-developmental perspective the sequence of adverse experiences that await a great number of black children conceived today by adolescents or adults in urban ghettos. This is the micro-level explanation for why successive generations within families live in these areas of concentrated poverty and suffer the personal problems that pervade them, regardless of what government programs exist to combat the structural problems and the personal dysfunctions. In simplest form, to provide a sense of the structure of this chapter: Children are born to marginal or dysfunctional adults in toxic communities at a high rate and get damaged very early in life, by their parents, their social and physical environment, or by the state's child welfare system. That personal damage makes them function poorly for the rest of their lives, including when they become parents. What public or private money is devoted to fixing damaged people is ineffectual.

That is it. If you investigate the life histories of the black individuals who make up a disproportionate percentage of the population in juvenile detention centers and prisons, homeless shelters, the juvenile court's maltreatment docket, and drug dens you will find some combination of: organic damage from maternal ingestion of drugs, alcohol, or tobacco during pregnancy, or from toxins in the environment after birth; parental disengagement or maltreatment; instability of caretaking during infancy; extreme stress from neighborhood conditions; and a community culture that induces life-limiting choices.[1] Anti-poverty programs—whether outright cash payments or job programs or "community-asset-building" investments—cannot end the inter-generational cycle, because the problem is not just lack of money and opportunity; it is primarily deeply-damaged people, concentrated together in disordered areas, and having babies they are unable to spare from also becoming damaged.[2] Existing programs targeting the children, such as Head Start and Nurse-Family Partnership, are also ineffectual in keeping them out of the cycle.

This chapter tracks the stages of child development, identifying hazards present in each for persons born to members of depressed black urban communities. It explains at each step the role *our* laws—that is the rules of life that *our* representatives create, with our explicit or implicit support—play in causing children to be subject to these hazards, effectively imprisoning children from birth in the toxic world of their parents. Later chapters propose reforms. Here the point is just this factual one: To stop the cycle, we would have to stop, as much as possible, what is going on at each of these stages.

Pre-natal harm

To begin with, most black babies born to mothers living in areas of concentrated poverty start life at some disadvantage because of influences on *in utero* development. How much disadvantage results from any individual influence is difficult to establish. This is in part because any particular influence necessarily interacts with others—other prenatal inputs and innumerable facets of children's experience growing up after birth. In addition, most types of research are dependent on maternal willingness to participate and on maternal reporting, so sampling bias and uncertainty about information accuracy plague the research, uniformly in the direction of underestimating unhealthy maternal behavior and adverse consequences from it. (ACLs, of course, latch onto any non-finding in a study and cite it as proof that maternal behavior does not harm babies, uninterested in the validity of the research design.[3]) We can, though, identify types of influence that the best research finds tend to result in worse outcomes for children.

First, these mothers live in a highly stressful social environment where maintaining a healthy lifestyle is quite difficult. For example, a "resident leader" in a Chicago housing project expressed to a researcher "that overwhelming stress had driven her to smoking two packs of cigarettes a day and that she was on medication for high blood pressure and anxiety," explaining: "If you're not a drug addict, you're going to end up on something because you got to have something, and sometimes you have to really, really not see … You got to turn and … look the other way … it's rough."[4] There is little that can be done about that short of transforming those communities, which is not going to happen. Second, most of these mothers do not receive prenatal care until late in pregnancy or not at all. Third, a substantial minority of these babies get alcohol, nicotine, and/or illegal drugs in their bloodstream *in utero*.

Medical professionals and advocates for women and children place great emphasis on pre-natal care, because pre-natal life is of great developmental importance. It is an important focus of advocacy among, for example, those who work with pregnant prison inmates. As a human being grows from a barely-perceptible zygote to a 20-inch long creature, the rudiments of all bodily systems develop—in particular, the brain that will regulate beliefs, attitudes, emotions, and behavior for the rest of life. The physical environment in which this occurs greatly influences the quality of these critical bodily systems, but that physical environment is part of the body of a presumptively-autonomous person, whose choices can greatly affect the quality of the environment, and law and policy must respect that person.

Only 60 percent of black expectant mothers overall receive prenatal care starting in the first trimester, compared with over three-quarters of white mothers.[5] Most of the rest receive care later in the pregnancy, but as much as 10 percent of black mothers overall receive none.[6] The rate of non-care is much higher among teen mothers and women suffering from addiction, mental illness, or domestic violence. Contrary to common claims from advocates for poor women, surveys of women who fail to get prenatal care suggest the primary reasons are mundane practical obstacles such as lack of transportation or child care rather than avoiding surveillance,[7] though substance abusers do also worry about being stigmatized or reported to authorities by clinic staff.[8] Failure to receive care creates danger of nutritional deficiencies (protein, zinc, iron, and certain fatty acids), which for the baby can "disturb brain functioning and thus predispose to antisocial behavior in children and adolescents."[9] Additional consequences are higher rates of preterm delivery, low birth weight, congenital malformations, and infant mortality, all of which disproportionately occur with black babies (e.g., over 40 percent are born preterm).[10]

The state's efforts to ensure pre-natal care for unborn children are largely limited to subsidizing the cost for poor women. Some state or local governments might also pay to advertise its importance. Several states protect substance-abusing women from CPS intervention after delivery if they have been receiving pre-natal care, which might incentivize a few, if they are aware of and trust the legal system to adhere to that promise.[11] There is no direct legal sanction for failing to obtain adequate nutrition or medical check-ups during pregnancy. (I am not suggesting here that there should be; this chapter is merely descriptive.)

In addition to needing positive inputs, fetuses need to avoid harmful inputs. The federal government and most states have criminal and civil laws aimed at protecting unborn children against harmful conduct by persons other than the mother, such as physical attack, reckless driving, or even creation of stressful or otherwise unhealthy conditions (e.g., domestic violence, shackling of pregnant prison inmates, pollutants in a work environment or water system).[12] Certainly, if someone (e.g., angry ex-boyfriend) snuck up on a pregnant women (e.g., while she was sleeping) and used a syringe to inject alcohol or heroin into her womb, the criminal law would punish that person severely.

Harmful inputs are bad for the child regardless of source, of course. Prenatal exposure to alcohol, certain drugs, or nicotine that mothers intentionally ingested elevates the risk of negative occurrences during pregnancy or at birth, of impaired brain development, and of behavior disorders in childhood and adolescence.[13] "80% of FASD [fetal alcohol spectrum disorder]-diagnosed children exhibit neurological deficits such as microcephaly (decreased brain size) or behavioral abnormality ... Poor attention capacity, judgement, memory, hyperactivity, negative conduct, and other behavioral issues are also noted within this population,"[14] as are lower IQs.[15] "The Centers for Disease Control and Prevention advocates abstaining from alcohol during pregnancy as the only way to reliably prevent FASDs."[16] Alcohol consumption is proportionately distributed among racial groups,[17] but heavier use occurs among people who suffer from depression or live in a stressful environment. There is little indication of alcohol abuse among young mothers in ethnographic work on black ghettos; families discourage them from "partying" once pregnancy is known.[18] Alcohol intake might therefore be a concern principally with somewhat older poor women, of any race, having their third or higher child. Significantly, "the cumulative effect of conditions commonly found amongst poor women—e.g., substandard living conditions, inadequate nutrition, and high levels of stress—[degrade] the ability of a mother's body to protect the fetus from the effects of alcohol."[19] One study found risk of fetal alcohol syndrome 16 times higher for babies of poor mothers than for babies with more affluent mothers who consumed similar amounts of alcohol.[20]

The worst damage from alcohol seems to occur in the first two months after conception,[21] when girls and women are less likely to be aware of the pregnancy. But consumption later in pregnancy is also quite damaging.[22] A 2014 research report found that a "moderate- to high-dose" of

> prenatal exposure to alcohol significantly altered the expression of genes and the development of a network of connections in the neocortex—the part of the brain responsible for high-level thought and cognition, vision, hearing, touch, balance, motor skills, language, and emotion.

"The changes were especially severe in the frontal cortex, which regulates motor skill learning, decision-making, planning, judgment, attention, risk-taking, executive function and social skills." Even for children with milder forms of fetal alcohol spectrum disorder, "behavioral issues such as hyperactivity, hyperirritability and attention problems" were "dramatic."[23]

Smoking, like alcohol consumption, is a legal activity for people 21 or older. Research shows an impact on fetal growth, but not on long-term growth after birth.[24] *In utero* infection with nicotine significantly increases risk of placental abruption, low birth weight, premature delivery, spontaneous abortion, and certain birth defects, and "has also been linked to decreased pulmonary function, sudden infant death syndrome, and harm to the child's mental and emotional functioning," as well as neonatal hyperactivity, which could interfere with feeding.[25] At least some of these effects can also result from second-hand smoke, so residing with smokers poses a risk to prenatal development.[26] Beyond enforcing the prohibition on underage consumption of alcohol and nicotine and disseminating information about their effects on unborn children (e.g., regulations requiring label warnings, public service announcements), government generally does nothing to address these problems.

Studies do consistently show higher incidence of illegal drug abuse among pregnant black women overall—in one eight-year study, 7.7 percent versus 4.4 percent for white women.[27] Research also shows greater cocaine and marijuana use among single, unemployed, and less educated pregnant women.[28] Combining these observations suggests a high rate of illegal drug use during pregnancy among black mothers in poor, urban areas, consistent with high numbers of babies born with positive toxicology in inner-city hospitals.

The most common illegal drug among pregnant women and among poor blacks is marijuana.[29] (Its now being legalized will likely increase its prevalence.) There is some evidence it causes modest deficits in children—reduced short- and long-term memory, poorer higher-order thinking skills, behavioral disorders, neuropsychiatric diseases.[30] Harder drugs—cocaine, heroin, and methamphetamines—appear much more problematic, having several serious effects on fetuses, especially if mothers abuse more than one substance. A 2015 study involving a group of cocaine users and a group that used other drugs was "the first to show that maternal drug use during pregnancy alters the brain's functional organization in newborns." MRIs showed the most severe impact was in babies of cocaine users, relating to "suppression of amygdala responses from the higher-order prefrontal cortex," which "may potentially underlie the arousal dysregulation" and "later behavioral outcomes."[31]

Meth use is associated with a long list of developmental deficits,[32] but appears to be still uncommon in black communities. Crack cocaine remains the third most commonly abused substance (after alcohol and marijuana) for blacks, and a normal dose "delivers at least ten times the amount of cocaine present in a standard 'line' of powdered cocaine." By constricting blood vessels and reducing oxygen supply to the baby, it creates heightened risk of obstetric complications and

> a variety of teratogenic effects, including killing parts of the fetal brain and intestines …, swelling of the kidneys …, a variety of cephalic and cardiac disorders, cleft palate, cleft lip, possessing an abnormal number of digits, down syndrome, and causing a fetus's intestines to stick out of his or her body.[33]

Moreover, post birth withdrawal symptoms "include seizures, tremors, sleep pattern disturbances, irritability and feeding problems."[34] Extended stays in the ICU, coupled with the inappropriateness of breast feeding if drugs remain in the mother's system, inhibit maternal bonding. Long-term effects are harder to discern, because so many other variables influence a child's development after birth. Many studies find, though, that because cocaine exposure interferes with neurotransmitter development, it manifests in adolescence in problems with learning, language, thought-process, and behavior.[35] Most cocaine users consume alcohol or benzodiazepines "to mediate the 'crash' following cocaine use," and the combination of toxic substances intensifies the effect of each.[36] Unlike alcohol, the harmful effects of cocaine are greater in the second and third trimesters than in the first.[37]

Opioid abuse is especially evident to birthing facility personnel because of the severe withdrawal babies manifest: One neonatal nurse explained:

> Even in your darkest, deepest imagination, you can't imagine their agony. You think you might know what one of these tremoring and screaming babies sounds and looks like, but it's nothing like a colicky baby. We have some who scream as if their limbs are being ripped off.[38]

In 2013, almost 1 percent of all newborns nationally, more than 27,000 altogether, suffered Neonatal Abstinence Syndrome (NAS) because of opioid exposure, and the numbers have been climbing steadily.[39] A St. Louis hospital saw the number increase by 52 percent in five years.[40] NAS lasts up to ten weeks, so the baby's experience of the world in the first month or two of life—imprinting an inchoate impression on his or her brain of what the outside world is like—is basically torture. In addition to NAS, heroin use during pregnancy impairs fetal growth, causing low birth weight in over 40 percent of affected pregnancies and smaller average head circumference.

There are two basic things the state might do to prevent prenatal harm: Prevent pregnancy among women whose situation makes it likely, and prevent it from occurring after a baby is conceived. As to the first, states provide funding for contraception, which is readily available for free to inner-city poor males and females. Lack of access to birth control is not an explanation for unwanted or unwise procreation.[41] There is some cultural bias against contraception use in black ghettos (it signals distrust in one's sexual partner or lack of commitment on one's own part), and many substance abusers are not sufficiently in control of their lives to get to the clinic regularly, take a pill every day, or keep condoms with them and insist on use of condoms when engaging in sex.[42] And other than subsidizing family planning, all the state does to prevent conception is maintain statutory rape laws on their books, while rarely enforcing them.

Most states also do little to prevent harmful inputs by pregnant women. There are laws criminalizing use of certain drugs by anyone; these are generally unenforced,[43] but police in some areas might use them to detain women they believe to be pregnant. A minority of states also or instead authorize charges of criminal or civil child maltreatment after birth when birthing facilities detect pre-natal substance abuse and report it to authorities.[44] (Most do not, because courts conclude that legislatures intended "child" to mean a person after birth when they enacted maltreatment laws.)

Advocates for women are likely correct in asserting that threat of criminal prosecution during pregnancy for substance abuse is likely only to make matters worse for the baby, not deterring substance abuse but potentially deterring a woman from going to a clinic for pre-natal care (though most would not go to a clinic regardless). I doubt the threat of post-birth maltreatment charges adds anything to the other reasons already causing a substantial percentage not to get pre-natal care—namely, fear of health care providers' berating them or reporting them to police simply for violating drug laws. More to the point: I am aware of no evidence showing, and I find it intuitively implausible, that such efforts deter substance abuse during pregnancy. Women suffering from addiction are unlikely to consider the uncertain possibility of being charged with maltreatment months down the road substantial enough to outweigh their current, intense desire to get drunk or high. Even if they thought "I am definitely going to get caught for doing this and might lose my baby as a result," it would likely be insufficient to stop them from abusing, as evidenced by the great number who test positive after delivery. Addiction is enormously powerful, and former addicts are forthright about how children became of secondary importance to their addicted self.[45] One mother explained,

> The funny thing about addiction is it doesn't matter how much you love your child. It doesn't matter how much you want to do good.… The addiction has this force that if you don't address what the issues are surrounding the addiction, you're always going to go back to it.

Another, who had entered prison pregnant three times, said that after each time she was paroled, she "did what I normally did on the outside because that's what addicts do. We're selfish … The babies aren't going to get us clean … I have six kids and that didn't cure me."

Apart from deterrence, the state could try to induce pregnant addicts to get treatment. There is some public funding of substance abuse treatment facilities. Liberals complain there is not enough. Even if treatment is available, though, at any given time most substance abusers do not want it, even if they are pregnant; they are not ready to try to stop using. Many inner-city areas have long waiting lists for certain forms of addiction treatment, but the lists represent a fraction of addicts. In some other areas, there are open spaces, and clinic and social workers who encounter pregnant substance abusers urge them to enter a program, but such exhortations are ineffectual with most; either they are ready or they are not.

Crucially, even substance abusers who get treatment are highly unlikely to achieve sobriety before the pregnancy is over. All these addictions are extremely difficult to overcome. Ethnographic work on drug addicts attempting recovery in areas of concentrated poverty is monotonously depressing, the occasional "success" usually temporary and dwarfed by the number of persistent failures.[46] A recurrent theme is that addicts face multiple obstacles to long-term functionality—not only chemical dependency but also traumatic life histories and home and community environments pushing them to find mental and emotional escape.[47] As liberals who complain about foster-care timelines in the Adoption and Safe Families Act (ASFA) emphasize, the path to non-abuse is neither short nor straight; there is a cycle of abstinence and relapse that typically repeats numerous times before an addiction can be deemed under control. In 2016, 64,000 people in the US died from drug overdose, commonly while relapsing.[48] The vast majority of people who seek treatment have been in treatment before, most more than once.[49] The medical consensus is that "it takes most addicts well over a year of skilled, intense inpatient treatment to even have a chance of recovery."[50]

> Effective treatment generally requires a combination of craving-reducing drugs (to give recovery a chance), time (for the brain to literally recover), counseling (for the

addict to understand what he or she is going through), mutual support (to maintain sobriety), and transition training (to prepare for reentering society).[51]

Moreover,

[s]cientists who study addiction understand how little the disease needs to return at full strength. Even brief flashing images of drug paraphernalia are sufficient to trigger a flood of dopamine in a recovering brain, which can, in turn, cause a relapse. The addict is all the more vulnerable when access to the drug is easy.[52]

Drugs and drug paraphernalia are ubiquitous in areas of concentrated poverty, and drug sellers have financial incentive to lure addicts back in.

Thus, even the best treatment programs, with all the facilities and services and encouragement experts typically recommend, have a success rate less than 20 percent.[53] Among the small percentage of alcohol abusers who enter treatment, only a small percentage complete it and avoid relapsing thereafter. AA's success rate is between 5 and 8 percent.[54] Many jurisdictions have implemented well-financed pilot programs to see how successful they could be in overcoming addiction with new and intensive approaches, and the results only reinforce how dim the prospects are for someone unable to curtail their substance abuse on their own. For example, a five-year demonstration project in Cook County, Illinois, provided 1500 randomly selected parents in the child protective system with comprehensive needs assessment, entry into addiction treatment within 24 hours, and a "Recovery Coach" to coordinate services, monitor progress, advocate for and encourage them. It secured recommended services very quickly for the vast majority of parents but raised the rate at which social workers thought it "safe" to return a child to parent custody only from 11.6 percent to 15.5 percent.[55] Moreover, treatment success rates are even lower for African-Americans than they are for whites.[56] As I explain in Chapter 6 and in an appendix, family drug courts have similarly abysmal success rates, and most serve only to further harm children by stringing out foster care. Even for those in these programs who succeed, it is unclear treatment made the difference; whatever caused them to decide to try (self-anger, threat of jail or TPR) might have been sufficient to motivate them to change on their own.

It is very difficult, therefore, to justify much social service spending on substance abuse treatment, especially if there are effective means of preventing people from ever becoming substance abusers, means that could be deployed extensively with additional funding. This will seem heresy to liberals, but children might benefit more if money were taken from this area of government budgets and reallocated to the child-centered proposals I will make in subsequent chapters. In a world of unlimited resources, sure, spend more on treatment facilities. Given that there is no more money, what little there is for combatting dysfunction should be directed to most effective use. Intensive substance abuse treatment is very expensive and has little pay off. More money for treatment is not the answer, and there is no more money anyway.

So is there nothing states can do about pre-natal harm from alcohol, drugs, or smoking? A small number attempt simply to disable pregnant women from obtaining and using harmful substances. Some do so by prosecuting women for illegal substance possession or use and either jailing them or making abstinence a condition of probation. This is not helpful from a child-welfare perspective. Treating the woman as a criminal helps no one, and placing a pregnant woman in any facility that does not specialize in dealing with withdrawal further endangers the baby.

Another means of disabling is civil commitment. Every state has laws authorizing this for individuals who, because they are mentally unable to control their behavior, pose a danger to themselves or others. Some might be too restrictive to apply to addiction. Virginia's law authorizes commitment only if a judge finds a "mental illness" and that "all available less restrictive treatment alternatives to involuntary inpatient treatment ... that would offer an opportunity for the improvement of the person's condition have been investigated and determined to be inappropriate ..." The fetus is either another person or part of the woman's self, so behavior posing a danger to the fetus is one or the other. However, addiction per se is not a "mental illness," and judges are likely to find some less restrictive treatment offers "an opportunity" for "improvement."

Some state laws, though, refer specifically to alcohol or drug abuse as a basis for commitment, and many local jurisdictions have been using these to commit people because of addiction, typically at the request of family members.[57] These laws recognize that substance abuse is harmful to self regardless of pregnancy. They generally require that commitment entails appropriate "treatment," however, and requires termination of commitment if treatment is not "working" of if no rehabilitative treatment is being given.[58] Commitment itself could be deemed "working" insofar as it safely stops the abuse, but if various reformative strategies, such as extensive counseling, must be provided, in addition to medical care, in order for "treatment" to be found, then this intervention is also expensive and using it more often would require taking funds from elsewhere in the state budget.

The state's bad parentage decision-making

This is the crux, the core problem with the legal system's treatment of children born to marginal or unfit biological parents who live in horrible neighborhoods. Prenatal adversity can be substantially ameliorated with high-quality post-natal parenting, but it is greatly exacerbated by marginal or dysfunctional parenting. Yet progress with improving at-risk children's postnatal life is extraordinarily difficult because, as with slavery in the nineteenth century, public discussion about this topic is riddled with unsupportable moral assertions by people who ultimately refuse to acknowledge the separate and equal personhood of another human being—in this case, the newborn child—and to open their minds to rational explanation of the rights that equal personhood entails.

A baby's caregivers largely determine the child's experience of the world outside the womb, and that experience has a tremendous effect on every aspect of the child's development and later life.[59] The state's creation of legal parent–child relationships is therefore life-determining, more momentous than its creation of any other legal family relationship. Comprehension of certain basic aspects of early childhood development is crucial to sound state decision-making in this realm.

In the first half year of life, what children need is a safe, low-stress environment in which their physical needs are promptly met, so they get what they need physically and feel the assurance that their needs will be met in the future—that the world is a hospitable place. That impression on their brains influences how they later approach other persons and make decisions about their lives. For that impression to be positive, babies need caregivers capable of quickly and appropriately responding to their signals, such as cries for food, warmth, sleep, attention, and contact, and who can provide a home that is not dangerous, chaotic, or highly stressful.

An important fact largely unknown to or ignored by child welfare workers and many participants in policy and legal debates about child protection is that it does not much matter at this earliest stage, prior to the critical period of attachment formation, *who* in particular is providing the baby's care.[60] Temporary caregivers, such as foster parents, can fully satisfy a newborn's needs so long as they have sufficient material resources (e.g., enough healthy food, stable and safe housing), concern, understanding of babies' signals, time, and capacity for giving positive attention to a very needy, non-lingual person in a peaceful environment. A caregiver who is not the biological mother might not be able to breastfeed the baby, which is nutritionally significant (but the birth mother might be unable safely to breastfeed anyway), and a baby's interactions in the earliest months can provide *some* psychological foundation for his or her later development of secure attachment to a permanent caregiver, as well as for the mother's bonding with the child, but otherwise there is little or no reason to prefer the birth mother. So if a particular birth mother is currently incapable of satisfying a newborn's needs even with available assistance that she is willing to receive, a good alternative caregiver is better for the baby in the short run. Widespread belief that a newborn simply must be with his or her mother reflect ideology or ignorance.

Conversely, what is *bad* for a child's earliest post-partum development includes physical abuse (e.g., from shaking) or neglect (e.g., malnutrition), and also social deprivation and stress. Physical abuse can cause severe and lasting neurological and psychological damage. Neglect, in addition to creating in the child a lasting sub-conscious sense that the world is not a nurturing place where one's needs are met, can retard cognitive and physiological growth, shrinking the child's life prospects. In addition, we know from studies of children who spent time after birth in institutional care that even if they are safe and have basic physical needs satisfied, if they receive little caregiver attention they incur "metabolic deficits in the areas of the brain believed to be involved in higher cognition, emotion, and emotion regulation."[61] Child development expert Pamela Alexander writes:

> Abandonment or even the careless inattention of a caregiver can lead to a child's realistic sense of terror—perhaps that is why parental neglect often has more deleterious effects than abuse.... The ability of the mother to accurately interpret and respond contingently to the infant's emotional cues is integral to the development of the right hemisphere of the brain as well as to the child's acquisition of identity.... Therefore, the mother's lack of awareness of her own internal states or her preoccupation with her own unresolved experience of trauma has the potential to seriously compromise the child's sense of self, lifelong ability to regulate emotions, and even neural substrate.[62]

Further, many babies—in particular, those impacted by maternal alcohol or drug abuse during pregnancy—require "super caregivers" who are extraordinarily attentive and capable of satisfying extraordinary needs, not merely average or normal caregivers.[63] As explained above, this is disproportionately true of black babies born in poor communities. These babies should not be in the care of marginal parents (very immature, cognitively impaired, lacking suitable and stable housing), let alone deeply-dysfunctional ones (mentally ill, substance abusing, criminally involved, etc.), yet birth mothers in the poorest communities are disproportionately marginal or dysfunctional. A substantial percentage are emotionally-needy and socially distracted teenage school dropouts living in an environment (parents' home) over which they have little control, and many older mothers are distracted and disabled by relationship and housing instability, poverty, substance abuse, abusive partners, having other children in foster care, or facing criminal charges. In the worst neighborhoods, a great number of parents can be found living illegally with their children in derelict apartments or in the stairwells or laundry rooms of housing projects.[64] It is no surprise then, that 30 percent of all child fatalities are among black children and that the infant mortality rate among blacks in inner cities is far higher than that for any other group; preterm, low-weight, neurologically-compromised babies are born and go home with poor women incapable, because of mental health, substance-abuse, or home-environment problems, to provide the superior care these babies need.[65]

An ever-increasing body of research provides a fairly clear picture of what sorts of birth-parent history, characteristics, and circumstances correlate with deficient parenting, and in particular with high risk of future abuse, neglect, abandonment, or accidental killing of children.[66] Yet despite having well-established knowledge about the profound importance of early infancy experience and of capable, nurturing caregivers, about the adverse consequences of abuse and neglect, and about parental characteristics that signal danger for a child, our government, applying laws we explicitly or implicitly endorse, places newborns into legal parent–child relationships with biological parents *in total disregard of their fitness and living circumstances*. A typical state parentage law confers legal mother status on whoever gave birth to the child, and confers legal father status on the basis of either biological paternity tests or a legal presumption as to who the biological father is. Period. No state's parentage statutes contain any exception even for biological parents who are manifestly and abjectly unfit—for example, having in the recent past killed or grotesquely abused another child, or having several other children in foster care because of maltreatment. (The singular "qualification"-type exclusion is for rapists in some paternity laws.) No matter how many children the state has already had to remove from a person's custody, and no matter how severe a drug addiction or mental illness is apparent at the time of birth, the state (our agent) forces the new child to be in a legal family relationship with such persons solely because they are the procreators, without requiring them to make any showing of rehabilitation. Indeed, state agencies are unlikely even to be aware of that history when they grant that person's application for a birth certificate establishing legal parenthood. Even if they know, it does not matter. You could have murdered five other children, but if your girlfriend was pregnant when you went to prison, the state will force that baby to be your legal child. Likewise with a 14-year-old who got pregnant to give her 16-year old gang-member boyfriend an exciting birthday present, and with the gun-slinging, drug-selling boyfriend—they are going to be the child's mommy and daddy.

Further, the state (our agent) confers a strong presumptive right to possess and control the life of the child on all legal parents (in some states, for some mothers, even if they are in prison). It thereby creates major obstacles to correcting this tragically foolish and disrespectful (to the child) initial parentage decision after the fact. The state does assume custody of some children immediately after birth, but this is a small fraction of those whose birth parents are high risk. The traditional and still dominant government approach to child maltreatment is *reactive* to *harms* that have already occurred to *this child*, rather than *proactive* in trying to *prevent* harm ever from occurring in high-risk families and environments. And once the damage is done, repair is extremely difficult, as evidenced by the multiple poor outcomes for mal-treated children. Moreover, the state's handling of maltreatment after it occurs is likely to inflict further damage on the child, as explained in the next subsection. The initial state decision of parentage is therefore fateful. This is when *we* throw them in the river. If we want to stop destroying black lives, we must reform parentage laws.

The federal government, thanks to Republican Congresses, has in the past two decades tried to push states toward a prevention approach, not by suggesting any change to parentage laws but rather simply by encouraging CPS contact with some high-risk birth parents. The Keeping Children And Families Safe Act (KCAFSA) of 2003 (as amended in 2009), requires as a condition of certain federal funding that states require birthing facilities, *if* they test a newborn child for drug or alcohol exposure and have a positive toxicology result, report this to the local CPS office, which in turn should react *in some way* to ensure the child's safety. This is crucial, because parental substance abuse dramatically increases the likelihood of a parent's maltreating a child and otherwise gen-erating bad outcomes for children.[67] In particular, "drug use during pregnancy has become a powerful predictor of subsequent child abuse reports."[68] In addition, as noted above, high-quality parenting in infancy can mitigate significantly the effects of toxic exposure in utero on brain development, so placing the child in high-quality foster care could make a great difference in his or her life prospects.[69] Conservative supporters of KCAFSA decried the fact that substance abusing mothers routinely take their children home without any safeguards in place, noting that a high percentage end up abused or neglected, and expressed belief that this legislation would spare a great number of chil-dren from having to suffer permanent damage before receiving proper attention from local child welfare agencies.[70] They criticized the reactive nature of CPS's traditional approach, and saw the Act as a significant step toward being more proactive.[71] Yet it does not appear to have accomplished much.

One obstacle to improvement is that birthing facilities are generally not required to test; no state mandates testing of all newborns, and only a handful mandate testing where physicians suspect substance abuse.[72] Whether to test is left to individual hospital policy or individual physician discretion. Further, even if they test, physicians generally endeavor to evade any legal requirements that could result in any legal action against their patients (and they view the mother as their patient), so some neglect to test even when they suspect.[73] In any event, many babies do not begin to exhibit withdrawal symptoms until more than 48 hours after birth, when hospitals typically have already discharged mother and baby.[74] One of the few benefits of racial bias *for black children,* is that, if the complaints of some liberal observers are correct, medical professionals exer-cise their discretion to test black babies at a higher rate than white babies (which adult-centered liberals decry as a wrong to "black people" rather than as a wrong to white babies). Further, the "some way" CPS responds to a report of positive toxicology can be so modest as to provide no real protection.[75] The babies go home with the mother anyway, typically with no monitoring, and some are never seen alive again.[76]

In any event, it appears most states have simply ignored this federal mandate; they have no provision in their reporting laws or maltreatment definitions directing birthing facilities to report positive toxicology.[77] The federal government agency overseeing child welfare law, the Children's Bureau in the Department of Health and Human Ser-vices, has exerted no meaningful oversight authority for many years,[78] presumably because Democratic administrations dislike the federal laws and Republican presidents get elected by trumpeting states' rights. These realities help explain why, in 2009, the Children's Bureau estimated that "90–95% of babies born prenatally exposed to alcohol or illegal drugs do not have that exposure detected at birth and simply go home with their birth parents."[79]

An additional legal step a few U.S. jurisdictions have undertaken, by way of identifying high-risk birth parents, is to conduct some form of "Birth Match." This is, along with the development of predictive analytics that I discuss below, arguably the most promising phenomenon in child welfare today. The basic idea with Birth Match is to try to avoid blithely sending a child home with a parent very likely to abuse or neglect him or her. In its currently-enacted forms, it is a very limited effort, but it is a start. It is far more modest than the investigation endured by applicants for adoption of a child or for jobs involving interaction with children, such as school teacher. Under programs that Michigan and Maryland instituted by statute in the first decade of this century, new births are reported to the state child welfare agency, which then does a cross-check against records of past maltreatment cases, to see if the birth parents of a newborn child have previously had their rights involuntarily terminated as to another child because of maltreatment. The history targeted is thus very limited and does not include, for example, having several other children already in foster care or having killed a child previously (which, if not intentional, might have resulted in little or no prison time). A positive match triggers a CPS assessment or investigation of the family.

New York City's child protection agency adopted an internal policy at some point, directing case workers to take action if and when they become aware that parents already in the child protection system have given birth to another child. A 2013 review of the Michigan, Maryland, and New York City efforts found they led to more protective removals of newborns, suggesting success in sparing some children at high-risk from damage.[80] Since then, Texas and Minnesota have enacted birth-match legislation.

The vast majority of US jurisdictions, however, make no such effort to learn when birth parents with serious maltreatment histories have another child, so that they can endeavor to protect the newborn from a similar fate, even though it could be easily done. Hospital employees might happen to know of a particular birth parent's history— for example, if they treated the previous child who was maltreated. Or CPS caseworkers might know certain parents in the system are expecting another baby. The happenstance of hospital or CPS awareness of parental history does not occur for many children, however. Moreover, hospital employees are required to report, and CPS is allowed to respond to, only what state law says constitutes abuse, neglect, or endangerment, and that generally does not include past conduct toward another child. (Note: Maltreatment definitions do not match grounds for TPR. Thus, although all states today must, to receive certain federal funds, make a past TPR a basis for a new TPR, that does not mean a state's laws will include 'prior TPR' in the definitional statute used to determine whether CPS may open a case file and conduct an assessment or investigation.)

State laws also do not include parental incarceration in the definition of abuse, neglect, or endangerment. So even if the birth mother is a prison inmate, CPS in nearly all states will not be alerted or get involved. The state will either place the baby in prison too, in the ten or so states that have prison nurseries, or it will leave mom free to pick anyone in the community to come collect the baby. Nor, in most states, does a state's definition of maltreatment include a current condition, such as addiction, that has not yet been observed to endanger *this child*—that is, the newborn. Even in states compliant with the KCAFSA, the law might authorize CPS only to contact the birth parents and offer services, which the parents are free to refuse. Only a handful of states go beyond the KCAFSA requirements and treat in utero exposure to controlled substances as abuse or neglect, or treat a birth mother's addiction as creating a situation of "endangerment," so that there is a legal basis for CPS to take protective action regardless of parental consent. And these states have come under heavy attack from liberal scholars and women's rights organizations for doing so, ostensibly based on supposed rights of parenthood and concern for discriminatory application of the law (which, as with drug testing, would mean disproportionately *benefiting* minority-race *children*). So, many local agencies and caseworkers in those states are likely reluctant to use that legal authority. Thus, although CPS agencies in the US do assume custody of thousands of newborns each year,[81] this is a small fraction of the number who are at high-risk of life-altering maltreatment (as well as adverse neighborhood effect). Regardless of birth parents' history with children, the state empowers them to leave the birthing facility with the child. CPS must wait for someone to report that the parent has harmed this child too.

Further, unless and until CPS takes custody of a child, or at least investigates, there is no way for a TPR as to a newborn child to get underway, and therefore no prospect of correcting through adoption what the state's ham-fisted paternity and maternity laws have done. Even if CPS agencies were inclined to make hard-nosed parentage decisions for newborns, the state law bases at their disposal for seeking TPR as to a birth parent and placing a newborn for adoption with fit caregivers are limited. As noted, all must include prior TPR, along with a limited range of other instances of past harm to a child (felony conviction for severe abuse of another child), and authorize TPR quickly (i.e., without having to make "reasonable efforts" to rehabilitate the birth parents) as to a new child, without prolonged foster care. But except in a handful of states, TPR grounds do not include maltreatment of other children that has not (yet) led to TPR or felony criminal conviction, nor do they include parental conditions that incapacitate them, such as addiction or incarceration. In addition, CPS workers are generally ideologically opposed to using any "fast-track" TPR authorization; they believe every parent deserves another chance. So even if they take protective custody of a newborn, they almost never move quickly toward adoption but instead park the child in foster or kin care and undertake lengthy efforts to rehabilitate the parents and transfer the child to birth-parent custody. They do this despite the fact that reunification success rates for parents unable to assume custody at a child's birth are abysmal.[82]

In, sum, despite their aim of promoting more proactive intervention, ASFA and KCAFSA have done little to change the conventional, reactive response to child maltreatment. The state (our agent) continues to repose legal-parent status and custody in parents it "knows" pose a heightened risk of maltreating a child. All the risk factors are disproportionately present in urban areas of concentrated poverty and therefore put a great number of black children born to parents living there at high risk of a developmentally deficient and traumatic neo-natal experience of life. Studies confirm that abuse and neglect rates are much higher for black children in general than for other children, with one fifth of all black children becoming victims of *substantiated maltreatment* at some point in their childhood,[83] which is likely only half or one third of the black children who actually suffer maltreatment.[84] Notes one observer: "black children are about as likely to have a confirmed report of maltreatment during childhood as they are to complete college."[85] The great majority of them are in poor households in impoverished neighborhoods.

Attachment failure

At about the seven-month mark, after a baby has developed the capacity to differentiate among caregivers and reached the stage of animate-object permanence (i.e., awareness that people still exist after leaving the room), and as they start to become physically capable of exploring the world, another crucial developmental need arises—to form a secure attachment to a permanent caregiver.[86] Secure attachment is fundamental to human flourishing.

Attachment involves children's coming to see one or more particular persons in the world as the source of their security and need-satisfaction, to whom they can turn when they have a physical, psychological, or emotional need. It is at this point, therefore, that it becomes important *who*, specifically, is a child's custodian and caretaker. It should be a person capable of filling that role competently and consistently throughout the child's pre-adolescent years, so that the attachment is secure and not disrupted. A secure attachment initially entails a desire to stay close to a strong, protective, and nurturing figure, and ultimately "its effective operation brings with it a strong feeling of security and contentment."[87] That security enables a child to explore the world without great anxiety, knowing he or she can always return to the safe and nurturing base the caregiver represents, and therefore to master tasks and develop a sense of competence and self-worth. It also "creates a positive expectation from the child's view that relationships can be fulfilling, helpful, and provide sufficient protection in a world that may at times be overwhelming,"[88] an expectation of trust that will later make possible positive peer and family relationships and healthy intimacy. As a result, securely attached children become "more independent, socially competent, inquisitive, and cooperative and empathic with peers; have higher self-esteem; and demonstrate more persistence and flexibility on problem-solving tasks."[89] They possess a "greater capacity for self-regulation, effective social interactions, positive self-representations, self-reliance, and adaptive coping skills."[90] Attachment thus plays an "essential formative role [...] in later social and emotional functioning."[91]

Whether a child forms an attachment at all and whether any attachment formed is secure largely depends on the child's interactions with caregivers and on the environment in which that interaction takes place, during the critical attachment phase of infancy—between seven or eight months and twenty-four months of age. In this period especially, babies need "sensitive and responsive care from familiar adults in the course of feeding, holding, talking, playing, soothing, and general proximity."[92] And they need this to take place in low-stress contexts. If they receive this, they should have the psycho-emotional foundation they will need successfully to traverse later developmental stages and attendant challenges.

Accordingly, it is not sufficient for a child's healthy development that a parent simply not physically endanger the child—safety is not enough. Even if a parent is consistently present and not dangerous, a child might fail to form a secure attachment as a result of poor parenting. Inadequate parenting can be manifest in the form of "disturbed family interactions, parental rejection, inattentive or disorganized parenting, [and] neglect."[93] Children can therefore fail to form a secure attachment, even when a parent is consistently present, if the parent is frequently changing environments, operating randomly rather than following a regular schedule, largely distracted, incapacitated for significant periods, or simply apathetic.

Such deficiencies in care are correlated with a parent's immaturity, substance abuse, mental health struggles, father absence, dysfunctional relationship with another adult, and trauma from violence against self, friends, relatives, neighbors; "[p]reoccupation with personal stressors diminishes the parent's ability to respond" in the ways that a baby needs.[94] Consider the exceedingly common case in black ghettos of the girl—16, 15, even younger—who gets pregnant to solidify her relationship with a boy she's been "together" with for a few months. She will drop out of school if she has not already, and have a baby while still a minor herself. Sometime during the critical attachment period her boyfriend is likely to leave her, creating a huge distraction as well as stress and conflict. If the baby has begun to view the boyfriend as a significant figure, he or she might experience some loss by "daddy's" disappearance. Once the girl/mother has recovered from the breakup, she will be distracted by the search for, and courting experience with, the next boyfriend, whose entrance into the household the infant/toddler will have to try to comprehend. Then the girl/mom will be distracted with a new pregnancy. Sometime after the second child's birth, the first child, having adjusted to Boyfriend 2's presence in their life, will experience his departure and mom's associated drama, stress, conflict, and distraction. Throughout this time, conflict will likely grow between mom and her own mother, because of financial strain or overcrowding, and eventually mom will have to try to find her own housing, with no job or co-parent and two or more children, and the first child will suffer from mom's heightened anxiety and perhaps also with lack of stability, food, clothes, privacy, safety, etc. Mom's choices from that point on, as she struggles to survive, could take the first child (and the second and…) on a truly destructive path, but already all her children are likely to have an insecure attachment to her, portending great struggles for them in the future even if mom's situation stabilizes at some point.[95]

Now consider parents who are already addicted to drugs when a baby is born. They are likely to be mired in a myriad of dysfunctional conditions—poverty, single parenthood, domestic violence victimhood, cohabitation with other substance abusers, unstable and substandard housing—that prevent them from parenting adequately and that create an environment for infants antithetical to healthy development—erratic behavior, high levels of conflict, drugs and weapons within reach, criminally-involved non-relative adults.[96] The adverse child rearing environment and poor parenting is likely to persist throughout early childhood, as addiction usually persists for years.[97]

> Dysfunctional features of drug-using women's parental role may include the tendency to ignore their child, negative affectivity dominated by feelings of anger, and ambivalent and incoherent attitudes. The parenting style can be shaped by rigidity and authoritarianism and characterized by low tolerance and the use of physical, punitive, and threatening disciplinary methods; this attitude may appear in alternation with passivity, permissiveness, and lack of supervision and control. The maternal attitude is also defined in terms of over-involvement, together with a tendency to isolate and refuse external influences, associated with intrusiveness and acceleration in the child's autonomy. The need to satisfy adult's expectancies and desires and the parental inability to fully play the parental role and function exposes drug-abusing women's children to the risk of reversing their roles. Limited knowledge of adequate care practices, wrong conceptions on both the pre- and postnatal developmental effects of exposure to drugs as well as on the normal developmental problems and needs contribute to the inadequacy of parental behaviors. These mothers are at risk of ignoring important emotional aspects of the relationship with their child, increasing the likelihood of later child maladjustment…. Finally, these

children are subjected to a strong discontinuity of parental care, and they deal with repetitive separations owing to abandonments that follow relapse into substances, recoveries, and incarcerations, and to a general mother's difficulty in guaranteeing herself as a constant and available presence, both physically and psychologically. Separations from the primary caregiver are often premature, and they happen in almost one-third of the cases, during the first 2 years, a crucial period for the establishment of the mother–child relationship.[98]

Also destined for insecure attachment are children of parents who are simply absent for long periods while chasing self-regarding gratifications or serving time in jail or prison.[99] And then there are the many parents in areas of concentrated poverty weighed down by severe anxiety and depression or carrying around rage from their own adverse childhood experiences.

These are all attachment failure scenarios, as well as conditions ripe for physical harm. Researchers have found that

insecure patterns are common in groups of drug-abusing women's children with rates of 68% higher than what has been attested in groups of children exposed to other maternal psychopathological disorders (55%), poverty (45%), and prematurity (39%). Instead, the percentages are equal to those reported in groups of children exposed to maternal alcoholism (65%) and lower only with respect to groups of children who are victims of maltreatment (86%).[100]

Children in these situations fail to form trust in a caregiver and, more generally, in the world, and so as an adolescent and adult will approach everyone with some distrust. The child fails to develop self-esteem, a sense of competence, a view of themselves as persons worthy of care, self-control, ability to concentrate on tasks, and ability to tolerate adversity. These psychological problems are the root cause of later educational failure and anti-social behavior in adolescence, and in turn a prelude to adult dysfunction, which is in turn a prelude to dysfunctional parenting of the next generation.[101]

As suggested by the reference to parent–child separations above, disruption of a developing or established attachment relationship also harms children.[102] Sudden long-term separation from an attachment figure is traumatic. It is difficult to re-establish an attachment once it is disrupted and very difficult for a child later to form an attachment to a new caregiver.[103] Thus, sending a baby home with a birth parent whose life is in turmoil, or waiting until an infant suffers maltreatment, means not only early developmental deprivation from neglect and/or damage from abuse, but also pronounced psychological disturbance if the birth parent separates from the child during the critical attachment period or later in childhood.[104] Thus, when the state has strong reason to believe a birth parent will abandon a child at some point—for example, because that person is a 16 year old who spent his or her own childhood bouncing among foster-care placements until ending up in juvenile detention, or is a 29-year-old addict living with a drug-dealing boyfriend or squatting in a condemned building with other substance abusers, it sets the stage for developmental disaster by making that birth parent a legal parent and custodian. Importantly, children are also adversely affected by being removed from foster parents if they have begun to attach to the foster parents, whether the removal is for the purpose of returning the child to a birth parent or for the purpose of changing non-parent placements—as is often done today to shift black children from white foster parents to kin who might be interested in adopting, when CPS finally acknowledges that reunification is highly unlikely.[105]

More on the concrete consequences of attachment disorders: Numerous studies of simply maternal deprivation (without abuse) have found "a variety of serious medical problems, physical and brain growth deficiencies, cognitive problems, speech and language delays, sensory integration difficulties and ... social and behavioral abnormalities."[106] Attachment failure retards psycho-emotional development and produces emotional withdrawal, a generalized distrust of people, reactive indiscriminate socializing, lack of impulse control, failure to internalize moral norms, and psychiatric disorders such as depression, anxiety, hyperactivity, and disruptive behavior. Some children subject to early deprivation recover some lost ground in some areas of development if transitioned early to a highly nurturing environment, but much damage is irreparable and less recovery in all aspects of development is possible the longer a child goes without permanence in a good home.[107] Merely providing services to neglectful parents or special educational programs for a child is not going to remedy the effects of a non-nurturing environment in infancy (more on this below).

A much larger body of social science research demonstrates a clear link between parental behavior that satisfies the state's definition of child maltreatment and numerous adverse effects and outcomes for maltreated children, because the maltreatment exacerbates attachment disorders. It shows a strong correlation between maltreatment and structural brain difference, cognitive impairment, delayed language development, poor school performance, poor physical health and development, psychiatric disorders, lack of self-control and behavioral disorders, failure to internalize moral norms, peer socialization problems, violence and other forms of delinquency, running away from home, youth suicide, substance abuse, prostitution, teen pregnancy, unemployment, criminality in adulthood, committing or incurring partner violence as an adult, and maltreatment of the next generation of children.[108] Many of these adverse outcomes are more pronounced the younger a child is when incurring the maltreatment. And of course an inhospitable neighborhood environment, which inflicts additional trauma and lacks resources for remedial services, intensifies and multiplies the bad outcomes for a maltreated child.

It is important to understand that adverse early childhood experience resulting in failure to form a secure attachment undermines not only a child's relationship with parents, but also the child's chances of forming positive bonds *with anyone*. This in turn makes the child ripe for later criminal involvement, because he or she will not be embedded in a positive social network that can constrain his or her choices. In other words, the child will later have little to lose in terms of personal relationships by rejecting positive norms and instead joining a criminal network that provides a form of success and possibly a semblance of social belongingness as well.[109] In fact, the correlation between early *neglect* and later criminality appears to be stronger than that between early abuse and later criminality. Schreck and Stewart write that "offenders are not socialized into crime, but rather they are *under*socialized into conformity..."[110] Any hope that children can be removed from the cradle-to-prison pipeline simply by stopping physical abuse in the home is therefore illusory. Children need secure attachment in order to find a positive path through life.

So what does the state do to promote secure attachment for children? Little to nothing. For the most part, the state is indifferent to the quantity and quality of parent–child interactions until someone reports that a parent has abused or neglected a child.

The law does not mandate or encourage parents to devote great attention to their infant children, nor discourage devoting attention to other pursuits (indeed, welfare reform pushed many mothers out of the house, to work). The state makes little or no effort to educate parents about the importance of attachment—in fact, most state officials, including many CPS directors and case workers, appear ignorant about it. Increasingly there is modest state financial support for "home visitor" programs that offer to help families identified as "at risk" with parenting skills and applying for government bene-fits. Only one of these programs, the Nurse–Family Partnership (NFP), has been proven to have a significant, lasting positive impact with any children, and it amounts to just modest improvements on a few measures for a narrow range of relatively low-risk fam-ilies (i.e., marginal rather than deeply dysfunctional).[111] Whether it is cost-effective is probably a close call.

The federal family leave mandate helps few children during the attachment period, because to the extent any parents are able to take leave that is unpaid, they are likely to do so only during the first months of their babies' lives. Any liberals whose next thought is "we just need to become more like Scandinavia" should stop and remember: This is not going to happen. There is no more money.

Further, when the state does directly separate children from parents in child protec-tion removals, proactively at birth or reactively after a maltreatment report, it pays little heed to the attachment needs of infants. One huge problem with child-protection law and practice is that it still fails to differentiate among children by age or developmental stage. It still takes a "one size fits all" approach, even though prominent child-welfare experts have been urging greater CPS responsiveness to children's stage of development for at least two decades.[112] Thus, when CPS removes a child at birth, it is likely to take precisely the same approach as it would if it removed a ten-year old. This is tragically nonsensical. Regardless of how dim are the parents' prospects for improvement, CPS places the baby with relatives or unrelated foster parents while it attempts to rehabilitate the parents, for as long as the law permits the agency to do so, intent on attempting reunification at some point—most likely, smack in the middle of the critical attachment period.

Currently, as a result of a federal mandate (also a component of ASFA), CPS in all states presumptively must petition for TPR if a child has been in foster care for 15 of the previous 22 months. This has substantially reduced the average length of time in foster care for children overall. But this timeline is far too long for a newborn or an infant removed in the first few months after birth. What is the experience of that infant going to be? The best case scenario is that the parents' problems are permanently resolved before the child reaches six months of age, the child goes home, and they live happily ever after. The odds of that happening are vanishingly slight.[113] The second-best scenario is somewhat more common, but not the norm: The baby is placed in a pre-adoption foster placement with concurrent planning, the child attaches securely to foster parents (despite their uncertainty about the future and about what CPS expects of them), and ultimately CPS petitions for, and a court grants, TPR of birth parents and adoption by those foster parents. Here are the more likely scenarios: (1) CPS transfers the child to parental custody fairly quickly, without problems fully resolved, and the child subsequently suffers maltreatment and re-removal, probably in the middle of the critical attachment period, thereby disrupting that process and traumatizing the child. (2) The baby remains in kin care for as long as the juvenile court will allow CPS to keep him or her there (relative placement means the ASFA timeline does not apply), not attaching to any caregiver, and at some point returns to a birth parent, with little prospect for secure attachment with him or her, or else CPS moves for TPR and hopes someone will adopt the child, which is increasingly unlikely as the child ages. This is part of the reason why black children stay in foster care almost twice as long as white children.[114] (3) The baby remains in non-relative foster care for 15 months and then CPS attempts "reunification" (a misleading term with a child never before in parental custody), disrupting any attachment the child has formed with the foster parents and traumatizing the child, and the child then experiences non-attachment, maltreatment, and possibly re-removal—again turning his or her world upside down. All these more likely scenarios resulting from CPS taking the standard approach with newborns spell attachment failure.

Yet ACLs loudly complain that the ASFA timeline is too short; it "represents federally mandated destruction of black families."[115] Parents need and deserve more time, they say, especially if parents are addicted to drugs or incarcerated.[116] Applying TPR rules to incarcerated parents "is symptomatic of family law's failure to evolve"; it "reveal[s] a view of family that remains unrealistically tied to the physical presence of a parent," writes a law professor in the *Berkeley Journal of Gender, Law and Justice*.[117] ACLs' call for extended timelines makes no distinction among cases based on the age of the child, and pays no attention to the impact on a child of changing homes and caregivers after living in one family for years. For them, the child protection system is about helping poor parents keep their rights, not about doing what is best for the children. And they have had some success convincing liberal legislators to enact such extra protections for the least fit parents.[118]

The reason why child protection law is oblivious to child development is that liberals in social work, child welfare policy, the legal academy, and legislatures resist any shorter timelines with any children. An early draft of ASFA would have created a much shorter timeline with children under six months of age, but liberal members of Congress, pushed by liberal advocacy organizations, blocked it, pushing for the longest possible timeline.[119] Individual CPS agencies could nevertheless adopt an internal policy to apply shorter timelines with newborns. But they do not. Why?

As Richard Gelles, a leading authority on child protection practice in the US, has repeatedly observed, CPS caseworkers view parents—not children—as their clients.[120] This has been evident to me from numerous conversations with CPS directors and case workers. They typically have little contact with children after the initial investigation, even if the children are placed in foster care, but are likely to have frequent contacts with parents. They might simply collect information about the child from foster parents, school officials, and service providers, such as a therapist for a child, rather than by interacting with the child. If they are operating in a family drug court, where the judge views herself also as coach and cheerleader for the parents (more on this in Chapter 6), this attitude will only be reinforced. Thus, in discussing policy reforms with local and state-level CPS officials in Virginia, I have only heard objections couched in terms of parents' rights rather than child welfare. When I have given presentations to CPS social workers and directors and I raise this concern, there are always a couple who approach me afterwards and, in hushed tones, say something like "it is so true; CPS is all about helping parents and giving them every last chance, not about doing what is best for the children."

If you view the parent as your client, then the child's age is largely irrelevant; in general terms, your client's interest, social workers suppose, is the same regardless—satisfy the state's rules for regaining possession of offspring (safe home, correct the conditions that led to maltreatment). (They implicitly assume parents have only self–regarding interests, not an interest in seeing their offspring have the best possible life.) So for many CPS caseworkers, sensitivity to age makes no sense unless relevant to safety or neglect (e.g., if children are not old enough to feed themselves); children's developmental needs per se are beside the point, and the law does not tell them any differently. All parents should get as much time as possible, in their view; "we never give up on our parents." Any who are more protective of children's interests have to worry about a parent-centered judge ordering them to give parents more time. For their part, guardians ad litem appointed to represent the child in agency and court proceedings are, at least in my observation in upstate New York (where I worked as a guardian ad litem (GAL)) and in Virginia (where I have sat in on innumerable child protection court hearings), generally passive (because if they want to keep getting assigned cases they had better go with the system's flow) and also ignorant about children's developmental needs.

So why any *different* treatment based on age? Why not a short timeline for all? Because once a child has lived with a parent for some years, (a) that parent is likely to be an attachment figure for the child, even if the attachment is insecure, and so there can be significant psychological cost to the child from severing the tie, (b) attachment to any other caregiver is highly unlikely, and (c) adoption is far less likely, so the upside potential of TPR for such a child is low. Newborns and infants, in contrast, are highly sought after by adoptive parents in large part precisely because there are good prospects for a normal, secure reciprocal bond. So the upside potential of TPR for a child in the first half year of life is huge. Thus, with a ten-year old child who has psychological ties, however frayed, to his or her birth parents, the standard CPS response to maltreatment makes much more sense, and the pleas of liberal scholars to give substance-abusing parents more time have purchase. Not so with newborns and infants.[121]

As noted, another aspect of ASFA designed in part to avoid attachment-precluding foster care placements was the requirement that states *authorize* proactive "fast-track TPR" (TPR without first trying (again) to rehabilitate parents, sometimes called "reunification bypass") with birth parents who have especially horrible maltreatment histories with other children. However, for the more common of those cases, involving a prior TPR or past civil finding of "aggravated circumstances" rather than felony conviction, state laws enacted in compliance do not require caseworkers ever to use this authorization. So CPS rarely does. It is contrary to the social work mentality; they are not trained to determine when efforts to rehabilitate parents would be futile, nor to determine when adoption would be better for a child than attempting to make it possible for the child safely to live with birth parents. They are trained to help their clients overcome problems, and so TPR represents failure for them, even when a great adoption placement is available.[122] An observer of ASFA's passage predicted social worker resistance to its aims:

> State agencies already have a proven record of undermining the Child Welfare Act because of their unyielding, one-sided belief in reunification ... [I]n 1997 Congress learned that states still sometimes sent children back into households that no amount of family preservation could help. Because funding for family preservation is so often paltry, this record can only reflect commitment to family reunification regardless of circumstance. Numerous studies confirm that social workers and judges often strain mightily to avoid severing a child's bonds to her parents, even

when doing so would ultimately benefit a child. To be sure, these attitudes have been changing, and ASFA will shift priorities further. But given the status quo inclination of bureaucracies and the bias of social workers as a professional group, such change can only come slowly. In fact, in the absence of new support for services, ASFA's effort to promote permanency through adoption may only steel professionals' resolve to resist rules apparently unconcerned about parental needs.[123]

This prediction of social worker parent-protective resistance to ASFA was borne out by a survey of CPS staff in California. Attempting to discover why CPS workers in that state rarely employed the state's extensive reunification-bypass law, Jill Berrick *et al.* found that many social workers expressed "ambivalence about its use due to philosophical perspectives on the social work profession." A representative comment by a social worker: "It doesn't fit with the social work ethic. We are social workers. We do this work because we think people can change."[124] In my own conversations with numerous CPS agency directors and social workers in Virginia, I heard the same perspective voiced. One big-city agency director told me emphatically that her agency would never use the fast-track TPR authorization, because "we don't give up on parents," and "you never know when someone might change."

Consistent with this strong alignment with parents, CPS directors and case workers often express what I call the "One Percent Philosophy"—that is, that unless they can say with certainty parent X will not reunify, then they should continue to try to rehabilitate that parent, provide more services, give more time, for as long as the law permits. If there is any chance, even one percent, they will persist. Is that good odds from a child's standpoint? That question never arises for them. The mentality arises partly from social work training, partly from blind faith in the power of human redemption, and partly from aversion to passing judgment on people, which for some reason is in our culture stronger in connection with parenting than with almost anything else people do. But this way of thinking should lead to a practice of *never* terminating, ever, which no one endorses. Even after five years of reunification efforts, one cannot say there is *no* chance *at all* of this parent changing soon. So adherence to this philosophy would result in—and did routinely result in before ASFA—children's remaining in foster care until adulthood, if not for the time limits ASFA imposed (and still thousands "age out" of foster care every year).

Making proactive TPR an effective tool for serving infants' pressing need for quick placement in a good permanent home would thus require a cultural transformation in the social work profession. Gelles has argued just that, most recently in his incisive book *Out of Harm's Way: Creating an Effective Child Welfare System*. And he is undertaking that challenge with students at the University of Pennsylvania, where he is dean of the School of Social Work and Social Policy. A handful of faculty members in other schools of social work are also undertaking that challenge. So there is hope that increasingly the profession will focus greater attention upstream. But for now, CPS is mostly flailing about in the life-destroying currents.

Hostile residential environment

For children who do spend their early years with marginal or dysfunctional parents in areas of concentrated parties, there is, in addition to the problem of attachment failure, the heightened probability of maltreatment by someone in the child's environment. In light of parents' housing instability, there is a much higher likelihood than with other children that a non-parent will abuse them, sexually or physically, or subject them to risk of dangerous instruments or of witnessing domestic violence. Abuse in their early years damages them in ways extremely difficult to remedy.[125]

Black Americans in prison tell life stories rife with instances of parents erupting into outbursts of physical and verbal abuse, beatings or molestation by mom's boyfriend to which mom was indifferent, growing up surrounded by family violence or criminal activity, multiple stays in foster care or shelters, evictions, and a neighborhood that offered only one anti-social path in life.[126] These experiences leave the great majority of them with lasting and serious mental health disorders,[127] in addition to contributing to school dropout, which in turn makes their life prospects dim.[128] In addition to brain injuries, physically abused children form intense distrust and confusion about relationships, become desensitized and dissociative, suffer diminished sense of self-worth, and have difficulty relaxing and concentrating, all of which disposes them to school failure, further victimization, teen pregnancy, and violent crime.[129]

Juveniles charged with delinquency also tell of parental disengagement and apathy, manifest in youths' disinclination to seek parents' assistance in dealing with police and court proceedings.[130] Even older children need custodians to provide a safe home environment and adequate food, clothing, supervision, and loving attention. This requires substantial effort by caregivers, and that effort is most likely to be lacking when parents have too many children, are still pursuing adolescent interests, or lack capacity because of substance abuse, mental illness, or diminished cognitive development themselves.[131] Older children of substance-abusing parents speak of being left alone at home, unsupervised and unprovided for, of leaving home at any hour to escape the sight of the parents or parents' companions, or simply running away.[132] Many end up occupying a parental role for younger children. Adequate parenting also requires resources, so children's needs are less likely to be met in households living below the poverty line. Deprivation of these things is a strong predictor of later dysfunction.[133]

The factors identified above have a cumulative effect, with many in combination creating a nearly 50 percent chance a boy will become a violent offender.[134] A great number of inner-city black households are characterized by a collection of such predictive factors—a single mother with multiple children she started having in early adolescence, living in cramped quarters with little income, much of it diverted to things other than good nutrition, clothing, and learning experiences for the children.

For its part, the state is even more exclusively reactive with older children, in terms of maltreatment policy. In contrast to the slight efforts the state makes at the time of a child's birth to identify high-risk birth parents, it is hard to think of proactive efforts with older children, or any looking for danger signs, other than allowing parents to ask DSS for help and modest investments in voluntary-home-visitor programs. Certainly there are events that do or easily could come to government attention that should raise a red flag—murder or arrest or release from prison of a household member, eviction, utility shutoff, parents' job loss, multiple school changes.[135] But the state is not sensitive to such signs of heightened family stress or danger, instead waiting until maltreatment is manifest—for example, in an emergency room visit, an event at school (outburst, absence, showing up malnourished or inadequately clothed, etc.), shoplifting, a 911 domestic violence call, running away, etc.

Foster care decision-making

Once older children have incurred maltreatment, there are no great options for them. Most maltreatment will not come to the state's attention and so will likely recur. When it is reported, state decision-making is, at best, a matter of damage control, of determining which is the least bad outcome for the children. Unfortunately, state decision-making is in many cases not at its best, largely because a liberal ideology of family preservation skews the rules and subjective decisions in a parent-protective direction.

First, CPS in many jurisdictions now will not even investigate most valid maltreatment reports, but will instead just offer assistance that parents are free to decline. I discuss further in Chapter 6 the now-widespread phenomenon of "differential response." Second, even when CPS does investigate, in a substantial percentage of cases it does not find sufficient evidence of maltreatment. Parent-protective liberal critics of CPS are wont to mischaracterize these as cases in which CPS found maltreatment did not occur, as a basis for alleging that false accusations against poor and minority-race people are rampant. They are wrong. As with any other legal complaint, it might be impossible to prove a case even when accusations are true, and this is especially so when victims are children. Many abusers are skilled at avoiding physical signs of their actions, the child is often the only witness, and other adults (including parents) might try to protect the person reported by disputing a child's account. Certainly some reports are false, but probably in most cases of "unfounded" allegations the maltreatment did occur, and will likely recur, as suggested by studies showing actual maltreatment is far greater than CPS substantiated cases.

When caseworkers do substantiate maltreatment charges, they face a choice between leaving the child in the home or asking a court to order removal. They are legally required to make "reasonable efforts" to avoid removal, and in most cases they leave the child in the home and work with the parents on correcting problems. In a significant percentage of cases in which caseworkers leave children in the home, maltreatment recurs and the children are further damaged. That does not mean leaving the child home was a mistake; it depends on the severity of the harm—whether it outweighs any negative impact the child would have experienced from being separated from parents. A child at this point is in a far-from-ideal situation, and CPS, at best, must make an educated guess as to which is the less bad next step in the child's life. The problem is that they are generally not completely child-focused, in part because of their inherent tendency to identify and sympathize with parents, and in part because the Left is constantly barraging them with ironic accusations of being anti-parent, overbearing, judgmental, racist, etc. They also have budgetary reasons to leave children home. The principal counteracting force is risk-averseness; foster care, despite common claims to the contrary, has far lower rates of child maltreatment than parental custody following a maltreatment report, and CPS agencies do not want to be blamed for a child being terribly injured or killed. Whether that all cashes out to optimal decision-making would be hard to assess.

In a small percentage of all cases of reported maltreatment, CPS takes custody of the child. Then it must choose a temporary placement and, in nearly all cases, will try to "rehabilitate" the parents. These children are highly vulnerable to further damage at this point if the placement chosen is insufficiently nurturing or unstable, or if children are put through unsuccessful reunification with parents and again maltreated and removed. The quality of the home environment into which CPS places children after taking custody matters greatly to the outcomes for those children.[136]

When black children are removed from parental custody, they are much more likely than white children to be placed in "kin care," with relatives.[137] Federal law requires that agencies *"consider giving preference"* to an adult relative over a nonrelated caregiver and attempt to identify and provide notice to relatives.[138] Consistent with this federal command, the law in most states does not require that CPS actually *give* priority to relatives at any stage of a child protective intervention, but rather only requires caseworkers to investigate whether there are relatives willing and able to take custody. Even if they do identify such relatives, they are supposed to choose the placement most conducive to the child's welfare, after considering both relatives and non-relatives.[139]

Nevertheless, social workers operate with a very strong bias toward relative placement with black children. Some even insist the law requires giving priority to any available and minimally-qualified relative, when in fact it does not. This reflects a widespread belief in the social work profession that a minority-race child belongs to kin and community (the same attitude motivating long-standing and continued opposition to trans-racial adoption among CPS administrators and caseworkers).[140] In addition, historically and still in most instances, relative placement saves the agency money; it is usually an alternative to state assumption of custody and not a formal state-supervised foster care arrangement, and the relatives are not vetted or prepared for surrogate care, nor provided financial or other support, to the same degree as foster parents. Moreover, when they choose relatives in an initial placement, there will typically be no one in a position to challenge their having done so, so there would be no occasion for a court to enforce a statute that rejects such prioritizing. In contrast, if they choose a non-relative foster home, relatives might complain. So avoiding legal challenge provides an additional reason to favor kin placements. In addition, some states have gone beyond the federal mandate and create a clear presumption in favor of kin placement, which results in much-higher-than-average kin placement rates.[141]

Is kin care inherently better? Widespread claims that it is are unfounded. Research on outcomes arising from kin care versus non-kin foster care has produced inconsistent results and, more to the point, is virtually impossible to design validly. Kin care is a multifarious phenomenon, with varying degrees of state involvement in selection and support.[142] There is never random sampling, and there is obvious reason to suppose children with willing and able kin caregivers are inherently in a lower-risk category than those whom no relative wants or who has no relatives fit to care for them. Additional problems with the research are that researchers do not differentiate among community contexts (e.g., do not focus specifically on kin care for children living in areas of concentrated poverty and crime), many also pay no attention to child's age as a variable, and most rely on caregiver reports to assess outcomes such as behavioral or mental health problems.[143] We do know that children placed in kin care take longer to achieve permanence.

In the absence of reliable research, there is only intuition as to the impact on a child of being with relatives rather than unrelated foster parents. There are child-centered reasons to suppose that, for older children, kin care is usually better, especially if a child already has a positive relationship with the kin caregivers—namely, familiarity and pre-existing affection. In addition, placement with relatives might give older children—whose prospects for adoption are generally much less than infants—a better chance than they would have in non-relative foster care, should their birth parents never regain custody, of completing childhood in a situation that comes close to being a "real" family. Familiarity and sense of normality are not pertinent, though, for a newborn or infant, and affection for them typically comes fast with any willing caregivers. They have only some interest in *later developing* family ties to biological parents and relatives, an interest whose significance is routinely exaggerated and that, in any event, they can satisfy later if they return to parental custody, are adopted by a relative, or have an open adoption with non-relatives. Further, newborns and infants stand an excellent chance of adoption if placed with unrelated foster parents, whereas relatives of the birth parents might well never want to take that step. The latter are more likely to prefer a long-term guardianship that does not bind them or offend the child's parents so much. Moreover, for children of any age there can be significant downsides to kin placement.

First, in some states, a child must be in CPS custody for CPS to petition for TPR,[144] so one consequence of placement with relatives in an informal arrangement is extended impermanence. In fact, placing a child with relatives, even if they are officially foster parents, allows CPS to avoid the mandatory TPR-filing requirement of ASFA for when a child has been in foster care for 15 of the past 22 months. Placement with relatives generally also results in less state oversight of a child's situation.

Another downside is that many relatives of children taken into state custody, whatever their merits as caregivers for a child, have troubling inter-personal dynamics with the parents. There could be deep-seated conflicts in some cases that interfere in one way or another with reunification efforts.[145] If you imagine your own child being removed from your custody and placed with your aging parents, because you "messed up," you can imagine what tensions could arise. Contrariwise, relatives might be unable or unwilling to enforce restrictions on parents' contact with the child while rehabilitation efforts are ongoing. They might, in fact, simply give the child over to the birth parents, without CPS authorization or awareness, so kin care can effectively amount to a return to parents, even though the parental conditions that originally necessitated removal still exist. Unless a caseworker makes unannounced visits, it is easy to avoid detection.

An additional downside is that relatives are more likely than non-relatives to become substitute caregivers suddenly without having previously wanted or planned to do that, out of a sense of familial duty or acquiescing to the importuning of an exhausted caseworker, and without fully appreciating the toll it will take. Kin caregivers are, on average, relative to non-kin foster parents, older, poorer, less well educated, less healthy physically and mentally, and far more likely to be single and disabled. Most are grandparents, and one-fifth to one-third of them are living in poverty.[146] Caring for grandchildren tends to intensify any struggles they have financially, socially, and mentally.[147]

Finally, dysfunction tends to run through families, rather than being isolated in a single individual—in particular, the struggling parent very likely had a troubled childhood also, and that parent's parents are the family members most likely to become the relative caregivers. As Elizabeth Bartholet explains:

> [W]e should be willing to face up to the fact that child maltreatment is only rarely aberrational. It ordinarily grows out of a family and community context. Keeping the child in that same context will often serve the child no better than keeping him or her with the maltreating parent.[148]

Couple this with the likelihood that, because of agency and social worker bias toward relative placement, they are likely to be less diligent or demanding in scrutinizing relatives, and there is reason for concern about the quality of kin care.

All that said, studies of kin care that have been done, though not providing valid comparisons with non-kin foster care or much contextual nuance, do not reveal great problems on the whole for children. As noted, the older a child is, the more intuitive sense it makes. However, as with timelines, CPS caseworkers, courts, and advocates for poor and minority-race communities who wade into child welfare policy (as well as many researchers) fail to recognize, or refuse to acknowledge, the very different situation of newborns and infants in this regard. What is clearly a damaging consequence of strong preference for kin placement is when it is the basis for suddenly severing a young child's relationship with, and possibly attachment to, unrelated, long-term foster parents. Yet agencies around the country are routinely doing this, and some courts are sanctioning it, using adult-centered language that makes the child seem like an object to be possessed rather than a person whose needs and rights should be controlling. For example, in a 2016 decision, Ellis v. Arkansas Dep't of Human Servs., 505 S.W.3d 678, the Arkansas Supreme Court overturned a decision of a trial court aimed at preserving a child's attachment relationship with foster parents, stating that

> it simply cannot be the law that strong bonds with a foster family can defeat the statutory preference for relative placement. If that were the case, then parents and relatives would always be at risk of losing permanent custody of a child in circumstances in which an infant resided with a foster family that provided good care for an extended period of time.

Related to this last point is the more general historical practice of changing placement from one foster home to another. In days hopefully gone by, CPS would do this to prevent foster parents from getting "too close," because that was viewed as antithetical to the objective of reunification with parents. Eventually, it became clear that multiple placements spelled multiple problems for foster youth. Repeated severance of relationships makes it all but impossible for children to trust or let themselves get close to anyone, resulting in an unhealthy mental isolation. Add to change of residence the problems of turnover among caseworkers and guardians ad litem assigned to a child's case, possibly change of school as well, and the foster care experience can be unbearably disorienting and disturbing for many children, leaving them no confidence about a positive future and in a state of constant anxiety that the rug will be pulled out from under them, and all this piled on top of worries about their parents—that the parents are sad, will fail, will be angry at them, etc.[149] Research suggests similar rates of placement stability overall as between kin care and non-kin foster care, but stability intuitively would be less likely with the subset of kin who are struggling with financial hardship, physical sickness and disability, and mental health problems (depression, stress, etc.), all of which are at high levels in poor inner-city areas.

Addressing the problem of multiple placements to some degree is another positive aspect of ASFA—a shift from discouraging "concurrent planning" to encouraging it, or at least authorizing it. Concurrent planning means case workers pursue two goals at once: while working with parents for reunification, they are also readying the backup plan, in case reunification fails, which can be guardianship (typically with a relative) or adoption (hopefully with the child's foster parents). This accelerates the process to permanency and, accordingly, an end to CPS involvement and court hearings. Further, if the concurrent plan is adoption by foster parents, the child is more likely to remain with them, not be transferred to another foster home. CPS directors and social workers appear to have readily bought into the idea of concurrent planning when the backup plan is kin guardianship. They have been highly resistant, though, to concurrent planning with a backup plan of adoption, which seems more conflictual to them. What I see repeatedly in TPR case histories in Virginia is that CPS initially places a child with kin and seeks a concurrent plan of long-term "relative placement," but the kin later change their mind, unable to bear the ongoing burden of caring full-time for a grandchild, niece, or nephew, and then CPS has to scramble to try to find non-relative foster parents who might be interested in adoption, a search that is more difficult the older the child.[150] There has also been some confusion among caseworkers about what concurrent planning is; some say they are doing it when in fact they are not—that is, not taking appropriate preparatory steps in the adoption process.[151] For this and a variety of other reasons, the time children remain in foster-care status following removal from parents is still longer than it should be and multiple placements remain common. Most adoptions do not occur until after a child has been in foster care more than two years, which is a very long time for a young child, from a child-development perspective.[152]

Lack of preparation for school

An important consequence of the high rates of deep poverty, single parenthood, teen parenthood, father absence, housing instability, over-crowded living quarters, substance abuse, child maltreatment, domestic violence, neighborhood violence, and other crime in impoverished urban black communities is that children are not prepared to learn when they attend school. One cannot reasonably expect academic success from children who come from chaotic homes with poorly educated, overworked, insufficiently motivated, dysfunctional, or maltreating parents in neighborhoods that have few or no role models and an oppositional culture.[153] Nor from children who are undernourished, distracted by traumatic events outside (and perhaps also inside) of school, and living with a persistently high level of personal stress. Nor for any child in a classroom in which such children predominate. Numerous studies show that a child's learning depends not only on his or her personal preparedness and family background and the competence of the teacher, but also on the composition of the rest of the student body.[154] A child surrounded by others who cannot maintain attention, who are too unprepared to accomplish at grade level, and who have emotional and behavioral disorders, has little chance of receiving an uninterrupted lesson in an environment that is conducive to learning. Thus, the concentration of children from poor family environments in any school inhibits the learning of all students regardless of how much money states give to such a school.

There was hope decades ago that getting children in impoverished inner-city neighborhoods into school programs earlier in their lives would help with long-term academic achievement. And still today, it seems to be the main proposal liberal politicians have to offer as a means of combatting the achievement gaps between wealthy and poor, and between white and black. The expectation is that teachers in Head Start, pre-Kindergarten, and other state-subsidized early childhood education programs can supply what parents and other caregivers have not been providing—reading to children, talking with them about what they are learning, laying the foundation for numeracy and problem solving, and so forth in a quiet and calm environment. Such programs typically also provide nutrition, so children's general health should be better and they should be undistracted by hunger. The idea has intuitive appeal. Unfortunately, studies of later school performance by children who enjoyed these opportunities do not confirm that appeal. Some programs show short-term improvements, but benefits disappear in early years of elementary school.[155] What these programs cannot do is change the children's home or community.[156] Consider the recollection one New Orleans man had of an incident in his early childhood:

> When I was four years old, I seen this pretty little girl, rolling on her little scooter, die in the drive-by. Just out of nowhere. The next thing you know, I see her jump crazy with blood, shot through the forehead, nose, and all this right here, bleeding all up on the mouth. And I'm shocked, I'm scared.[157]

On another occasion, the child heard a man shot in an alley, and on still another he woke up to find a dead body on his grandfather's porch. How is a preschool program going to help that child? Head Start and subsidized preschool are Band-Aids on the broken arms and legs and hearts and psyches of children coming from dysfunctional homes and blighted, traumatizing neighborhoods.

What Head Start and subsidized pre-K do accomplish is reduction of maltreatment rates, simply because they separate children from parents for substantial periods and give parents respite. That respite is also reflected in observation of parents' providing more positive nurturing at home. Wealthy parents need respite, too, and that is part of the reason they pay for preschool or hire a nanny. Parents struggling to make ends meet need it at least as much. And relative to the Family–Nurse Partnership programs, the free preschooling programs are likely to reach much deeper into poverty and dysfunction, because even parents who are barely surviving are likely to find attractive, and take advantage of, the offer to let them drop off their small children for free daycare. No one comes to your home, no one tries to change you, no one asks probing questions. You just drop off your child and have a free morning or free day. In addition, programs such as Head Start are simply offered more broadly; they are not limited to first-time parents, do not exclude children of parents who are substance abusing or mentally ill, and do not require parents first to attend a clinic or other service outlet. Thus, there is definitely some payoff from spending on Head Start and preschool for the poor, but it is not academic, and if simple daycare would be much less expensive per child than Head Start, then our limited public funds might be better spent by shifting them from Head Start to day care. Academic achievement is a lost cause for the great majority of children living in urban ghettos.

Bad schools

The lack of school-readiness among poor urban black preschool children becomes manifest and multiplied in later years, as they go through (or drop out of) elementary, middle, and then secondary schools. In large urban school districts, the worst performing schools are predominantly black. Many are objectively failing as measured on state performance evaluations, and many are chaotic and dangerous for students and teachers.[158]

The overall achievement gap is partly a reflection of relative affluence, and increasingly it is affluence that correlates most strongly with academic success; children of all races perform more poorly if in low-income households, and the achievement gap between poor and rich students has grown.[159] Viewed at the school-district level: "The richest and poorest districts have average performance levels more than four grade levels apart."[160] But researchers believe the gap between races also partly reflects black students' self-image and culture. Black students in all economic classes express feeling less capable and embrace the anti-academic and anti-mainstream components of black ghetto culture.[161] Whatever the full explanation, the gap between races remains "gaping"; a 2016 study found: "The average 12th grade black student ... placed only in the 19th percentile"[162] (a figure that would be much worse, naturally, if the huge number of dropouts were tested and included). Lower school performance translates to a greater chance of dropping out, the next step in the cycle for a high number of black children in impoverished urban areas, and less opportunity for employment in adulthood.

What does or can government do to improve educational attainment among the poorest black Americans? The prevailing liberal answer, of course, is more money. Researchers have found, however, that increased spending for schools has no effect on black children's academic achievement.[163] Funding across school districts has become much more equal in recent decades, mostly as a result of court orders, yet the achievement gap remains.

What about threatening school administrators? The federal No Child Left Behind Act attempted that, tying federal funding to reaching certain goals for academic progress by African-American children and other groups, on the assumption that poor performance was a reflection of relative neglect of poor-performing students. The Act is widely regarded as a failure, especially for children from the poorest backgrounds, having accomplished nothing more than eliminating music, art, and gym classes in many schools and adding a lot of instruction in how to take standardized tests.[164]

The dismal rates of high school graduation and college attendance among blacks who grow up in poor inner-city neighborhoods does partly reflect the poor quality of the schools they attend—bad facilities, poorly administered, staffed by teachers who are there because no other school would hire them. Giving the schools more money would enable them to improve their facilities, purchase new equipment, and hire more security officers. However, there is, first, the problem that there is no more money. Legislation to increase substantially funding of inner-city public schools has no political purchase today.[165] The legislative trend in this millennium has been to drain money from public school systems, which in the inner city are viewed as a lost cause, with good reason. The appointment of Betsy DeVos as Secretary of Education made clear the Trump Administration's disinclination to do anything for public education. At best, any new funding gets redirected to voucher programs intended to facilitate attendance at a better school for some students (the least needy—those whose parents are motivated and capable of going through the steps to obtain and use vouchers and possibly pay part of private-school tuition, and those whom private schools are willing to accept, i.e., well-behaved, will not need special attention). There is no evidence or reason to believe voucher programs have put a dent in rates of poverty in urban black neighborhoods, even if they have given some children somewhat better life prospects.[166]

In addition, schools are failing in part because the most cynical administrators and least capable teachers work in them, and injecting more money into those schools is not going to change that. With rare exception, even the most altruistic and enthusiastic teachers run away from these schools.[167] Anyone who grows up in these communities and manages to get to college and become qualified as a teacher or administrator is likely to live and work elsewhere. Outsiders fear driving into these neighborhoods each day, leaving their car in a lot, walking alone from car to school in the early morning and from school to car late in the day, facing a room full of unprepared and potentially dangerous students with little or no support from administrators or parents. Students in a Santa Ana school described what sort of classroom and student body would await an idealistic young teacher:

> There were kids with guns in the school, lots of fights, people throwing stuff in class, being very disrespectful to the teachers. Kids would spit in their faces, tell them off, start arguments, be really rude. It was nasty.[168]

Touch any student in an effort to control or console, and you are likely to trigger an opportunistic lawsuit by parents.[169] Such is the relationship between school and parents with which teachers must contend. Thus, schools in bad neighborhoods struggle to fill positions with minimally qualified people and fight against a major burnout problem with any good employees they do manage to hire, and this is so even if they are able to pay above-market salaries.

Third, even if urban school districts could offer large salary premiums (big "if") to attract "high value added" teachers, and even if many such teachers were sufficiently attracted by the money or driven by missionary zeal (big "if"), research suggests that *also* would not much help children in these neighborhoods.[170] Harvard sociologist Robert Putnam explains that the biggest obstacle to academic achievement for children in impoverished areas is the general academic unpreparedness of the student body. Even if an individual child's parents have spent time reading, providing experiences that stimulate cognitive development, and instilling in their child the importance of education, it is extremely difficult for that child to learn and grow intellectually if surrounded in school by other students who are not similarly prepared.[171] More school funding is not going to erase ghetto students' unpreparedness—a reflection of their early developmental deprivations and current preoccupations with hunger, disorder, danger, and death. As children in dysfunctional homes and neighborhoods get older, more suffer from physical and sexual abuse in addition to neglect,[172] and they spend more time outside the home unsupervised and so witness more terrifying events and get caught up in conflicts and illegal activities in the neighborhood.[173] Many go through a gang recruitment process before dropping out, and that leads to violence in the schools. Teachers and researchers describe urban ghetto schools as chaotic, highly stressful environments, with individual or gang-based hostilities routinely breaking out into fighting.[174] All of this distracts the children while they are in school as well as at home, preventing them from concentrating on school work or even sitting still for any length of time. It also adversely affects their health, causing them to miss many days of school. Even in a home free of child abuse, drugs, and violence, doing homework is likely to be difficult simply because apartments are small and dominated by television, people coming and going, and other distractions. In addition, as children get older, lack of parental engagement or availability becomes an increasing problem, as teachers are assigning homework and trying to deal with more serious behavioral problems. Even engaged parents have difficulty meeting with teachers, because of work and lack of transportation. Teachers dealing with poor populations routinely lament parent absence, which forces them to take on the entire burden of education for an over-crowded classroom and also to act as a surrogate parent for children struggling with emotionally and psychologically disturbing events and situations in their lives outside schools.[175]

In part because schools are of poor quality and youth do not experience rewards of achievement, a high percentage of black students either choose to drop out or engage in misbehavior that gets them expelled. Schools can initiate CHINS proceedings, but there is little school or the legal system can do if parents are unresponsive. If youths are defiant, school officials and judges are likely simply to threaten commitment to a detention facility, which if carried out would counter-productively immerse the children in an environment full of youthful offenders. When young people violate school rules, schools anywhere, and especially in the poorest neighborhoods, are less inclined today to take the traditional approach of calling parents and having them impose discipline, and are also less inclined simply to impose detention or extra work. Instead, "zero tolerance" dictates removal, possibly also referral to the school "resource officer," which results in a huge number of disaffected urban youths, mostly of minority race, facing expulsion and delinquency charges for fairly minor misbehavior, often simply displays of willingness to defend themselves so as not to be labeled weak and become a chronic target inside and outside of school.[176]

Disciplinary actions thus generally lead to the same result as dropping out, putting black youth on a path to prison. Over a third of black children overall in grades 7–12 get suspended or expelled at some point, so likely over half in inner-city schools, compared with just 15 percent of white children and 20 percent of Hispanic children.[177] Once excluded from school, where can they obtain better-than-poverty income except in criminal activity?

Direct neighborhood effects

Noted above were several ways conditions in the worst neighborhoods indirectly cause problems for children. For example, substance abuse by women who are or could become pregnant, and by men and women who produce children and are likely to commit maltreatment, arises in part from the stress and despair that pervades the community, as does parental exhaustion or apathy. The conditions undermining parenting also adversely affect children in direct ways that channel them into poverty and dysfunction, and the maltreatment or chaos they experience at home drives many out into this milieu without parental supervision. Outside home, conflicts, dangers, lack of role models, and fatalistic attitude (what many observers call a "culture of despair" or "collective hopelessness") pervading the worst neighborhoods demoralize and traumatize children.[178] The chronic, severe stress directly interferes with children's brain development—in particular inhibiting proper growth of the prefrontal cortex, which regulates "executive functions" that include concentration, impulse control, and mental flexibility.[179]

In recent years, child development experts and journalists have paid greater attention than in the past to the trauma children are incurring in urban ghettos. Life for these children is very much like life in a war zone; indeed, a CDC physician reported to Congress in 2012 that children living in inner cities, who get no break from being in a combat area, experience higher rates of PTSD than combat veterans.[180] They regularly see guns and hear shots. Many see people shot in front of them.[181] Many more hear adults talking about who was the latest to be killed. They attend funerals of young people. The director of a grief support center in Baltimore observed: "You hear about the shootings, but you don't hear about the aftermath. It's like you're killing 10 other people when you kill one."[182] Children see the fear in the eyes and bodies of their parents and neighbors. They walk past windows and walls with bullet holes when they go to school or the corner store. They are kept inside on "lock down" when not in school, if they are lucky.[183] Before setting foot outdoors, they have to do surveillance to see who is out there and what is happening.[184] They hear that you have to carry a gun to protect yourself when you go out, and so many are doing that by middle school, and shootings by and of teens are becoming daily events in some cities.[185] They do not carry books to school, because they might have to run when a gunfight breaks out or when someone comes after them with a knife.[186] They might, though, go to school wearing necklaces with cards bearing faces and names of murdered classmates, friends, and relatives.[187] They have to worry that any word they speak or write or any look they give could offend someone and get them and their family and friends shot or knifed; "Arguments start on Facebook and Twitter between young people age 12 to 17 and are frequently settled with guns…. One shooting often begets another, and another."[188] They and their peers operate every day at a heightened level of anxiety, so it takes little to trigger violent outbursts. One concrete manifestation: "In 2013, there were 47 recorded lockdowns in Oakland public schools."[189] Children say they do not expect to live long.

In addition to the violence and fear, there is the pervasive hopelessness. High rates of unemployment and abandoned properties and low rates of home ownership shape children's expectations for their own lives and their conception of what a community is like.[190] More foreboding is that the social and economic life of many such neighborhoods is dominated by gangs, who establish a prevailing normative structure that is intense and toxic. One of the reasons drugs and violent crime are so pervasive in these neighborhoods is that those wielding de facto regulatory power are the leaders of the groups selling drugs and enforcing their rule with guns. Sociologists have documented the highly-effective strategies gangs use to recruit boys from the earliest possible age, beginning with generous payments for performing lawful tasks such as going to the store to get snacks for gang members, then paying even more for minor forms of assistance with the drug selling, such as keeping lookout, and going through a series of promotions after that until eventually the boys are making the deals on the streets with a gun in their belt, transporting shipments of drugs, and defending territory. And throughout this process there is an implicit or explicit threat that refusing the work could make life very difficult for a boy. Boys without a strong adult protecting them from this recruiting have little ability to resist, and if they have dropped out or been expelled from school they have little reason to do so. Gang leaders in fact take the place of parents for many, providing a male authority figure and protector to boys who have not had that in their lives; this might be the most vivid and tragic manifestation of the pervasive absence of fathers in these communities. Horizontal gang relationships give young people companionship and a sense of belonging to a team, something larger than themselves, much like the military.[191] Not joining, on the other hand, puts one at odds with the gang, likely necessitating violent action as a display of strength; there is no neutral ground for anyone the gang tries to recruit.[192] In other words, one must become a "thug" in order to survive, and parents teach their children from an early age that they have to be "hard," not "soft."[193] The violence, though, might also land one in prison, or dead. Boys in these neighborhoods simply see no way out of this destructive dynamic, no way to broaden their severely constrained life options.[194]

Thus it is that most black males who grow up in urban areas of concentrated poverty become criminally involved and half end up in jail or prison. Diversion programs in juvenile justice are little used; the safe route for prosecutors with political aspirations is to lock up youthful offenders, in detention centers where little rehabilitation occurs, recidivism rates are high, and youth establish lasting relationships with other criminals rather than with positive role models.

Black girls in impoverished neighborhoods might also be recruited for lower level drug-trade work for gangs, but more often are pressed into sexual service for male gang members, making early teen pregnancy inevitable, or into sex work on the streets to generate income for the gang. Girls who have been sexually abused or pimped at home will run away and discover that serving a gang with sex in one way or another is preferable to doing it for a parent or step-parent and better than being homeless and penniless.[195] Many end up living on the streets anyway, trying to survive on their own, vulnerable to predation and attack. Any of these choices for girls who leave home put them at risk of arrest and incarceration, if not for prostitution then for getting entangled in boyfriends' work in the drug trade. Girls who do not feel compelled to leave home are likely to get pregnant early anyway, in a normative environment where "waiting till you are established in a career" is not part of the lexicon. They are likely to stay with their mothers until old enough to start collecting welfare benefits and housing assistance on their own, then move out and replicate the lives of their mothers.

The worst thing that can happen to a child is to be killed. Whereas car accidents are the leading cause of death among white teens, for black teens getting shot is the most common cause; youths account for nearly half of all child and teen gun deaths. Children in America's worst neighborhoods express doubt that they will survive to adulthood. What is rare in black ghettos is for young people to finish high school and either find long-term employment that will allow them to be self-sufficient or go on to college and pursue a career. Few leave, few have stable jobs, few can maintain a healthy and legal lifestyle. For most, there is just the prospect of remaining in the stressful, blighted environment with meager income for the rest of their lives. That and any pain remaining from childhood maltreatment or trauma lead so many to substance abuse. And to having babies either accidentally or as a means of bringing some light into an otherwise bleak existence. And then their babies go through the same sequence described above.

Summary

The several stages in the cradle-to-prison pipeline in impoverished urban communities are well documented, and nothing we are now doing to address the phenomenon is successful at diverting a significant number of black children out of the pipeline to a more positive life course. Few can escape, and the great majority that do not escape end up constituting the new generation of damaged adults who procreate at above-average rates, passing on the dysfunction they inherited.

Now recall the point made in the Introduction, that what happens in the ghetto does not stay in the ghetto. The spillover effect of this dysfunction in impoverished black neighborhoods is manifest in the most horrendous ways today throughout America, as law-abiding black individuals everywhere are susceptible to brutality and murder by police or civilians in situations where a white person whose behavior was exactly the same would not be.[196] In more moderate form, the stereotypes of the black criminal (murderer, thief, prostitute, welfare scammer, etc.) and the black drug addict, cause law-abiding, hard-working black people to be denied employment and housing. The stereotype is continually fed by the fraction of black Americans who fit the stereotype. Our historically-ingrained inclination to associate negative traits with non-white people—aided by the media's exploiting our dread of 'the Black Menace'—causes us further to exaggerate the rate of criminality and other negative behaviors among blacks as a whole.[197] The black urban thug stereotype is further fed and spread by other African-Americans' imitation of the criminal image; young black males in high-violence neighborhoods, whether likely to commit any crimes or not, feel compelled to take on a menacing demeanor to avoid being preyed upon, and the urban thug "look" became an oppositional fashion that black males of all economic classes throughout the country have adopted.[198] This magnifies the stigmatizing and stereotyping effects that reports of actual violent crime have. White America, especially the large portion of it that is not at all attuned to youth, urban, or black culture generally, sees black males generically as angry and lawless, presumptively violent.

These stereotypes explain why a black Harvard law professor can be stopped by police for aggressive questioning simply because he is walking home from the store in sweatpants; police (and residents) consciously or unconsciously associate 'unknown black man in baggy clothes' with 'criminal.' They explain why America has been content to watch its prison population rise to shocking levels; too many people believe that is where most black people need to be kept, and the prison population is disproportionately black.[199] They explain why even affluent African-American parents must tell their children that the white world will assume they are dangerous, deceitful, lawbreaking, and uneducated,[200] a well-warranted admonition that causes the children to carry an anxiety with them throughout life, a felt need always to counteract the stigma and stereotype, or that drives them to embrace it defiantly.[201] The stereotypes explain why every African-American has to worry about being denied housing or employment on account of their race; landlords and employers associate blackness with stealing, irresponsibility, bad education, and threat of violence should any conflict arise.[202] This "guilt by imputed association" is pervasively destructive. Ending the inter-generational cycle of dysfunction in impoverished urban areas might therefore go a long way toward improving the social experience and life prospects of all black people in this country.

Notes

1 See, for example, Popkin (2016), 21; Curtis (2014); Wagmiller (2007, 164).
2 See Besharov and Call (2009).
3 For example, in a law-journal article entitled *Criminalizing Pregnancy*, Cortney Lollar (2017, 951) boldly proclaims: "In the vast majority of cases, exposure to drugs in utero does not result in the negative long-term effects legislators, and most of us, presume." And "our laws assess harm based on the social meaning of different drugs" (i.e., we ascribe harm to whatever black people do) (Lollar 2017, 967). Lollar (2017, 968) claims this is proven by "a national large-scale, longitudinal study." The study she cites (Betancourt *et al.* 2011), was actually very small-scale and very local. It assessed 120 adolescents, including the control group, "recruited at birth from a single inner-city hospital" (Betancourt *et al.* 2011, 38). The authors of that study acknowledged that their not finding a statistically significant difference between test group and control group on three of five measures (they did find a difference on two other child-welfare measures) could be because of small sample size (Betancourt *et al.* 2011, 43). In addition, the study suffered from severe selection bias: Test-group members were a small subset of all women at that hospital who admitted to cocaine use during pregnancy. The researchers excluded any women who were not native English speakers or who were mentally ill, 45 percent of women invited to participate in the study on the basis of a positive drug test refused the invitation (so those most incapable of or averse to interaction with strangers were also excluded), 12 percent of those who did participate had not tested positive for cocaine at time of childbirth (suggesting greater control

over consumption, or misunderstanding when asked if they had used cocaine); and 40 percent of study subjects who started dropped out (and attrition in child-welfare studies tends to occur disproportionately with children faring the worst).

4 Popkin (2016, 21).
5 Office of Minority Health (2017).
6 Child Trends Data Bank (2015, 3).
7 Roberts and Pies (2011).
8 Roberts and Pies (2011); Duso and Stogner (2016, 636–40).
9 Peskin *et al.* (2012, 90).
10 MacDorman and Matthews (2011); Harmon (2011); Office of Minority Health (2017).
11 See, for example, Minn. Stat. § 626.5561(b).
12 See, for example, 18 U.S. Code § 1841—Protection of unborn children; Tex. Civ. Practice & Remedies 71.001 (defining "person" to include "an unborn child at every stage of gestation from fertilization until birth" for purposes of state wrongful death law); Ammons (2012).
13 See Hwang (2017) ("After controlling for maternal characteristics and preterm birth, SUD [substance use disorder] -exposed neonates were more likely to have intrauterine growth restriction, cardiac, respiratory, neurologic, infectious, hematologic, and feeding/nutrition problems, prolonged hospital stay, and higher mortality" as well as being "more likely to be rehospitalized"); Ross *et al.* (2015); Peskin *et al.* (2012, 74, 87–8); Duso and Stogner (2016, 624–7) (summarizing and citing studies).
14 Duso and Stogner (2016, 627); Ji *et al.* (2010) (documenting behavioral problems and depressive symptoms in youths who had been adopted and who experienced pre-natal drug exposure).
15 Weisberg and Vandervort (2016, 671).
16 Weisberg and Vandervort (2016, 671).
17 Wallace, Myers and Osai (2005) (citing The National Survey of Drug Use and Health Report, 2004) (finding heavy alcohol consumption among three percent of pregnant women across the board); SAMHSA (2012) (finding that 12.8 percent of black women had used any alcohol in the past month, similar to the 12.2 percent figure for white women).
18 See Edin and Kefalas (2011, 53).
19 Weisberg and Vandervort (2016, 675).
20 Weisberg and Vandervort (2016, 675 n.148).
21 Duso and Stogner (2016, 625).
22 Duso and Stogner (2016, 625).
23 Newswise (2014).
24 See Behnke and Smith (2013, 1016).
25 Weisberg and Vandervort (2016, 676–7); Wickström (2007) (stating: "A large number of studies confirm that maternal tobacco smoking during pregnancy adversely affects pre- and postnatal growth and increases the risk of fetal mortality, morbidity, cognitive development, and behavior of children and adolescents" and citing sources).
26 Grant (2005).
27 SAMHSA (2012).
28 Wallace *et al.* (2005).
29 Weisberg and Vandervort (2016, 678).
30 Weisberg and Vandervort (2016, 678–9). Cf. Mark and Terplan (2017) (concluding from review of literature that effects are "subtle" but include "decrease in weight among cannabis-exposed newborns with a pooled mean difference of 109 g," greater likelihood of admission to a neonatal ICU, and "impaired visual acuity, verbal reasoning and comprehension and short term memory as well as poorer test scores."); Behnke and Smith (2013, 1016) ("Although there have been studies revealing subtle abnormalities in infant neurobehavior related to prenatal marijuana exposure, there have been no significant effects documented for fetal growth, congenital anomalies, or withdrawal").
31 Newswise (2015).
32 See, for example, Kwiatkowskia (2018) ("PME [prenatal methamphetamine exposed] children scored significantly worse than controls on the measures of IQ, learning and memory, confrontation naming, visual-motor integration, and fine motor coordination. Hierarchical

regression analyses that included potential confounding sociodemographic, co-exposure and anthropometric variables confirmed that PME impacts negatively on cognitive performance").

33 Weisberg and Vandervort (2016, 680–1). See also Fraser (2016, 57–9) (finding from a review of the literature clear, repeated research findings that cocaine, principally because it constricts blood vessels, in a significant number of babies causes miscarriage, stillbirth, preterm delivery, diminished fetal growth, defective or absent limbs, cardiac defect, bowel defects, insufficient intracranial growth, decreased gray matter, decreased cortical thickness, and increased volumes of cerebrospinal fluid).

34 Fraser (2016, 58). See also Fraser (2016, 59) (stating most mothers do not visit the child in the ICU, because they feel ashamed and afraid of contact with CPS).

35 Fraser (2016, 58–9) ("Long term effects of prenatal cocaine exposure have been well documented," and "many well conducted longitudinal studies" focus on "a child's developmental and physiological wellbeing after prenatal cocaine exposure." "Results showed that prenatal cocaine exposure had significant impacts upon syntax and phonological language processing abilities … subsequently impacting upon literacy skills (Lewis et al., 2013)." Another "study found that prenatal cocaine exposed children had decreased sleep duration and poor sleep pattern organisation (Stone et al., 2010)." Another found higher "reported delinquent behaviour during adolescence including reduced problem solving and reasoning abilities" and "those exposed to cocaine during the first trimester had a smaller head circumference, weighed less and were shorter than other participants at 15 years of age (Richardson et al., 2015)."); Cain et al. (2013) ("The use of cocaine alone or in conjunction with other illicit drugs, combined with the normal physiological cardiovascular changes in pregnancy, leads to a myriad of pathophysiological changes, thereby placing the life of the pregnant cocaine user, as well as the health status of their unborn fetus and neonate at risk for adverse outcomes."); National Institute on Drug Abuse (2016) ("Babies born to mothers who use cocaine during pregnancy are often prematurely delivered, have low birth weights and smaller head circumferences, and are shorter in length than babies born to mothers who do not use cocaine…. Using sophisticated technologies, scientists are now finding that exposure to cocaine during fetal development may lead to subtle, yet significant, later deficits in some children. These include behavior problems (e.g., difficulties with self-regulation) and deficits in some aspects of cognitive performance, information processing, and sustained attention to tasks—abilities that are important for the realization of a child's full potential. Some deficits persist into the later years, with prenatally exposed adolescents showing increased risk for subtle problems with language and memory. Brain scans in teens suggests that at-rest functioning of some brain regions—including areas involved in attention, planning, and language—may differ from that of non-exposed peers."); Weisberg and Vandervort (2016, 681) (cocaine exposure manifests in "lack of attention span and the loss of visual memories" and "scor[ing] lower on intelligence tests").

36 Fraser (2016).

37 Fraser (2016, 57) ("During the second trimester, the foetus is exposed to greater amounts of cocaine as maternal metabolic functionality is decreased, leading to an increased half-life of cocaine (Cain et al., 2013). With this in mind, the availability of cocaine to the foetus is threefold via placental blood flow, placental membranes and within the amniotic fluid").

38 Munz (2016).

39 Munz (2016); Shiffman (2015).

40 Munz (2016).

41 See Edin and Kefalas (2011, 38).

42 Edin and Nelson (2013, 24); Edin and Kafales (2011, 37–42).

43 See Baradaran (2013, 175).

44 See, for example, 750 Ill. Comp. Stat. 405/2–18(2) (2008) (treating as prima facie evidence of neglect fetal alcohol syndrome and "a medical diagnosis at birth of withdrawal symptoms from narcotics or barbiturates"), 750 Ill. Comp. Stat. 50/1 (creating a rebuttable presumption that the birth mother is unfit "where there is a confirmed test result that at birth the child's blood, urine, or meconium contained any amount of a controlled substance … and the biological mother of this child is the biological mother of at least one other child who was adjudicated a neglected minor …"); Minn. Stat. § 626.556(f) (2006 & Supp. 2007)

("'Neglect' means … prenatal exposure to a controlled substance, as defined in section 253B.02, subdivision 2, used by the mother for a nonmedical purpose, as evidenced by withdrawal symptoms in the child at birth, results of a toxicology test performed on the mother at delivery or the child at birth, or medical effects or developmental delays during the child's first year of life that medically indicate prenatal exposure to a controlled substance…"); Tenn. Code. Ann. §§ 39–13–107 (infamous "fetal assault" statute; Tex. Fam. Code Ann. § 161.001(1)(R) (authorizing TPR as to a parent who has "been the cause of the child being born addicted to alcohol or a controlled substance," if TPR would be in the child's best interest).

45 See Dwyer (2014).

46 See, for example, Fairbanks (2009).

47 See, for example, Engstrom *et al.* (2012, 366–76) (reporting results of study of women in methadone treatment, including that 57 percent had suffered childhood sexual abuse and 90 percent of them had experienced domestic violence as adults); Choi and Ryan (2007, 1402) (finding that 76 percent of substance-abusing mothers in the child welfare system "had more than four different needs present," including 52 percent who had mental health needs, and 29 percent of the mothers "presented with more than 7 different needs"); Smith (2008, 512, 515) (finding from review of literature that 46 percent of frequent meth users have psychiatric problems).

48 Almost a quarter were heroin addicts. Winnefeld (2017).

49 Winnefeld (2017).

50 Winnefeld (2017).

51 Winnefeld (2017).

52 Winnefeld (2017).

53 Loveland Driscoll (2014); Tzilos *et al.* (2009) (reporting 38 percent completion rate for a program providing methadone and cognitive-behavioral therapy, and 6-month relapse rate of 44 percent among those who completed, for a 6-month-post-treatment success rate less than 20 percent); Miller *et al.* (2001, 216) (noting two previous large multi-site studies that showed a 12-month client-retention rate of 45 percent and 44 percent respectively); Miller *et al.* (2001), 216 (finding that combined results of seven studies, of over 8000 people who sought treatment for alcoholism, 17 percent of persons could not be located at follow-up (which most likely means they dropped out of treatment), and only a third of the rest had achieved either abstinence (24 percent) or sufficient reduction in drinking to avoid "alcohol-related problems" (10 percent), though most reduced their drinking significantly while in treatment); Otero *et al.* (2016, 12–13) (stating that only 23.3 percent of meth users complete treatment, and half of those relapse within a year and a half after completing treatment).

54 See Dodes and Dodes (2014) (based on extensive review of data on AA retention and studies on sobriety).

55 Ryan (2006, 1–1 to 1–11, 3–3).

56 See Guerrero *et al.* (2013).

57 See, for example, Wis. Stat. § 51–20; Mindock *et al.* (2012) (finding an average of five commitments per year for alcohol abuse across 44 of Wisconsin's 72 counties); Orlando (2012).

58 See, for example, Orlando (2012) ("The court may not order commitment unless it determines that the treatment facility is able to provide adequate and appropriate treatment for the respondent and that the treatment is likely to be beneficial (CGS § 17a-685(d))").

59 See, for example, Peskin *et al.* (2012, 90) (noting that a study of juvenile delinquents in detention found that one-third suffered from iron-deficient anemia) and 91 (noting a study of public-school children finding that "children given a daily vitamin and mineral supplement showed a reduction of 47% in antisocial behavior after four months compared with children given the placebo" and another showing that fatty acid supplements reduced conduct disorders by 43 percent).

60 See Mercer (2010, 69–75).

61 Zeanah *et al.* (2003).

62 Alexander (2015), 21.

63 See Ji *et al.* (2010, 433) (describing research showing "adverse home environment" compounded the effect of pre-natal exposure to alcohol in producing psychiatric symptoms);

Ji *et al.* (2010, 439) (finding from study that even if they are adopted, "children who were prenatally exposed to drugs are at risk for behavioral problems").

64 Popkin (2016, 41).

65 Commission to Eliminate Child Abuse and Neglect Fatalities (2016, 36); MacDorman and Matthews (2011).

66 See Gelles (2017, 109) (describing statistical models that, when applied to maltreatment reports CPS has already received, could predict which would be substantiated with a high degree of accuracy—90 percent for one model and roughly 75 percent for another).

67 See Barth and Lloyd (2010, 50) (describing research showing parental substance abuse is correlated with violence and depression, which are antithetical to healthy child development).

68 Barth and Brooks (2000, 24).

69 Barth and Brooks (2000, 25).

70 See, for example, 148 Cong. Rec. H1511 (daily ed. April 30, 2002) (statement of Rep. Greenwood) ("Today, children are born all over this country to mothers who have substance abuse problems. Their mothers are alcoholic or their mothers are drug addicts. These babies are born in hospitals, they are frequently underweight, they are frequently frail.... [T]hey are sent home from hospitals every day in this country and it is only a matter of time in so many instances until they return back to the hospital abused, bruised, beaten, and sometimes deceased. That is because we have not developed a system in this country to identify these children and intervene in their lives. The amendments that we put in this bill for the first time require the States to set up programs so that when these children are born to these addicted families that there is intervention.... In those cases where the mother is refusing or unable or unwilling to get help to protect her child, to mother properly, to parent properly, or where the home situation is just too chaotic and too violent for the child to be safe, then there can be intervention and the child can be placed in foster care. Over and over again, the newspapers of our country are replete with these cases of terribly, terribly abused, battered, sexually abused and sometimes beaten-to-death children who could have been saved if only we had intervened when we knew there was a problem, when we could see that this child was born to a dysfunctional family where substance abuse is the issue. Now we will be able to do that").

71 See, for example, 148 Cong. Rec. H1513 (daily ed. April 23, 2002) (statement of Rep. Holt); 148 Cong. Rec. H1509 (daily ed. April 23, 2002) (statement of Rep. Miller).

72 See, for example, § Minn. Stat. 626.5562 (requiring a toxicology test of a pregnant woman "within eight hours after delivery to determine whether there is evidence that she has ingested a controlled substance, if the woman has obstetrical complications that are a medical indication of possible use of a controlled substance for a nonmedical purpose," and of a newborn "if the physician has reason to believe based on a medical assessment of the mother or the infant that the mother used a controlled substance for a nonmedical purpose during the pregnancy").

73 See, for example, Wilson and Shiffman (2015b) (noting that in December 2015, the chair of the American Academy of Pediatrics told a reporter: "If you're in a state where a report is made and social services are great, they're going to help this mom and get home health care, then that's great. But if it's a punitive kind of state, what's the point? So I think some of us just say, 'Let's don't' "); Wilson and Shiffman (2015b) (noting that the director of Healthy & Free Tennessee told the reporter: "Nationally we are seeing a push to put a newborn or a fetus's needs above the mother, and I think that's wrong. This goes to some of the same issues related to controlling women's bodies and their reproductive choices."); Wilson (2015b) ("doctors say they are sometimes reluctant to refer drug-dependent mothers and newborns to authorities. They don't want to report women who seem to be doing their best to overcome addictions to heroin or painkillers"); Wilson (2015b) (describing instance in 2014 when a woman went to a hospital in North Dakota, a day after smoking meth, to deliver a baby, the same hospital where she had secured large quantities of hydrocodone after complaining of dental pain three times in a 17-day period, who was caught by a nurse in a lie about having a doctor's approval for use of another drug, whose baby was born premature and noted to be visibly shaking; the doctors declined to test the baby and sent the mother home with the baby and a prescription for more hydrocodone, and at home the mother got high and suffocated the baby); Munz (2016) ("Providers say it is heartbreaking

to learn that a mom who worked hard to stay clean during pregnancy has lost custody of her child…").

74 See Wilson (2015b).
75 See Dwyer (2008). Minnesota is unusual in requiring an investigation if the mother refuses assistance. Minn. Stat. § 626.5561.
76 See Wilson (2015a) (discussing deaths of newborns in custody of drug addicts).
77 Nine states and DC include the mandate in reporting laws. Wilson (2015d). Fourteen include prenatal exposure in definitions of child abuse and make medical professionals mandatory reporters of child abuse in general. See Kelly (2017). Thus, the actual number compliant, if only indirectly or implicitly, is somewhere between 14 and 23 (depending on overlap between the two groups). And some of those reporting laws have major loopholes. Minnesota's, for example, effectively excludes marijuana and alcohol, the two most commonly abused substances. See Minn. Stat. § 626.5561(1)(a) ("A health care professional or a social service professional who is mandated to report … is exempt from reporting under paragraph (a) a woman's use or consumption of tetrahydrocannabinol or alcoholic beverages during pregnancy if the professional is providing the woman with … healthcare services").
78 Cf. Wilson and Shiffman (2015a) ("Despite the widespread lack of compliance, Reuters found that no state has ever lost federal funding for failing to meet the law's provisions").
79 Young et al. (2009, 32).
80 Shaw et al. (2013, 219).
81 Nearly 50,000 according to the latest federal government count. Children's Bureau (2017).
82 See, for example, Huang and Ryan (2011, 322) (stating that "such families rarely achieve reunification and are at an increased risk of experiencing a subsequent substance related allegation of maltreatment," citing an Illinois study of substance exposed infants in which "only 14% of substance exposed infants achieve reunification with their biological parents within 7 years," and finding from a study of predominantly poor African-Americans that even with residential rehabilitation followed by outpatient transitional services less than 10 percent of substance-abusing mothers achieved reunification within 18 months of the child's birth).
83 See that by the time children have turned age 18 in any given birth cohort, roughly 1 in 8 children have been substantiated as a victim of abuse or neglect. And the prevalence for different groups is much higher in some cases; the prevalence for black children is over 1 in 5.
84 See Putnam-Hornstein et al. (2014) ("rates of child maltreatment in the United States may be 2 to 3 times higher than the number of identified victims in any given year."); Wildeman et al. (2014, 710) ("The cumulative prevalence determined from self-reports of victimization is roughly three times the cumulative prevalence of confirmed maltreatment").
85 Wildeman et al. (2014).
86 See Mercer (2006, 59–62).
87 Bowlby (1991, 293).
88 Goldsmith et al. (2004).
89 Kelly and Lamb (2000).
90 Goldsmith et al. (2004).
91 Kelly and Lamb (2000).
92 Kelly and Lamb (2000, 298); Mercer (2006, 58–62).
93 Mercer (2006, 302).
94 Alexander (2015, 60–1) (on consequences of father absence); Goldsmith et al. (2004, 3); Goldsmith et al. (2004, 4) (noting that repeated changes in caregivers, as might occur when parents come in and out of a child's life, can produce Reactive Attachment Disorder); Kelly and Lamb (2000, 302) (discussing impact of parental discord); Kelly and Lamb (2000, 305) (discussing locational stability and its importance for infants and "predictable comings and goings of both parents, regular feeding and sleeping schedules, consistent and appropriate care, and affection and acceptance"); Wagmiller (2007, 164) ("Children in high-poverty neighborhoods, regardless of their own family economic circumstances … experience poorer home environments, less maternal warmth, and less cognitive stimulation from their mothers."); Leventhal et al. (1997) ("Studies show that mothers who use cocaine have difficulties interacting with their infants, in particular, demonstrating more intrusive and hostile behaviors toward their infants."); Children's Bureau (2003) (noting that substance-abusing

parents have a diminished capacity to function as parents because of drug-related activities and are often also afflicted with mental illness, high levels of stress, and dysfunction in their larger family).

95 Cf. Huston *et al.* (1994) (documenting higher rates of insecure attachment among the poor).

96 See Huang and Ryan (2011, 323).

97 Huang and Ryan (2011, 322) ("two third of primary caregivers in the drug-exposed group continue to use cocaine and/or opiates at follow-up, 4–5 years after the child's birth").

98 Parolin and Simonelli (2016, 2).

99 See Howard (2011); Mercer (2006, 63).

100 Parolin and Simonelli (2016, 4).

101 See Farrington (2012).

102 See Mueller (2010, 3038) (observing "severe physiological stress response" resulting from separation from the primary caregiver); Schuengel *et al.* (2009, 1) ("the risks of severe disruptions of attachment are profound"); Schuengel *et al.* (2009, 2) ("parent-child relationships support a range of regulatory processes … Separation from the parent results in a complete withdrawal of these regulatory influences").

103 See Kelly and Lamb (2000, 300–1).

104 See Mercer (2006, 60–4).

105 See Goldsmith *et al.* (2004, 1) (warning of the severe risks to, and long-term effects on a child associated with separation from the caregiver); Kelly and Lamb (2000, 304) ("[T]he loss or attenuation of significant relationships in childhood can cause anxiety and a profound sense of loss, particularly in the first 2 years, when children have limited cognitive and communicative resources to help cope with loss").

106 Zeanah *et al.* (2003); see also Wagmiller (2007, 164); Nelson and Zigler (2000, 210, 216) ("[I]solation rearing also results in a host of behavioral impairments, including hyperactivity, abnormal responses to novelty and stressors, and cognitive deficits in adulthood").

107 See Putnam (2015, 112); Dwyer (2008, 422).

108 See Alexander (2015, 96–8, 120–2, 130–1, 140–1); Dwyer (2008, 424).

109 See Schreck and Steward (2012, 56–61).

110 Schreck and Steward (2012, 61).

111 See Stoesz (2016). At least one study explicitly excluded women who were substance abusing, had a DSM-IV psychotic disorder, or had AIDS (Sadler *et al.* 2013, 391). Further, FNP operators recruit participants at a pre-natal clinic, where the most dysfunctional pregnant women are unlikely to be found. Mothers who end up subjects of the studies are referred by clinic staff, which could further skew the sample. The most studied programs invite only women or girls having their first baby, which in a poor community means very young mothers who are less likely to suffer from addiction, depression, or domestic violence victimization than are older mothers having their third or eighth child. Olds (2014); Olds *et al.* (2014); Kitzman *et al.* (2010, 416–17). One study done on use of FNP with parents who have already maltreated a child found no benefits (MacMillan *et al.* 2005). In addition, a problem that plagues all human-subject research afflicts FNP research as well: Persons who qualify for participation refuse at the outset or later drop out, and the reasons they do so could mean the study sample is unrepresentative. For example, in the study of the Denver program, the number of subjects in the treatment group was less than half of those originally invited to participate. Those remaining were likely the cream of a select crop among poor women.

112 See, for example, Berrick *et al.* (1998).

113 According to the AFCARS Report for 2016 (Children's Bureau 2017), of the 273,539 children who entered foster care that year, 49,234 were less than one year of age. During that same year 11,153 children under age one exited foster care. The report does not indicate what percentage of those exited to parental custody, but according to a Casey report, "[c]hildren under the age of one are reunified with their parents only 35 percent of the time (Murray 2011). So it seems less than 10 percent of children who enter foster care when under age one (including an unknown number who enter immediately after birth) are transferred to parental custody before they turn one, mostly likely after the seven-month mark. And a substantial percentage of those likely re-entered foster care later after being maltreated (again), given that foster-care re-entry rates are generally high.

114 The Annie E. Casey Foundation (2002).
115 White (2006).
116 See, for example, Murray and Luker (2015, 328) (asserting that ASFA has "gone awry" because it "has produced devastating consequences for incarcerated women"); *idem*, 322 (complaining that "federal laws like" ASFA somehow "further exacerbate the difficulties that incarcerated women face" upon reentry); Mitchell (2012); Kennedy (2011, 84) ("This Article proposes deconstructing the family ideology at work in parental termination cases and rethinking the policy and practice of state and judicial intervention in families with an incarcerated parent. It suggests that courts adopt a higher standard of proof than is typically required in deciding parental termination cases").
117 Kennedy (2011, 83).
118 See, for example, N.Y. Soc. Serv. Law § 384-b (adding as another exception to the 15/22 rule "parents are incarcerated, or participating in a residential substance abuse treatment program").
119 See Somini (2000).
120 See Gelles (2017, 75–7, 82–5, 88–90).
121 See Dicker and Gordon (2004).
122 See Dwyer (2008, 441–2); Bartholet (2012, 1358).
123 Gordon (1999, 678–9).
124 Berrick *et al.* (2008). See also Bartholet (2012, 1361–3) (documenting this attitude among CPS agency directors).
125 See Lederman *et al.* (2001, 33–4) ("For young children who have the misfortune of entering the juvenile court system in their first few years of life, preventive interventions are often too late").
126 See, for example, Ross (2015, 27–31). Ross (2015, 28) ("The vast majority have been raped"); Ross (2015, 39) ("Almost all girls incarcerated in Los Angeles will be poor girls of color…"); Ross (2015, 39–40) (in California "92 percent of girls [in detention] have been sexually and/or physically assaulted…"); Ross (2015, 65) ("Up to 73 percent of juvenile justice-involved girls have histories of physical and sexual violence"); Ross (2015, 108, 116, 121, 124–5, 127, 132) ("The majority of girls in correctional settings have experienced physical and sexual abuse, and nearly 4 out of 5 had run away from home"); Ross (2015, 133).
127 Ross (2015, 69).
128 Farrington (2012, 161–2).
129 Farrington (2012, 159–60).
130 Woolard (2012, 117).
131 Farrington (2012, 160–1).
132 Ross (2015, 78, 107).
133 See Farrington (2012, 158).
134 Farrington (2012).
135 See, for example, Slack *et al.* (2011).
136 Cf. Ji *et al.* (2010, 439) (reporting from a study of 379 adoptive parents and their children: "Results demonstrate that the adoptive family environment, namely family sense of coherence, may have a strong influence on adoptees' psychosocial adjustment. The conclusion is consistent with findings from previous studies…"); Ji *et al.* (2010, 433) (defining "family sense of coherence" as "the degree to which a family perceives family life as comprehensible, manageable, and meaningful"); Ji *et al.* (2010, 435) (stating that family coherence includes "degree of predictability and explicability of family life," "extent to which family resources are available to meet the demands posed by family stressors," and "the degree to which family perceives the demands are worthy of investment by family"); Ji *et al.* (2010, 433) (describing prior research finding that quality of family environment following removal of a child from parental custody largely determines child welfare outcomes—specifically, attachment security with caregivers, "maternal sensitive responsiveness," positive communication with parents, openness about adoption, low parental stress, high levels of "parental supports," and "highly organized, expressive families").
137 See Farrow *et al.* (2011).
138 42 U.S.C. § 671(a)(19).

139 See, for example, Ellis v. Arkansas Department of Human Services, 497 S.W.3d 720, 728 (Ark. App. 2016) ("it is axiomatic that the child's best interest must be the paramount consideration in every decision the court makes at all stages of juvenile court proceedings."); In re Lauren R., 148 Cal. App. 4th 841, 855 (2007) ("[R]egardless of the relative placement preference, the fundamental duty of the court is to assure the best interests of the child, whose bond with a foster parent may require that placement with a relative be rejected."); Va. Stat. 16.1–281 ("The child's health and safety shall be the paramount concern of the court and the agency throughout the placement, case planning, service provision and review process").

140 See, for example, Farr (2013); Adler (2001, 18–19); Bartholet (1991, 1169–70, 1179–82); Roberts (2003, 180) (noting the National Association of Black Social Workers' opposition to transracial adoption on the grounds that it constitutes "a form of 'genocide' ").

141 See, for example, Arizona Statute § 8–514.03.

142 See Berrick and Hernandez (2016, 24–33).

143 See generally Reece et al. (2014, Chs. 9, 10).

144 See, for example, Kan. Stat. Ann. § 38–2365(h); S.C. Code Ann. §20–7–768; S.D. Codified Laws § 26–8A-26; Utah Code Ann. § 78A-6–314; Va. Stat. § 16.1–283.

145 This might be why "[p]lacement with kin, and limited or no parental visiting, are associated with non-reunification." See D'Andrade and Berrick (2006), 36.

146 Berrick and Hernandez (2016).

147 See Musil et al. (2009, 389–408).

148 See Bartholet (1999, 93).

149 Gnau (2015).

150 Cf. Virginia Dept. of Social Services (2015) (stating that local DSS offices "should diligently recruit [an adoptive] home as soon *after TPR* as possible") (emphasis added).

151 See, for example, Frame et al. (2006, 361–2).

152 Children's Bureau (2015), 2.

153 See Tanner (2017) (quoting a pediatrician as saying " 'The damage that happens to kids from the infectious disease of toxic stress is as severe as the damage from meningitis or polio or pertussis,' " and a preschool teacher as saying that children "living with parents struggling to make ends meet or dealing with drug and alcohol problems, depression or domestic violence … come to school in 'fight or flight' mode, unfocused and withdrawn or aggressive, sometimes kicking and screaming at their classmates"); Putnam (2015, 78) (discussing how the "kaleidoscopic, multi–partner, or blended family" negatively affects children's academic performance and other outcomes).

154 See Wells et al. (2015, 87–87–116).

155 See, for example, Chaudry (2017, 106); Gibbs (2013); Puma et al. (2012); Puma et al. (2010); Curtis and Nelson (2003, 463, 464) ("[O]ver the past four decades, scores of enriched preschool intervention programs have been implemented … [T]he hoped-for and expected enduring effects on IQ have largely not been obtained").

156 See Besharov and Call (2008, 28–35) ("Debate rages about how best to close the achievement gap, but all specialists agree that to be successful, programs must be focused on the children's deep needs and be intense enough to make a difference. That means multiple years of educational and support services for the parents as well as the children—and that simply is not something pre-K and its three or four hours of school-based services will provide").

157 Putnam (2015, 103).

158 See, for example, Putnam (2015, 153–4).

159 Tavernise (2012). The achievement gap between children at the 90th percentile of family income and children at the 10th percentile increased 30–40 percent between 1976 and 2001. Reardon (2011).

160 See Scott (2016, 65–7) (discussing research of sociologist Sean Reardon).

161 See Putnam (2015).

162 See Camera (2016).

163 Camera (2016); Ryan (2010). Cf. Baker (2012, 19) (finding evidence-increased funding can result in higher *short-term* performance for schools in the aggregate, via smaller class sizes, better teachers and teacher retention, services for children having special needs, better

equipment and curricular materials, improved security, and adequate building, but stating "limited evidence about the connection between funding and *longer-term* outcomes," "it remains difficult to tie district-level expenditure data to specific schools, programs and class-rooms, limiting the ability of researchers to explore more closely the relationship between spending patterns, resource allocation choices and student outcomes," and "we know that such opportunities are inequitably distributed across children" (emphasis in original)).

164 See Schneider (2017, 30, 37–40); Eskelsen and Thornton (2015); McCluskey (2015); Cas-selman (2015) (suggesting that the law's main positive effect was the increased data collec-tion that exposed the relatively poor performance of poor and minority-race students, which in some more affluent school districts provoked greater attention to the small number of students from less privileged backgrounds).

165 Some advocates for poor public school districts have tried a litigation route, but this is a major undertaking and rarely produces appreciable positive change: "State school finance victories repeatedly have encountered entrenched resistance by state legislatures and the public and thus often require decades of litigation to achieve any results." Ogletree and Robinson (2015, 269). And any improvements are always vulnerable to being undone when the affluent find the coast is clear to take back their money.

166 Whether they have helped many children is quite doubtful. See Carey (2017).

167 See, for example, Kaplowitz (2003).

168 Putnam (2015), 172.

169 See Kaplowitz (2003).

170 See Chetty *et al.* (2014) (showing effects of good teachers are much greater in higher SES families and concluding that "teacher quality … is complementary to family inputs and resources").

171 See Putnam (2015, 165–72).

172 Ross (2015, 34) (finding a common life history among teen girls committed to juvenile detention is that sexual abuse at home distracted them from school work and forced them to focus on escaping the abuse, in many cases by running away from home).

173 See McDaniels (2014); Smith and Fong (2004, 214–15).

174 Shedd (2017, 74).

175 See, for example, McDermott and Rothenburg (2000).

176 See Eckholm (2013).

177 Ross (2015, 61).

178 See Wagmiller (2007, 164).

179 Putnam (2015, 110–13).

180 See CBS SF Bay Area (2014).

181 McDonald and Richmond (2008).

182 McDaniels (2014).

183 See, for example, Shedd (2017, 74); Popkin (2016, 49).

184 See Horn (2017) ("'Every time you go outside, you have to think about it: Is somebody gonna shoot you today? Are you gonna get robbed today?' asked a 17-year-old who has lost a brother and a best friend to the city's gun violence.'" "'Is this gonna be the last time you see your mom?'").

185 See Horn *et al.* (2017).

186 Shedd (2017, 74).

187 CBS SF Bay Area (2014).

188 Horn (2017).

189 CBS SF Bay Area (2014).

190 See Timberlake and Michael (2007).

191 See Anderson (2008).

192 See Anderson (2008, 17–18).

193 See, for example, Putnam (2015, 96).

194 See Foreman (2017, 225–7); Duck (2008).

195 Ross (2015, 51–6).

196 See Correll *et al.* (2007); Peruche and Plant (2006).

197 See generally Ghandnoosh (2014).

198 Anderson (2008, 17–18).

199 Anderson (2008); Hetey and Eberhardt (2014).
200 See, for example, Nelson (2013); McRady (2014).
201 See Lenhardt (2004, 843–4).
202 See Luo (2009).

Bibliography

Adler, Libby S. "The Meanings of Permanence: A Critical Analysis of the Adoption and Safe Families Act of 1997," *Harvard Journal on Legislation* 38(1) (2001): 18–19.

Alexander, Pamela C. *Intergenerational Cycles of Trauma and Violence: An Attachment and Family Systems Perspective*. New York: W.W. Norton & Company, 2015.

Ammons, Jackie. "Texas' Prenatal Protection Act: Civil and Criminal Fetus Fatality Protection," *Texas Journal of Women and the Law* 21(2) (Spring 2012): 267–80.

Anderson, Elijah. *Against the Wall: Poor, Young, Black, and Male*. Philadelphia, PA: University of Pennsylvania Press, 2008.

Annie E. Casey Foundation. *Race Matters: Unequal Opportunity within the Child Welfare System*. AECF.org: The Annie E. Casey Foundation, 2002.

Baker, Bruce D. *Does Money Matter in Education?* Washington, DC: Albert Shanker Institute, 2012.

Baradaran, Shima. "Race, Prediction, and Discretion," *George Washington Law Review* 81(1) (January 2013): 157–222.

Barth, Richard P. and Devon Brooks, "Outcomes for Drug-Exposed Children Eight Years Postadoption." In *Adoption & Prenatal Alcohol and Drug Exposure*, edited by Devon Barth *et al.* Washington, DC: Child Welfare League of America, 2000.

Barth, Richard P. and Christopher Lloyd. "Five-Year Developmental Outcomes for Young Children Remaining in Foster Care, Returned Home, Or Adopted." In *How does Foster Care Work?: International Evidence on Outcomes*, edited by Elizabeth Fernandez and Richard P. Barth, 58–9. London and Philadelphia: Jessica Kingsley Publishers, 2010.

Bartholet, Elizabeth. "Where do Black Children Belong? The Politics of Race Matching in Adoption," *University of Pennsylvania Law Review* 139(5) (1991): 1169–82.

Bartholet, Elizabeth. *Nobody's Children: Abuse and Neglect, Foster Drift, and the Adoption Alternative*. Boston, MA: Beacon Press, 1999.

Bartholet, Elizabeth. "Creating a Child-Friendly Child Welfare System: Effective Early Intervention to Prevent Maltreatment and Protect Victimized Children," *Buffalo Law Review* 60 (2012): 1323.

Behnke, Marylou and Smith, Vincent C. "Prenatal Substance Abuse: Short- and Long-term Effects on the Exposed Fetus," *Pediatrics* 131(3) (2013): 1009–24.

Berrick, Jill Duerr and Julia Hernandez. "Developing Consistent and Transparent Kinship Care Policy and Practice: State Mandated, Mediated, and Independent Care," *Children and Youth Services Review* 68 (2016): 24–33.

Berrick, Jill Duerr, Barbara Needle, Richard P. Barth, and Melissa Johnson-Reid. *The Tender Years: Toward Developmentally Sensitive Child Welfare Services for Very Young Children*. New York: Oxford University Press, 1998.

Berrick, Jill Duerr, Young Choi, Amy D'Andrade, and Laura Fram. "Reasonable Efforts? Implementation of the Reunification Bypass Provision of ASFA," *Child Welfare* 87(3) (2008): 163–82.

Besharov, Douglas J. and Douglas Call. "The New Kindergarten," *Wilson Quarterly* 32(4) (2008): 28–35.

Besharov, Douglas J. and Douglas M. Call. "Income Transfers Alone Won't Eradicate Poverty," *The Policy Studies Journal* 37(4) (2009): 599–631.

Betancourt, Laura M., Wei Yang, Nancy L. Brodsky, Paul R. Gallagher, Elsa K. Malmud, Joan M. Giannetta, Martha J. Farah, and Hallam Hurt. "Adolescents with and Without Gestational

Cocaine Exposure: Longitudinal Analysis of Inhibitory Control, Memory and Receptive Language," *Neurotoxicology and Teratology* 33, 20(1) (2011): 36–46.

Blumberg, Marvin L. "Treatment of the Abused Child and the Child Abuser." In *Child Abuse: A Multi-disciplinary Study*, Vol. 6, edited by Byrgen Finkelman. New York: Routledge, 1995.

Bowlby, John. "Postscript." In *Attachment across the Life Cycle*, edited by Colin Murray Parkes, Joan Stevenson-Hinde and Peter Marris, 293. London: Routledge, 1991.

Cain, M.A. *et al.* "The Maternal, Fetal, and Neonatal Effects of Cocaine Exposure in Pregnancy," *Clinical Obstetrics and Gynecology* 56(1) (2013): 124–32.

Camera, Lauren. "Achievement Gap Between White and Black Students Still Gaping," *U.S. News & World Report* January 13, 2016.

Carey, Kevin. "School Choice: Dismal Voucher Results Surprise Researchers as DeVos Era Begins," *New York Times*, February 23, 2017, sec. TheUpshot.

Casselman, Ben. "No Child Left Behind Worked: At Least in One Important Way," *New York Times*, December 22, 2015 at 6:03 a.m., 2015, sec. FiveThirtyEight.

CBS SF Bay Area, "Inner-City Oakland Youth Suffering From Post-Traumatic Stress Disorder" (May 16, 2014).

Chaudry, Ajay *et al. Cradle to Kindergarten: A New Plan to Combat Inequality*, 106. New York: Russell Sage Foundation, 2017.

Chetty, Raj, John N. Friedman, and Jonah E. Rockoff. "Measuring the Impacts of Teachers II: Teacher Value-Added and Student Outcomes in Adulthood," *American Economic Review* 104(9) (September, 2014): 2633.

Child Trends Data Bank. *Late or No Prenatal Care: Indicators of Child and Youth Well-Being*. 2015.

Children's Bureau. *Substance Abuse and Child Maltreatment, Child Welfare Info. Gateway*. Washington, DC: Child Welfare Information Gateway, Children's Bureau/ACYF, 2003.

Children's Bureau. *Child Welfare Outcomes 2010–2014: Report to Congress: Executive Summary*. Children's Bureau, 2015.

Children's Bureau. *Trends in Foster Care and Adoption*. Washington, DC: Children's Bureau, An Office of the Administration for Children & Families, 2016.

Children's Bureau. *The AFCARS Report: Preliminary FY 2016* (No. 24). Washington, DC: Child Welfare Information Gateway, Children's Bureau, Administration for Children & Families, U.S. Department of Health & Human Services, 2017.

Choi, Sam and Joseph P. Ryan. "Co-occurring Problems for Substance Abusing Mothers in Child Welfare: Matching Services to Improve Family Reunification," *Children and Youth Services Review* 29(11) (2007): 1395–410.

Commission to Eliminate Child Abuse and Neglect Fatalities. *Within Our Reach. A National Strategy to Eliminate. Child Abuse and Neglect Fatalities: Final Report*, 2016.

Correll, J., B. Park, C.M. Judd, B. Wittenbrink, M.S. Sadler, and T. Keesee. "Across the Thin Blue Line: Police Officers and Racial Bias in the Decision to Shoot," *Journal of Personality and Social Psychology* 92(6) (2007): 1006.

Curtis, Henry Pierson. "Death on Tarpon Street: Family's Cycle of Violence, Child Abuse, and Drugs." *Orlando Sentinel*, September 2, 2014.

Curtis, W. John and Charles A. Nelson. "Toward Building a Better Brain: Neurobehavioral Outcomes, Mechanisms, and Processes of Environmental Enrichment." In *Resilience and Vulnerability: Adaptation in the Context of Childhood Adversities*, edited by Suniya S. Luthar, 463, 464. Cambridge: Cambridge University Press, 2003.

D'Andrade, Amy and Jill Duerr Berrick. "When Policy Meets Practice: The Untested Effects of Permanency Reforms in Child Welfare," *Journal of Sociology & Social Welfare* 33(1) (2006): 31–6.

Dicker, Sheryl and Elysa Gordon. "Building Bridges for Babies in Foster Care: The Babies can't Wait Initiative," *Juvenile & Family Court Journal* 55(2) (April, 2004): 29–30.

Dodes, Lance M. and Zachary Dodes. *The Sober Truth: Debunking the Bad Science behind 12-Step Programs and the Rehab Industry*. Boston: Beacon Press, 2014.

Duck, Waverly. "Young, Black, and Male: The Life History of an American Drug Dealer Facing Death Row." In *Against the Wall: Poor, Young, Black, and Male*, edited by Elijah Anderson, 38–52. Philadelphia, PA: University of Pennsylvania Press, 2008.

Duso, Adam J. and John Stogner. "Re-Evaluating the Criminalization of In Utero Alcohol Exposure: A Harm-Reduction Approach," *William. & Mary Bill of Rights Journal* 24 (2016): 621–41.

Dwyer, James G. "The Child Protection Pretense: States' Continued Consignment of Newborn Babies to Unfit Parents," *Minnesota Law Review* 93 (2008): 407–24.

Dwyer, James. "Jailing Black Babies," *Utah Law Review* 465(3) (October, 2014).

Eckholm, Erik. "With Police in Schools, More Children in Court," *New York Times*, April 12, 2013, sec. Education.

Edin, Kathryn and Timothy J. Nelson. *Doing the Best I Can: Fatherhood in the Inner City*. Berkeley, CA: University of California Press, 2013.

Edin, Kathryn and Maria Kefalas. *Promises I Can Keep: Why Poor Women Put Motherhood Before Marriage*. Berkeley, CA: University of California Press, 2011.

Engstrom, Malitta, Nabila El-Bassel, and Louisa Gilbert. "Childhood Sexual Abuse Characteristics, Intimate Partner Violence Exposure, and Psychological Distress among Women in Methadone Treatment," *Journal of Substance Abuse Treatment* 43(3) (2012): 366–76.

Eskelsen, Lily Garcia and Otha Thornton. "'No Child Left Behind' Has Failed." *Washington Post*, February 13, 2015, sec. Opinions.

Fairbanks, Robert P. *How It Works: Recovering Citizens in Post-Welfare Philadelphia*. Chicago, IL: University of Chicago Press, 2009.

Farr, Stephani. "Workers Fired for Recommending Interracial Adoption." *Philadelphia Daily News* July 2, 2013.

Farrington, David P. "Predictors of Violent Young Offenders." In *The Oxford Handbook of Juvenile Crime and Juvenile Justice*, edited by Donna M. Bishop and Barry C. Feld, 152–61. Oxford University Press: Oxford Handbooks Online, 2012.

Farrow, Frank, Susan Notkin, Dennette Derezotes, and Oronde Miller. *Racial Equity in Child Welfare: Key Themes, Findings and Perspectives*. Washington, DC; New York: Center for the Study of Social Policy, Alliance for Racial Equity in Child Welfare, and The Annie E. Casey Foundation, 2011.

Foreman, James Jr. *Locking Up Our Own: Crime and Punishment in Black America*. New York: Farrar, Straus and Giroux, 2017.

Frame, Laura, Jill Duerr Berrick, and Jennifer Foulkes Coakley. "Essential Elements of Implementing a System of Concurrent Planning," *Child and Family Social Work* 11 (2006): 361–2.

Fraser, Alyssa, Karen Walker, and Janet Green. "Maternal Cocaine Abuse—An Evidence Review," *Journal of Neonatal Nursing* 22(2) (2016): 56–60.

Gelles, Richard. *Out of Harm's Way: Creating an Effective Child Welfare System*. New York: Oxford University Press, 2017.

Ghandnoosh, Nazgol. *Race and Punishment: Racial Perceptions of Crime and Support for Punitive Policies*. Washington, DC: The Sentencing Project, 2014.

Gibbs, Chloe *et al.* "Head Start Origins and Impacts." In *Legacies of the War on Poverty*, edited by Martha J. Bailey and Sheldon Danziger. New York: Russell Sage Foundation, 2013.

Gnau, Thomas. "Abandoned by Parents for Heroin." *My Dayton Daily News*, November 7, 2015, sec. Local.

Goldsmith, Douglas F., David Oppenheim, and Janine Wanless. "Separation and Reunification: Using Attachment Theory and Research to Inform Decisions Affecting the Placements of Children in Foster Care," *Juvenile & Family Court Journal* 55(2) (April, 2004): 1, 3.

Gordon, Robert M. "Drifting through Byzantium: The Promise and Failure of the Adoption and Safe Families Act of 1997," *Minnesota Law Review* 83 (1999): 637–702.

Grant, Stephen G. "Qualitatively and Quantitatively Similar Effects of Active and Passive Maternal Tobacco Smoke Exposure on In Utero Mutagenesis at the HPRT locus," *BMC Pediatrics* 5(1) (2005).

Guerrero, Erick G. *et al.* "Disparities in Completion of Substance Abuse Treatment between and within Racial and Ethnic Groups," *Health Services Research* 48(4) (2013): 1450–67.

Harmon, Katherine. "U.S. Stillbirths Still Prevalent, Often Unexplained," *Scientific American* (December 13, 2011).

Hetey, Rebecca C. and Jennifer L. Eberhardt. "Racial Disparities in Incarceration Increase Acceptance of Punitive Policies," *Psychological Science* 25(10) (2014): 1949.

Horn, Brittany. "Blood on Wilmington Streets is mostly from Young People," *The New Journal* (Wilmington, Del.) September 8, 2017.

Horn, Brittany *et al.* "In a New Era of Gang Warfare in Wilmington, Insults on Social Media Lead to Bloodshed in the Streets," *The New Journal* (Wilmington, DE) September 9, 2017.

Howard, Kimberly. "Early Mother-Child Separation, Parenting, and Child Well-Being in Early Head Start Families," *Attachment & Human* Development 13(1) (2011): 5–26.

Huang, Hui and Joseph P. Ryan. "Trying to Come Home: Substance Exposed Infants, Mothers, and Family Reunification," *Children and Youth Services Review* 33(2) (February 2011): 322–9.

Huston, Aletha C., Vonnie C. McLoyd, and Cynthia Garcia Coll. "Children and Poverty: Issues in Contemporary Research," *Child Development* 65(2) (1994): 275–82.

Hwang, Sunah S., Hafsatou Diop, Chia-ling Liu, Qi Yu, Hermik Babakhanlou-Chase, Xiaohui Cui, and Milto Kotelchuk. "Maternal Substance Use Disorders and Infant Outcomes in the First Year of Life among Massachusetts Singletons, 2003–2010," *The Journal of Pediatrics* 191 (2017): 69–75.

Ji, Juye, Devon Brooks, Richard P. Barth, and Hansung Kim. "Beyond Preadoptive Risk: The Impact of Adoptive Family Environment on Adopted Youth's Psychosocial Adjustment," *American Journal Orthopsychiatry* 80(3) (2010): 432–42.

Kaplowitz, Joshua. "How I Joined Teach for America—and Got Sued for $20 Million," *City Journal* (Winter, 2003).

Kelly, Joan B. and Michael E. Lamb. "Using Child Development Research to make Appropriate Custody and Access Decisions for Young Children," *Family and Conciliation Courts Review* 38(3) (July, 2000): 297–8.

Kelly, John. "Beyond Last Week's News about Increasing Foster Care Rates: More Adoption, Indiana in Crisis, Long Term Foster Care and More." *Chronicle of Social Change.* December 7, 2017.

Kennedy, Deseriee A. "Children, Parents & the State: The Construction of A New Family Ideology," *Berkeley Journal of Gender, Law & Justice* 26(1) (Winter 2011): 78–138.

Harriet J. Kitzman, David L. Olds, Robert Cole, Carole Hanks, Elizabeth Anson, Kimberly Arcoleo, Dennis W. Luckey, Michael D. Knudtson, Charles R. Henderson, and John Holmberg. "Enduring Effects of Prenatal and Infancy Home Visiting by Nurses on Children," *Archive of Pediatric and Adolescent Medicine* 164(5) (2010): 412–18.

Kwiatkowskia, Maja A. *et al.* "Cognitive Outcomes in Prenatal Methamphetamine Exposed Children Aged Six to Seven Years," *Comprehensive Psychiatry* 80 (2018): 24–33.

Lederman, Cindy S., Joy D. Osofsky, and Lynne Katz. "When the Bough Breaks the Cradle Will Fall: Promoting the Health and Well-being of Infants and Toddlers in Juvenile Court," *Juvenile and Family Court Journal* (Fall 2001).

Lenhardt, Robin A. "Understanding the Mark: Race, Stigma, and Equality in Context," *New York University Law Review* 79(3) (June 2004): 803–25.

Leventhal, John M., Brian W.C. Forsyth, Keqin Qi, Lyla Johnson, Donna Schroeder, and Nancy Votto. "Maltreatment of Children Born to Women Who used Cocaine during Pregnancy: A Population-Based Study," *Pediatrics* 100(2) (August, 1997): 1.

Lollar, Cortney E. "Criminalizing Pregnancy," *Indiana Law Journal* 92 (2017): 947–1005.

Loveland, David and Hilary Driscoll. "Examining Attrition Rates at One Specialty Addiction Treatment Provider in the United States: A Case Study Using a Retrospective Chart Review," *Substance Abuse Treatment, Prevention and Policy* 9 (2014) 9, 11.

Luo, Michael. "In Job Hunt, College Degree Can't Close Racial Gap." *New York Times*, November 30, 2009, sec. U.S.

MacDorman, M.F. and T.J. Matthews. *Understanding Racial and Ethnic Disparities in U.S. Infant Mortality Rates*. Hyattsville, MD: National Center for Health Statistics, 2011.

MacMillan, Harriet L., B. Helen Thomas, Ellen Jamieson, Christine A. Walsh, Michael H. Boyle, Harry S. Shannon, and Amiram Gafni. "Effectiveness of Home Visitation by Public-health Nurses in Prevention of the Recurrence of Child Physical Abuse and Neglect: A Randomised Controlled Trial," *Lancet* 365 (May 2005).

Mark, Katrina and Mishka Terplan. "Cannabis and Pregnancy: Maternal Child Health Implications During a Period of Drug Policy Liberalization," *Preventive Medicine* 104 (2017): 46–9.

McCluskey, Neal. *Testimony: Has No Child Left Behind Worked?* Committee on Education and the Workforce: Democrats, US House of Representatives. Washington, DC: Center for Educational Freedom, CATO Institute, 2015.

McDaniels, Andrea K. "Collateral Damage: Advocates Aim to Save Baltimore Children from Impact of Violence," *The Baltimore Sun*, December 13, 2014, sec. Health.

McDermott, Peter and Julia J. Rothenburg. "Why Urban Parents Resist Involvement in their Children's Elementary Education," *The Qualitative Report* 5(3/4) (October 1, 2000).

McDonald, Catherine C. and Therese R. Richmond. "The Relationship between Community Violence Exposure and Mental Health Symptoms in Urban Adolescents," *Journal of Psychiatric and Mental Health Nursing* 15(10) (2008): 833–49.

McRady, Rachel. "Django Unchained Star Daniele Watts Handcuffed on Suspicion of Prostitution After Kissing Her White Boyfriend," *US Magazine* (September 14, 2014).

Mercer, Jean. *Understanding Attachment: Parenting, Child Care, and Emotional Development*. Westport, CT: Praeger, 2006.

Mercer, Jean. *Child Development: Myths and Misunderstandings*. Washington, DC: Sage Publications, 2010.

Mindock, Susan, *et al.* "Prevalence of Involuntary Commitment for Alcohol Dependence," *WMJ* 111(2) (2012): 55–7.

Miller, William R., S.T. Walters, and M.E. Bennett. "How Effective Is Alcoholism Treatment in the United States?" *Journal of Studies on Alcohol* (March 2001): 211–20.

Mitchell, Caitlin. "Family Integrity and Incarcerated Parents: Bridging the Divide," *Yale Journal of Law & Feminism* 24 (2012): 175.

Mueller, Sven C. "Early-life Stress is Associated with Impairment in Cognitive Control in Adolescence: An fMRI Study," *Neuropsychologia* 48 (2010): 3037–44.

Munz, Michele. "Rapid Rise in Newborns Dependent on Opioids Has Hospitals Scrambling." *St. Louis Dispatch*, August 29, 2016.

Murray, Andrea, Tracey Campfield, Susan Dougherty, and Kerrin Sweet. *Timely Permanency through Reunification*. Casey Family Programs, 2011.

Murray, Melissa and Kristin Luker. *Cases on Reproductive Rights and Justice*. St. Paul, MN: Foundation Press, 2015.

Musil, Carol, Camille Warner, Jaclene Zauszniewski, May Wykle, and Theresa Standing. "Grandmother Caregiving, Family Stress and Strain, and Depressive Symptoms," *Western Journal of Nursing Research* 31(3) (2009): 389–408.

National Institute on Drug Abuse. "Why Are Cocaine Users at Risk for Contracting HIV/AIDS and Hepatitis?" National Institute of Health (May 2016).

Nelson, Charles A. and Edward F. Zigler. "The Neurobiological Bases of Early Intervention." In *Handbook of Early Childhood Intervention*, edited by Jack P. Shonkoff and Samuel J. Meisels. 2nd ed., Ch. 10, 204–10, 216. Cambridge: Cambridge University Press, 2000.

Nelson, Charmain. "Getting Arrested for 'Shopping while Black'," *Huffington Post*, October 28, 2013, sec. The Blog.

Newswise. "Prenatal Exposure to Alcohol Disrupts Brain Circuitry," *Child Law Practice* 33(1) (January 2014): 14.

Newswise. "Functional Brain Organization of Newborns Altered by Prenatal Cocaine Exposure," *Child Law Practice* 34(5) (2015): 79.

Office of Minority Health. *Infant Mortality and African Americans*. Office of Minority Health, 2017.

Ogletree Jr., Charles J. and Kimberly J. Robinson. *The Enduring Legacy of Rodriguez: Creating New Pathways to Equal Educational Opportunity*, edited by Charles J. Ogletree Jr., Kimberly J. Robinson. Cambridge, MA: Harvard Education Press, 2015.

Olds, David. "Effect of Home Visiting by Nurses on Maternal and Child Mortality: Results of a 2-Decade Follow-up of a Randomized Clinical Trial," *JAMA Pediatrics* 168(9) (2014): 800–6.

Olds, David L., John R. Holmberg, Nancy Donelan-McCall, Dennis W. Luckey, Michael D. Knudtson, and JoAnn Robinson. "Effects of Home Visits by Paraprofessionals and by Nurses on Children: Follow-Up of a Randomized Trial at Ages 6 and 9 years," *JAMA Pediatrics* 168(2) (2014): 114–21.

Orlando, James. *Commitment for Substance Abuse Disorders*. Connecticut General Assembly: Office of Legislative Research, 2012.

Otero, Cathleen, Sharon Boles, Nancy Young, and Kim Dennis. *Methamphetamine Addiction, Treatment, and Outcomes: Implications for Child Welfare Workers*. Lincoln, NE: Center on Children, Families, and the Law (2006): 12–13.

Parolin, Micol and Alessandra Simonelli. "Attachment Theory and Maternal Drug Addiction: The Contribution to Parenting Interventions," *Front Psychiatry* 7 (2016): 1–14.

Peruche, B. Michelle and E. Ashby Plant. "The Correlates of Law Enforcement Officers' Automatic and Controlled Race-Based Responses to Criminal Suspects," *Basic and Applied Social Psychology* 28(2) (2006): 193.

Peskin, Melissa, Andrea L. Glenn, Jianghong Liu, Yu Gao, Robert A. Schug, Yaling Yang, and Adrian Raine. "Personal Characteristics of Delinquents: Neurobiology, Genetic Predispositions, Individual Psychosocial Attributes." In *The Oxford Handbook of Juvenile Crime and Juvenile Justice*, edited by Donna M. Bishop and Barry C. Feld. OxfordHandbooks.com: Oxford Handbook Online, September 2012.

Popkin, Susan J. *No Simple Solutions: Transforming Public Housing in Chicago*. Lanham, MD: Rowman & Littlefield, 2016.

Puma, Michael, Stephen Bell, Ronna Cook, Camilla Heid, Gary Shapiro, Pam Broene, Frank Jenkins *et al. Head Start Impact Study Final Report*. Washington, DC: Office of Planning, Research and Evaluation, Administration for Children and Families (ACF), US Department of Health and Human Services, 2010.

Puma, Mike, Stephen Bell, Ronna Cook, Camilla Heid, Pam Broene, Frank Jenkins, Andrew Mashburn, and Jason Downer. *Third Grade Follow-Up to the Head Start Impact Study Final Report, Executive Summary*. Washington, DC: Office of Planning, Research and Evaluation, Administration for Children & Families (ACF), US Department of Health and Human Services, 2012.

Putnam, Robert D. *Our Kids: The American Dream in Crisis*. New York: Simon & Schuster, 2015.

Putnam-Hornstein, Emily, James David Simon, Andrea Lane Eastman, and Joseph Magruder. "Risk of Re-Reporting among Infants Who Remain at Home Following Alleged Maltreatment," *Child Maltreatment* 20(2) (November, 2014): 92–103.

Reardon, Sean F. "The Widening Academic Achievement Gap between the Rich and the Poor: New Evidence and Possible Explanations." In *Whither Opportunity?: Rising Inequality and Children's Life Chances*, edited by R. Murnane and G. Duncan. New York: Russell Sage Foundation Press, 2011.

Reece, Robert M. *et al. Treatment of Child Abuse: Common Ground for Mental Health, Medical, and Legal Practitioners*. 2nd ed. Baltimore, MD: Johns Hopkins University Press, 2014.

Reed, Judith. "Working With Abusive Parents: A Parent's View." In *Child Abuse: A Multidisciplinary Study*, Vol. 6, edited by Byrgen Finkelman. New York: Routledge, 1995.

Roberts, Dorothy E. "Child Welfare and Civil Rights," *University of Illinois Law Review* 2003(1) (2003): 171–80.

Roberts, Sarah C. and Cheri Pies. "Complex Calculations: How Drug Use during Pregnancy Becomes a Barrier to Prenatal Care," *Maternal and Child Health Journal* 15 (2011): 333–41.

Ross, Emily J. *et al.* "Developmental Consequences of Fetal Exposure to Drugs," *Neuropsychopharmacology Reviews* 40 (2015): 61–7.

Ross, Richard. *Girls in Justice*. 1st ed. Santa Barbara, CA: The Image of Justice, 2015.

Ryan, James. *Five Miles Away, a World Apart: One City, Two Schools, and the Story of Educational Opportunity in Modern America*. New York: Oxford University Press, 2010.

Ryan, Joseph P. *Illinois Alcohol and Other Drug Abuse (AODA) Waiver Demonstration: Final Evaluation Report*. Urbana, IL: Children and Family Research Center, 2006.

Sadler, Lois S., Arietta Slade, Nancy Close, Denise L. Webb, Tanika Simpson, Kristopher Fennie, and Linda C. Mayes. "Minding the Baby: Enhancing Reflectiveness to Improve Early Health and Relationship Outcomes in an Interdisciplinary Home Visiting Program," *Infant Mental Health Journal* 34(5) (2013): 391–405.

Substance Abuse and Mental Health Services Administration (SAMHSA). *Substance Use during Pregnancy Varies by Race and Ethnicity*. Rockville, MD: Center for Behavioral Health Statistics and Quality, 2012.

Schneider, Jack. *Beyond Test Scores: A Better Way to Measure School Quality*. Cambridge, MA: Harvard University Press, 2017.

Schreck, Christopher J. and Eric A. Steward. "The Victim-Offender Overlap and its Implications for Juvenile Justice." In *The Oxford Handbook of Juvenile Crime and Juvenile Justice*, edited by Barry C. Feld and Donna M. Bishop, 47–69. OxfordHandbooks.com: Oxford Handbooks Online, September 2012.

Schuengel, Carlo, Mirjam Oosternan, and Paula S. Sterkenburg. "Children with Disrupted Attachment Histories: Interventions and Psychophysiological Indices of Effects," *Child and Adolescent Psychiatry and Mental Health* 3(1) (2009): 26-1-2.

Scott, Sam. "The Gravity of Inequality." *Stanford Magazine* (November/December 2016): 65–7.

Shaw, Terry V., Richard P. Barth, John Mattingly, David Ayer, and Steve Berry. "Child Welfare Birth Match: Timely use of Child Welfare Administrative Data to Protect Newborns," *Journal of Public Child Welfare* 7(2) (2013): 217.

Shedd, Carla, "From Perceiving Injustice to Achieving Racial Justice," In *Racial Reconciliation and the Healing of a Nation*, Charles J. Ogletree Jr. and Austin Sarat. New York: New York University Press, 2017.

Shiffman, John. "In the Heart of U.S. Opioid Epidemic, Help Finds Mother and Baby." *Reuters*, December 7, 2015.

Slack, Kristen Shook, Lawrence M. Berger, Kimberly DuMont, Mi Youn Yang, Bomi Kim, Susan Ehrhard-Dietzel, and Jane L. Holl. "Risk and Protective Factors for Child Neglect during Early Childhood: A Cross-study Comparison," *Children and Youth Services Review* 33(8) (2011): 1354–63.

Smith, Brenda D. "Methamphetamine Use and Child Welfare: Review and Research Agenda," *Journal of Public Child Welfare* 2(4) 2008, 511–29.

Smith, Margaret G. and Rowena Fong. In *The Children of Neglect: When No One Cares*, 216–17. New York: Brunner-Routledge, 2004.

Somini, Sengupta. "Campaigns Soft-Pedal on Children and the Poor." *New York Times*, October 29, 2000, sec. N.Y./Region.

Stoesz, David. *The Dynamic Welfare State*. New York: Oxford University Press, 2016.

Tanner, Lindsey. "Stress Can Affect a Child in a Major Way." *U.S. News & World Report*, July 12, 2017.

Tavernise, Sabrina. "Education Gap Grows between Rich and Poor, Studies Say." *New York Times*, February 9, 2012, sec. Education.

Timberlake, Jeffrey M. and Joseph Michael. "Children's Exposure to Neighborhood Poverty and Affluence in the United States, 1990–2000." In *Child Poverty in America Today: Families and Children*, edited by Barbara A. Arrighi and David J. Maume. Vol. 1. Westport, CT: Praeger Perspectives, 2007.

Tzilos, Golfo K., Gary L. Rhodes, David M. Ledgerwood, and Mark K. Greenwald. "Predicting Cocaine Group Treatment Outcome in Cocaine-Abusing Methadone Patients," *Experimental and Clinical Psychopharmacology* 17 (2009): 320–5.

Virginia Department of Social Services. *Child and Family Services Manual* 2015.

Wagmiller, Robert L. "Children and the Changing Social Ecology of Economic Disadvantage in Urban America." In *Child Poverty in America Today: Families and Children, Volume 1*, edited by Barbara A. Arrighi and David J. Maume, Vol. 1, 163–4. Westport, CT: Greenwood Publishing Group, 2007.

Wallace, John M., Valerie L. Myers, and Esohe R. Osai. *Faith Matters: Race/Ethnicity, Religion and Substance Use*. Canada: The Annie E. Casey Foundation, 2005.

Weisberg, Andrew J. and Frank E. Vandervort. "A Liberal Dilemma: Respecting Autonomy While Also Protecting Inchoate Children From Prenatal Substance Abuse," *William & Mary Bill of Rights Journal* 24(3) (2016): 659–708.

Wells, Amy Stuart, Lauren Fox, and Alana Miles. "Still Separate, Still Unequal in a Post-*Milliken* Era: Why *Rodriguez* Would Have Been Good But Not Enough." In *The Enduring Legacy of Rodriguez: Creating New Pathways to Equal Educational*, edited by Charles J. Ogletree Jr., and Kimberly Jenkins Robinson, 87–116. Cambridge, MA: Harvard Education Press, 2015.

White, Christina. "Federally Mandated Destruction of the Black Family: The Adoption and Safe Families Act," *Northwestern Journal of Law & Social Policy* 1(1) (2006): 303.

Wickström, R. "Effects of Nicotine during Pregnancy: Human and Experimental Evidence," *Current Neuropharmacology* 5(3) (September 2007, 2007): 213.

Wildeman, Christopher *et al.* "The Prevalence of Confirmed Maltreatment among US Children, 2004 to 2011," *JAMA Pediatrics* 168(8) (2014): 706–13.

Wilson, Duff. "As Social Services Stand Back, Mother and Baby Fall 'into Hell'." *Reuters*, December 7, 2015a.

Wilson, Duff. "Hospital Fails to Test for Drugs; Days Later, a Newborn is Dead." *Reuters*, December 7, 2015b.

Wilson, Duff. "Infant Deaths Prompt Changes at Methadone Clinic." *Reuters*, December 7, 2015c.

Wilson, Duff. "Most States Ignore U.S. Law Protecting Drug-Endangered Newborns." *Reuters*, December 7, 2015d.

Wilson, Duff and John Shiffman. "Newborns Die after Being Sent Home with Drug-Dependent Mothers." *Reuters*, December 7, 2015a.

Wilson, Duff and John Shiffman. "State Policies Deter Doctors from Reporting Drug-Endangered Babies." *Reuters*, December 7, 2015b.

Winnefeld, James. "No Family is Safe from This Epidemic." *The Atlantic*, November 29, 2017.

Woolard, Jennifer L. "Adolescent Development, Delinquency, and Juvenile Justice." In *The Oxford Handbook on Juvenile Crime and Juvenile Justice*, edited by Donna M. Bishop and Barry C. Feld, 117. Oxford University Press: Oxford Handbooks Online, 2012.

Young, Nancy K. *et al.* Substance-Exposed Infants: State Responses to the Problem. HHS Pub. No. (SMA) 09-4369. Rockville, MD: Substance Abuse and Mental Health Services Administration, 2009.

Zeanah, Charles H., Charles A. Nelson, Nathan A. Fox, Anna T. Smyke, Peter Marshall, Susan W. Parker, and Sebastian Koga. "Designing Research to Study the Effects of Institutionalization on Brain and Behavioral Development: The Bucharest Early Intervention Project," *Development and Psychology* 15 (2003): 885.

Part II

Breaking the cycle

In simplest terms, the way to end this cycle and dramatically reduce the rate of adult dysfunction among African Americans, and incidentally thereby to eliminate a major cause of the persistent racism and racial stereotyping that plagues all black Americans, is to enact legal and policy reforms that cause fewer children to be raised by unfit parents in dysfunctional communities. It is really no great mystery which particular reforms could accomplish that. The main difficulty lies in overcoming political resistance to enacting them, and most of that political resistance comes from liberals.

For black Americans trapped in areas of concentrated poverty and dysfunction, what would be necessary to transform life positively *for all*, to restore health to communities and to both adults and children in them, helping everyone and hurting no one—if that were even possible given the deep damage already done to so many individuals—is so great and so costly that liberals have been unsuccessful in getting government to commit to it, or anything resembling it. That is not going to change.

And here is the rub: Perhaps because they are in denial about this political reality, liberals are almost uniformly unwilling to endorse or even allow the next-best alternative for children born into the worst social circumstances. The next-best alternative is to interrupt the inter-generational cycle with hard-nosed measures that, regardless of the impact on current adults, prevent today's children from incurring the same damaging early-childhood experiences suffered by so many of today's adults. And in light of the circumstances, these measures are not merely morally permissible; they are morally requisite. Children have a right to them. For the most part, they entail ordering state officials (our agents) to stop doing to children the tragically damaging things they are now doing.

I describe in this Part a coherent set of legal and policy reforms that would effectively spare a great number of children from having to endure maltreatment and life in a hostile home and neighborhood environment, and therefore reduce dramatically the number of future adolescents and adults inclined toward substance abuse and criminality and unprepared for lawful self-sufficiency. I will also explain, based on decades of philosophical and legal study of children's rights, why these are morally correct things to do despite the inevitable additional suffering they might occasion for already-damaged adults.

And I will describe the resistance most other liberals mount to each one of those potential reforms. After battling that resistance for over two decades, encountering it in one child welfare policy context after another, I have reluctantly come to the conclusion that liberals constitute a major obstacle to ending the inter-generational cycle of destroyed lives that plagues black America. They are, in effect, imprisoning black children in a destructive environment, holding them hostage even, by blocking all attempts to remove the children from these destructive environments, insisting that America pay an enormous price to effect economic justice for all today, adults and children alike, when it is obvious that America will not pay.

My description of necessary reforms proceeds from the real-world assumption that, because currently damaged adults and dysfunctional communities cannot be transformed in time to spare children born today from also becoming damaged by them—in part because America will not invest in such a transformation and in part because we simply do not know how to fix deeply-damaged people—there is a conflict of interest between those adults and the children born to them, and to some extent also between children and the survival of particular local communities. The best thing for a large number of today's newborn children is for the state not to force them into a relationship with their biological parents and their biological parents' communities, and to impose substantial restrictions on the freedom of those whom the state does make legal parents—for example, to prevent them from taking drugs or living in places not minimally suitable for raising children.

And let me reiterate: There are millions of well-functioning adults living in well-functioning neighborhoods in this country, a substantial portion of whom are African-Americans, who wish to adopt an infant, the vast majority of whom express indifference to the child's race. The number of US-born newborns or infants under age one currently available for adoption each year is miniscule by comparison. That is why there was tremendous growth of international adoption in the latter part of the twentieth century, including from African countries; so many who seek to adopt a newborn or infant in this country give up hope. And now the international options have been severely reduced, because many countries, at the urging of UNICEF, have shut down their foreign adoption systems. Conversely, there are too few Americans willing to adopt an older child who has already been damaged by adverse experience in infancy and beyond. That is why there are over 100,000 children in the US—disproportionately black children—in foster care and "awaiting adoption."[1] For too many, the state was too late in affording the possibility of having fit parents.

Either of those preventive strategies, though—choosing persons other than biological parents to be a newborn child's caregivers or constraining the liberty of birth parents who do become legal parents, *appears* bad for the biological parents and might also further weaken the parents' already-struggling communities. I emphasize "appears" because, in fact, biological parents unable to care adequately for a child might themselves be better off on the whole if the state did not put them in a position to harm their offspring, just as we suppose self-destructive individuals are better off if prevented from harming themselves. As one parent put it: "We don't like being child abusers any more than society likes the problem of abuse."[2] Or another:

> I am a child abuser. That is difficult enough to admit, even harder to accept. Even more incredible to me is that my son's life ended as a result of a beating I gave him. Although this happened over seventeen months ago, time has not erased my pain.[3]

Conversely, aiming first and foremost to minimize the suffering and maximize the liberty of dysfunctional parents, and to shore up struggling communities, which has been the predominant liberal response to entrenched poverty and disorder, entails ascribing to birth parents and communities a possessory right to newborn children regardless of whether that is best for the children, and that immoral approach has been extremely damaging for countless children in one generation after another. That approach is why the cycle churns on. It must stop.

I therefore present below a multi-pronged approach to keeping children out of the cycle, in the hope it might increase openness in some quarters to such child-focused measures—many proposed by others as well and even instantiated in law in some places, even if most liberals would paint them as imperialist, neo-colonial, slavery re-enacting, anti-women oppression. Legislators can continue cowering before such adult-centered ideological ad hominem attacks and let the cycle continue grinding up generations of black Americans, or they can decide to shift their focus to children and do what is needed to stop the cycle. Even in the absence of political support, though, it is worthwhile to articulate this approach, to identify the measures that would actually work, because it might be possible through litigation, predicated on the constitutional rights of children, to compel states to adopt some of these measures. I offer in the chapters below hints as to what the constitutional claims would look like.

The normative framework

The chapters to follow will display a way of thinking about children's rights you have probably never before encountered, a way that treats children not as needing special sorts of rights entirely different from those we guarantee adults, as if children were a different species, but rather as persons who should possess rights equivalent (even if not identical) to the rights we adults insist on for ourselves. In various contexts in which children have important interests at stake, I will ask what rights adults have in similar contexts when they have similar interests at stake, and then whether children should have comparable rights, simply exercised for them by a proxy (such as a court or child protection agency). For example, when the legal system chooses legal parents for a child, as in adoption (and also, I emphasize, in applying parentage laws at a child's birth), it is making on behalf of that child a kind of decision—that is, with whom to form a legal family relationship—that adults also make—for example, when deciding whether and whom to marry. So we should ask: What is the nature of adults' rights in the context of family formation? If we adults have an absolute right to refuse a family relationship with someone we think unfit to be a spouse, someone we think will repeatedly harm us and provide little of the good that spouses are supposed to provide, should not newborn children have a comparable right against being forced into a family relationship with someone unfit to be a parent?

This analytical device has the potential, I think, to wear down liberal resistance. When children are accorded only "special rights," if any, it is easy to engage in ad hoc, unprincipled reasoning about what the content of those rights should be. And so it is easy for liberals to say,

> well, yes, children should have some rights, but those rights have to be balanced against parents' interests and rights, and against the interests and rights of communities, and against the aims of promoting equality for women and overcoming our history of brutal racist oppression, and against…

And so it is that children's rights, and indeed children themselves, fade from view in liberal social policy. Liberals (and conservatives) need to confront the gross disparity between the robust rights they defend for adults and the cramped rights they begrudgingly allow children. Adults exercising their own rights are not required to compromise their own interests in the ways liberals would compromise the interests of children born to dysfunctional parents. For example, if a woman meets and has an initial attraction to a man, but then learns the man has a substance abuse problem and a history of mistreating intimate partners, or lives in a horrible neighborhood and refuses to leave, or is about to begin a five-year prison sentence, she has an absolute right to refuse to form a relationship with him. There is no balancing of rights that occurs, and she is under no obligation to factor into her decision the man's happiness, or what impact the decision could have on the strength of his community or racial group, nor to give him years to attempt rehabilitation so long as there is any chance he might turn himself around. Nor is there any requirement that he be blameworthy; it is entirely appropriate to say to someone "I'm sorry, I don't blame you for your condition, but forming a family with you is not the right decision for me."

Liberals therefore need to confront squarely the question why only children must have their welfare compromised for the sake of other people and for so-called progressive causes, when it comes to deciding with whom they will live and share family life, especially given that children have more fundamental interests at stake than do adults in this regard and much less ability to protect their own interests. Why must children born to dysfunctional adults be denied real, nurturing parents during the crucial attachment stage of development, and instead go home with persons incapable of properly caring for them or else be parked in the foster-care system, solely because social workers believe there is "some chance" their birth parents can become minimally adequate caregivers if given enough time, and like to pat themselves on the back for "never giving up on our parents"?

A preliminary point, about Slippery Slopes. I am repeatedly astonished by how readily otherwise rational people react to proposals for greater protection of children's welfare against parental choices, actions, or unfitness by conjuring up the most extreme extensions of an idea or approach, making arguments of the sort "If we start doing X, then what's to stop us from doing other, horrible things that bear some remote resemblance to what you are proposing?" For example, if someone proposes paying female drug-addicts to accept long-term contraceptive implants, the Left will inevitably accuse them of favoring forced sterilization of all poor people and fling the frightful "EUGENICIST!" epithet at them. Slippery-slope arguments are generally unsound and a sign of analytical weakness. Such arguments impute to opponents assumptions no one has made, rest on assumptions that are unstated and undefended, overlook relevant distinctions across decision contexts, and aim to shift the conversation away from what someone has actually proposed to something else that they have not proposed, because the latter is an easier target.

Children need us all to be honest, fair, and open minded in our reading of others' ideas. Look at what I actually say and do not impute to me assumptions, attitudes, or positions I do not state. I will aim to do the same with the people whose views I challenge. After all, slippery slope arguments can always be turned around on their proponents, so I could impishly charge liberals with favoring a return to the ancient Roman law of *patria potestas*, under which fathers were free to kill their children if they wished. But that would be intellectually lazy and irresponsible, so I will not do it. This is an extremely sensitive subject, and what I propose will seem radical, even though our legal system is already committed in theory to many of the fundamental ideas underlying my proposals. In this context, it is especially important for everyone to proceed cautiously, respectfully, and honestly. And to bear in mind that the strongly adult-centered American electorate will always scrutinize skeptically any new proposals to protect children's interests at the expense of parents' happiness.

Chapter 3 addresses the pre-natal period, during which the state (and private organizations) might adopt measures aimed at (1) discouraging substance abusers from procreating and (2) preventing pregnant women from substance abusing (by targeting suppliers for criminal prosecution, giving pregnant women priority for voluntary admission to residential rehabilitation, and, if nothing else works, in extreme cases pursuing civil commitment). Chapter 4 addresses the neo-natal period, when the state should (3) mandate efforts (Birth Match and toxicology screening) to identify unfit birth parents, (4) allow unfit birth parents a far shorter time to rehabilitate themselves, (5) place a far greater number of newborns and infants in adoptive homes or pre-adoptive foster care placements, and (6) add several additional bases for "fast-track" termination of parental rights. If the state placed far fewer children into legal relationships with, and in the custody of, unfit parents, it could concentrate its limited social-service resources on parents who are marginal rather than those who are deeply-dysfunctional. Chapter 5 addresses the "neighborhood effect" and suggests measures—one fairly radical (no-child zones), others modest (e.g., giving priority in distributing relocation vouchers to custodial parents of infant children)—to (7) prevent custodial parents from locating their children's home in any of America's worst neighborhoods.

I am more confident about Chapter 4's recommendations than about certain possibilities discussed in Chapters 3 and 5. Prenatal issues are normatively more challenging. Any efforts aimed at women's behavior before giving birth obviously could infringe important individual rights of those women, whereas ascribing rights to any children in that context runs up against conceptual challenges. As for Chapter 5, though I find it normatively easy to defend a right of children against the state's empowering their parents to make them live in a life-destroying environment, the practicalities of effectuating that right in concrete policies are extremely complex. I welcome constructive responses to all the proposals by readers capable of offering special empirical expertise or of engaging insightfully with my normative analyses.

Notes

1 There are over 400,000 in foster care, but only a quarter are available for adoption. Children's Bureau (2016, 1).
2 See, for example, Reed (1995, 26).
3 Blumberg (1995, 205).

Bibliography

Blumberg, Marvin L. "Treatment of the Abused Child and the Child Abuser." In *Child Abuse: A Multi-Disciplinary Study, Vol. 6*, edited by Byrgen Finkelman. New York: Routledge, 1995.

Children's Bureau. *Trends in Foster Care and Adoption: FY 2007–FY 2016*. Washington, DC: US Department of Health and Human Services, Administration for Children and Families, Administration on Children, Youth and Families, 2016.

Reed, Judith. "Working with Abusive Parents: A Parent's View." In *Child Abuse: A Multi-Disciplinary Study, Vol. 6*, edited by Byrgen Finkelman. New York: Routledge, 1995.

Chapter 3

Conception and pre-natal life

One means of reducing in the future the number of adults and adolescents incapable of adequate parenting, because of personal problems such as drug addiction, alcoholism, and mental illness, or because of bad life circumstances such as incarceration or being trapped in an abusive relationship, would be to minimize the number of children born today to such adults and adolescents. This could be done by encouraging persons who now have such dysfunctions or circumstances not to procreate, and by ensuring that if such persons do conceive a child they do not inflict lasting damage on the child during pre-natal life. These are factual observations. What people disagree about is what, if anything, the state should do to pursue these aims.

Prevent people unfit to parent from conceiving

This brief section is a digression from the book's general children's-rights-based analysis. It is conceptually incoherent, I believe, to speak of possible future children having a right not to come into existence. Even if it made sense conceptually, it would be substantively implausible to ascribe such a right, if we assume it is better to exist than not, even if one incurs some detriment before being born. It is conceptually coherent to speak of existing children benefiting from their parents' not having more children—for example, if the children are in foster care and need their parents to focus on rehabilitation. Or of existing children who need state assistance having an interest in state resources not being further diluted by new entrants into the child-protection system. But I am not going to take the position that any existing children have a *right* to anyone's forbearance from procreating. So here I offer simply a few points of social policy regarding child welfare.

There are important limits on what the state can do in this realm. Nonconsensual sterilization, absent paternalistic justification (which I think absent in this context), is an affront to human dignity and infringes on a very strong moral right of persons to bodily integrity.[1] Prohibiting certain adults from having sex presents a whole host of moral, legal, and practical problems. However, there are policies and practices states and private organizations can adopt to reduce the rate at which dysfunctional adolescents and adults conceive children, without infringing basic liberties. They can do so by creating incentives and disincentives less oppressive than the threat of criminal prosecution, attempting to influence decision-making but respecting individuals' self-determining right to choose. In fact, encouraging people who are unprepared to parent to take steps to avoid pregnancy is quite common. The government already does this by providing sex education and/or abstinence encouragement among minors in public schools.

Private organizations (schools, churches, Scouts, etc.), service providers (e.g., doctors), and parents do the same with teenagers in their care. Any of us might urge a sibling or friend or even casual acquaintance struggling with addiction or mental illness to try to avoid procreating, for that person's own good as well as to avoid setting up a child for an adverse early experience. We would find it impertinent, I think, if that person protested: "Stop infringing my liberty!" We would say: "I'm not, I'm just urging you to make this choice for yourself." We would also be perplexed if some third party accused us of implicitly saying to that person: "You're not worthy of reproducing the human race," and "You're not worthy of being treated as a human being."[2]

Neither government nor private remonstrance, though, is likely to reach or be effective with the population in danger of having the most problematic pregnancies— namely, adolescents and adults living in the community (i.e., not institutionalized) who suffer from drug addiction, alcoholism, mental illness, mental disability, or great immaturity. These are people debilitated in ways that make adequate parenting very unlikely, yet paradoxically also people especially likely to procreate, because they are (a) more likely to have sex impulsively and (b) generally not careful about avoiding unintended pregnancy. The lack of efforts to avoid pregnancy could reflect a general carelessness or lack of self-control or it could be because the opportunity cost of pregnancy is so low (i.e., they see little reason not to conceive a child). Substance abusers are also unlikely to have family or friends looking after them and counseling them about family planning. For this population in particular, some other means of incentivizing use of effective birth control would be needed.

Some private organizations in the US have attempted this. Project Prevention might be the most well-known. It is a non-profit operating in many states, providing direct assistance of two kinds to men and women addicted to drugs or alcohol: (a) referrals to treatment facilities and (b) cash incentives ($300) to use long-term birth control (e.g., vasectomy, IUD, Implanon).[3] The organization has made some bad PR moves. (The two instances frequently cited by liberals hostile to its mission are a comparison its founder made to sterilizing dogs and billboards saying "Don't let a pregnancy ruin your drug habit.") But disrespect toward persons who have lost control of their lives is not an inherent feature of such an effort, and to suggest that it is amounts to evasion. One could bring a "least of my brothers" or "but for the grace of God" attitude to this work.

In any event, many thousands of men and women have accepted both kinds of assistance, and there can be no denying that Project Prevention accomplishes what it says:

> We are lowering the number of children added to foster care, preventing the addicts from the guilt and pain they feel each time they give birth only to have their child taken away, and preventing suffering of innocent children, because even those fortunate enough to be born with no medical or emotional problems, after placed in foster care, often face a lifetime of longing to feel loved and wanted.

It seems clear that the program reduces the number of children born who have incurred organic damage in utero or who suffer an early childhood experience likely to make them also drug addicts one day. We cannot see the damage and suffering it prevents, but it is undoubtedly enormous.

Nevertheless, no legislator is likely these days to propose supporting such private efforts or doing anything similar through any state agency (a Louisiana Congressman tried in 2008 and was soon removed from his leadership position). Expanding such programs would therefore require increased private giving.

The predominant liberal reaction to such programs aimed at inducing voluntary acceptance of long-term contraception is, of course, uniformly and unqualifiedly hostile, in predictable ways. They mischaracterize it: One article cites Project Prevention as an example of a "category of undesirables" being "legally pressured or forced not to have children."[4] Another says it imposes "financial penalties for pregnancy."[5] Still another says it is "using coercion to buy women's reproductive capacities."[6] (If I pay my neighbor not to blare his stereo when I have company, have I bought his stereo?) They assert without basis that it targets minority-race women.[7] From their ideological and adult-centered perspective, the facts (fewer children suffering, grateful recipients) are irrelevant. What matters is the symbolism: These programs are a classist, racist, misogynist attack on poor black women, simply because drug addicts are disproportionately poor and black and because it is women who bear babies (and despite the fact that the program also serves men) and because the founder made a comparison to spaying and neutering of dogs. They raise the boogeyman of "EUGENICS";[8] if you think substance abusers should not be having children, then you must think no black people should be having children (which says more about the mindset of those leveling the eugenics charge than about anyone else). They are not critical of any parents who create incentives of various kinds for their child to avoid pregnancy (even if a parent is white and the child black or mixed race), but they villainize private organizations who step in where family influence is missing.

Reasonable people can disagree about the moral issues this practice raises. To make headway with intractable social problems such as substance abuse and child maltreatment, though, policy needs to be based on what a thing is, in and of itself, not what it resembles in ACLs' post-modern imaginings. One possible scenario critics describe would certainly be troubling—namely, persons' being so desperate for cash for a drug fix that they agree to do something relating to their bodies that they would prefer not to do. If it is permanent sterilization, that seems a substantial loss, and of course doing that to someone who is consenting only because of overwhelming immediate physical need is wrong. But how would that ever happen? Are we to imagine a physician waiting in the operating room, scalpel in hand, while a Project Prevention staff member dangles money and a consent form in front of an addict outside the room. The process of consulting, scheduling, prepping, and undergoing such a procedure takes far too long to fit this scenario. And if it is a realistic concern, it can be addressed with regulations imposing a waiting period before any sterilization, as some states have done (and not in reaction to Project Prevention).[9] Other scenarios, I think, are not sufficiently troubling to condemn unless one grossly exaggerates the value and entitlement of being able to procreate intentionally at any and every moment, radically discounts the autonomy of people who accept the deal, and adopts an extreme form of anti-paternalism.[10] It might be that critics also need to have a little more respect for the men and women who have participated in the program; to assume they are all so hapless they would sell away their Basic Human Rights and "reproductive capacities" for $300 is itself arguably demeaning.

Liberals likewise categorically condemn judicial no-procreation orders, something a few jurisdictions have tried, most often as a condition for probation in criminal cases (i.e., 'if you have another child, your probation will be revoked').[11] The most defensible instance of attaching negative consequences to procreation, in my view, is informing a parent whose child has been removed because of maltreatment that rehabilitative efforts will end, and a petition for TPR will be filed, if they procreate again before they have completed the treatment and services the court orders and if the judge concludes having another baby will be too great a distraction from their rehabilitation. This is essentially what an upstate New York trial court judge did in 2004, in a case that made national headlines, with a mother who was

> a homeless, unemployed drug abuser and prostitute, [who] has given birth to seven children, apparently with seven different fathers … [and all of whose] children were removed from her care and custody because she could not and did not take care of them.[12]

The justification in such a case is the impact on the existing child, who is waiting to see if the parent cares enough about getting him or her back to complete the plan of rehabilitation. It is no different from telling such a parent that if he or she resumes cohabitation with a certain person (sex offender, drug supplier, pimp) then the permanency plan will change. ACLs would characterize it as "punitive," but it is not. It is an adjustment in proxy decision-making for the child in foster care. But for most liberals, all that matters is that it is a state effort to influence reproductive choices, and abortion-rights hyper-vigilance brooks no exception to their blanket opposition to any such effort.[13] Some CPS directors have actually ordered their caseworkers not even to discuss birth control with parents in the system.[14]

Prevent pregnant women from harming the fetus

Dwarfing the number of drug- and alcohol-abusers who accept the assistance of programs such as Project Prevention, or who come under a no-procreation order, is the number who get pregnant, most likely without having made a deliberate autonomous choice to do so. Giving such women priority in voluntary entry into a residential facility, with medical treatment to end abuse in the best way possible for the unborn child, is justifiable and sound policy. The impact of substance abuse on involuntary recipients of toxic substances (babies) justifies such preferential treatment morally, and the cost to the state of compromised child development is great. (The average cost for treating a newborn with neonatal abstinence syndrome, for example, approaches $100,000, typically paid for by the state.)

Just as obvious as the superiority of voluntary residential treatment, however, are obstacles to its happening. The great shortage of rehabilitation facilities is not going to change. Giving pregnant women priority would still leave many waiting, and legislators or program administrators might oppose this policy for fear some addicts would get pregnant intentionally to jump the queue. Further, only a small percentage of addicts are ready to stop at a given time, so most would not voluntarily enter, and those who do enter voluntarily are unlikely to stay and maintain abstinence for a prolonged period; as explained in Chapter 2, these programs are not very effective.

Something more would be needed, then, to prevent prenatal exposure to toxic substances. My first recommendation is to target the supply source. James Winnefeld has argued that even persons who buy and use illegal drugs should be viewed as victims of a violent crime, citing the danger of overdose for a user; "the deadliest link in the overdose supply chain is the street dealer who looks an addicted person coldly in the eye and sells what he or she knows could be the person's last high."[15] The same could be said of a dealer who sees a woman who is clearly pregnant and coldly sells her illegal drugs. It should be viewed as a crime of violence against the unborn child—a new and separate offense, an extension of existing assault or conspiracy laws, or at least an aggravating factor in sentencing for drug distribution. At present, only a few states do anything along these lines. Illinois doubles the maximum penalty for "delivery" of a controlled substance for anyone who delivers "to a woman he knows to be pregnant," and it charges with a separate offense, a Class 2 felony, "[a]ny person who sells or delivers for a commercial consideration any item of drug paraphernalia to a woman he knows to be pregnant."[16] In North Carolina, "selling or delivering a controlled substance to … a pregnant female" is a more serious crime (Class D felony) than selling or delivering to other persons.[17] These laws might well have a racially or socio-economically disparate impact, but a search via Westlaw and Google turned up not a single complaint about them.

For a more effective approach, I recommend states extend the criminalization to any intentional transfer, directly or indirectly, of illegal drugs to a woman, or alcohol or tobacco products to a female less than 21 years of age, if the female happens to be pregnant (regardless of whether the transferor knew or had reason to know of the pregnancy). If the penalty were severe enough, it might cause many drug sellers to stop selling to women, or to men they know share with a woman, and it might cause some men not to share what they buy with any woman. Alternatively, police could simply make it known on the street that enforcement efforts concerning distribution henceforth will focus on suppliers to pregnant addicts. Criminal law experts could refine this idea. The state's interest in the health of the unborn children seems to me sufficient to justify the greater effort to prevent transfer to pregnant women. Some state courts have also treated a father's supplying of drugs to a pregnant mother as a form of child abuse warranting post-birth TPR against the co-parent,[18] or even his not preventing the mother from substance abusing as a form of child neglect (failure to protect).[19] I see no reason not to do that, though I doubt it has any deterrent effect.

With respect to the choices of pregnant women, unborn children have a substantial interest both in their mothers' receiving prenatal care and in their mothers' not ingesting large quantities of toxic substances. Satisfying the first might in some cases lead to satisfying the second, so a concerted effort to increase rates of prenatal care is in order. Conceptually, this would be done by making it as attractive to substance abusers as possible to get prenatal care, and/or by making it unattractive for them not to get it. One essential way to make it attractive is to make it completely non-threatening. Thus, contrary to the impulse of some 'law and order' conservatives, I recommend that states actually prohibit clinic staff from ever reporting patients' substance abuse to authorities, and if any violate that prohibition then the agency they contact should be legally required to reject the report. Women and girls should be immune from arrest or other state intervention while they are traveling to and from the clinic as well. As noted in Chapter 2, however, fear of being reported is not the main reason substance abusers cite for not getting prenatal care, so this might not raise the rate of care much even if substance abusers can be convinced that the clinic is a legal "safe zone." Other efforts to make prenatal care attractive (e.g., free transportation and care for other children, hot meals) would require more money, which is not likely to be forthcoming from the state.

The flipside—making failure to get prenatal care unattractive—might be accomplished partly by making it known that if there is any post-birth hearing on parental fitness, a parent's pre-birth conduct will be considered. The law does this in some contexts with fathers already; failure to provide material assistance to the woman carrying one's child can count in favor of terminating one's parental rights through an adoption proceeding, if the mother wants to place the child for adoption. And most likely, when CPS seeks state custody of a newborn, the mother's prenatal conduct is considered in assessing her ability and willingness to care for the child. So I am suggesting here that the state might send a clearer message to pregnant women about that. Coupled with a strong message that the clinic is a safe zone, this might motivate some.

With respect to substance abuse during pregnancy, a criminal-law response is not, from my liberal perspective, morally appropriate at any time with conduct stemming from sickness. Threatening civil child abuse charges after birth, if a toxicology test of the child is positive, seems to me highly unlikely to have a deterrent effect during pregnancy; against it are addicts' generally short-term horizon (i.e., securing the next high) and people's unrealistic optimism about their ability to quit bad habits later when they really need to. Civil child abuse charges during pregnancy, which some jurisdictions have tried or considered, seem to me unnecessary. The legitimate aim is simply to improve the health of mother and unborn child, and this could be done by using existing civil commitment laws or creating a new one specifically addressing substance abuse and pregnancy. Wisconsin uses a CHINS-type proceeding rather than a maltreatment proceeding, such that the mother need not have a record of child abuse afterward nor any interaction with CPS. It treats a baby in utero whose mother is drug dependent or suffering from alcoholism as "an unborn child … in need of protection or services" and authorizes courts to order a civil commitment to an inpatient care facility.[20] A great practical obstacle to civil commitment, however, would be identifying the pregnant substance abusers, given that clinics (or any other providers of assistance the state should want these women and girls to receive) would not be the source of such identification.

Supposing any pregnant substance abusers could be identified, there should be important substantive limitations on the commitment rule. One necessary finding for a commitment order should be that the facility the mother would enter would in fact improve her health and that of the baby rather than the opposite—that is, it has expertise in and provides special care needed during withdrawal. An additional necessary finding should be that, based upon evidence of how much of which substance the mother is using, her behavior meets some research-backed standard of threatened harm to the fetus (e.g., a substantial risk of significant adverse impact on brain development), sufficient to outweigh the likely stress and life disruption that this coercive proceeding would cause her (which could in turn negatively affect the baby). In other words, this approach should be used only in more serious cases, with the burden of proof on the state.

Any sort of detention is costly, however, and we cannot assume any new funding would be forthcoming to pay for it. I would suggest shifting to this civil commitment approach some state funding now devoted to supporting drug or alcohol rehab per se; as explained in Chapter 2, rehab programs do not have sufficient proven efficacy to warrant devotion of scarce recourses. In addition, as with voluntary entry into residential facilities, priority in assignment of beds could be given to pregnant women who are involuntarily committed. For some pregnant substance abusers, measures short of commitment might suffice and be much less costly—for example, offering to forego involuntary commitment if she agrees to remain at home except for trips to an outpatient treatment facility, to abstinence, and to monitoring.

The prevailing liberal response, however, to any efforts to stop substance abuse during pregnancy that target the women themselves, even civil commitment to a residential treatment facility, is uniformly and unqualifiedly hostile.[21] There is no reason to think it would be any less hostile to more modest forms of coercion, such as confinement to the home with monitoring, even though existing law might authorize the far worse reaction of jailing a user of illegal drugs. As in other realms, what motivates the liberal response is a visceral opposition to 'the optics'; no matter what the intervention is called, it looks to them like blaming and punishing women for having a sickness, targeting particular women because of their pregnancy, and treating women like things—incubators. Because only women can bear children, there is a gender equality element to it that disturbs feminists.[22] (They typically express no reservations, however, about criminal prohibitions on forcible rape, even though those apply almost as exclusively to only one gender.)

Again, we could imagine a comparable attempt by family members to stop someone from doing something destructive, something they are likely to regret—for example, an "intervention" with a sister or adolescent daughter who knows she is pregnant but continues to drink heavily or take high-dose opioids. We would not feel that we were blaming or punishing her, or treating her like a mere incubator, or less respectful of her autonomy just because she is female, if we reluctantly take aggressive action to get her in treatment. We would likely assume she is not acting autonomously, because she is doing something she undoubtedly will one day regret, and regardless we would feel we have a moral obligation to the baby.

Some advocates for women contend that biological fathers per se also endanger babies by their drug abuse and yet are not subject to criminal or civil child endangerment charges, but to the extent that premise is true what follows is not necessarily a gender-equal hands-off approach; one could, and from a child-centered perspective likely would, instead proceed to endorse a gender-equal program of coercing abstinence. The most plausible charge with respect to men arises when they supply pregnant women with drugs or alcohol, and so my second recommendation above was to punish that behavior severely. But such attempts to make the legal response even-handed in gender terms do not move liberal feminists, who insist nothing coercive should be done with pregnant women, that instead the state should only offer assistance and spend a lot more on high-quality pre-natal care and eliminating the underlying conditions of poverty and sexual abuse that lead girls to become drug or alcohol abusers and so forth with a completely non-coercive alternative plan that is unrealistic.

Moreover, rather than acknowledge that there might be a conflict of interests between substance-abusing pregnant women and their unborn child, which might require them to think in a rational way about whose interests are more compelling, advocates for women stretch their minds to find some basis for maintaining that their position is actually best for children as well. The basis they arrive at, in this and many other contexts, is that if the legal system in any way inflicts suffering or loss of freedom on women for the sake of their babies, then the women will do something even worse—either have an abortion or continue the pregnancy but forego pre-natal care.[23] I have already addressed the concern about prenatal care by recommending clinics be prohibited from reporting. And I have seen no citation to any evidence of women having abortions to avoid arrest for "pre-natal child abuse" (which I have rejected), let alone to avoid civil commitment to a withdrawal-treating facility.

In sum, to address the problems of pregnant women and girls failing to get prenatal care or ingesting substances that will cause significant brain damage and other developmental harms to babies inside them, which presumably none of them want, I recommend:

1   Giving pregnant females priority in substance-abuse treatment programs.
2   Amending criminal codes to severely punish those who are the source of illegal drugs for a pregnant girl or woman, or of alcohol for a pregnant female under 21.
3   Prohibiting prenatal care providers from reporting maternal substance abuse to any state agency, and making this known in the community.
4   In more severe cases, civil commitment of substance-abusing pregnant women and girls to secure addiction-treatment facilities, without charging them criminally nor alleging child maltreatment.

Following implementation of the best-possible version of these proposals (preferably with constructive input from professionals who work directly with the substance-abusing population), the thought process for men who interact with pregnant women should be:

> I am not going to take my chances with getting caught selling or giving drugs or alcohol to anyone I know or have strong reason to believe is pregnant. If I am selling, I can make plenty of money selling only to other people. If I am giving, maybe it is time for me to move on to a different relationship.

And the thought process for any pregnant woman or girl should be:

> I don't want to poison my baby. My boyfriend or dealer could get a long prison sentence for giving or selling me drugs. I don't want that, and he will probably stop supplying me. I would be given priority at a residential treatment facility, where I would have medical care during withdrawal. The prenatal care clinic is a safe place for me to start on the path to abstaining at least until the baby is born. If I can stay clean till the birth, the state won't take away my baby right after birth based on toxicology tests. If I don't stop and I get caught, I could be involuntarily committed and might have less choice about which facility I go to. Or CPS will probably take the baby at birth. So I might as well go whole-hog for rehab and admit myself to a treatment facility.

From the baby's standpoint, that is a good thought process.

Justifying pregnancy-related coercion

Deliberation about these proposals could be enhanced by greater clarity about certain normative assumptions. With respect to becoming pregnant, many people refer to a right to have children. Breaking down this idea of "having a child" into component parts reveals that it actually consists of several things, and that there is much less moral or legal support for some parts than for others. One part of "having a child" in a conventional sense is engaging in sex, another is conceiving a distinct human being, another is carrying any child conceived until birth, and finally there is having custody of a child after birth. The first, intimacy among consenting autonomous persons, is a component of normal and natural individual liberty, and so is rightly constitutionally protected. The third—not being forced to have an abortion—is and should be legally protected.

The second component of the concept of "having a child," however—that is, creating another human being, is a very peculiar subject for a right, and courts have actually not recognized it as a right under the constitution. The Supreme Court has recognized a negative right against the state's preventing individuals from securing the means to *avoid* conceiving a child, incidental to a right to preserve one's bodily integrity. It *should* recognize (though it has not) a right against forced sterilization. And it might say there is also a liberty or privacy right against being forced to use contraception when having sex. But it seems highly unlikely that the Court would ever rule that individuals have a constitutional right to create another human being per se, such that, for example, laws limiting assisted reproduction are constitutionally impermissible. In fact, there are no established substantive-due-process constitutional limitations on state restriction of the various forms of assisted reproduction. Most states refuse to enforce surrogacy agreements, and many that do allow them restrict them to persons who pass a mental-health or parental-fitness evaluation,[24] without being ordered by courts to liberalize their rules.

And after all, what would be the moral basis for having a god-like right to create a person? Another person is not part of oneself, by definition, so it is not an aspect of self-determination. It is also not a mere thing, like a song or painting, so assimilating it to rights of expression is problematic. And creating another life is not a fundamental interest for anyone; it is not the sort of thing one must be able to do in order to carry on in life and pursue any other aims. It is rather an ulterior and rather rarified objective people pursue. Certainly many people attach great subjective importance to it, and some pursue it by spending a substantial amount of wealth on technological assistance, such as in vitro fertilization and implantation. But many people also attach enormous importance to, and spend a great deal of money on, winning elections and attracting mates, yet we do not say they have a fundamental interest, and therefore presumptive right, to hold political office or to be married to a particular person (even if that person does not reciprocate). Thus, if the state prohibited assisted reproduction, we should not say the state has completely undermined some people's ability to carry on in life, just as we do not say that of anyone who simply cannot afford reproductive assistance, or someone denied the opportunity to adopt a child. And if what is at issue is simply a state or private effort to influence some persons' decision-making about contraception, to create an incentive for people to choose to use some form of birth control, any suggestion that this violates a right is fanciful. Even a highly coercive offer to suspend a prison sentence in exchange for a convicted criminal's agreement to avoid pregnancy per se (as opposed to sex) is morally and constitutionally defensible. The far more modest offer of a few hundred dollars, or a greater chance of reuniting with an existing child, certainly cannot be said to violate anyone's rights or otherwise constitute a wrong.

At the same time, the case *in favor* of incentivizing some people to use contraception is also not extremely compelling, because, again, it is difficult to see how anyone is *harmed* (i.e., wrongfully made worse off) by conception per se. Yet the case is strong enough. There are sound policy reasons for creating such incentives—namely, preventing the existence of persons likely to incur physiological damage in utero, with all the suffering and societal costs that entails, and sparing women who suffer from addiction and mental illness from the physical and psychological burdens of being pregnant while addicted. Those reasons are not as compelling as an aim of protecting some existing person from being harmed. But given the absence of any established or defensible right to create another person, these policy reasons suffice to justify the work of Project Prevention and any similar efforts by other private agencies or the state—that is, merely extending a financial inducement to addicted men and women to accept long-term (but not necessarily permanent) contraception.

When it comes to protecting children in utero once they have been conceived, the normative case for punishing men who supply harmful substances to pregnant women is easy. Once a child exists and is expected one day to be born, whether viewed now as a person or a potential person, the state has a strong interest in preventing damage to the child, and there is no countervailing interest worthy of respect on the other side in favor of tolerating facilitation of fetal drug or alcohol exposure. An enhanced penalty for a supplier most likely would include a loss of liberty above and beyond that simply for distributing illegal drugs or for giving alcohol to an underage person, and liberty interests are strong. But it is well settled in our legal system that such a severe penalty as incarceration may be used to deter even relatively minor harms to innocent persons (e.g., property crimes that cause a loss for which the victim might have ample insurance), or even simply to try to induce fulfillment of a financial obligation owed to the state (e.g., jailing of child-support delinquents). Existing laws already criminalize other third-party behaviors that inflict harm on fetuses, such as physically assaulting the mother or committing vehicular manslaughter.

The stakes are higher on both sides in connection with stopping a pregnant woman from abusing drugs or alcohol. Civil commitment is a substantial deprivation of personal liberty. Yet no one would maintain that involuntarily committing a mother to a residential treatment program for nine months or less would be an excessive reaction to her injecting heroine or whiskey into a baby *after* birth. Opposition in the case of pregnancy must therefore rest on an assumption that the state has a dramatically lesser interest in protecting a fetus. The effect on the woman is actually less in the case of pregnancy, because it would not entail separating her from the child she harmed. And the blameworthiness of the woman could be the same in the two cases—for example, if she injects a baby after birth while in a delusional state because she is high or drunk. So what would have to be different between the two cases, for someone to insist that what is an appropriate state reaction in the post-birth cases is not appropriate in the pregnancy case, is the interests being protected.

Yet if we assume the child will one day be born, because we respect the woman's decision *not* to have an abortion, the damage to the child per unit of drug or alcohol the child ingests is actually *greater* in the pregnancy case, when the most basic structures of the brain and other organs are forming. Accordingly, the state's interest is actually stronger. What the US Supreme Court has said about the state's interest regarding fetuses does not detract from this conclusion, because (a) it recognized a compelling interest on the part of the state in the third trimester, which is when most of the commitments would occur (simply because pregnancy is more evident then, to the woman and to the rest of the world) and (b) what it said about the state's lesser interest in the first two trimesters was within the context of the abortion decision—that is, whether the state must allow a woman to terminate a pregnancy, an action that could not lead to the sort of harm at issue here (damaged personhood suffered for decades).

In addition, many people are confused about the relevance of Roe v. Wade for "personhood," believing the Court established for all purposes that a fetus is not a person and may not be treated as such. What the Court said was that the original intent concerning the word "person" in the Fourteenth Amendment of the US Constitution likely did not include treatment of unborn children as persons. Thus, a fetus does not have federal constitutional rights. But the Court did not say, and has no authority to say, that a state may not treat a fetus as a "person" under state law, a human being with sufficient legal and moral status that its interests matter. A state simply may not make its view of an unborn child as a person trump a woman's right to have an abortion, until the point of viability, and the abortion right is not at issue here. Moreover, on any defensible philosophical account of moral status, it is undeniable that human beings have some moral status well before birth, and so that their interests matter morally and should matter legally.[25]

From another perspective: Abuse of drugs and underage consumption of alcohol are crimes. To the extent such prohibitions are morally justified, it is most clearly so on grounds of potential harms to other. Someone out of control because of cocaine or heroin use might pick up a gun or knife or get behind the wheel of a car and seriously injure another person. Or they might cause another person also to ingest the illegal drug, as many substance-abusing parents have done accidentally or intentionally with their infant children, and this is especially bad if the other person is highly vulnerable to toxic substances. For any other behavior that is criminal because it poses a danger to others, the state places people who do it in detention to stop the dangerous behavior, and it does this regardless of whether a person has a mental health problem that creates a compulsion to engage in the behavior—in other words, whether it can be character-ized as "a disease." Those who oppose any state restraint of pregnant women who abuse drugs or alcohol therefore bear the burden of demonstrating why there should be an exception only for that illegal behavior. To say that restraint in this case involves "tar-geting" will not suffice, because there is an obvious justification for targeting pregnant substance abusers, just as there is obvious justification for targeting drug abusers and drunk drivers who have post-birth children in their custody, for targeting people who are drunk in public rather than at home, and for targeting people (nearly all men) who have a prostitution or child pornography habit.

Thus, the two measures recommended in connection with pregnancy that entail some coercion—namely, to extend financial inducements to dysfunctional people to use some form of birth control and to civilly commit drug- or alcohol-abusing pregnant women—find adequate normative support in a proper assessment of the interests at stake and in comparison with other well-established child-protection laws. Yet few pol-iticians would endorse them, because they would come under fire from liberals, who would characterize them as misogynist oppression of women and part of a master plot to overturn *Roe v. Wade*.

Notes

1 The US Supreme Court has not yet translated that moral right into a constitutional right, but most legal scholars who speak of Buck v. Bell, 274 US 200 (1927) seem to assume the Court would overturn it if presented with an opportunity. That decision rejected a Fourteenth Amendment substantive due process challenge to the Virginia Sterilization Act of 1923, which authorized the superintendents of the state's several psychiatric hospitals and of the State Colony for Epileptics and Feeble-Minded to arrange for surgical sterilization of any "patient confined in such institution afflicted with hereditary forms of insanity that are recur-rent, idiocy, imbecility, feeble-mindedness or epilepsy."

2 See Open Society Foundations (2013, 2) (interview with Lynn Paltrow, executive director and founder of National Advocates for Pregnant Women, asserting that this is what Project Prevention is telling substance-abusing men and women).

3 See Thyer (2016).

4 Purvis (2017, 431).

5 Persad (2014, 283).

6 Roberson (2009, 91).

7 See Open Society Foundations (2013) (interview with Lynn Paltrow making this allegation); Smith-McKeever *et al.* (2006) (study contradicting claims that Project Prevention targets minority-race women). See also Maillard (2013), 1382 (asserting that "Project Prevention disproportionately impacts low-income, minority communities" but then citing statistics showing that its participants are 57 percent white, which is pretty close to the percentage (61 percent) of the US population on the whole that is white).

8 Hale-Kupiec (2016, 450); Maillard (2013, 1382) ("The organization's goals reiterate eugenic thought").

9 See Tazkargy (2014, 161–2).

10 Cf. Conly (2012).

11 See Dillard (2009).

12 In re V.R., 6 Misc. 3d 1003(A), 800 N.Y.S.2d 358 (Fam. Ct. 2004).

13 See, for example, Flavin (2009, 41) (criticizing the order in In re V.R. as "old eugenic wine in new bottles").

14 See, for example, McMillan (2012, 139) ("Child welfare workers said they were prohibited by policy to discuss birth control or family planning with clients").

15 Winnefeld (2017).

16 720 ILCS 570/401; 720 Ill. Comp. Stat. Ann. 570/407.2; 720 Ill. Comp. Stat. Ann. 600/3.

17 N.C. Gen. Stat. Ann. § 90–5.

18 See, for example, In re Joshua E.R., 2012 WL 1691620 (Tenn. Ct. App. May 15, 2012); CASI Found., Inc. v. Doe, 128 P.3d 934 (Idaho 2006).

19 See, for example, In re G.A., 2012 WL 1068630 (Tex. App. 2012); Dept. of Human Services v. J.S., 182 P.3d 278 (Or. App. 2008).

20 Wis. Stat. 48.135, 51.20.

21 Examples include Bridges (2009); Fentiman (2009).

22 See, for example, Oberman (1992, 6, n. 24).

23 See, for example, ACLU (2018).

24 See, for example, Utah Code § 78B-15–803 (requiring persons seeking approval of a surrogacy contract to undergo a home study and satisfy the standards of fitness applied to adoptive parents); New Hampshire Revised Statutes §§ 168-B: 13–18 (requiring, inter alia, a "non-medical evaluation" that considers "[t]he ability and disposition of the person being evaluated to give a child love, affection and guidance … [and] to provide the child with food, clothing, shelter, medical care and other basic necessities").

25 See Dwyer (2012).

Bibliography

ACLU. *Coercive and Punitive Governmental Responses to Women's Conduct during Pregnancy. Arresting the Pregnancy Police.* aclu.org: ACLU (2018).

Bridges, Khiara M. "Quasi-Colonial Bodies: An Analysis of the Reproductive Lives of Poor Black and Racially Subjugated Women," *Columbia Journal of Gender & Law* 18(2) (2009): 609.

Conly, Sarah. *Against Autonomy: Justifying Coercive Paternalism.* New York: Cambridge University Press, 2012.

Dillard, Carter. "Child Welfare and Future Persons," *Georgia Law Review* 43(2) (2009): 367–446.

Dwyer, James G. *Moral Status and Human Life: The Case for Children's Superiority.* New York: Cambridge University Press, 2012.

Fentiman, Linda C. "Pursuing the Perfect Mother: Why America's Criminalization of Maternal Substance Abuse is Not the Answer—A Comparative Legal Analysis," *Michigan Journal of Gender & Law* 15(2) (2009): 389–465.

Flavin, Jeanne. *Our Bodies, Our Crimes: The Policing of Women's Reproduction in America.* New York: New York University Press, 2009.

Hale-Kupiec, Thomas. "Immortal Invasive Initiatives: The Need for a Genetic Right to Be Forgotten," *Minnesota Journal of Law, Science and Technology* 17(1) (Winter 2016): 441–88.

Maillard, Kevin Noble. "Serial Paternity," *Michigan State Law Review* 2013(4) (2013): 1369–84.

McMillan, Heidee. *Therapeutic Justice and Addicted Parents: A Family Treatment Court Evaluation.* El Paso: LFB Scholarly Publishing LLC, 2012.

Oberman, Michelle. "The Control of Pregnancy and the Criminalization of Femaleness," *Berkeley Women's Law Journal* 7(1) (1992): 1–12.

Open Society Foundations. "Transcript: 'Project Prevention, Child Welfare, and Junk Science," 2013.

Persad, Govind. "Libertarian Patriarchalism: Nudges, Procedural Roadblocks, and Reproductive Choice," *Women's Rights Law Reporter* 35 (2014): 273–98.

Purvis, Dara E. "The Rules of Maternity," *Tennessee Law Review* 84(2) (Winter 2017): 367–446.

Roberson, Lynette. "Paid Sterilizations for Poor Women: Coercing Them Out of Poverty," *Southern Region Black Law Students Association Law Journal* 3 (2009): 84–98.

Smith-McKeever, C., C.-M. Hsieh, and R. Harris. "CRACK/Project Prevention: Providing a Social Service or Promoting Social Control?" *Journal of Obstetrics and Gynaecology* 26(4) (2006): 339–43.

Tazkargy, Ariel S. "From Coercion to Coercion: Voluntary Sterilization Policies in the United States," *Law and Inequality: A Journal of Theory and Practice* 32(1) (Winter 2014): 135–68.

Thyer, Bruce A. "Project Prevention: Concept, Operation, Results and Controversies about Paying Drug Abusers to Obtain Long-Term Birth Control," *William & Mary Bill of Rights Journal* 24(3) (March 2016): 643–58.

Winnefeld, James. "No Family is Safe from This Epidemic." *The Atlantic*, November 29, 2017.

Chapter 4

Sparing children from unfit parents

We adults would not choose a spouse without making any inquiry into the other person's histories or current capacities. The legal system would not appoint guardians for incompetent adults with complete disregard for a potential guardian's criminal record, history of abusing vulnerable people, current ability to provide care, and living situation. The harm to children of an unfit custodian is far worse than the harm to an adult of being in a relationship with a comparably unfit spouse or guardian, because early childhood experience is so fundamental to basic health and wellbeing. Yet, as shown in Chapter 2, the state now severely undermines many infants' psycho-emotional and physiological development by placing them into legal and custodial relationships with biological parents incapable of providing adequate nurturing. It does this disproportionately to black children.

It is imperative—morally and constitutionally—that states stop doing this to children. They must make much greater effort to get parentage right at the outset for all children. If they did so, money spent assisting those whom the state does make legal parents could be targeted at parents capable of adequate parenting with some assistance, rather than at persons who are deeply dysfunctional and extremely unlikely to transform themselves within the timeframe that newborns' developmental needs require. Incidentally, the societal costs of addressing various individual dysfunctions (substance abuse, criminality, mental health problems, school dropout, etc.) more generally would dramatically shrink. Tellingly, in selecting adoptive parents for a parentless child, the state exercises far greater care; it would not knowingly qualify for adoption anyone who has a history of child maltreatment, a current drug addiction, or a serious mental illness or who is very immature. It would not approve a home for a new-family adoption (as opposed to relative or step-parent adoption) if the home were in a hellish neighborhood. The state's failure to exercise any care whatsoever in selecting children's first parents is patently unjustifiable.

Steps to appropriate state parentage decision-making for newborns

In most basic terms, to stop forcing newborns into family relationships likely to cause them fundamental harm, the state must: (a) Identify at or before a child's birth, biological parents who pose a high risk of maltreatment to a baby placed in their custody. (b) Expeditiously assess whether those biological parents so identified can, in fact, currently provide an adequate home environment for a baby. If not, then (c) take protective custody of the child, (d) place the newborn in a pre-adoptive placement, (e) operate on a shorter permanency timeline than that now applied to all children, and (f) pursue fast-track TPR and adoption when that is in a newborn's best interests all things considered (including children's interest in being raised by their biological parents but also their crucial need for secure attachment and their other developmental needs), after (g) encouraging such biological parents voluntarily to relinquish their rights. As documented in Chapter 2, there can be no question that a newborn child is highly likely to have a far better life if placed immediately in family relationships with persons qualified for adoption instead of remaining legally tied to biological parents who will not be able adequately to care for the child at or soon after birth.

Identifying at-risk newborns

The notion that state employees would make judgments in advance about individuals' parenting ability (rather than waiting until they actually maltreat the child in question) troubles many people. ACLs, in particular, react with indignation; it is "profiling" and "a gross breach of human rights."[1] Their reaction rests on failure to see or acknowledge certain undeniable realities:

a   The government is already profoundly involved in family formation, choosing legal parents for all newborn children via maternity and paternity laws.
b   Most people would justify biology-based legal parentage on the basis of a prediction that children's lives will go well if raised by their biological parents.
c   Universal biology-based parentage is a reckless approach to legal parentage, one that predictably destroys many children's prospects for a decent life, and *that* is an egregious abuse of state power;
d   State child-welfare workers and courts already routinely engage in prediction of the future parenting ability of many legal parents (after they have damaged a child), it would be impossible for them to operate without doing so, and they do this now on the basis of factors that could be used to assess biological parents at the time of a child's birth—namely, past parenting, past efforts to rehabilitate, current dysfunction, mental health, maturity, and residential situation.
e   The state already conducts a background check on people who seek legal-parent status as to a child who is not their biological offspring (i.e., in qualifying people for adoption), even though that group of people is on average better prepared for parenting than is the rest of the adult population,[2] as well as on anyone who applies for any kind of job in a school or day care; and
f   The identification I am urging here is largely based on past maltreatment, so it is not really 'in advance of' demonstrated unfitness, but rather only in advance of inflicting abuse or neglect on *another* child.

I am not proposing anything like placement of every child with the best available parents. In the regime proposed here, the default is and would remain that the state makes biological parents the first legal parents of a child. However, the state already "knows," because of records it keeps of past child maltreatment and criminal convictions, that certain birth parents have a high likelihood of harming a child just born. In addition, the state can easily identify other birth parents who are likely incapable of caring adequately for a child, by conducting toxicology testing on all newborns. For the state to force a vulnerable newborn child to be in a legal relationship with and custody of such persons, without first ensuring the child will be safe and receive proper care, is a clear violation of a right we all take for granted for ourselves—that is, a right against the state's forcing us to be in a relationship with someone likely to harm us. Yes, the state must choose legal parents and custodians for newborn children; there is no other way for a legal relationship to arise. But this inevitability in no way licenses the state to carry out this function in such a reckless way, to place children into relationships with complete indifference to whether the persons it chooses are fit to care for a child.

Below I describe feasible ways the state could fulfill the duty it owes newborn children to exercise reasonable judgment in choosing legal parents and custodians, why these precautions are morally and constitutionally required, and why most liberals oppose them.

Birth match

What the state "knows" about most biological parents is their history of child maltreatment and criminal conduct (which for the vast majority of birth parents is "none"). The state maintains records of persons who have in the past been found to have abused or neglected a child, had their rights to a child terminated, or committed crimes such as violent felonies or drug abuse, distribution, or manufacture. The state also knows who is currently incarcerated and who has been involuntarily committed to a psychiatric facility because they pose a danger to self or others. And the state knows which birth parents were themselves victims of maltreatment as children, which, sadly, makes them high-risk parents themselves, especially if they experienced a lot of instability after that in foster care.

State and private agencies routinely consult such databases to do background checks on anyone who applies to become a parent of a child who is not their biological offspring—that is, through adoption. In fact, to become a parent by adoption, even if one has no child maltreatment or criminal history, one must also go through a home study, interview, and post-placement supervision. People who have adopted can attest to how extensive and detailed that investigation is—far beyond what I am urging here. Agencies also routinely consult these databases to do background checks on anyone who applies to be a school teacher, daycare worker, coach for youth recreation programs, or even janitor in a school. Any applicant for any of these employment or volunteer positions who had previously had rights to a child terminated because of maltreatment would be rejected instantly, with no opportunity for appeal, regardless of what suffering that caused them. Indeed, simply having had a founded report of child abuse or neglect in the past would likely disqualify a person from any of these positions. Were an agency to hire such a person anyway, the public would demand that it be held accountable for any harm that person subsequently caused a child.

Yet, traditionally, the state has not used this information in its possession, except in connection with adoption, to avoid the far worse danger to children of placing them into legal relationships with and custody of persons who have seriously troubling backgrounds, even though it could easily do so. State actors might explain the greater care in connection with adoption by saying "well, in that context, the state is choosing the parents and creating the relationship," but the reality is that the state is doing exactly that also when it makes biological parents a child's legal parents and custodians. It only seems like the state is not involved because biology-based legal parentage is so universal and happens so routinely in the majority of cases simply by issuance of birth certificates in accordance with agency implementation of a statute, rather than by individualized agency or court decision. (Although, of course, the latter happens in a great number of paternity cases.)

Promoting birth match in Virginia

Invoking these comparisons to state and private agency practices, a dozen years ago I proposed, in my book *Children's Relationship Rights* and in discussions I had with Virginia legislators, CPS directors, social workers, and attorneys, that the state begin to do a cross check of new births reported to the state's Office of Vital records against the state's records of past terminations of parental rights (TPRs) and serious violent crimes. I held a conference at my university to discuss with the various players in Virginia's child welfare system this and other proposals for making that system more proactive and preventive of child maltreatment rather than only reactive.

The conference audience, made up mostly of child protection agency officials, lawyers who work as guardians ad litem for children, and liberal legislators, was almost uniformly opposed to this proposal. There were a couple of child-centered local CPS directors who urged me to expand the proposal, so the computer matching program would also identify birth parents who currently have one or more children in foster care, even if they have never had a TPR or serious criminal conviction. They routinely see parents who have lost custody of children, but not had a TPR, procreating again and again and maltreating another child and another. However, most of the rest of the audience expressed reflexive opposition, entirely on parent-centered grounds. Some stated such a program would violate birth parents' privacy rights, even though all the information is already in the state's hands and it is just a matter of two agencies putting together information each already has. Some raised the specter of Big Brother licensing people to be parents, even though that is not what I proposed and even though those persons had no qualms about rigorous scrutiny of people who want to be parents by adoption or foster parents (or teachers, coaches, day care workers, etc.). Some said that for the state to take custody of any newborns based on parents' history would amount to adding a new "punishment" for past behavior already fully addressed by the criminal or civil child maltreatment proceedings as to the prior child—as if protecting children should be viewed as depriving adults of a property right. There were also vague assertions that this data cross-check would somehow infringe parental rights, assertions with no basis in constitutional doctrine or any plausible moral view.[3] And, of course, there was the usual disparate-impact objection, that the proposal would disproportionately identify birth parents who are poor and therefore predominantly of minority race. As in other contexts, this objection betrays the adult-centered mindset of most liberals, because it overlooks the fact that *children* of minority race would disproportionately *benefit* from the program, as they are disproportionately at high risk.

Thus, even though the audience predominantly comprised people whose professional focus is supposed to be children's welfare, all objections were adult-centered, adult-protective, ACLU-type responses. Not a single person offered a single reason why this proposal could be in any way detrimental to any child. Nor did anyone deny that this practice would spare many children from terrible harm. Nor was anyone swayed by comparison with our own, self-protective efforts to learn the history of any person with whom we contemplate forming an intimate relationship. Or with adoption, hiring of school teachers, etc.

Existing birth match programs

As noted in Chapter 2, a handful of jurisdictions have by now adopted a version of this practice, starting with Michigan in 2001. In 2016, the National Commission to End Child Abuse and Neglect Fatalities endorsed Birth Match in its final report. Richard Barth, Dean of the School of Social Work at the University of Maryland and President of the American Academy of Social Work and Social Welfare, has spearheaded the state legislative effort. The approach in his home state, Maryland, is very limited—looking only for prior TPRs and prescribing merely offers of assistance. A more robust proposal was watered down because liberal advocacy groups made the same sort of objections I heard at the conference. Barth recommends identifying all "prior failed cases" and currently open cases.[4] Failed cases could include, as in Michigan, also birth parents who previously *would have been* terminated except that CPS or a court found that unnecessary because (a) the abused child died, (b) the child was placed in a permanent guardianship, or (c) the child would remain with the other parent and a no-contact order was in place. It would also include parents whose child was killed or very seriously harmed by a non-parent adult in the household (e.g., a custodial parent's partner).[5] Michigan's program identifies over a thousand children per year who are at high risk but otherwise would not have come to the attention of CPS.[6]

Texas's Birth Match is similar to Maryland's—prior TPRs only, offer services only—and struggled to get off the ground because of legislative reluctance to fund it.[7] As usual, adult-centered liberals resisted. At a Council Meeting of the Texas Department of Family and Protective Services, a representative of the Parent Guidance Center peppered the Council with questions, which she insisted be answered before the program was implemented, including: "Will the agency look only at parents who receive government assistance of some sort?" (i.e., is this discrimination against poor adults?); "Is this a civil rights issue? Are there constitutional problems that may exist?" (i.e., does this violate some rights of the adults?); "Are the parents being chipped, not physically chipped in the system, but psychologically chipped?" (i.e., is Big Brother stigmatizing poor parents?); "Is it discrimination against mothers in these cases where the fathers are not tracked?" (i.e., is this part of the master patriarchal plot to subordinate women); and "What kind of information will [home visitors] record?" (i.e., will this violate adults' "privacy" rights?). The representative worried "birth match could result in a psychological sterilization for parents who will be afraid to change, move on, and have another child" and "fears it will appear that the Department is waiting at the ends of hospital beds."[8] I wonder whether she would want the government to tell her if someone who once brutally beat or sexually abused a child had moved in next door to her own house.

Minnesota has the most robust program. The database comparison identifies birth parents who have had a prior involuntary TPR or even just had a child placed in foster care, or who have a record of causing egregious harm to any child.[9] A match is treated as a maltreatment report and can trigger assessment or investigation. If the caseworker concludes the child will be safe, CPS can still provide services, and in appropriate circumstances ask a court to find the child is "in need of protection or services" in order to accomplish that. If CPS determines the child is not safe, it *must* petition a court for termination of the birth parents' rights and place the child in a pre-adoptive home, unless the agency can convince the court that some other permanency plan is in the child's best interests.[10]

An ideal birth match program

Ask yourself what you would want to know about a person you have begun dating. It would certainly include past instances of divorce resulting from that person's abuse of a spouse (the equivalent of a TPR). But presumably you would also want to know if that person had at some point simply been subject to a protective order to stay away from a partner after a judicial finding that they had committed domestic violence. You would likely also want to know whether the person had any previous criminal convictions for any type of felony, and especially violent ones. In fact, you would undoubtedly want to know if they had ever been charged with certain especially serious crimes, even if never convicted. And you would want to know if the person currently has a drug or alcohol addiction, or a mental illness, because that could seriously adversely affect you in many ways, even though you are infinitely more capable of self-protection than is a newborn. It would be obvious whether the person is in prison, and for nearly everyone the fact that someone is in prison is a compelling reason not to initiate a relationship with him or her. Pause for a moment to think about why these various background facts would matter to you in deciding whether to form a relationship.

Now ask yourself if those reasons are ones also pertinent to the parent–child relationship. If such histories or current conditions and behaviors would make you worry greatly about *your welfare* if in a relationship with such a person, and highly pessimistic about the prospects for the person's changing, how can you be sanguine about the state's putting a helpless and profoundly needy newborn child into a legal relationship with such a person and making the child's fate dependent on a very unpromising gamble that the person can transform himself or herself?

Indeed, imagine it is your child. Imagine you have a fling with someone you do not know well that results in an accidental pregnancy, the child is carried to term and born, and then you face a custody decision. Would you ask for a custody evaluation, looking into the other person's past? Suppose in the course of such evaluation it turns out that this other person a couple of years ago had a founded report of child abuse, which led to foster care and then a TPR. Or that when you met, that person had recently left prison after serving time for a violent felony conviction, or has a serious mental illness or drug addiction. Would you be glad you found that out? And would you argue in court that that person should not have custody of the child? What if he or she expressed willingness to accept rehabilitation services and the court said to that person "okay, if you do what we ask, then on the child's first birthday we will switch custody to you and see how that goes"? Would that sound like a good plan to you? Or would you be incredulous that a court would propose changing custodians of a one year old who has been in the constant care of, and become securely attached to, another parent figure? And would you be likely to oppose even unsupervised visitation until the child is old enough to call you on the phone? Perhaps you would even think it best for your child that the state deny that other person legal-parent status?

What parental and circumstantial factors are reliable predictors of child maltreatment? Some of the best child–welfare researchers are now focused on this question and developing tools CPS can use to assess risk to children with a high degree of accuracy in the different circumstance of screening hotline maltreatment reports.[11] The *New York Times* recently reported:

In August 2016, Allegheny County became the first jurisdiction in the United States, or anywhere else, to let a predictive-analytics algorithm—the same kind of sophisticated pattern analysis used in credit reports, the automated buying and selling of stocks and the hiring, firing and fielding of baseball players on World Series-winning teams—offer up a second opinion on every incoming call, in hopes of doing a better job of identifying the families most in need of intervention.[12]

Emily Putnam-Hornstein, of the University of Southern California, and Rhema Vaithianathan, at the Auckland University of Technology in New Zealand closely analyzed 76,964 allegations of maltreatment made between April 2010 and April 2014 in Alleghany County to build the algorithm. In doing so, they discovered a high rate of error in screener's subjective decisions—both cases labeled high risk that should not have been and cases labeled low risk that were actually high risk. In eight of the latter set of cases, the child ended up dead. Now when a report comes in, screeners go through a checklist of factors and the computer program yields a risk score. Many pediatricians and others who work with maltreated children welcome this new approach as "finally bringing some objectivity and science to decisions that can be so unbelievably life-changing."[13]

The *Times* story about Alleghany County does not reveal the content of the computer checklist. Research done by Putnam-Hornstein, Barbara Needell, and others shows substantial correlations between child maltreatment and parent's substance abuse, mental illness, cognitive impairment (specifically, deficit in "social information processing"), prior maltreatment of another child, immaturity, lack of education, not receiving prenatal care, poverty, lack of paternity establishment, partner abuse, prior criminal convictions, having three or more children, and having been a foster child.[14] An especially disturbing finding in a California study was that 40 percent of children born to a teen mother who herself had been a victim of substantiated child maltreatment (and 30 percent born to a teen mother who was the subject of an unsubstantiated report) ended up reported as maltreated themselves by age five.[15]

We also know certain of these conditions—substance abuse, mental illness, and intellectual disability in particular—are extremely difficult to correct, especially within a newborn child's development timeframe, and highly likely to result in removal and non-reunification if the parent takes the child home after the birth.[16] Moreover, parental incarceration creates an obvious obstacle to adequate child rearing and, as discussed further in Chapter 6, such biological parents are at very high risk of maltreatment and abandonment after release from prison.

Parent-protective liberals nevertheless resist use of predictive instruments. Some view the very idea of "judging" someone based on what we think he or she will do to a child as a terrible violation of human rights,[17] even though we all make judgments about people all the time based on what we think they might do to us. Many in the child welfare field have an instinctive aversion to triage, and the idea of making predictions about parents—even those already reported for maltreatment—strikes them as "presuming guilty until proven innocent." Gelles observed the head of a social workers' union assert that child welfare workers would use "Structured Decision Making," which relies in part on identification of maltreatment-predictive factors, "over my dead body."[18] At a conference some years ago, I suggested that agencies might be able to shift some funding to effective prevention programs if they adopted a triage approach to reported maltreatment, systematically moving to TPR immediately after assessment parents whom predictive tools show are highly likely to end up terminated eventually anyway. None of the many CPS people in the room were interested, and the director of a large city's child protection agency said "I'm not going down that road. I'm not going to start making predictions about people."

The mindset of many is thus clearly muddled by what I call "The Myth of Non-prediction"—that is, the supposition that CPS work is not already thoroughly suffused with predicting parents' future behavior. In fact, agency involvement with families today is based entirely on predictions, only very subjective and less reliable ones. Why does a child welfare agency exist at all? Because we predict agency actions will improve parenting (a prediction not always correct, but correct in a number of cases CPS thinks sufficiently high to rely on). Why does CPS invite and respond to reports of maltreatment? Based on a (not always correct) prediction that the report reflects reality. Why does CPS sometimes not remove a particular child after investigating? Based on a (not always correct) prediction that the parent will not in the future maltreat the child. Why does CPS sometimes remove children after substantiating a maltreatment report? Certainly not to punish parents for past behavior; that is not CPS's purpose. Rather, it is to protect the child from future harm, based on a (not always correct) prediction that that parent will in the future maltreat the child. Then each day CPS implicitly decides whether to continue the status quo with that child rather than reunifying, again based on a case worker's prediction about the parents. Why does CPS at some point decide to reunify as to a certain child? Based on a prediction about that child's parent in the future. And why go to TPR as to another child? Based on a prediction that the parent cannot safely assume custody within some unspecified time frame. And on and on.

CPS directors should explain, before we give their opposition to triage decision-making any weight, why it is an unacceptable (from a child-welfare perspective) departure from agency practice to make a more objective decision, based on research-verified rates of maltreatment and unsuccessful reunification for parents who have certain constellations of characteristics, to move for immediate TPR as to a subset of children identified at birth as at high risk if placed in parental custody. It is really the same decision CPS typically makes after years of unsuccessful reunification efforts, based on a prediction, but too late to spare children from a deeply damaging early-childhood experience. And there is no "non-decision" possibility, no way for the state to wash its hands. If CPS does not immediately petition on behalf of a child for TPR as to birth parents, it is thereby deciding to put the child at risk of all the negative effects of impermanence and maltreatment. And on what basis? If not a prediction about the parents, that they are sufficiently likely to become capable of adequate parenting, then what? Some basis entirely other than the child's welfare? I doubt they would admit that.

There needs to be a conversation among child-welfare experts, with true advocates for children in the room, about the confidence level the state should have in biological parents with problematic histories or current dysfunctions who seek legal-parent status, before the state confers legal parenthood on them at a child's birth. Looked at another way, child welfare experts should be deliberating about what likelihood of maltreatment or abandonment is sufficient to say the state would be throwing the child in the river by conferring legal-parent status on a particular biological parent at the time of a child's birth. But that conversation has not even begun, because of the dominance of this supposed aversion to "making predictions," coupled with the social work ideology of redemption: "never give up, you never know."

There are also adult-centered objections vaguely citing civil liberties. *The Times* article notes, for example:

> During a 2016 White House panel on foster care, Gladys Carrión, then the commissioner of New York City's Administration for Children's Services, expressed worries about the use of predictive analytics by child-protection agencies. "It scares the hell out of me," she said—"especially the potential impact on people's civil liberties."

In that regard, it is worth noting that the legal system has long been using predictive instruments to decide whether and for how long people should go to prison; in criminal sentencing, parole board decision-making, and juvenile dispositions, they make predictions about future dangerousness.[19] And, recall, the state is routinely doing background checks and disqualifying people from a host of other roles connected with children on the basis of a supposition that certain past conduct creates too great a danger of future conduct harmful to children.

In sum, I would urge application of a Birth Match program that compares birth records with all public records of history or characteristics that research shows are strongly correlated with maltreatment—parents' CPS history (including having been a child victim of maltreatment), parents' criminal history, any accessible state database of commitments to psychiatric facilities, prior births, and child fatalities. All such information could go into an algorithm that generates a risk score. Some past events would be sufficient in and of themselves to raise the score above the threshold for investigation (e.g., prior involuntary TPR within the past three years). Others would not, so there would have to be a combination of past events in order to launch an investigation. As with the Minnesota program, CPS might offer services to some parents whose risk score does not rise to the investigation threshold.

Mandatory, universal toxicology testing

The state could easily identify an additional group of newborn children at high risk of maltreatment or not having special needs met simply by adding to the medical tests already mandated for newborns a test for drugs and alcohol in the baby's blood system. The purpose would not be to punish in any way for past maternal conduct. The purpose would be solely forward looking, to protect the newborn child from future harm. The likelihood that a baby who has been exposed to toxic substances either (a) needs special care and treatment, or (b) would be in danger if sent home with birth parents, dwarfs the likelihood that he or she has any of the metabolic disorders for which universal screening is done. There is compelling reason for the state to take this simple step of requiring that all birthing facilities perform one more test on newborn fluid samples. Moreover, a baby is a distinct person, so a newborn's doctor stands in a direct physician–patient relationship with him or her, and the parents' patent conflict of interest means their consent should not be required.[20]

Yet no state does this. As noted in Chapter 2, a handful of states require testing if maternal substance abuse is suspected, but hospital staff in those states are inclined to ignore signs of addiction because they sympathize so much with mothers and do not want to bring any adverse legal consequences upon them. And the vast majority of states never require testing. This is not because lawmakers are ignorant of the ability to detect fetal exposure to drugs or alcohol or of the dangers that substance-abusing parents present to newborns and infants. The Keeping Children and Families Safe Act is testament to Congress's awareness, and it communicates its rationale clearly to the states. More likely the lack of a mandate reflects legislative cowering in the face of widespread and vociferous resistance from advocates for women.[21]

So it is left to individual medical facilities to decide whether they routinely conduct toxicology testing, and many leave it to the discretion of medical personnel, which of course leads to liberal complaints about biased decisions regarding whom to test—asserting, of course, that it is unfair to poor and minority-race mothers rather than to the children who do not get tested. If any facility said 'we will no longer provide meta-bolic screening or hearing tests in connection with Medicaid-covered births,' liberals would be incensed at this denial of benefits to children of the poor, but with any testing as to which there is a potential conflict of interests between parents and babies, liberals instinctively try to protect the parents. A legal mandate of universal testing, requiring physicians to document in every newborn's hospital file the test results, along with mandatory reporting, should eliminate both physician resistance and the bias issue. (Though liberals will still complain about disparate impact on three dimensions—race, gender, and socioeconomic status, 'surveilling the black family,' the state's 'punishing' mothers who are victim of structural injustice, etc., and so likely still demand no chil-dren be tested.)

As in other contexts, feminists will also tack on the boilerplate, ostensibly child-centered claim that universal toxicology screening will cause drug- or alcohol-abusing women to react in a way that creates even greater danger for children—in this context, giving birth in back alleys rather than in medical facilities. But testing is already wide-spread, and reputed to target poor, minority-race women, and reporting of positive toxicology is now legally mandated in many states, yet no study has shown this feared result has occurred. Nor, again, do liberal opponents devote any time to trying to figure out a way to deter such a maternal reaction while still mandating the testing, because that would likely entail some restriction on maternal liberty or threat of bad con-sequences for doing something relating to pregnancy, and that is unthinkable to these liberals.

Nor do they stop to think about what they are implicitly saying about the poor, predominantly minority-race, women whose dignity they purport to defend. These privileged critics imply that poor black mothers either (a) care so little about their child's welfare that they would choose to put the child at grave risk rather than suffer themselves, or (b) are not in control of their lives, not rational actors, not autonomous. Either view would support denying these women legal parenthood. Advocates for poor, substance-abusing women should clarify what exactly is their view of the women; is it (a) that they are unable to do what is best for their child, or (b) that they are able to do what is best for their child but will nevertheless, for selfish reasons, choose to harm their child?

Evaluation

After Birth Match and toxicology screening identify a birth parent whose history or current condition signals a high risk of child maltreatment, a court hearing should be scheduled and CPS should conduct a fuller examination of the birth parents' history and current circumstances, in order to formulate an informed recommendation for the court. Depending on how long the investigation will take and the baby's condition (e.g., premature or enduring drug withdrawal), the baby might remain in the hospital while this takes place. If only one parent is identified as having a problematic history or current condition, the other presumptively would be allowed to assume custody of the baby at the point of normal discharge from the birthing facility, and CPS should seek a temporary protective order disallowing or requiring supervision of contact between the baby and the identified parent. If both birth parents have been identified or a non-identified parent does not wish to assume custody, then the CPS might need to request a temporary custody order and place the child in foster or kin care.

The agency investigation and court evaluation should take into account factors substantially correlated with future maltreatment in addition to those identified with public records—for example, failure to complete high school, current substance abuse by a biological father, having supplied illegal drugs to the mother. If a court finds that conditions underlying the past events or the current circumstances that triggered the investigation have been corrected—for example, a mother has ended a relationship with a man from whose abuse she had failed to protect a child, then it should close the case. If, however, investigation of the home and interviews with the parent(s) do not alleviate the concern raised by parental history, the court should make a temporary placement decision based on the child's best interests and undertake the permanency planning approach discussed below. The law should make clear that one of the red flags noted above does not necessarily mean a parent is currently unfit, especially if the substantive bases for raising a red flag are very broad, erring on the side of over-inclusion.

Caseworker and court assessments should take into account not only correlations between parental characteristics or circumstances and child maltreatment in the absence of rehabilitation but also rates of successful rehabilitation with different sorts of dysfunction and whether relapse would endanger the child or could be managed using existing resources in a way that avoids trauma to the child. In addition, assessments should take into account any information birth parents can supply about their particular capacities, support systems, or anything else in their individual circumstances not captured by the predictive instruments.

Order protective custody of children in high-risk situations

Legislatures must explicitly authorize courts to order state custody of newborns based on biological parents' criminal or child-maltreatment history or current incapacity (including incarceration). They must fill the gap in the existing law of many states between grounds for termination of parental rights—in particular, the federally-mandated grounds relating to past history with other children—and legal bases for initial CPS action regarding a newborn child. State laws make past egregious conduct toward another child a basis for fast-track TPR when that is in a child's best interests,[22] but most states' laws do not authorize CPS to do anything with respect to a new child solely on the basis of that history—remove or petition for TPR and adoption. In that context, CPS would have to wait until the new child is placed in foster care for some other reason. Making such a history in and of itself a basis for removal is necessary so that those more proactive grounds for TPR—designed to make it possible for a child immediately to join a family that is not mired in dysfunction—are not meaningless.

It is difficult to imagine what plausible argument could be made against doing this, in and of itself, given that the real policy choice has already been made—that is, to allow for TPR and adoption *before* a child suffers maltreatment. This further step of authorizing state custody based on conduct toward another child simply makes it possible to effectuate that policy choice. If you were going to be born again tomorrow, to parents who previously killed a child, you would certainly want in place a system for having a hearing on your birth parents' fitness and your best interests, before the state blithely placed you in your birth parents' custody.

Why have states not done this? The explanation for legislative inaction is often more mysterious than the explanation for legislative action. It could simply be parsimonious state responses to ASFA; the federal Act did not direct states to amend their definitions of child endangerment or their rules for taking a child into custody, to sync with the new TPR rules, so perhaps legislators simply did not think to do it. Or it might be that liberal advocacy groups in some states recognized they could undermine the federal mandate by blocking legislation authorizing the steps that lead up to proactive TPR. As a general matter, ACLs are highly resistant to "removal" of children from biological parents, and they generally make no distinction among children based on developmental stage or needs. For example, Dorothy Roberts, a prominent critic of the child-protective system, writes:

> Think for a moment what it means to rip children from their parents and their siblings to be placed in the care of strangers. Removing children from their homes is perhaps the most severe government intrusion into the lives of citizens. It is also one of the most terrifying experiences a child can have.[23]

What Roberts describes is simply inapplicable to children taken into state custody at birth or within the first half year of life. Those children are not attached to their birth parents and experience no terror in the absence of their birth parents. (Even at a later stage, children will not manifest distress from separation if the parents' have been emotionally neglectful or abusive and as a result the children have no attachment to the birth parents or an avoidant-dismissive attachment.) Newborns also do not yet have a sense that some place is "home," so it is nonsense to suggest the state causes them a "terrifying experience" by assuming custody of them. Additionally, it is at best misleading to characterize state assumption of custody as "removal" or as disruption of a family relationship, and it is inapt to characterize state efforts at rehabilitating unfit birth parents of newborns as "reunification." A newborn has not been in a relationship with the birth parents that could be disrupted, and so cannot logically be reunited with them. Roberts is also to be faulted for failing to acknowledge that placing a child in a home with dangerous biological parents is a severe government intrusion into a child's life, one that might indeed lead to terrifying experiences for the child.

Other parent-protective liberals make broad claims about how harmful foster care is to children, citing research on poor outcomes for children who have been in foster care,[24] not understanding or acknowledging that (a) such research does not show foster care—as opposed to the maltreatment preceding it—caused the poor outcomes, and (b) the impact of a foster placement is going to be completely different for a newborn than it is for an older child. A foster parent—who could be the baby's grandmother—can give "kangaroo care" at least as well as a birth mother who has a mental illness or is in drug withdrawal herself in the post-natal period. ACLs also launch ad hominem attacks against anyone who proposes separating babies from dysfunctional birth mothers—typically, that they are acting solely on the basis of a racist and sexist view of black women as unworthy of procreating and deserving punishment for simply wanting to be parents.[25] And then there is always the disparate impact (on adults) complaint and the charge that "this problem would not exist if the government would end structural injustice"[26]—a charge with which I agree, but that cannot support a conclusion that the state should place a child in the custody of a very high-risk birth parent.

Pre-adoptive placements and concurrent planning

Whenever the state does take protective custody of a baby, the law should mandate that CPS give strong preference in selecting temporary caregivers to those who commit to adopt a child placed with them if "TPR and adoption" becomes the permanency plan for the child. That is consistent with a preference for qualified kin; they would simply have to make that commitment. Further, once CPS has placed a baby with temporary caregivers, the law should give those caregivers priority in selection of adoptive parents if and when adoption is to occur, if at that point a child has been in the current placement for a substantial period and is doing well. Legislators must make clear to agencies that a preference for kin placement must not override the preference for continuation of established caregiver–child relationships. Some states now actually do the opposite, in complete disregard of children's developmental needs.[27] Thus, if no fit relative steps forward at the time of a child's birth, then the preference for placement with relatives should become inoperative for that child. If a relative expresses willingness to take custody only when TPR is immanent, in order to "keep the child in the family," that is too late, if the child is in the midst of forming, or has already formed, an attachment to the non-kin caregivers.

Instituting these additional preferences would also stop the common current practice of removing a baby and parking him or her in the home of any willing relative, or the homes of a succession of relatives, where no one is acting like a real *parent* to the child—that is, with the singular devotion to the child's needs and the permanent commitment that parents give. That practice makes secure attachment exceedingly unlikely for a child. The enormous literature on the bad outcomes for children raised by kin while parents are in prison makes all too plain that being in the same home as biological relatives is not nearly enough for infants. The tragic path of these children's lives is paved not so much by the knowledge that they have a birth parent in prison (which they would not even comprehend until age 3 or 4) as by the turmoil in their living situations—that is, by the lack of a stable living environment and a consistent, permanent parent figure to whom they can attach securely.

As noted, it is not crucial that caregivers during a child's first six months of life be their permanent caregivers. After the first half year or so of life, however, it becomes extremely important that a child's placement be with good *permanent* caregivers, and given the inherent imperfections of agency and court processes, there is substantial danger that a placement immediately after birth with uncommitted kin, even if intended to be only for six months, will in fact be prolonged inadvertently until well into the second half year, or even second year, of the child's life, undermining the prospects for secure attachment and for adoption.

CPS workers have been resistant to concurrent planning, however. Because of the allegiance they form to parents, whom they view as their clients, it feels like an underhanded betrayal to them to be planning at the same time for someone else to become the child's parents. If the fost-to-adopt placement is not with relatives, it cuts against social workers' view of children as property of the biological family. If the birth parents are black and foster parents white, then their view of children as property of "the black community" and their intense distaste for trans-racial adoption produce further obstructionism.[28] Legislatures might therefore need to wade into the details of agency practice and specify a timeline for accomplishment of specific tasks on the adoption track (state-level administrative rule-making also cannot be trusted; it is generally done by people elevated from local CPS agencies, steeped in the same 'child as property' ideology). In doing so, they would likely encounter opposition from ACLs, who view concurrent planning as another card in the deck stacked against poor or otherwise disadvantaged parents.[29]

CPS agencies in many parts of the country have experienced difficulty recruiting fost-to-adopt parents. That is largely because people interested in adopting accurately observe that the law is so protective of biological parents until a TPR occurs, and so disregards the bonds that form between foster parents and a child that the adoption-through-fostering route is a torturous one for caregivers and child. They fear they will bond with a child and then CPS will remove the child, an experience all the more painful when the would-be adopters see little hope that the child, whom they have come to love, can have a decent life with the biological parents. Applicants for adoption naturally prefer to have placed with them a child whose legal relationship to biological parents has already been severed. At the same time, they want to adopt an infant because an infant is far more likely to attach securely to them. But the number of children in the US fitting both those criteria is currently miniscule relative to the number of couples who want to adopt such a child; hence the enormous interest in adopting from other countries. Implementing the further child-focused reforms detailed below should go a long way toward making a fost-to-adopt placement of newborns more appealing to Americans seeking to adopt.

Shorter timelines for newborns and infants

The law must force CPS to operate on a much shorter timeline with children who come into foster care at birth or in the first year of life. Their urgent developmental needs demand it, but CPS will not on its own alter its conventional approach of giving all parents, regardless of children's age, a year and a half to two years to reunify. As explained, ASFA required states to enact laws mandating that CPS petition for TPR if the child has been in foster care for 15 of the past 22 months, but waiting until a child is 15 months old to ask a court to decide whether they should keep trying with the parents is far too long for a newborn; it spells attachment disaster. Yet CPS caseworkers will wait until the 15 month mark almost every time, so they can tell parents "we tried so hard for you, but this horrible law forces us to do this." Indeed they will exploit ASFA's exceptions to the 15/22 rule (child is placed with relatives or documentation that TPR is not in the child's best interests) whenever they can. In Virginia, the policy manual that the state-level child-welfare agency issues to local CPS offices actually makes "any progress" an additional exception, in blatant contravention of ASFA. It misstates the legal rule regarding mandatory TPR petitions to say CPS must file "when a child has been in the care of the agency for 15 of the last 22 months *and there has been no progress toward reunification with the parent from whom the child was removed*."[30]

Social workers will not act on the basis of an infant's attachment needs unless legislatures order them to do so. Their sympathy for parents, their identification with the adult community from which the parents come, and/or their liberal guilt rule them regardless of the age of the children—in fact, probably more so when the children are newborns. This even though the ASFA mandate is just to file a petition, which a judge can reject.

An early draft of ASFA would have created a much shorter timeline with children under six months of age, requiring a petition after six months in foster care, but liberal members of Congress, pushed by liberal advocacy organizations, blocked it, pushing for the longest possible timeline.[31] Their position did not rest on any empirical evidence about the needs of infants or the rehabilitation prospects of parents of infants, but rather on their basic adult-centered opposition to any timelines for parents. They opposed the 15/22 rule for children in general, and they opposed the 6-month limit for newborns simply because it was another timeline, and a shorter one. From a parent-protective perspective, it does not matter how old a child is; the parents' interest is presumed always the same—to have more time rather than less.

Since ASFA's enactment, as noted, liberal legal academics have complained incessantly about its rehabilitation timelines,[32] and they have argued for generous exceptions to the timelines—ironically, particularly for parents least likely ever to be able to fulfill a child's need for permanent nurturing caregivers (those addicted or in prison). In doing, so they fail completely to acknowledge that the child's needs differ based on developmental stage. They might well be correct with respect to children placed in foster care at an older age, children who have already formed some sort of relationship with their biological parents and who have become very difficult to place for adoption, that giving some parents two or three years to turn themselves around is consistent with children's welfare. But existing TPR rules accommodate that possibility; they require courts to find that a TPR would be in a child's best interests, all things considered. But these academics are absolutely mistaken in advocating this approach with respect to infants, who constitute a large portion of all children taken into state custody. That approach creates too great a danger that a child will experience turmoil during the attachment stage. At best, it merely causes a child's caregivers (foster parents) prolonged anxiety and uncertainty about bonding with the child, fearing CPS might sever the bond at any moment should the birth parents show any significant signs of improvement, which is likely to affect children adversely. At worst, it results in complete turmoil for the child during the attachment stage, if removed from foster parents after beginning to attach to them and placed with parents who are only minimally nurturing and likely to separate from the child again, thus dooming any prospects for the child to form the foundation for lifetime wellbeing that a secure attachment constitutes.

Hence, biological parents of a newborn who comes into state custody as a result of an assessment that follows a Birth Match notification or positive toxicology test should have just six months to demonstrate ability to care for a child, and even that six months they should have *only if* a court determines at the time of birth that there is a reasonable prospect of that occurring, *and only if* the parents demonstrate immediately a determination to make their best effort.[33] The rule might be the same for infants who come into state custody before four months of age.[34] With infants between four months and two years of age, decision-making might need to be more nuanced and situation-specific, and so the law might require CPS case workers to present to the court a child-specific plan for achieving secure attachment, and might list considerations the agency and the court should address—for example, biological parents' motivation, their ability to relocate out of a bad home or neighborhood environment (see Chapter 5), success rates for overcoming particular personal problems, and sources of support. In addition, all states should mandate (it seems only a few do now)[35] that CPS caseworkers receive training on early childhood development and decision-making with newborns' attachment needs in mind.

For the shorter timeline to be effective, the law must require CPS to petition for TPR in advance of the six-month mark, without exception. This does not mean TPR will occur in every case. It simply means that before the critical attachment period begins, a court will review the child's situation, with parents on notice TPR could occur, and render a timely permanency decision in the child's best interests. Given the delays that routinely occur in child welfare legal proceedings, the law should actually require CPS to petition for TPR at or even before a child's birth in cases where the prescribed assessment reveals that parental rehabilitation is unlikely.

This shorter timeline for the youngest children would certainly be incompatible with some of liberals' favorite family-preservation programs, discussed in Chapter 6. And they would holler that transformation in six months is simply impossible for birth parents with certain problems. From a child-centered perspective, though, that means forcing the child to wait six months is unjustified.

Expanded TPR grounds and mandatory petitions

Every TPR rule should have two prongs, and in most states now does. The first prong requires some parental-fitness-related reason to consider a TPR at all, and the US Supreme Court, though never purporting to dictate the content of this reason, has held that state law must impose at least a 'clear and convincing' evidentiary burden on CPS regarding this prong, whatever its content might be. The second prong requires the state to show TPR would be in the child's best interests. The second does not necessarily follow from the first; I have seen plenty of cases where a parent satisfies one or more of a state's standards for unfitness, but the child would gain little or nothing by a TPR, because he or she is very unlikely to be adopted and has some interest in maintaining a relationship with the parent even though he or she cannot live with the parent. In some cases, the child is in the custody of another parent, who is a good caretaker, and it is unclear what the child gains by TPR as to the "unfit" parent.

So the first prong essentially acts as a predicate for doing a best-interest-based reconsideration of the state's initial parentage decision. As a general matter, we do not second guess this state decision on a regular basis; we do not ask repeatedly of all parents "are you really the best available for that child." And we should not. But I have identified a number of parental histories or current conditions that make it appropriate and morally requisite (as a right of the child) to be more circumspect at the time of a child's birth, rather than waiting until a manifestly unfit parent damages the child.

As explained in Chapter 2, however, TPR rules traditionally included in the first prong only bad things the parent had already done *to the child in question*. They provided no basis for acting proactively before a child was damaged, by the parent or by prolonged state custody. The child had to be thrown into the river first, then the legal system would react. ASFA was revolutionary in a modest way, if that makes sense. As explained in Chapter 2, it required states to *authorize* TPR in a limited set of cases based on a parent's prior maltreatment of a different child, to spare the new child from maltreatment, if that is what is best for the child. It marked a dramatic shift in attitude, from reaction to prevention, based on the obvious reality that a parent might already have proven themselves irremediably unfit in connection with another child and the common sense conclusion that we should not wait until they prove it again with a new child. However, it pushed this preventive approach only in a very limited set of situations (prior TPR, prior felony conviction based on conduct toward a child, prior maltreatment with aggravated circumstances).

Many of the bases identified above for a "Birth Match" should also be predicates for triggering judicial *consideration* of whether TPR would be in a child's best interests (*not* automatic TPR). Though, as I noted, many states already go beyond the preventive grounds that ASFA mandated, none cover all those that are sufficient reason to consider a TPR, so all states would need to expand their TPR unfitness prongs in some ways. They should include incarceration currently or in the recent past (e.g., three years), commitment for mental illness currently or in the recent past, other children in foster care now or in the recent past, having been found by a court in the recent past to have committed domestic violence toward a co-parent, current substance abuse problems that makes it highly unlikely (not all such problems do so) the birth parent could become capable within six months of safely assuming custody and adequately caring for the child (taking into account any special needs created by in utero exposure to the substance), and a history of chronically being a victim of domestic violence while a custodial parents (e.g., three or more prior reports in which a child's presence was documented). There are terms here that require further specification, but the basic idea is that many more children need for the state to be much more careful in creating their legal family relationships. Again, the consequence of having these additional bases for *considering* TPR is not automatic granting of TPR; it is simply to have courts do a best-interests evaluation of legal parentage for a lot more children, and state laws can require courts to be comprehensive and transparent in conducting that evaluation.

When I presented the idea of expanded TPR grounds at the William & Mary conference I mentioned earlier (at that time, I suggested just incarceration and addiction, grounds which some other states already had), the reaction was almost uniformly hostile, and it arose entirely from sympathy for adults and vague suppositions of parental entitlement. The loudest proponents of parents' rights were, as usual, so-called child-protection officials. One attorney who does exclusively guardian ad litem work was also incensed on behalf of birth parents. As I noted earlier, some CPS agency directors have told me they simply will never use the ASFA-driven authorization of proactive TPR petitions that already exist. Advocates for children in other states, such as the Lullaby Project in Arizona, have observed the same aversion among CPS officials and employees.[36]

Mere authorization of TPR on any grounds is therefore inadequate. To overcome resistance of liberal, adult-focused social workers and agency directors, provisions regarding *petitions* for termination of parental rights need to be mandatory and without exception. As noted above, ASFA already requires mandatory filing of a TPR petition in two circumstances over a parent's objection—that is, 15/22 and prior felony child abuse conviction. The exceptions to the 15/22 mandate need to be eliminated, so courts are pushed to consider (but not necessarily to order) TPR within that time frame for older children. The shorter timeline for newborns should, as noted, also entail mandatory petitioning. And all other proactive grounds just identified should also leave CPS no discretion as to petitioning when the grounds exist. Though courts also operate imperfectly, and though many judges are as protective of parents as CPS workers are, misuse of discretion seems less likely in the courts, whose decision-making is more public and susceptible to appeal, than in a caseworker's cubicle.

In addition, the federal agency charged with ASFA enforcement needs to play a far more active role in enforcing the federal mandates that already exist. Virginia, incredibly, did not even enact the 15/22 rule in its Code until 20 years after ASFA was passed, and the federal oversight agency never troubled the Commonwealth about this. I mentioned the blatant non-compliance to a Deputy Attorney General in Richmond I know who is very devoted to improving child welfare in our state, and he saw to it that legislation was passed to fix the statute. Many states for many years did not institute the requirement of a TPR petition in cases of prior violent felonies against a child, with impunity. And I noted earlier that most states have ignored KCAFSA. Passing federal laws without enforcing them sends a false message to the child welfare community that certain steps have been taken when they actually have not, and it encourages local agencies to ignore new legal requirements for their work.

What I have proposed here is essentially a lot more up-front work, for which there would be a substantial state cost, but if done properly would, within a year, reduce downstream agency expenses as well as a whole lot of damage to children (CPS response to reports, longer foster care stays, more court proceedings, dealing with the dysfunctional adolescents and adults who emerge from the current system). Legislators generally do not respond to "this will save you money in the long run," but if the proposal is "take money from these parts of this year's social services budget and put it here instead," or "stop having your caseworkers devote so much time to futile efforts with parents who have already damaged their children and shift them to time-of-birth assessments and proactive TPRs," then proposals become more politically feasible, at least from a budgetary standpoint. (There is still the liberal uproar for legislators to deal with.)

And, indeed, ACLs would resist every one of these steps. The standard liberal response to manifest parental unfitness at any point in a child's life, and regardless of parents' history, is, as discussed in Chapter 6, that we must instead spend a lot of money trying to fix people. And they keep that position plausible by coming up with one experimental program after another promising miraculous transformation of the parents, oblivious to what happens to the child in the meantime, so averse are liberals to states' ever choosing anyone other than birth parents (or, more precisely, birth mothers) to raise a child when the birth parents want to be legal parents. The standard objections to more expedient permanency decisions is "you never know," "we need to give them a chance," and "it is unfair to pile this suffering on top of what they have already endured in life."

In addition, even though I stipulate that a best-interests finding must be an absolute prerequisite to termination of parental rights, liberal resisters will struggle to find some way to argue that what I propose is bad for children. For example, some will likely object that more expansive grounds for TPR or increased use of them will only create many more "legal orphans"—children with no legal parents and no prospect of getting any.[37] They will overlook the fact that I am focusing on newborns and infants, and refuse to acknowledge that those children—just born and not damaged by post-birth maltreatment—would be adopted in a heartbeat and have a far greater chance for a flourishing life as a result.

As noted, the prevailing liberal attitude toward parental incarceration, or at least maternal incarceration, toward substance abuse, and toward chronic domestic violence victimization is the complete opposite of what I propose. It insists that these things should be treated as *an excuse* for the parent's failure to care for a child, and so that the law should extend a child's stay in foster care to wait for the parent to get out of prison, overcome addiction, break a pattern of dysfunctional intimate partnerships. As if all that should matter is whether the mother is to blame for her incapacity. A number of sympathetic judges have agreed.[38] Nearly every law review article or student note written about incarcerated parents begins with the sad (and true) story of how America willfully incarcerates blacks instead of making life fair for them so that they will not live in the condition of deprivation and desperation that leads to criminal activity. With incarcerated mothers, in particular, the starting point for analysis is that they do not really deserve to be in prison, that the crimes most committed were minor or instigated by a male partner, and that American society has failed them by not using therapeutic facilities and constructive services instead of prisons and, of course, by not making life fair in the first place. I agree with that premise, but the conclusion ACLs arrive at following this premise is, from a child-centered perspective, invalid and immoral.

Resistance will also arise from the tendency of social workers and liberal scholars, agency heads, and politicians to treat children of minority race as the property of, or a resource for, minority-race communities. Complaints about race disproportionality in the foster care system mention not only the impact on individual black parents but also the impact on "the black community" from removal of many children from their home neighborhoods. How retaining children in abusive or neglectful environments helps any community they never spell out; there is instead a vague suggestion that disproportionate CPS removals are part of a systemic effort to wipe out the black race. This is ironic given that most CPS employees in heavily-black urban areas are themselves black and manifest family-preservation extremism and categorical preference for kin in substitute care and adoption. And it overlooks that there are a great number of African-American couples wanting to adopt a newborn or infant.

Promote voluntary relinquishment

An alternative to involuntary TPR that might spare many newborns from early childhood deprivation is to encourage birth parents whose personal characteristics or circumstances would seriously impair their ability to care for a child, voluntarily to waive their statutory parental rights so that persons who have passed scrutiny to qualify for adopting can serve as the newborn child's parents. They deserve to be told the truth about adoption:

> If your child is made available for adoption immediately after birth, people with good homes in good neighborhoods will be falling over each other to try to get first in line. Many would be interested in an open adoption, allowing you to have a relationship with the child as he or she grows up. But if your child goes into foster care and the plan is to keep him or her there until you have overcome your problems, the child will be at much greater risk of emotional problems in the future, we will place a lot of demands on you, and most parents in your situation do not succeed. So think about whether you think you can commit yourself absolutely to a plan of rehabilitation immediately, with six months to get your problems under control. If yes, then that is what we will do. If not, then voluntary relinquishment now is a good, available option for the child.

ACLs, however, have made it taboo to suggest to anyone that she or he do such a thing, release one's legal claim to a relationship with and custody of a child. The mere suggestion of adoption counseling raises cries of "oppression," classist arrogance, and even genocide. They will object that this hypothetical conversation with the birth parent is coercive or demeaning or in some other way disrespectful. And, in fact, one would thus be hard pressed to find any state laws, agency regulations, or institutional policies directing any public or private facilities that deal with mentally ill, substance abusing, immature, or incarcerated parents-to-be simply to make those persons aware of the availability of adoptive parents.

But is not the opposite actually true? Is it not unwarranted paternalism to assume, as CPS now implicitly does, that every parent must want to gain custody of their off-spring, and not even present the full range of options to them? Is it not presumptuous to impute to every birth parent a profound interest in raising a child, in "keeping their own," so great as to outweigh the pain they are likely to endure from CPS's coercion of their behavior and from recognition of their own failings? Is it not demeaning to assume these birth parents could not possibly make a free, informed, altruistic decision for their child, to give him or her a better life, out of love?

Justifying better parentage decision-making

I reiterate here the crucial and obvious points that legal parent–child relationships arise from laws and the state makes those laws. Thus, the state creates legal parent–child rela-tionships, and those legal relationships constitute the practical basis for formation of the social parent–child relationship, because the state attaches to them legal custody, legal liberties, and legal decision-making powers. This is most apparent to us when we do something such as enroll a child in public school. We must show the child's birth cer-tificate, establishing that we are his or her legal parents, with legal custody and the legal authority to decide where the child lives and goes to school. Hopefully an occasion you will never face: Suppose someone else decides he wants to raise your child and walks off with him or her from the playground. You call the police and say "go get that child and bring him back to me!" The police officer says "Why? Are you the child's legal parent?" If you say "no, but I am the child's biological parent and God has given me rights," the officer will not recapture the child for you, but more likely will warn you to stay away from the child.

The laws conferring legal parenthood identify specific bases for doing so. Thus, the state effectively chooses who each newborn child's first legal parents will be, with all the powers, privileges, and rights that go with that status. As with any other state action, the state should be morally and constitutionally constrained in how it carries out its choosing of persons to be a child's legal parents. The state's current approach through-out the US is, as explained in Chapter 2, to confer legal parent status almost exclusively on the basis of biological connection, with no effort to avoid placing a baby into a legal relationship with someone manifestly unfit to serve as a parent.

What no one else seems to have recognized, yet what cannot be denied, is that chil-dren must have a moral and constitutional right against the state's doing this profound thing to them in such a reckless manner. Liberal legal scholarship sees only parents' rights in this context.[39] To see clearly why this is so, it will help to broaden the scope of discussion to family relationships more generally.

State creation of legal family relationships

In addition to the parent–child relationship, the state creates legal marriages and it creates guardianships for incompetent adults. The rules governing these other two relationships reflect sound general principles as to the proper approach to state involvement in family formation, and those principles presumptively should apply also to parent–child relationships.

Marriages arise only by mutual voluntary consent. Every individual has an absolute right to refuse to enter into this kind of legal family relationship with a particular other person, based on nothing other than a judgment that it is not in his or her best interests. Conversely, a person who is generally unfit for this kind of family relationship has no basis for complaint if denied the opportunity for this kind of relationship. Such a person has a right to marry in the abstract, but it depends crucially on reciprocal choice, it is entirely ineffectual in the absence of such reciprocation, and the state cannot compel anyone to reciprocate.

Guardian–ward relationships closely resemble the parent–child relationship; they similarly arise without the wards themselves giving present actual consent, precisely because the ward has been deemed incompetent. Like the parent–child relationship, the guardian–ward relationship can prejudice or adversely affect the welfare of the dependent person, because it likewise entails substantial powers and duties for the carer. Both relationships preclude the dependent party from having that same legal relationship with other persons. A guardian is less likely than a parent to live with the person under care, but many guardians do so. And depending on how much direct care a guardian provides, the guardian role can be more or less burdensome than parenthood typically is. Yet it is not uncommon for some family members of an incompetent adult to have a very strong desire to serve as guardian, which occasionally creates disputes over who will serve in that role.

The law governing appointment of a guardian for an incompetent adult, however, is starkly different from that governing initial parentage. The former approximates marriage law, as described above, to the extent possible given the incompetence of one party to the relationship. It respects the dependent individual's personhood by insisting that the relationship arise exclusively on the basis of some appropriate form of reciprocation—namely, a finding either that the ward chose it before becoming incompetent, in an advance directive of some kind, or that the ward would now choose it if able. The law makes the state decision-maker a surrogate for the incompetent adult, directing the appointing court effectively to give proxy consent to a legal relationship on behalf of the non-autonomous person. And that proxy consent amounts to a "best interests" determination—that is, an assessment of which competent adult, among those willing to serve, would be the best caregiver for the incompetent adult. Satisfying any applicant's desire for the position, no matter how intense, is not a permissible aim in making this decision on behalf of the dependent person, and a judge aware of something rendering particular applicants unfit to serve as guardian—for example, that they previously abused another incompetent adult or that they are now incarcerated—most certainly would not appoint them. This regime, we believe, is morally and constitutionally required; it would be wrong in both senses for the state to create these relationships in total disregard of prospective guardians' fitness and for purposes other than serving the welfare of the incompetent adult.

Parentage law, to respect the personhood of children, should likewise be understood as effecting a proxy choice on behalf of someone unable to choose for himself or herself. The attitude underlying existing law, viewing parentage rules as satisfying a proprietary interest of parents, is morally indefensible. Certainly one could characterize existing parentage laws as effectuating in most cases what newborn children would choose if able, in terms of who their legal parents will be, given the social and emotional significance of biological ties. However, unlike guardianship laws, maternity and paternity laws do not contain an overarching best interests standard that controls when statutory priorities are inconsistent with it. Yet a baby is at much greater risk of harm in a parent–child relationship than a ward typically is in a guardian–ward relationship. This state practice must end.

Constitutional limitations on state parentage choices

The constitutional argument against the state's forcing newborn children into legal relationships with and custody of manifestly unfit parents is fairly straightforward: The Supreme Court has repeatedly stated that children are, once born, persons and bearers of rights under the federal Constitution. As a general matter, individuals have a constitutional right to freedom of intimate association, which entails both freedom to associate and freedom from forced intimate association. Parentage laws, coupled with custody laws, force children into an intimate association, and thereby infringe this right, so the state must have compelling justification for doing it in each instance. If the state analogously started forcing us competent adults into unchosen intimate relationships, we would certainly demand extraordinary justification.

In the vast majority of instances, *there is* compelling justification for the state's placing newborn children into a legal relationship with their birth parents—namely, that children need to be in some such relationship for their survival and healthy development, and it is in general best for children to be raised by their biological parents. But in a significant percentage of cases, when the state knows or has reason to suspect a birth parent is unfit, that justification is inadequate, or simply inapplicable, especially given that there are plenty of alternative potential parents, and there is no other justification that can possibly serve.

Significantly, courts have recognized a constitutional right of children in a different context of forced intimate association—that is, when the state places children in the custody of foster parents. Courts have established that there is state action when CPS places a child in a foster care relationship and that the state, though not precluded from placing children into such unchosen associations, because children need for the state to do this, is constitutionally required to do so with care. The constitutional lens in this context is not intimate association so much as substantive due process under the Fourteenth Amendment Due Process Clause, which the Supreme Court has said serves the broad purpose "to secure the individual from the arbitrary exercise of the powers of government."[40] Some courts apply a "professional judgment" standard, whereas others impose liability on an agency that acts with "deliberate indifference" to dangers the placement might pose for the child.[41] Thus, were a state to select foster parents with the same disregard for child maltreatment history, drug addiction, severe mental illness, or incarceration that it shows when making birth parents legal parents, courts would conclude that it violated a constitutional right of any children harmed as a result. Accordingly, state statutes require child protection agencies to investigate any applicants for foster parent positions and require that courts find foster parents fit and qualified prior to placing a child with them. They must do this also when they place a child in "kin care" or approve a child's relatives as foster parents.

Conversely, biological parents have no constitutional right to be placed into a legal relationship with a child regardless of their fitness. As described above, federal law now mandates that states authorize preventive TPR as to birth parents with certain histories, and that is practically equivalent to denying the birth parents legal parenthood in the first place as to a newborn. So long as there is a hearing to assess current fitness, as my proposal entails, this is clearly constitutional.[42] No court has ever held in any context that the state has a constitutional obligation to try to rehabilitate unfit parents. In addition, in custody disputes between legal parents, states can deny custody or even unsupervised contact to a parent based solely on a best-interests determination. No court would say that use of the best-interest standard in the context of custody disputes between parents violates any parent's constitutional rights, and some say it fulfills a right of the child.

One can also easily posit hypothetical laws that everyone would recognize as violating children's constitutional rights. Suppose, for example, that a state's laws were to declare that doctors must euthanize babies born with only four fingers on a hand, or that newborns with red hair should be shipped immediately to Ireland, or that the first legal parent for any newborn left at a safe haven depository shall be an unmarried male sex-offender just released from prison. In any of these hypothetical cases, we would charge the state with an atrocious abuse of state power and a violation of the babies' rights against the state. Notably, in the case of sex offenders adopting children, it would not matter that legislators were motivated in passing such laws by compassion for such men, who were likely abused as children themselves and who might otherwise never have an opportunity to raise a child, given their relative unattractiveness to women as potential partners. The Constitution simply does not permit legislatures to use babies in that way to ease the suffering of adults. This is so even though we recognize that the state must establish *some* legal rules as to who will be the legal parents and custodians of newborn children. That the state inevitably must intrude into babies' intimate lives to the extent of choosing legal and custodial parents for them does not mean that it is constitutionally unconstrained in how it does so.

The state action question

In *Deshaney v. Winnebago County* (what I refer to as the "Dred Scott" of child welfare law), the US Supreme Court held that a county child protection agency did not violate the constitutional rights of a boy whose father beat him to the point of causing severe brain damage, by failing to remove the boy from his father's custody even though the agency had strong reason to believe the boy was in danger. The basis for the Court's rejection of the § 1983 claim was that there was no state action, but rather only a failure to act, and a supposition that the Constitution imposes no affirmative obligation on the state to protect individuals from private violence.

The *Deshaney* Court failed to acknowledge the CPS agency's role in creating the situation in which Joshua Deshaney was harmed—that is, by repeatedly removing Joshua from a safe foster home and depositing him in his abusive father's home. It was also oblivious to the fact that the state conferred legal parent status on Randy Deshaney in the first place. (The family's attorney did a very poor job framing the complaint.) Accordingly, the Court treated the claim as one to state-agency protection from a private harm that the state played no role in creating, and held that the Constitution does not confer such positive rights to state assistance. The Court indicated that the outcome would likely be different if Joshua's attorney had shown that the state had by affirmative conduct created a danger or vulnerability for the child. Following *Deshaney*, most lower courts have adopted a "state-created danger" rule for a § 1983 claim that is based on harmful private conduct, and the most common articulation of the rule requires a plaintiff to show state actors assisted in creating or increasing danger of private harm when they knew or should have known of the danger.

A challenge to parentage laws would focus directly on affirmative conduct by the state—namely, the state's enactment and implementation of statutes determining every child's first legal relationships and bestowing custodial rights on the adult parties to that relationship. The initial creation of a legal and custodial parent–child relationship is as much state action as is creating a guardian–ward relationship, whether it occurs by operation of a statute over a large number of cases or by judicial decision in an individual case. Similarly, if a state passed a statute declaring that any two adults who live in the same household are ipso facto legally married, and are therefore subject to all the legal duties that marriage entails, no one would have difficulty seeing the state action, even though it comprised automatic operation of a statutory rule over a large number of cases.

Further, state creation of legal and custodial parent–child relationships is a state action that, in the case of unfit parents, creates a danger for the child that would not otherwise exist, because those adults would not otherwise be legally free to take the child into their household and assume control over the child's life. And, because of the exclusivity and plenary power that the state injects into legal parenthood, such state action entails cutting off potential private sources of protection, including assumption of custody by other adults who are prepared to provide a very nurturing upbringing. Analogously, if the state gave legal effect to private marriage ceremonies between men and ten-year-old girls, few would have difficulty perceiving how this state action endangers and potentially violates the constitutional rights of the children, because of the liberties and rights that marriage would confer on the men.

Further, few people would have difficulty seeing how the creation of legal parent–child relationships constitutes potentially wrongful state action in the case of adoption—that is, if a social services agency and court were to grant adoption of a newborn to persons the state knew to be grossly unfit to parent. Imagine an adult, reported in the newspapers today for throwing a crying baby against a brick wall, going tomorrow to a local social services agency and applying to adopt any available baby. Were the agency and a court to approve such an adoption, we would readily discern state action and would ascribe responsibility to the state if that adult then threw the adopted baby against the same brick wall. We should do so equally if that same person gave birth to another child and the state conferred legal-parent status on the person as to that child. That is certainly more clearly state action than is a state agency's declining to create a legal relationship desired by private parties, such as a legal marriage between persons of the same sex, yet the courts unhesitatingly treated such refusal to create a legal relationship as state action subject to constitutional constraint in the same-sex marriage cases. No one argued to the contrary.

Can states justify their current parentage laws?

If babies, like us, have a fundamental substantive due process right against the state's placing them in family relationships with people very likely to harm them, then a challenge to maternity and paternity laws as applied to a newborn whose birth parents are manifestly unfit would put the state in the position of having to show that such laws, without exceptions for unfitness, are narrowly tailored to serve a compelling state interest. The state would need to demonstrate that placing newborn babies into legal and custodial relationships with birth parents without regard to fitness is necessary to avoid some other great and overriding cost. Below I refute several possibilities likely to be suggested.

Difficulty of more careful parentage decisions

Avoiding additional administrative costs is not sufficient justification for infringing fundamental rights. Even if it were, there would be little additional administrative burden from identifying presumptively unfit parents at the time of birth rather than after they have damaged a child. To identify birth parents presumptively unfit by virtue of past conduct, state-level child protection agencies need simply install a computer program that cross-checks databases the state already possesses—namely, birth records and records of past child maltreatment or domestic violence or of violent felonies. To identify birth parents presumptively unfit by virtue of current substance abuse, states need only mandate testing of all newborns for drug or alcohol exposure, which some hospitals already routinely do (cost does not seem to be what is stopping the rest from doing so). Any court proceeding triggered by such identification, would likely substitute for and obviate the need for the several court proceedings that ordinarily ensue after unfit parents maltreat children. Prevention is much easier and cheaper for the state than remediation.

Harm to others

A truly compelling state interest might be avoiding substantial and unwarranted injury to society generally or to other individuals. However, given the enormous social cost of child maltreatment, and given that the state already severs many children's legal relationship with unfit parents (after maltreatment occurs), it would be implausible to suggest that limited pre-parentage screening aimed at preventing child maltreatment would on the whole harm societal interests.

Rather, the most obvious candidate for a compelling state interest is avoiding the impact on biological parents who wish to be the legal parents of their offspring but are denied their wish because they are unfit. It is far from clear that persons who are biological parents are benefited by having responsibility for a child's fundamental well being placed upon them when they are unprepared to fulfill it or, in other words, by being given the opportunity permanently to damage their offspring. I imagine Joshua Deshaney's father would acknowledge that he himself (as well as Joshua) would be better off today if the state had never made him Joshua's legal parent and custodian. Recall the statements I quoted earlier of parents burdened with guilt about the harms they have caused children. But let us suppose for sake of analysis that being denied legal parenthood as to one's off-spring is always on the whole a bad thing for a biological parent.

We might first ask whether that denial is so bad as to thwart substantially a funda-mental interest. The term "fundamental" is bandied about in our culture, and especially in the legal system, with little understanding of what it means. It does not mean "some-thing I strongly desire." It means foundational, the base upon which the edifice of a life sits, prerequisite to pursuing one's other aims in life. Parenthood is not that, as evidenced by the commonness of putting it off until one's 30s and by the many people who choose never to do it. Conversely, the child does have fundamental interests at stake in connection with the state's parentage decisions, because what a child needs from parents—nourishment, nurturing, secure attachment, protection, etc.—are prerequisites to a flourishing life, to healthy development that will enable the child to pursue particular aims later in life.

Many people speak as if there is a well-recognized constitutional right of biological parents per se to become legal parents, and if there were then states would have to respect it, but there is not. The US Constitution, of course, contains not a word about parenthood, and the Supreme Court has never held that there is such a right. In fact, the Court has implied that biological parents who are *unfit* to care for a child should receive no constitutional protection for their desire to be a legal parent. The most relevant precedents concern unwed biological fathers' "substantive due process" right—that is, interest protection under the Fourteenth Amendment's Due Process Clause—to become legal parents. The Court established in four decisions in the 1970s and early 1980s that constitutional protection attaches to a fit biological father's interest in legal paternity if and only if he "demonstrates a full commitment to the responsibilities of parenthood by coming forward to participate in the rearing of his child."[43] In two of those cases, the Court held that the biological father had no constitutional right against state approval of an adoption of his offspring by another man, because the biological father had not demonstrated sufficient commitment to parenting.[44] In the other two cases, the Court found sufficient involvement in the child's life. In none of these unwed fathers' rights cases was there an allegation that the adult asserting rights was unfit to be a parent, but the Court implied that unfitness would be a proper basis for denying the right.[45] This is an aspect of the unwed father cases that family law scholars have overlooked. In *Stanley v. Illinois*, the Court suggested the state could constitutionally require a hearing on an unwed father's fitness, even after finding that he had been substantially involved in raising the children, prior to conferring on him legal parental status, and indeed could put the onus on the biological father to initiate such a proceeding to demonstrate fitness.[46] Lower courts relying on the early fathers' rights cases have consistently indicated that unfitness obviates a biological parent's claim to a constitutional right to a relationship. [47]

Courts might come to a different conclusion with respect to mothers, but cases have not arisen to test that possibility. The Supreme Court might hold that pregnancy in and of itself entails sacrifice sufficient to show commitment to parental responsibility, so that any fit birth mother per se has a presumptive constitutional right to become her offspring's legal parent. But there is no reason to suppose the Court would hold fitness is irrelevant with respect to mothers. In fact, constitutional norms of gender equality presumptively would require the Court to hold that unfit birth mothers, as much as unfit biological fathers, have no constitutional right to become legal parents and custodians of their offspring. This would be consistent with Supreme Court doctrine relating to termination of parental rights, which has implicitly approved of severing an existing relationship based on whatever a state deems unfitness.[48]

It is also noteworthy that the Supreme Court's constitutional jurisprudence relating to the family has shifted emphasis somewhat, from biological relationships to social relationships that generate emotional and psychological benefits for their members. In particular, the most recent Supreme Court decision analyzing a claim to a constitutional right to be a parent, *Michael H. v. Gerald D.*,[49] which resulted only in a plurality opinion (no majority analysis, but a combination of minority opinions in favor of a particular result), rejected such a claim by a biological parent who had an established relationship with the child in question and was not unfit. The Court upheld a California law that established an irrefutable presumption of paternity in favor of a mother's husband. The opinion with the most support, that of Justice Scalia, explicitly denied that biology plus commitment are sufficient to generate a constitutional right. It insisted that the Court's past holdings instead established constitutional protection for "the relationships that develop within the unitary family," not for biological relationships. The three dissenters in *Michael H.* would have applied the biology-plus-commitment test, but they also rejected the notion that biology alone gives rise to constitutional protection, stating that "although an unwed father's biological link to his child does not, in and of itself, guarantee him a constitutional stake in his relationship with that child, such a link combined with a substantial parent–child relationship will do so."[50] So as of 1989, when the Supreme Court last addressed the rights of biological fathers to become legal parents of a child, there was virtually no support for the notion that biology alone gives rise to a right.

Consistent with this more recent emphasis on family relationship as social rather than merely biological, courts have generally accorded less weight to an interest in initiating a relationship than to an interest in maintaining an already-established social family relationship.[51] For example, in 1998 the California Supreme Court rejected an unwed father's claim to constitutional guarantee of an opportunity to demonstrate commitment to parenthood, joining other state courts in concluding from the plurality and dissenting opinions in *Michael H.* that "a biological father's mere desire to establish a personal relationship with the child is not a fundamental liberty interest protected by the Due Process Clause."[52] With adults who are not biological parents, there are many more examples of courts differentiating continuation of an existing relationship from a desire to initiate a relationship.[53]

In addition, the Supreme Court has declined to require states to apply any particular substantive legal standard of parental fitness when they order TPRs, even after a legal parent–child relationship exists with a mother or father. The Court has established procedural rights for parents in TPR proceedings—namely, the clear and convincing evidence standard and a right of indigent parents in some cases to a state-provided lawyer. But it has never held that the state must find misconduct of a particular kind or severity before severing such a relationship. This further undermines any attempt by a state to justify infringing newborns' due process rights relating to legal parentage on the grounds that it is respecting birth parents' constitutional rights. They are entirely free to say that a birth mother's incarceration renders her presumptively unfit to be the legal mother of a newborn or that a biological father who has repeatedly lost custody of two or more older children because of maltreatment is presumptively unfit to become the legal parent of another offspring just born.

In sum, a state would not thwart a fundamental interest nor infringe any established constitutional right of biological parents by changing its parentage statutes to exclude unfit biological parents from legal parenthood. Even if the Court were to conclude that some constitutional right exists for biological parents per se with respect to legal parentage, its statement in numerous contexts that protecting the welfare of children is a compelling state interest suggests it would find no violation of such right in a state's excluding from legal parenthood birth parents the state has good reason to suppose will seriously damage a child.[54] Significantly, lower courts have pretty uniformly rejected constitutional challenges to state laws that authorize TPR on the basis of a parent's prior TPR as to another child,[55] and to CPS decisions to seek TPR without first attempting rehabilitative efforts.[56]

Thus, states are not justified by any concern for adults' interests or rights in infringing the substantive due process right of newborn children not to be forced into relationships that are likely to be quite harmful to them. State lawmakers and social service agencies can do much better than they currently are in effectuating children's rights with respect to parentage, and courts should compel them to do so.

Conclusion

Even the best parentage legal regime, one that screens out manifestly unfit parents, will not completely eliminate child maltreatment. Many first-time parents could not feasibly be identified in advance as posing a high risk to a child, and some parents do not commit maltreatment until they have had two or more children. For that reason, I have also urged in this chapter some reforms relating to CPS response to reports of abuse or neglect by legal parents. Above all, the law should force child-welfare agencies to act in a manner sensitive to children's developmental stage—in particular, respecting the urgency for infants of creating the conditions necessary for formation of a secure attachment to permanent caregivers. Like adults, children should be deemed to have an absolute right to exit a relationship expeditiously if that is, all things considered, best for them. Thus, the state should place children in foster care while undertaking parental rehabilitation only if, and to the extent that, this is making for children the best of a bad situation, and that is less likely to be the case with infants than it is with older children. I have also urged that when CPS does appropriately place an infant in foster care, it should try to make this a fost-to-adopt situation, to enable continuity of care, stability, and preservation of bonds in the event that parental-rehabilitation is unsuccessful. The rate of successful reunification after removal of a child is low, just as is the rate of successful reunification of spouses who separate because of partner abuse or neglect, and the state, as agent for the child, must prepare for the more likely outcome.

Notes

1 Richard Gelles discusses liberal "blowback" to proposals for using predictive instruments to improve CPS decision-making, citing the director of the National Coalition for Child Protection Reform and a UNICEF official in New Zealand, in Gelles (2017, at 110–12).

2 See, for example, Park *et al.* (2013, 21) (reviewing studies showing that adoptive parents on average are better educated, spend more time with their children, manifest more positive attitudes and affection toward their children, have stronger family cohesion, invest more in their children, and provide more social, cultural, and interactional resources to their children).

3 Perhaps the most bizarre response was in a long letter I received from an attorney after the conference, conveying that he was "troubled" that "forcing every woman who gives birth to subject herself to a criminal background check and national child abuse and neglect check may serve to deter procreation."

4 Barth *et al.* (2016, 12).

5 See *PSM 712–6* (2017); *PSM 713–09* (2017).

6 See Bladen (2014, slide 9).

7 See Dexheimer and Ball (2015); Aaronson and Ura (2014).

8 See Texas Department of Family and Protective Services (2013, 8–9).

9 Minnesota Department of Human Resources (2015, 31).

10 Minn. Stat. §§ 626.556, Subd. 2(p)(q), 260C.503, Subd. 2.

11 See Gelles (2017, 104–9) (discussing the research); Putnam-Hornstein et al. (2015, 496–503).

12 Hurley (2018).

13 Idem (quoting Rachel Berger, a pediatrician who directs a child-abuse research center at Children's Hospital of Pittsburgh).

14 See, for example, Putnam-Hornstein and Needell (2011, 1337–44); Putnam-Hornstein et al. (2011, 256–73); Slack et al. (2011, 1354–63).

15 See Putnam-Hornstein et al. (2015, 496–503); Putnam-Hornstein (2013, 4).

16 See Huang and Ryan (2011); Dwyer (2008, 424–6).

17 Cf. Gelles (2017, 100) (citing statements by Richard Wexler and by a UNICEF official in New Zealand).

18 Idem, 111–12.

19 See Gaudet et al. (2016, 503–31); Kelly (2015).

20 See Ferguson v. City of Charleston, S.C., 308 F.3d 380, 395–6 (4th Cir. 2002), cert. denied 539 US 928 (2003) (rejecting argument that testing of baby violates mother's rights: "We are aware of no decision holding, or even suggesting, that a mother has a reasonable expectation of privacy in her newborn child's bodily fluids. Indeed, such a holding would conflict with the general rule that an expectation of privacy does not arise from one's relationship to the person searched").

21 Cf. Weber (2007, 789–95); National Abandoned Infants Assistance Resource Center (2006, 2) (hereinafter NAIARC, citing opposition by American Academy of Pediatrics to universal testing of newborns for drug exposure); Roberts (1991, 1419).

22 See, for example, Ariz. Stat. §§ 8–456, 457; Va. Code Ann. § 16.1–283(E) (West 2018); Wash. Rev. Code Ann. § 13.34.132 (2017).

23 Roberts (2003, 173); see also Federle (2014, 710) ("there can be little doubt that paternalism inflicts violence … children in state care experience very real psychological pain through the loss of connection with parents, sibling, friends, and community … That we inflict this level of pain on thousands of children every year seems almost inconceivable").

24 See, for example, Lollar (2017, 986–7, 947–1005).

25 See, for example, Lollar (2017, 999–1000); Roberts (1997, 938–64).

26 Roberts (1997, 953–4).

27 See, for example, Ark. Code Ann. § 9–27–355(b)(i)(E)(iv) ("The court shall not base its decision to place the juvenile solely upon the consideration of the relationship formed between the juvenile and a foster parent").

28 See Baeder (2013) (describing CPS worker's explicitly discouraging white foster parents from adopting black child in their care and ultimately moving the child to an aunt); Banks (2009).

29 See, for example, Smith (2015, 328).

30 See Virginia Dept. of Social Services (2015, 9.5.4, emphasis added).

31 See Bevan (2016, 719); Somini (2000).

32 See, for example, Cohen (2006); Mabry (2000, 665) ("Congress has proposed a quick fix for the foster care system—terminate parental rights within a few months").

33 Cf. Lullaby Project (2018) (suggesting detailed requirements for parents demonstrating substantial compliance with a rehabilitation plan).

34 Colorado has taken a step in this direction, mandating that if a child is under age six when entering foster care, then a permanency hearing must take place within three months rather than the usual 12 months, and at that first permanency hearing the court has the authority to demand that CPS show cause why it should not petition for TPR. See Colo. Rev. Stat. Ann. §§ 19–3-702(1), (2.5) (2017).

35 Zero to Three (2013, 4) (listing Alaska, Hawaii, and South Dakota).

36 See Lullaby Project (2018).

37 Vandewalker (2008, 423); Guggenheim (1995, 137).

38 See, for example, 797 S.E.2d 740, 743 (S.C. Ct. App. 2017) (overturning TPR as to incarcerated father, on the grounds that the father's lack of care and contact was not "willful" but rather a result of his imprisonment).

39 For a recent example, see Sankara (2017, 699).

40 Daniels v. Williams, 474 U.S. 327, 331 (1986); cf. Youngberg v. Romeo, 457 US 307, 314–19 (1982) (holding that persons involuntarily committed to a state institution for the

mentally retarded have a substantive due process right to safe conditions, freedom from unreasonable bodily restraint, and minimally adequate training); Ingraham v. Wright, 430 US 651, 673 (1977) (upholding the practice of corporal punishment in public schools, but acknowledging that the Due Process Clause does confer on children's a right vis-à-vis the state "to be free from and to obtain judicial relief, for unjustified intrusions on personal security").

41 See Larsson and Talbot (2017).

42 See Sankara (2017, 698–700). At most, a parent-protective state court has held that the state must bear the burden of proving the parent currently would pose a substantial risk to the child if given custody. Fla. Dep't of Children and Families v. F.L., 880 So. 2d 602, 609 (Fla. 2004). Others have simply required that the parent has an opportunity to rebut a presumption of unfitness arising from the past findings. For example, In re Gach, 889 N.W.2d 707, 715–16 (Mich. Ct. App. 2016) ("As written, MCL 712A.19b(3)(l) provides no way to rebut this presumption of unfitness, assuming the fact of the prior involuntary termination").

43 Lehr v. Robertson, 463 US 248, 261 (1983).

44 Idem, at 248, 261–2, 266–7; Quilloin v. Walcott, 434 US 246, 254–6 (1978).

45 See, for example, Stanley v. Illinois, 405 US 645, 652–3 (1972) ("We do not question the assertion that neglectful parents may be separated from their children.... What is the state interest in separating children from fathers without a hearing designed to determine whether the father is unfit in a particular case?").

46 Stanley v. Illinois, 405 US 645, 656–7 & n. 9, 658 (1972).

47 See, for example, Adoption of Kelsey S. v. Rickie M., 823 P.2d 1216, 1236 (Cal. 1992) (en banc); In re Kirchner, 649 N.E.2d 324, 334, 339 (Ill. 1995); In re Baby Girl Clausen, 502 N.W.2d 649, 666–7 (Mich. 1993); In re Raquel Marie X., 559 N.E.2d 418, 424 (NY 1990).

48 See Dwyer (2009, 819).

49 Michael H. v. Gerald D., 491 US 110 (1989) (plurality opinion).

50 Idem, at 142–3 (Brennan, J., dissenting); see also idem, at 143 n.2 ("[A] mere biological connection is insufficient to establish a liberty interest on the part of an unwed father."); Smith v. Org. of Foster Families for Equal. & Reform (OFFER), 431 US 816, 844 (1977) (stating that "the importance of the familial relationship, to the individuals involved and to the society, stems from the emotional attachments that derive from the intimacy of daily association" and noting that for a child who has never known his biological parents, a relationship with other caregivers "should hold the same place in the emotional life of the ... child, and fulfill the same socializing functions, as a natural family"); idem, at 845 n. 53 ("The legal status of families has never been regarded as controlling...").

51 See Meyer (2006, 878) (indicating that a birth parent's interest in becoming a legal parent might receive less constitutional protection than the interest of someone who has already served for a time as a child's legal parent (whether a biological parent or an adoptive parent) in remaining in that role); Meyer (2006, 891–5) (showing that as a general matter the Supreme Court has interpreted the privacy right to protect already existing familiar relationships from government interference and not as a right to state's affirmative assistance in forming relationships).

52 Dawn D. v. Superior Court, 952 P.2d 1139, 1144–5 (Cal. 1998); see also Lisa I. v. Superior Court, 34 Cal. Rptr. 3d 927, 937 (Ct. App. 2005) ("[W]hen there is no existing relationship between the claimed biological father and the child, courts must defer to legislative choices reflected in paternity statutes."); Callender v. Skiles, 591 N.W.2d 182, 188 (Iowa 1999) (citing decisions in numerous other states refusing to recognize a due process right on the basis of biological fatherhood). Some state courts have held that biological fathers per se have a protected liberty interest under state constitutions. See Callender, at 187–90 (concluding that there is such a right under Iowa's state constitution and citing similar decisions in Colorado and Texas).

53 See, for example, Mullins v. Oregon, 57 F.3d 789 (9th Cir. 1995).

54 See, for example, Hodgson v. Minnesota, 497 US 417, 444 (1990) ("The State has a strong and legitimate interest in the welfare of its young citizens."); Lassiter v. Dep't of Soc. Servs. of Durham Cty., NC, 452 US 18, 27 (1981) ("[T]he State has an urgent interest in the welfare of the child..."); Prince v. Massachusetts, 321 US 158, 166–7 (1944) (describing ways in which, "[a]cting to guard the general interest in youth's well-being, the state as parens patriae may restrict the parent's control").

55 See, for example, In re Custody and Parental Rights of A.P., 172 P.3d 105 (Mont. 2007); Renee J. v. Superior Court, 28 P.3d 876, 878, 886 (Cal. 2001); In re Baby Boy H., 73 Cal. Rptr. 2d 793, 796, 799 (Ct. App. 1998); In re G.B., 754 N.E.2d 1027, 1030–2 (Ill. 1981); State ex rel. Children, Youth & Families Dep't v. Amy B., 61 P.3d 845 (N.M. Ct. App. 2002); cf. Sheneal W. Jr., 728 A.2d 544, 546, 552 (holding that the retroactive application of a statute providing for termination of parental rights when a parent has intentionally assaulted another child of the parent did not violate the parent's due process rights); Winnebago Cty. Dep't of Soc. Servs. v. Darrell A., 534 N.W.2d 907, 909–10 (Wis. Ct. App. 1995) (holding that the termination of parental rights pursuant to a statute making intentional homicide of parent grounds for termination did not constitute *ex post facto* law, did not violate the father's due process or equal protection rights, and did not constitute double jeopardy).

56 See, for example, Matter of S.G. v. Indiana Dep't of Child Servs., 67 N.E.3d 1138, 1140 (Ind. Ct. App. 2017); In re Baby Boy H., 63 Cal. App. 4th 470, 73 Cal. Rptr. 2d 793 (1998).

Bibliography

Aaronson, Becca and Alexa Ura. "Data Effort Aims to Help Reduce Child Deaths." *The Texas Tribune,* February 20, 2014.

Baeder, Ben. "Studies: Disproportionate Number of Black Children Wind Up in L.A. Foster Care." *Los Angeles Daily News,* March 23, 2013.

Banks, Ralph Richard. "The Multiethnic Placement Act and the Troubling Persistence of Race Matching," *Capital University Law Review* 271(38) (2009): 271–90.

Barth, Richard D. *et al. Safe Children: Reducing Severe and Fatal Maltreatment,* American Academy of Social Work and Social Welfare (2016), 12.

Bevan, Cassie Statuto. "The Impact of Liberal Ideology on Child Protection Reform," *William & Mary Bill of Rights Journal* 24(3) (2016): 709–19.

Bladen, Stacie. *Birth Match System Presentation to the Federal Commission to Eliminate Child Abuse and Neglect Facilities* (August 28, 2014), slide 9. (On file with author.)

Cohen, Laurie. "A Law's Fallout: Women in Prison Fight for Custody." *Wall Street Journal,* February 27, 2006.

Dexheimer, Eric and Andrea Ball, "Missed Signs, Fatal Consequences: Part 3: Agency Has Faced Uphill Battle, State Moves Toward Intervention before Tragedy Strikes," *Austin American-Statesman,* January 13, 2015.

Dwyer, James G. "The Child Protection Pretense: States' Continued Consignment of Newborn Babies to Unfit Parents," *Minnesota Law Review* 93 (2008): 407–24.

Dwyer, James G. "A Constitutional Birthright: The State, Parentage, and the Rights of Newborn Persons," *UCLA Law Review* 56 (2009): 755–835.

Federle, Katherine Hunt. "The Violence of Paternalism," *Wake Forest Law Review* 49 (2014): 703–12.

Gaudet, Lyn M. *et al.* "Can Neuroscience Help Predict Future Antisocial Behavior?" *Fordham Law Review* 85 (2016): 503–31.

Gelles, Richard. *Out of Harm's Way: Creating an Effective Child Welfare System.* New York: Oxford University Press, 2017.

Guggenheim, Martin. "The Effects of Recent Trends to Accelerate the Termination of Parental Rights of Children in Foster Care–An Empirical Analysis in Two States," *Family Law Quarterly* 29 (1995), 121–40.

Huang, Hui and Joseph P. Ryan. "Trying to Come Home: Substance Exposed Infants, Mothers, and Family Reunification," *Children and Youth Services Review* 33(2) (2011): 322–9.

Hurley, Dan. "Can an Algorithm Tell When Kids Are in Danger?" *New York Times* January 2, 2018.

Kelly, John. "Florida's New Predictive Risk Tool Likely to Drive Down Juvenile Incarceration." *The Chronicle of Social Change* 23 June, 2015.

Larsson, Eric M. and Jean A. Talbot. "Cause of Action for Negligent Placement in or Super-vision of Foster Home," *Causes of Action* 2d 1(43) (2017).

Lollar, Cortney E. "Criminalizing Pregnancy," *Indiana Law Journal* 92 (2017): 947–1005.

Lullaby Project. Rocket Docket, 2018.

Mabry, Cynthia R. "Second Chances: Insuring That Poor Families Remain Intact by Minimiz-ing Socioeconomic Ramifications of Poverty," *West Virginia Law Review* 102 (2000): 607–66.

Martin, Nina. "This Law is Supposed to Protect Babies, But It's Putting Their Moms Behind Bars: The War on Women Meets the War on Drugs—and Women Are Screwed." *Mother Jones* (September 23, 2015).

Meyer, David D. "A Privacy Right to Public Recognition of Family Relationships? The Cases of Marriage and Adoption," *Villanova Law Review* 51 (2006): 891–920.

Minnesota Department of Human Resources, *Minnesota Child Maltreatment Intake, Screening and Response Path Guidelines*. Saint Paul, MN: Minnesota Department of Human Resources, 2015.

National Abandoned Infants Assistance Resource Center. *Substance Exposed Infants: Noteworthy Policies & Practices*, September 2006, 2.

Park, Hyeshin, *et al.* "Factor Structure of Adoptive Parent-Child Relationship Items from the National Study of Adoptive Parents," *Journal of the Society for Social Work and Research* 4(1) (2013): 20–30.

PSM 712–6, CPS Intake—Special Cases, Children's Protective Services Manual. State of Michigan: Department of Health & Human Resources, February 1, 2017.

PSM 713–09, Completion of Field Investigation, Children's Protective Services Manual. State of Michi-gan: Department of Health & Human Resources, November 1, 2017.

Putnam-Hornstein, Emily. Research Brief, CDN Vo. 1–3: "California's Most Vulnerable Parents: Adolescent Mothers and Intergenerational Child Protective Service Involvement," Hilton Foundation (2013): 4.

Putnam-Hornstein, Emily and Barbara Needell, "Predictors of Child Protective Service Contact between Birth and Age Five: An Examination of California's 2002 Birth Cohort," *Children and Youth Services Review* 33 (2011): 1337–44.

Putnam-Hornstein, Emily *et al.* "A Public Health Approach to Child Maltreatment Surveillance: Evidence from a Data Linkage Project in the United States," *Child Abuse Review* 20 (2011): 256–73.

Putnam-Hornstein, Emily *et al.* "A Population-Level and Longitudinal Study of Adolescent Mothers and Intergenerational Maltreatment," *American Journal of Epidemiology* 187 (2015): 496–502. doi:10.1093/aje/kwu321.

Roberts, Dorothy E. "Punishing Drug Addicts Who Have Babies: Women of Color, Equality, and the Right of Privacy," *Harvard Law Review* 104 (1991): 1419–82.

Roberts, Dorothy E. "Child Welfare and Civil Rights," *University of Illinois Law Review* (2003): 171–82.

Roberts, Dorothy E. "Unshackling Black Motherhood," *Michigan Law Review* 95 (1997): 938–64.

Sankara, Vivek S. "Child Welfare's Scarlet Letter: How A Prior Termination of Parental Rights Can Permanently Brand a Parent as Unfit," *N.Y.U. Review of Law & Social Change* 41 (2017): 685–705.

Slack, Kristen Shook *et al.* "Risk and Protective Factors for Child Neglect during Early Child-hood: A Cross-study Comparison," *Children and Youth Services Review* 33 (2011): 1354–63.

Smith, Charisa. "The Conundrum of Family Reunification: A Theoretical, Legal, and Practical Approach to Reunification Services for Parents with Mental Disabilities," *Stanford Law & Policy Review* 26 (2015): 307–48.

Somini, Sengupta. "Campaigns Soft-Pedal on Children and the Poor." *New York Times*, October 29, 2000, sec. NY/Region.

Texas Department of Family and Protective Services Council Meeting: Minutes, October 18, 2013. Austin, TX: Texas Department of Family and Protective Services, October 2013.

Vandewalker, Ian. "Taking the Baby before It's Born: Termination of the Parental Rights of Women Who Use Illegal Drugs While Pregnant," *N.Y.U. Review of Law & Social Change* 32 (2008): 423–63.

Virginia Department of Social Services. *Child and Family Services Manual.* Virginia: Virginia Department of Social Services, 2015.

Weber, Ellen M. "Child Welfare Interventions for Drug-dependent Pregnant Women: Limitations of a Non-Public Health Response," *UMKC Law Review* 75 (2007): 789–845.

Zero to Three, *A Survey of State Child Welfare Policies and Initiatives* (Child Trends, 2013), 4.

Chapter 5

Separating children from bad neighborhoods

Chapters 1 and 2 explained why children's fate depends substantially on the quality of the larger social environment of their neighborhoods. Most biological parents in areas of entrenched poverty are not dysfunctional to such a degree as to be unfit. On the other hand, there are distressingly few adults in America's worst neighborhoods whom one could call "high functioning" or "successful." Those who grow up in such places and do develop the wherewithal to secure a good job and live a healthy family life typically leave the neighborhood, not wanting their own children to grow up there, and well-functioning people who did not grow up in such a place would not move into one. Yet there is a large range between unfit and high functioning, much of it occupied by parents who are simply terribly immature and lacking any sensible life plan. Children whose parents are in that range are at risk principally because of destructive aspects of their community—violence, toxic stress, coercion into gang membership, pervasive substance abuse, bad schools, etc.[1] When a child is born to biological parents who live in a horrible neighborhood, there are two basic approaches the state might take to avoid consigning the child to life in such neighborhood. One is to spend massive amounts of money trying (with little prospect of success) to transform the community (rather than simply relocate it). That is, of course, the preferred solution of most liberals (at least so long as "the rich" are paying for it, not them) and is hopelessly unrealistic. The other is to ensure that the child lives somewhere else, someplace safer and healthier. Most liberals would reject this more realistic (though still very challenging) approach.

Failure of the liberal approach

The primary liberal idea for addressing the "neighborhood effect" has been a large redistribution of wealth in the form of government spending on "revitalizing" America's worst urban areas, in the hope that this will eliminate crime, poverty, substance abuse, etc. One hears little of this idea these days, perhaps because liberals have recognized the money is not there and poor adults in urban areas have become jaded about "urban renewal," which, as James Baldwin quipped, typically amounts to "black removal." President Obama claimed some success with his Promise Neighborhoods Initiative, but he was able to secure only modest funding for programs in a small number of locations, and similar but better-funded "place-based" anti-poverty programs of the past, such as President Clinton's Empowerment Zone initiative, produced only modest improvement in some economic indicators in some of the targeted urban areas (and in those places it might have been because of gentrification).[2] Larger-scale efforts at transforming "communities" (as opposed to physical spaces), by creating strong social structures in disorganized neighborhoods, have generally been ineffective.[3] When urban renewal has "succeeded," it has been by gentrifying the physical space and relocating, not transforming, the dysfunctional community—that is, by forcing existing residents to move *en masse* to another location.[4] It also takes many years to have much effect. So if we were to ask about a child just born *today* to biological parents who live in the worst area of Baltimore or Cleveland or Detroit: Can urban renewal spare that child from being at high risk for many years of physical and psychological trauma, of abandonment or maltreatment, of developmental deprivation, and other ills of a toxic urban environment, the answer is emphatically "no." When an individual home presents such dangers to a child, the law does not say "leave the child there while we try to change it, even if it takes a decade." The law says "get that child out NOW."

Liberals, in theory, also support greatly increased infusion of public money into failing public school systems. Again, the money is not there and, as explained in Chapter 2, a lack of funding is not actually the problem with bad urban schools. There is a "neighborhood effect" within the classroom that increased school funding will not remove. Giving more money to schools cannot alleviate the personal obstacles to learning so many individual children bring into the classroom—exhaustion from living in a high-stress, overcrowded home; frequent change of residence; post-traumatic stress disorder from witnessing or incurring violence; inability to do any homework because they are not allowed to take books home and there is no one to supervise at home or the electricity has been cut off or they are afraid to be at home while mom's boyfriend is there; preoccupation with abuse they are suffering at home or conflicts they have with a gang member; worry about their grandmother who is in the hospital or their big brother who just went to prison; etc.[5]

Recognizing the importance of student body composition to the learning of any individual child, some propose creating unitary districts combining inner-city and suburban schools in metropolitan areas.[6] If this is merely a way of making more money available to inner-city schools, it can have little effect, for the reason just stated. If it is instead a strategy for changing the composition of the student body in the worst schools, by spreading out the children from the poorest backgrounds, the strategy has somewhat greater potential for having an impact. There are other ways of transferring children from bad schools to better as well, such as magnet schools and voucher programs. With these programs, too, though, there are concerns that the worst schools will only become worse, as the best students (i.e., those with the highest-functioning parents) leave and take state education money with them. The sad reality is that there is little chance for the kind of major transformation needed in the schools lying in impoverished black communities. The various school choice strategies reflect the idea I am suggesting, that when an environment is chronically toxic for children the most sensible policy is to remove them from it. Some conservatives would go farther and recommend completely shutting down the failing institutions, just as failed private businesses shut down. It might well be that children living in America's worst neighborhoods would be better off if local public schools were demolished and the money that has been used to finance them were instead used to pay for all children to attend *academically successful* private or public schools elsewhere. Liberals resist this idea in large part because they foresee further deterioration of the larger community, which they implicitly suppose must be saved no matter what. But that mindset leads to, in a sense, holding children hostage in bad schools for the sake of some aim other than enhancing their education and life prospects. (Conservatives, on the other hand, have successfully opposed any state effort to ensure private schools are succeeding before channeling state money to them.)[7]

Busing is another way of removing children from a bad environment, for part of the day. But there is little appetite for busing among Americans today, rich or poor. Even if more busing occurred, there would remain the problem that so many children from the poorest neighborhoods are hindered by their home and neighborhood environments, and if those hindrances manifest themselves in behavioral problems in a suburban school they will very quickly lead to expulsion. That is an obstacle to private school attendance with vouchers as well.

Finally, any major school-system reforms would take many years, even decades, to be implemented and show results. That means that they cannot be the answer for a child born today into a dysfunctional community where the schools are terrible, even if a better school environment could make up for much of the destructive influences of life in the rest of the community (which it cannot). Those schools cannot be changed overnight, nor is any new governance structure likely to take shape with any speed. In any event, there is far too little political support for additional spending on urban school systems. The only reforms that have garnered sufficient political support are public-school opt-outs and more intensive standardized testing, neither of which has helped the neediest black children.[8] In short, school reform is not the solution these children need.

For their part, conservatives have favored policies aimed at stopping or relocating criminal behavior, to at least make inner-city areas safer. The efficacy of intense policing practices such as "broken-window policing" and "stop-and-frisk" in reducing crime is much contested, but no one maintains that they have made targeted communities safe for children. In any event, liberals generally oppose such practices, and civil liberties groups have successfully sued to stop them in some jurisdictions.[9] From a perspective that considers only adult members of the community, one might reasonably conclude, as liberals generally do, that the balance of costs (including the incursion on civil liberties) and benefits cuts against such practices, even if they are effective. This is in important part, I think, because potential victims (and recall that in America's worst neighborhoods, any given person every year stands a one-in-ten chance of being the victim of violent crime) can in theory choose to exit.

However, when I focus on the children who are living in those neighborhoods, without having chosen to live there and without the legal or practical freedom to leave on their own, the balance tips the other way. If intense policing of adults would make children safer, then it is justifiable. We accept this in a school environment, and a neighborhood with hundreds of children is not so different. Lest this line of reasoning justify any incursion on adults' liberties anywhere and everywhere, there must be some threshold level of danger to warrant extraordinary restrictions on adults' freedom. By analogy, the law limits choice of residence for those who have been convicted of a sex offense, but not everyone who could conceivably molest a child. The law authorizes unannounced CPS home inspections only where serious child maltreatment or high risk of it has been documented, not every home where maltreatment could occur. It seems to me that when the number of murders children suffer or witness in a given neighborhood reaches some level, the state is justified in infringing the adults' normal liberties. But even if intensified policing made neighborhoods somewhat safer, it would not in and of itself reduce other life-limiting features of our worst urban areas.

Other efforts to improve life in inner-city neighborhoods have entailed relocating the people believed to be causing disorder to places where they can do less harm. Law professor Nicole Stelle Garnett explains that historical and contemporary programs have either concentrated the disorderly—for example, designating certain areas where vice will be tolerated or creating "human services campuses" to draw the homeless away from downtown areas—or, conversely, dispersed the disorderly from places where they have concentrated—for example, by intense "regulatory sweeps" (inspecting for code violations) in those places or prohibiting people with certain criminal histories from residing in them.[10] Creation of "adult-use zones" in big cities is especially interesting, because it shares with my "no-child zones" proposal below the premise that we might best protect children by separating them from places where dysfunctional or disorderly adults congregate. Garnett found courts more tolerant of coercive land-use approaches to addressing disorder than they are of preventive policing, generally upholding the former against constitutional challenges. Community resistance, though, can be just as great, and has caused legislators and regulators to retreat from such practices, and some are simply too troubled by the intensity of vice in designated zones (e.g., Boston's Combat Zone). Community objections echoed by liberal academics and advocacy groups have centered on perceived infringement of civil liberties and disparate racial impact. I suggest below reasons why both practical and moral concerns should be less with my proposal than with these regulatory approaches that focus on disorderly adults.

All the proposals below rest on the empirical premise that what children born to biological parents living in America's worst neighborhoods truly need is to get out. Most liberals might react to that statement by accusing me of being ignorantly judgmental and elitist. I would respond by suggesting they listen to the people who live in them, and that they contemplate living in one of these neighborhoods themselves with a child they love, and see if that changes their mind. Or even just go for a stroll in such a neighborhood some evening with their child, grandchild, niece, etc. Of course, they would never do even that, and they could contribute more constructively to the conversation if they thought concretely in their comfortable places about why they never would. What are the things that would discourage them from causing a child they love to spend even an hour, let alone an entire childhood, in such a place? Do those things not matter so much for black children whose parents are already living in such places?

Harvard economist Raj Chetty and others have documented, in studies of the Moving To Opportunity (MTO) program of the 1990s, which randomly assigned applicants for relocation vouchers to treatment and control groups, that a variety of welfare outcomes for children improve dramatically when their families relocate voluntarily and with government financial assistance while the children are still young, from high-poverty neighborhoods to low-poverty (<10 percent) neighborhoods. Welfare gains rose steadily the more years a child spent in the better neighborhood.[11] This substantiates neighborhood effect, insofar as the control group also consisted of parents who wanted to move out, and who therefore are generally also among the more protective of parents in poor inner-city areas; selection bias was minimized. Similarly, Leonard Rubinowitz and James Rosenbaum found, in their study of the voluntary-relocation program in Chicago following the Supreme Court's decision in Hill v. Gautreaux, the success of which partly inspired MTO, that children whose parents were randomly assigned vouchers for housing in suburbs were much more likely to remedy past educational deficiencies, finish high school, and go to college than were youth whose parents were randomly assigned vouchers for urban housing. In addition, parents in the suburban group were far more likely to find employment and get off of welfare.[12] There were difficulties in moving to predominantly-white suburbs, of precisely the sort one would expect (tensions with existing residents, discriminatory treatment by businesses, tracking in schools), but relocating families overcame these, and the benefits for them—safety, order, opportunity, services–greatly outweighed those transitional costs.

Would benefits also accrue to children of parents *forced* to move out of an extreme-poverty neighborhood? At least one significant experience supports an affirmative conclusion. When Chicago demolished some buildings within housing projects but not others, and offered the dislocated families a housing voucher that could only be used outside of public housing (but were not restricted to low-income areas), along with moving expenses (but no other assistance), researchers compared the long-term outcomes for children (all ages) in those families with children who remained behind in undemolished buildings. They found the relocating families moved to neighborhoods that on average had a 20–point lower poverty rate, and the children ultimately experienced significantly higher earnings and employment rates in adulthood, especially those who were under age 13 when they relocated.[13] Another study of this relocation, based on interviews of relocated families, found "the vast majority … ended up reasonably well-off," experienced "a vast improvement in the quality of their housing," and "believed they were far better off."[14] Of course, for adults and adolescents, a forced move can be quite upsetting, and the transition can be difficult. For children, age and gender would greatly influence outcomes; a 15 year-old boy is far less likely to separate socially and psychologically from the old neighborhood and to be welcomed into a more well-ordered community than is an infant or a 10 year-old girl. I return to this consideration below. And, naturally, receiving communities are less welcoming to "alcoholics, drug addicts, drug dealers, gang bangers, mentally ills, and families whose violent conflicts spilled out of their apartments,"[15] which reinforces the arguments in the preceding chapters about not forcing children to be in the custody of such persons.

Most liberals support offers of assistance for those who want to relocate, as with the MTO program, although some wag their finger even at that ("Why do black people have to leave their communities to be safe?"). But most would oppose any measures that in any way coerce parents into relocating to a better neighborhood. Rich white people are not coerced into moving or limited in their choice of where to relocate, they would say, so why should that be done to poor black people?[16] Are adults irrational if they do not wish to move out? So what, says the liberal. Jennifer Hochschild confidently asserts: "'ghetto residents' reasons for preferring to remain in an impoverished community are immaterial, because they are none of our business."[17] That adult-centered view overlooks that adult ghetto residents now are "preferring" not just for themselves but also for other persons—namely, children. And children's growing up in such places, because of the power *we* collectively bestow on their parents to dictate this aspect of their lives, is absolutely our business. Indeed, it is our fault.

As discussed below, however, the law does in various, uncontroversial ways already coerce some parents into moving, from one home to another and even from one residential area to another, and has done so for many decades, presumably because this has improved life on the whole for children. It would certainly be preferable if parents voluntarily chose to move to better neighborhoods with their children, but it is difficult to see how parental unhappiness with the relocation would outweigh the value for a child of living in a neighborhood that does not traumatize and demoralize them—where there are not drugs being sold or guns being fired in the streets, where gangs are not dominant, where there are many positive role models, and where they are surrounded in school by a critical mass of children who come prepared to learn. Parents who see those benefits for their children should ultimately embrace the relocation.[18] Those who do not have no legitimate basis for complaint about being coerced.

I begin my recommendations with the more tepid and less debatable, which boil down to taking neighborhood into account in any of the decisions the legal system already makes concerning children's residence. Throughout the chapter I press the point that sensitivity to social and physical environment in a neighborhood in child-welfare decision-making is no different conceptually or normatively from sensitivity to social and physical environment in a home.

Family law decisions that can relocate children

In various family law contexts, courts decide with whom a child will live. To some extent, the law already directs courts to consider when making those decisions where potential custodians live—that is, the quality of their neighborhood as well as the quality of their home. Judges can and should use that discretion to steer children, one at a time, toward better neighborhoods. They can, and many already do, routinely invite evidence about the larger environments in which particular parents live and what effects any dysfunction in the neighborhoods has had or is likely to have on children in those locations. Quality-of-life ratings by census tract or other unit can simplify such assessments.[19] Courts might even apply a very strong presumption or absolute bar against awarding or returning custody to a parent living in a community with a rating below a certain level, just as they would categorically deny custody to parents living in homes that fall below a certain level of health and safety.

Even when no parent or potential parent appearing before an agency or court lives in a neighborhood below a specified level of minimal adequacy, the relative quality of parents' or potential parents' neighborhoods should be factored into legal-parenthood and custody decisions. As a factual matter, it is clearly relevant to the empirical question of what is best for a child. Some neighborhoods might not be so bad as to warrant strong presumptions against or categorical prohibitions on residence by children, yet still be much less desirable places for children than other available options. This consideration comes into play now in domestic relations and child protection proceedings with older children, when parents or agency workers express concern about a youth being or becoming involved in illicit neighborhood activities, or when judges inquire about a child's academic progress as a result of being in one school rather than another. Legislatures should instruct courts to consider it directly and routinely and with infants as well as older children and adolescents. Many already have; a typical statute governing child custody disputes between parents includes something like "adjustment to neighborhood" in its list of best-interests factors, and adoption laws typically require the home study of applicants to include neighborhood quality.

In some contexts, liberals are likely to object that this consideration will have a disparate impact on poorer parents, which in most communities (but not the poorest) means on mothers. To their minds, then, it should not be done unless and until we eliminate poverty and gender inequality, so no one is at an unfair disadvantage in satisfying their desire to parent. This adult-centered objection is impertinent. As explained further below, judges deciding child custody should be viewed as agents for the child, making for the child a decision he or she cannot make but needs someone to make in his or her behalf. Judges have no other justification for injecting themselves into the child's intimate life in this way, so they must focus on nothing but what is best for the child. Differences in parental resources are often irrelevant or outweighed by other considerations, but it obviously matters to a child's wellbeing that one parent or potential parent lives in a high-crime area with failing schools whereas the other lives in a low-crime neighborhood with well-regarded schools.

In its work, CPS should also always consider the effects a particular neighborhood has had or is likely to have on a child in deciding whether to remove a child from parental custody, where to place a child after removal, and whether to return a child to parental custody. Thus, a parent living in a highly dysfunctional community would be more likely to lose custody of a child, and less likely to regain custody, all else being equal, than a parent living in a healthy community who had engaged in the same abusive or neglectful behavior. The rationale would be partly that the overall quality of life for a child of the former parent is substantially lower than that of a child of the latter parent, because of neighborhood effects, and so the former child stands in greater need of assistance and would benefit more from removal to another residential situation. And it would be partly that parents in a dysfunctional community with many stressors are less likely to correct their behavior than are parents in a community with greater social supports and fewer stressors. To the extent agencies already do this, it would provide at least partial explanation and justification for any observed differences in rates of removal as between black and white children even after controlling for type of maltreatment and parental income; poor urban blacks on average live in more dysfunctional neighborhoods than do poor urban whites.[20]

Especially after an agency and court have found parents to be abusive or neglectful and informed them that their neighborhood environment is an obstacle to proper care for their children, parents' choosing to remain in that neighborhood should count against return of the child, if it signals lack of full commitment to doing what is best for their children. (I address below the concern that some are incapable of relocating.) At a minimum, such parents would have to show a major transformation in their parenting capacity or home environment in order to make it in the child's best interests, or even acceptably safe, to return to live with them. In effect, if not explicitly, this could amount to CPS making parental relocation a condition of return. This would not be so different from a practice now routine for CPS—namely, telling parents they must move away from their drug source, abusive partner, or other problematic influences or social situations if they want the agency to recommend reunification as the permanency plan for a child. A parent might be inherently capable of providing minimally adequate care for a child but in a dysfunctional environment not able to give the child a satisfactory quality of life, either because of the effect the environment has on the parent or because the parent is unable to shield the child from the dangers the community presents.

Lastly, in deciding whether to terminate a parent's legal rights with respect to a child, in a child protective or adoption proceeding, courts should take into account not only what efforts parents have made to rehabilitate themselves, or what effort a birth parent objecting to adoption has made to assume parental responsibilities, but also whether the parent now lives in a safe neighborhood or has put in place strong protections against any dangerous elements in the community. Parents who have had to work hard to overcome addictions and other mental problems are likely to continue to be marginal parents even if they do successfully complete a rehabilitation program, and living in a community where violence, despair, and substance abuse are pervasive greatly increases the likelihood of relapse by the parent and of harm to the child.

The decision context in which it would be most difficult to inject consideration of community fitness is parentage law, because individualized best-interests decision-making is virtually non-existent in this context currently. For the state to address the unfitness of the communities in which some birth parents live would therefore require a larger revision of maternity and paternity laws. I argued in Chapter 4 for such revision—specifically, withholding legal parent status in the first instance from birth parents who are manifestly unfit. Those parents would be required to demonstrate to a court that they have or soon could overcome the conditions that triggered state scrutiny. In deciding whether to confer legal parent status on such birth parents, courts would take into account parental characteristics creating or lessening risk of harm to the child, and they could also take into account the neighborhood and social circle in which these presumptively unfit parents live. Community environment could count *in favor of* conferring legal parent status for some struggling with addiction or mental health problems, if the community is well-functioning and offers supportive services and positive social connections for parents.[21] Liberals readily acknowledge, even emphasize, the relevance of community environment when it is positive in this way, but they must also acknowledge that a parent's residential location can be a negative influence, making successful parenting even less likely.

This type of scrutiny immediately after birth is already occurring to a limited extent; as explained in Chapters 2 and 3, detection of alcohol or illegal drugs in a newborn's system in some states triggers a report to CPS, which must assess the birth mother's situation. In doing that assessment, case workers would naturally take into account the mother's living situation, and they might commonly extend that to include observations of or knowledge about the neighborhood, even if agency regulations do not explicitly direct them to do so. Case workers in jurisdictions conducting Birth Match might do this as well. The law should explicitly require consideration of this important factor in these evaluations.

In addition to simply making neighborhood quality a factor in decision-making, the state might use categorical negative assessments about particular neighborhoods in the various domestic relations and child protection decision contexts. The state might shortcut decision-making by establishing a presumption against granting legal parent status or custody of a child to persons who live in certain communities. For example, in the parentage context, a prior public determination that a birth parent's neighborhood is categorically unsafe or life-prospects-destroying for children (e.g., half of all males end up in prison) could constitute a "red flag" in a Birth-Match program, leading to a court hearing in which birth parents are asked if they are willing to relocate and, if not, to demonstrate that conferring legal parenthood on them would, all things considered, nevertheless be better for the child than the available alternatives, such as adoption. Or it could constitute strong evidence against a birth parent brought into court by some other unfitness trigger, such as a maltreatment history. Likewise, in the adoption context, state laws could impose a strong presumption against, or an absolute bar to, adoption by persons who live in certain neighborhoods, so that agencies need not even bother conducting a home study for such applicants. Such an automatic exclusion would occur today as to any applicant with, for example, a prior conviction for a violent felony against a child.

Readers already incensed by my neighborhood-related recommendations should consider that we adults engage in this sort of categorizing of people by geography when we make decisions about forming intimate partnerships. If only unconsciously, most adults in this country probably know that they would never date someone who lives in—and insists on continuing to live in—a dangerous, impoverished inner-city neighborhood, regardless of what positive attributes that person might have. What right does the state have blithely to place helpless, needy newborns into a legal relationship with and custody of those persons living in such places?

In the child maltreatment context, after removing a child from parental custody, in choosing foster homes for children whom they remove from parental custody, child protection agencies could categorically exclude from eligibility homes in horrible neighborhoods. Recall that under current law, the state can be held liable for harm stemming from a foster-care placement decision that is reckless or reflects deliberate indifference to dangers. In some cases, this will rule out kin placement, as all or most of a parent's extended family might live in the same or comparable neighborhoods. Further, legislatures might even amend their statutory definitions of neglect to make a parent's remaining in or moving into a neighborhood after it has been declared unsuitable for children per se neglect. This would be a form of "failure to protect," a concept now applied to parental decisions to remain in or move into a household with some person the parent knows to present a danger to the child, such as a convicted child molester or a person operating a meth lab. Significantly, it is a concept applied ostensibly without regard to the voluntariness of the parent's choice to be in such a household; it is no defense to a "failure to protect" charge to say that one could not afford or was afraid to live elsewhere.

In any of these contexts, the adults involved could avoid unfavorable treatment by moving. Agencies and courts could inform the individuals of that, but at some point the individuals would simply become aware that neighborhood quality matters and therefore realize they could improve their chances for a favorable outcome in family-law and child-protection proceedings by relocating. Not all would choose to do so, and for some that would be because of a perceived inability to relocate. But probably many would choose to do so who would not have otherwise, so the aggregate effect of both types of reforms should be an improvement in average quality of neighborhood in which children grow up—not because places change as a result, but because fewer children live in the bad places. To the extent relocations require higher expenditures on housing and transportation, this shift would necessitate a reallocation of resources by parents, but costs of living are not necessarily lower in blighted inner-city neighborhoods than in some safer and healthier areas outside of cities; as discussed below, it is a myth that poor people cannot afford to live anywhere but deeply-dysfunctional neighborhoods.[22]

To ACLs, the foregoing is simply insanity. The government passing judgment on where poor people live? And "punishing" individual parents because of behavior by other people in their neighborhood? This is piling one injustice on top of another. But wait, I have saved the best for last.

No-child residential areas

Beyond injecting consideration of neighborhood into individualized family-law decision-making, the legal system could simply declare that some neighborhood environments are unsuitable for children and no child may live there. As radical as this sounds, it is just an extension of what the state already does with families who inhabit home environments unsafe for children. The state provides limited assistance to parents to remedy problems in the home, but unless and until conditions improve, the state ensures the children live elsewhere, either requiring that a fit custodial parent move with the child to a different, healthy home environment, or placing the children in a home with other caregivers. Current law might be viewed as embodying the view that children have a right not to live in a home marked by violence, drug abuse, or co-residence with a known child abuser. If they could competently decide for themselves, they would choose to get out, and the agency, acting on behalf of the child, makes that decision for him or her. It is a straightforward enlargement of this idea to say children have a right not to be forced (by parents, using power the state confers on them) to live in neighborhoods marked by rampant violence and drug abuse, gang dominance, and a substantial number of co-residents who prey on children.

What I propose, concretely, is basically this: Relying on criteria of neighborhood quality, including rates of poverty, violent crime, gang activity, substance abuse, con-demned properties, vacancy, evictions, home ownership, single-parent households, and unemployment, as well as school quality, and availability of public services, health care, and healthy food, government at the state or local level could identify the worst resi-dential areas for children within its jurisdiction. A computer program with an algorithm for incorporating various types of data as to community conditions relevant to child welfare could generate a neighborhood quality index by census tract. This is something government agencies and private companies in fact already do. For example, the Citizens' Committee for Children of New York, Inc. has published a "community risk ranking" that "combines data from across multiple dimensions of child well-being" to rank New York City's 59 "community districts." It found most of the worst neighbor-hoods were in the Bronx, where blacks and Latinos make up the great majority of the population, having extraordinary rates of infant mortality, low birth weight, family homelessness, overcrowding in rental properties, violent felonies, teen idleness (i.e., not in school nor working), teen births, and other indications of danger or disadvantage for children.[23]

Using such metrics, government officials in any city can readily identify neighbor-hoods at the extreme negative end of the scale. A legislative body could specify some objective standard or "tipping point" at which the neighborhood quality is so low (e.g., less than 10 on a 100 point scale, or greater than 60 percent poverty rate) as to render an area categorically unsuitable for children. The threshold would not be a ranking but an absolute number, so even some large cities might not have any neighborhoods deemed unfit for children at a particular point in time. Based on such calculation, the state or local government could publicly declare particular communities unfit for child rearing and alter local zoning laws to designate those areas adult-only residential areas. A legislative body might also establish another standard (e.g., below 20 points or above 40 percent poverty rate) for identifying areas as to which an administrative body should undertake a more comprehensive and nuanced assessment, with community input, to determine whether the environment is so bad and timely improvement so improbable as to justify the disruption that would result from declaring the community unfit. Some communities, for example, might have very high rates of poverty and single parenthood yet not the high rates of violence, child maltreatment, gang activity, or substance abuse that tend to (but do not always) co-occur with concentrated poverty and single parent-hood. Accordingly, they might have a score that is low but not among the very worst, and further investigation might reveal that community members, despite the struggles poverty entails, have created a sufficiently safe and healthy environment for children.

(The numbers stated above are meant to be simply suggestive; reasoned, fact-based, child-centered deliberation might well show different numbers to be more appropriate. More generally, I am here just sketching how the idea might be implemented, not drafting legislation.)

Following such a finding and declaration, the state could take any number of steps toward making such areas childless. Most starkly, it could simply order that by a certain date no household in the area may contain children, and no children may enter the area. It would be like a combination of a round-the-clock juvenile curfew and a prohibition on parents living with their children in an unsuitable household. Or like condemnation of an area as "blighted," except eviction orders would be directed only at persons with custody of children. Courts would stand ready to respond to any noncompliance, ordering parents to move or else face loss of custody (as they commonly do in cases of unsuitable households).

Of course, I would urge governments at every level to provide every sort of relocation assistance displaced families might need (vouchers for renting a moving truck, help finding housing in another location, financial counseling, priority for rent subsidies, payment of security deposits, employment advising, social worker visits to link relocated families with services and social networks, etc.). One might hope the shock of governments declaring communities unfit would trigger more legislative support for financial assistance than now exists. Many parents would cheer this rezoning if it were coupled with such assistance, just as some were happy when given relocation assistance after being forced to move from a condemned building in the Chicago experiment mentioned earlier. Of course, the need for financial supports is not even close to being met now;[24] a huge number that would like to move do not even bother to apply for Section 8 vouchers, because they believe it is futile. And there might be little support for increased spending on these things among more affluent citizens, who would fear they would have to (a) pay for it, and (b) welcome into their own neighborhoods those exiting the places that in their minds are breeding grounds for thugs. Yet absence of assistance cannot justify continuing to authorize parents to make their children live in these hellish neighborhoods. The children have a right, like you, not to be forced to live there, regardless of whether there is money to help people relocate.

Why would any state or local government want to do this rezoning, especially if the people impacted would demand relocation assistance? One reason is that, in the worst neighborhoods, most families with children probably constitute a net financial cost to society, short-term and long-term. Most children in these neighborhoods are born to single, head-of-household mothers with little or no income, no financial support from fathers, and/or too little education, and it is unlikely the children will later pay back in taxes or other contributions to the community the expense to the government of paying for various aspects of their upbringing (schooling, food, healthcare, etc.), given the high likelihood that they will ultimately drop out of school, become criminally involved, and/or die before reaching adulthood if they grow up in those neighborhoods. Move these families to better neighborhoods, and the mothers are more likely to find work, thus producing an immediate benefit to the government in reduced welfare spending, and the children are more likely to stay in school and on a positive life trajectory, with a great long-term financial improvement for society.

On the other hand, although politicians always want to claim they have generated public benefits, above all they want to avoid alienating their voter base, which would be a big concern for many local-government officials—in particular, big-city mayors dependent on the black vote. Moreover, even if generous relocation assistance were offered, the rezoning would trigger fierce opposition and would be challenged in court, and that might outweigh for political actors any benefits they might see in the change. Liberal advocacy groups would characterize the rezoning as a condemnation of people rather than places, as a racist attack on 'the black community,' charge that it "undervalues the social capital of even poor communities" and "unfairly stigmatizes poor people."[25] In essence, they would demand (again) that the state spend massive amounts of money to fix these places or else leave them as they are. And most people who normally advocate for children would be silent, so as not to become targets of ACLs' attacks themselves.

I am not sanguine, therefore, about the possibility of any governments' actually voluntarily adopting this "No-Child Zone" proposal. Consider it a thought-provoking theoretical idea, intended to get readers to view the plight of children in impoverished urban areas in a new way—in particular, seeing how it reflects a choice by the state (us) to empower parents to cause their children to grow up in a hell on earth, a choice we implicitly renew every day. And that it is a choice the state could reverse simply by withdrawing the authorization, by adding something like "neighborhoods with a quality of life index lower than 10/100" to the existing list of places where parents are not empowered to house their children (e.g., industrial zones, under bridges, brothels, houses with meth labs).

However, the arguments for the proposal I present below might provide fodder for impact litigation that would force state and local governments to adopt it, a legal cause of action on behalf of children against states' empowering parents to house them in a toxic environment. I urge child-advocacy organizations to give it a try. Certainly it should be possible to get a court to enjoin the state from authorizing parents to do *some* things to children. Imagine, for example, if a state passed a law declaring that henceforth parents in the state may infibulate their daughters. One would expect lawsuits quickly filed against the state challenging that law on behalf of young girls whose parents want to infibulate them, and those lawsuits would likely succeed. Thus, courts should entertain a cause of action of the sort outlined below, and they would simply need to analyze whether authorizing parents to locate their children in very dangerous and toxic neighborhoods is sufficiently analogous to authorizing parents to do other things to children, such as infibulation, such that it, too, violates a constitutional right of children. If such a lawsuit should succeed, and a court ordered a state or local government to identify and designate certain neighborhoods as unfit for children, or were any government voluntarily to do this, then a court might also order that government to provide adequate relocation assistance to all affected families, as compensation for the harm the state has already caused the children by placing them in this predicament, or for defeating a reliance interest on parents' part.[26]

My proposals and argument here might also simply provide support for those who argue that existing housing-voucher programs should limit the use of housing vouchers to low-poverty areas where the child would attend a well-functioning school.[27] Currently, recipients can use vouchers in any neighborhood. The apartment or house must itself be of minimum quality, but it is irrelevant if the residence lies in a very dangerous and dysfunctional neighborhood, even if the recipient has minor children. In fact, most participants in the Housing Choice Voucher program use the vouchers in high-poverty, high-crime neighborhoods, many remaining in the very units they occupied before receiving the subsidy and not moving at all.[28] In other words, not only does the state confer legal-parent status on people it knows live in very bad environments, and authorize those people to take a newborn child to live in that very bad environment; the state is also *paying for* those people to make the child live in that very bad environment. In contrast, as noted above, the Gautreaux and Moving To Opportunity relocation programs were most successful for families whose vouchers were restricted to use in low-poverty areas—specifically, census tracts with less than a 10 percent poverty rate.

One widely-noted shortcoming of MTO was that the location restriction only applied for one year, and many recipients moved back to high-poverty neighborhoods after one year.[29] My rezoning proposal corrects this deficiency, as well as the Housing Choice phenomenon of rent-subsidy recipients' simply staying put, because it precludes remaining in or returning to any neighborhood designated as unfit for children. It seems an obvious improvement to an existing voluntary program like the Housing Choice Voucher program to impose exactly the same restriction on any participants who will have minor children living with them. Social scientists have developed criteria for identifying residential areas that constitute "communities of opportunity" within, as well as outside of, major cities—that is "neighborhoods that offer proximity to jobs (and job growth), quality schools, good child care, safety, and transportation access."[30] (Although research shows children do better the farther the new residence is from the old neighborhood.) A similar appropriate tweaking of existing housing policy would be to exclude families with young children from public housing developments that concentrate the poor within a small area.

ACLs would disapprove of even these more modest reforms, however, because they entail further limiting the life options of "the poor" (even though it would greatly expand life options for the children). For most liberals, restricting poor parents' choices is (unless to protect public school systems) never the answer; the answer is always more spending to support any positive choices poor people make. Perhaps that is why such restrictions are not in existing programs, but children are morally entitled to such limitations on the power over their lives that the state gives parents, and courts would certainly uphold such a condition on government assistance. The one child-centered reform ACLs might support is to put custodial parents with young children at the head of waiting lists for housing vouchers[31] (though conservatives might object that this incentivizes strategic procreation) and to provide relocation counseling that informs them about communities of opportunity and assistance available to help them move to one.

Still, I would defend the more ambitious plan of making entire neighborhoods childless—that is, to let adults remain living in places rife with violence, addiction, and other problems if they wish, but to separate children from them. Though the idea is novel, it is not as radical a departure from existing law and policy as it might at first seem. It is analogous to many things governments already do without much controversy. As noted above, the state declares households unfit for children and makes them childless through child protection proceedings. Adults may remain in the home, but not children. Governments routinely judge the suitability of particular spaces for habitation by any humans—zoning areas for industrial use only, condemning individual buildings, declaring neighborhoods "blighted" for urban renewal grant purposes.[32] Many states' definitions of "blight" include an unhealthy social environment—in particular, chronic criminal activity.[33] The restricted MTO vouchers reflected assumptions that "place matters," government is able to identify better and worse places, and it is legitimate for government to exert coercion on people to relocate to better places. The Obama administration successfully experimented in Dallas with an even more coercive housing-subsidy policy, under which residents of the city's worst neighborhood were offered high subsidies if they moved to a fairly affluent suburb, whereas those currently using housing vouchers in that worst neighborhood were told they would be cut off unless they moved to a lower-poverty neighborhood.[34] HUD was declaring it would no longer pay parents to keep their children living in an unsuitable neighborhood. There are also neighborhoods that themselves choose to exclude children (e.g., retirement communities), albeit for their own supposed enjoyment. The practice of excluding just children from public spaces is also common—for example, juvenile curfews, prohibitions on bringing children into bars, casinos, and betting parlors. (And surely the danger to children is far greater from living in a neighborhood where gang violence frequently breaks out than from walking through Caesars Palace). Such discriminations are understood to reflect differences between children and adults in vulnerability to, and capacity to avoid, dangers in the environment. They also reflect awareness that many parents are unable or insufficiently motivated to take protective measures themselves.

Further, the state now exerts substantial coercion on adults regarding their residential choices, in some ways to protect children. I noted above CPS conditioning of reunification on relocation, restrictions on residential choices of convicted sex offenders, and child removal from parents living on the streets. Affluent white people have no qualms about severely limiting other people's liberties in order to ensure no one who might pose any danger comes anywhere near their own children.[35] In addition, occasionally governments quarantine people to prevent the spread of disease, and governments force some convicted criminals to live in one particular place—a jail or prison—for extended periods.

Moreover, governments also already endeavor to disperse people from areas of concentrated poverty. I noted above experiments with various types of programs (small in scope because of lack of funding) relocating *willing* people from high-poverty, urban neighborhoods to low-poverty urban, suburban, or rural areas, using relocation vouchers, housing subsidies, and employment assistance.[36] Those that had greatest success dispersed families to many mixed-income areas and made it possible for them to remain there long-term, rather than moving a large number all to the same, only-marginally-better location with a high rate of turnover.[37] In some places, political or community resistance from receiving jurisdictions created obstacles, but in others families moving out of high-poverty, inner-city neighborhoods generally found acceptance and assistance.[38]

The novelty of my proposal lies in its peculiar combination of features. It would entail government (rather than private parties by mutual agreement) imposing the concept of an adult-only (rather than nonresidential for anyone) place on entire communities (rather than just an individual home) for the purpose of child protection (rather than for the benefit of people who wish not to live with children). What is novel about the idea makes it in some ways more difficult to defend against objections and in other ways easier to defend, as explained below.

Is there money in existing government budgets that could be shifted to implementation of No-Child Zones, or private money that could be leveraged? I noted above giving parents of young children the highest priority in existing housing and relocation assistance programs, shifting money now helping the childless. Federal law now sets aside some housing subsidy funds for use in facilitating reunification of children in foster care with parents whose homes CPS had found unsuitable, so that could be devoted to this purpose.[39] States might require that public and private efforts at "urban renewal" (i.e., gentrification) include a dispersal-aimed family-relocation component; the city and private developers must put some money into an MTO-type program pot, effecting a more veiled taxing of the rich. I would endorse shifting money from policing to relocation; government might justifiably have less concern about conditions in places inhabited only by autonomous adults, who are presumed to live there voluntarily (a presumption I evaluate below) and to be better able than children to guard their own welfare. (In other words, allow a Combat Zone to arise by moving out children rather than by asking the criminal element to move their businesses.)

Will receiving communities welcome relocators? Existing families in urban ghettos include youths of all ages. As noted, teenage boys are difficult to move, especially if they are black, in part because of the urban-thug stereotype. I would therefore recommend defining "children" for this purpose as persons aged 12 or younger. Sixteen-year-olds who want to move with their parents and younger siblings to a better neighborhood would, of course, be free to do so, but any so tied to a peer group that they refuse to go would not be forced by the rezoning per se; they might remain with another parent or other family member in the neighborhood. Importantly, after the initial evacuation period, further relocations would involve only newborn babies and the parents living with the babies, and they are the families most likely to be welcomed into a new neighborhood and supported by a new community, as well as the least costly to move. In other words, resistance from receiving communities should be mostly a transitional problem. It should help those communities be welcoming to know past relocation programs have generally not led to increased crime in places to which poor families moved.[40] Moreover, the life improvement for a child who relocates to a low-poverty neighborhood right after birth and remains there would be immense.[41]

I am not suggesting relocation is a panacea or costless for black children born to poor inner-city parents. They will likely face some aversion by established residents (regardless of color), some discrimination, some isolation.[42] They might have weaker ties to extended family. But they will not be risking their lives on a daily basis, will not be surrounded by toxic influences, will not be on a path to dysfunctional adulthood. They will have safety, services, opportunities, and role models not available in blighted inner-city neighborhoods. And they will have hope.

Justifying separation of children from blight

ACLs might concede that similar state practices already occur, but contend they should not, or that my extension of them goes too far. To them, what I have proposed amounts to punishing adults for things beyond their control and to unconstitutional and immoral state coercion of adults' choices about where they live with their children. "Dwyer gets to live wherever he wants with his kids, but poor black parents should not have the same freedom?" Or: "The price of freedom for poor people should be loss of custody of their children?" Of course, parenthood in some ways limits the freedom of everyone who enters into it, and every parent would be subject to the exclusion from no-child zones. But my proposals go to a central aspect of an adult's life—where one lives, which tends to determine with whom one regularly associates. The overwhelming majority of parents do not suffer from being excluded from horrible neighborhoods, because they have no reason or desire to live in such places. My proposals would have a significant disparate impact on a particular group of people that already suffers from many limitations on their freedom imposed by law, the economy, and attitudes of more privileged members of society.

Yet the justification for my proposals is obvious once one recognizes the state's role in creating families and the moral fact of children's distinct and equal personhood, and once one seriously contemplates the analogy to rules governing adult relationships. My proposals are not merely optional for the state, but in fact morally and legally obligatory. Children have a right, against the state, that it make decisions about where and with whom they live in a more careful way, one that is responsive to the seriously adverse impact that poor neighborhood quality can have on children's well-being.

Children's right against state-supported compulsion to live in horrible places

The state now plays an essential role in the series of events by which children come to live in particular places. It is not solely the result of private choices that the world for some children is filled with danger, disease, and dysfunction. Rather, it is also a result of the state's deciding, when a child is born, who the child's legal parents will be (through parentage laws) and what the scope of acceptable residential choices for parents is (through zoning laws). Similarly, the state knows that some adults in our society would like to infibulate any girl they are raising, and if it confers legal-parent status on those adults and also confers on them a scope of freedom as to choices about what is done to the child's body that includes the choice to infibulate, then we should ascribe responsibility to the state for the end result of girls' suffering infibulation; parents would be legally free to do it only because the state conferred this power and privilege on them. In fact, human-rights organizations condemn governments of other countries whose laws empower parents to do this; they do not only condemn parents. Likewise, if the state were to eliminate prohibitions on parental sexual abuse of children, thereby implicitly authorizing parents to do that, the state's responsibility would be evident. As feminist scholar Frances Olsen has pointed out:

> One of the main things a power-holder gains from successfully characterizing his power as "private" is a degree of legitimacy and immunity from attack. Thus it is predictable that people will try to characterize their use of power as "private" and to characterize power deployed against them as "not private"—that is, as public, oppressive, unjustified and unconstitutional.[43]

Thus, imagine an advocate for a newborn child objecting to application of a state's maternity law, for example, on the grounds that the birth mother lives in a hellish place and is unwilling to relocate even if she receives state assistance in doing so. Imagine the advocate presents compelling evidence that the state's making that woman the baby's legal mother would result in a much worse life on the whole for the child than would making some other willing adult the child's legal mother, even after taking into account the value of biological connection. Or that it would be in the child's best interest for the state to make the birth mother the baby's legal mother only on condition that she move to a very different neighborhood. On the basis of that evidence, the advocate would argue that the child has a moral and a Fourteenth Amendment substantive due process right against the state's forcing the child to be in a legal family relationship with, and in the custody of, the birth mother, so long as she insists on continuing to live there. This would *not* be a positive rights claim—that is, a plea for state assistance, or for gratuitous state protection against private harm.[44] It would be a negative rights claim— that is, a demand that the state not do something harmful to the child. This is a perfectly intelligible claim, entirely consistent with prevailing constitutional doctrine. And it would be a claim with great moral force, in essence objecting to abuse of state power: "How dare you, the state legislature and courts, force this child to live with that birth parent in that place, when you know that you are consigning the child to a life lived in a hell on earth?"

It is easier to recognize the state's active role in creating a child's living situation when one considers certain other analogous cases where the state action is well recognized. Again we can consider appointment of guardians for incompetent adults. Imagine you become mentally incompetent suddenly, as a result of illness or injury, while remaining physically fit, and the state needs to make a decision about your care, including who will serve as your guardian, with power to take you into his or her home. Suppose two persons, both blood relatives, wish to assume control of your life at that point and both petition to become the guardian. Suppose further that one of them lives in a safe and well-functioning suburban community with good services for persons of diminished capacity whereas the other lives in a crime- and drug-infested inner-city housing project where residents are afraid to leave their homes and stray bullets come through apartment windows. The state can easily elicit information about where each petitioner lives and where he or she intends for you to live.

If the state chose to place you, as a ward, in the care and custody of the petitioner who lives in a horrible environment and who intends to stay there, we would readily recognize that state action is involved in creating your overall living situation, including your location in a dangerous and dysfunctional community. We would expect the state to justify its seemingly inappropriate decision—for example, by explaining that the other petitioner was wholly unsuited to the guardian role, that there was no reasonable alternative placement, and that it has strongly encouraged this petitioner to move to another location. Absent adequate justification, we would think the state has abused its power and violated your moral and constitutional rights. And it would not be sufficient justification if the state explained that it simply chooses not to inquire about the residential circumstances of any petitioners for guardianship, lest it discriminate against or stigmatize the poor, let alone that it sympathized with the applicant whose life is otherwise so miserable. We would say that if the state is going to involve itself in a non-autonomous person's life to the extent of conferring on someone else legal power over the person's life, it must do so with care, based solely on what is best for that person, and in a manner designed, at a minimum, to avoid putting the non-autonomous person in danger.

Also analogous are selections of foster parents and adoptive parents; sometimes the state must choose such caretakers for a child, and when it does there clearly is state action and we expect the state to do so with some care.[45] If, for example, the state adopted a policy of *preferring* applicants for "new family" adoptions (i.e., adoptions of children with whom the adopters have no connection by biology or marriage) who live in the poorest urban neighborhoods, as a matter of sympathy for those people, we would surely recognize state action subject to constitutional challenge. As explained in Chapter 4, it is just as much state action, requiring justification, whenever the legislature or a court decides who a child's first legal parents and custodians will be, whether the reason for choosing particular persons is biological connection or something else.

And as with foster care, adoption, or adult guardianship, it is no justification for the state to say that it simply chooses not to inquire about first parents' living situation. The state should not assume control over persons' private lives in this way unless it does so with care. Some children might be better off if no legal relationships with adults were established and they simply remained in a birthing facility or if a nurse or doctor present at the birth took them home and assumed de facto custody.

Moreover, the reality is that the state typically does have information about birth parents' residential location, just as they have information about birth parents' child-maltreatment history and criminal record. So the state cannot plausibly claim to be innocent by virtue of ignorance. Birthing facilities report all births to a state department of health or vital records and include identifying information as to birth parents, including home address. A simple computer program at the receiving state agency could flag births to biological parents who live in unfit communities, a simple addition to a Birth Match system.

There is also clearly state action when the state designates particular spaces as appropriate for residence by all persons, knowing some adults who are parents will choose to live there with children, and it legally empowers parents to choose to locate children there, even though it is aware some such spaces are truly unfit for residence by children. Analogously, if the federal government authorized soldiers to take their infant offspring into war zones abroad, the state would be playing an essential and deliberate causal role in some children's living in a dangerous environment. It is because state governments in the US confer on parents legal authority to determine children's residence that legal parents can call upon the state to enforce their choices as to where children live, as against other private parties (e.g., an extended family member, a teacher) or against government actors who might wish to cause particular children to live in different places. It is because the state has made the adults with whom children in horrible inner-city neighborhoods live the legal parents of those children and has empowered them to house the children in those neighborhoods that a person concerned about the children's welfare cannot drive through the neighborhood with a bus, collecting the children and bringing them to live in a safe and attractive group home in the suburbs or out in the country. If someone did that, the parents could call the police, and the police would track down and return the children and throw the do-gooder in jail.

Thus, the state's position with respect to children living in hellish neighborhoods is not one of a passive, inactive onlooker; rather, it is one of active participant, consigning children to the custody of adults who live in such neighborhoods, empowering the persons it selects as legal parents to decide where children will live, and designating places as suitable for residence by all persons, children and adults alike. Even if one is inclined to defend this entrenched state practice, on grounds such as those I consider below, one should acknowledge that state actions and state decisions are playing a crucial role in where children live. And the state must always defend its actions and decisions, especially when they have such a profound effect on the fundamental wellbeing of vulnerable, politically powerless persons. Viewing the state as an active participant makes it easier to see the plausibility of a claim that any child's residing in a very dangerous neighborhood reflects a state violation of the child's moral and constitutional rights. The suggested moral claim against the state on behalf of a newborn child whose birth parents live in a horrible neighborhood is not: "Please save me from private dangers you played no part in creating." It is, rather: "You must not put me into a legal relationship with or in the custody of people who insist on living in that place, and you should not be telling the citizenry that that place is suitable for children to live."

In terms of constitutional rights, the state infringes the substantive due process rights of children under the Fourteenth Amendment of the Constitution of the United States when it places them into a legal relationship with and custody of legal parents who live in unfit communities, empowers legal parents to choose where children will live from among all areas zoned residential, and encourages parents to live in unfit communities by designating them as suitable for residence by all private individuals, including children, despite their unfitness. A representative for a newborn child should be permitted to assert such a claim and to seek injunctive relief against the state's abusing its power in that way. A court should require the state either to assign the child to legal parents who would not choose to live in an unfit community or else to prohibit whomever it makes the legal parents from taking the child to live in an unfit community. In this context, as in selection of guardians or private care facilities for incompetent adults and selection of foster and adoptive parents for children, we should view the state as a proxy decision-maker acting on behalf of a non-autonomous person, constrained by the Fourteenth Amendment to exercise care in making such momentous decisions about vulnerable private individual's lives—at a minimum, not acting with deliberate indifference to the fate likely to result for those individuals from the state's decisions, not blithely consigning newborns to grow up in horribly unhealthy and unsafe neighborhoods.

Objections

Despite my proposals' resemblance to numerous existing government practices, many will find them jarring. The idea of a territory in which children may not live or even visit could be the premise of a science fiction movie. To recommend denying or diminishing a parent–child relationship because of the neighborhood in which an adult lives might sound like urging parents be punished for being poor, which is especially troubling because their poverty can plausibly be traced to race-based historical and contemporary injustices. In addition, it seems unfair implicitly to fault people for adverse neighborhood conditions they themselves might have played no part in creating. Further, what I propose puts the government in the position of being judgmental toward and appearing callously indifferent to the parents and other adults living in bad areas. Moreover, coercing any people to move, although governments do it fairly routinely, does implicate their constitutional liberties, and threatening to deny or terminate parental status to people because of where they choose to live implicates other constitutional rights under current doctrine—that of parents to raise their offspring and to do so as they wish. There are also humanitarian and pragmatic concerns that arise from disrupting people's ties to a community and their daily interactions with extended family, some of which entail provision of needed care to family members, such as elderly parents.

Punishing parents for things other than their own conduct

Denying people legal parent status or custody of a child is a quite substantial cost to impose on them, and effectively forcing them to relocate also imposes a substantial cost. The state would appear to be imposing one cost or the other because of conduct by people other than those incurring it—that is, because other people commit crimes, sell drugs, fail to care for their property, do not supervise their children, and so forth. It is a widely-shared basic moral principle that people should not suffer for the wrongs and choices of others. In contrast, a parent's or potential parent's home environment is typically something over which he or she does have control, and so we feel more comfortable holding parents responsible for problems in it. This objection is unpersuasive for many reasons.

First, the assumption that the cost would be imposed solely because of other people's conduct is likely false in many cases, perhaps most. The adults on whom the cost would be imposed presumptively have chosen to live in the community and/or to have a child, and they can be held responsible for either choice. Underlying the objection, though, might be an additional assumption that many people who live in communities unsuitable for children are incapable of living elsewhere, because they cannot afford to live elsewhere or they need the support of others in those communities. There is a shortage of low-income housing in many places, many landlords will not accept housing vouchers, finding employment in new locations can be difficult, low-poverty communities might be unwelcoming toward poor people, and some poor people do rely on neighbors and family members for child care, elder care, and other needs (though, as noted in Chapter 1, residents of impoverished urban areas report social isolation and lack of supportive network).

But surely it is not true of every parent living in an unfit community that they cannot move to better neighborhoods, and it might not be true of any. Certainly many have the means but choose to remain in familiar surroundings and near family and friends because it is gratifying in some ways.[46] Those who can move might be faulted for not putting their child's welfare first. In reality, there are many places in the United States that are not crime- and drug-ridden and where people live with very little income, even just welfare benefits.[47] It might not be especially difficult financially for parents to move themselves and their children to a small town or rural area. In a recent ethnographic study of housing-unstable families in Milwaukee, Matthew Desmond found the going rate for a two-bedroom flat was around $550,[48] an amount that would secure a two-bedroom apartment in many of the small cities in Wisconsin that line Lake Michigan between Milwaukee and Green Bay, as well as many inland towns. Residents of Hunts Point, NY, are surely paying much more than that per month and could find similar rentals at a similar price in far better neighborhoods in upstate New York, where there are many small, safe cities (Cohoes, Watervliet, Mechanicsville, Amsterdam, etc.) with multi-racial downtown populations and low rents. In Williamsburg, VA, a wonderful place for persons of any race to raise children, with ample job opportunities, whose population is 15 percent black and whose schools are good and well-integrated racially and economically (most public schools' free-and-reduced-lunch population is in the 30–40 percent range), there are two-bedroom apartments in mixed-race complexes in low-crime, healthy neighborhoods available for $775 per month, which is comparable to what people are paying in the worst neighborhoods of Richmond and Norfolk. The same is undoubtedly true in thousands of other smaller communities across the nation, not to mention rural areas.

Most likely, many inner-city residents simply do not consider moving to another city, and those who do might reject the idea for normal non-financial reasons—familiarity, fear of the unknown or of boredom, existing relationships. But they should—if they have chosen to be custodial parents—be forced to consider it, for the sake of their children. Moreover, the cities where the nation's worst neighborhoods lie, generally also have mixed-income, mixed-race neighborhoods that are affordable.[49] Parents currently receiving government housing subsidies can use them at a new location anywhere in the country.[50] Further, there are public and private employment agencies in many communities to help people find employment.[51] Many parents might have connections through family and friends with persons living in better communities who could help them adjust and identify opportunities for work, daycare, friendships, etc. Lastly, currently many families living in poverty are forced to move often anyway, as rents change or buildings are condemned or renovated, so do not have much stability in their lives as it is. Relocation to entirely different environments, to better functioning communities, might allow them greater stability in the long run.

In short, a blanket assumption that every parent living in a horrible neighborhood is incapable of moving elsewhere is unwarranted; in fact, it is more realistic to assume the opposite, that they are living in unfit communities by choice or unreflectively. Their choices might be understandable, but they are nonetheless choices, and they might be unacceptable choices for their children. Moreover, probably most children who live in terrible neighborhoods were conceived and born when their parents already lived in those neighborhoods, so the parents presumptively made at least that voluntary decision—that is, to have a child, or to risk creating a child by having sex, despite knowing the child would live in the terrible place—which can be a basis for justifying imposing costs on them, just as such a decision is the normal justification for imposing the cost of a child support obligation.

Second, even if we assume some people cannot afford to relocate, at least not without substantial government assistance that might not currently be available, and therefore that some people are not responsible for the fact that they live in one community rather than another, it does not follow that imposing costs on them, in terms of their parental interests, is punitive or unfair punishment. Not every cost people incur at the hands of the state or private parties is a punishment. Typically, we view as punishment taking away from persons a good they currently possess, as opposed to declining to give persons a good they do not possess but want to have. Some of the state decisions discussed above are of the latter sort. Birth parents who fill out an application for a birth certificate and adults who apply for adoption are asking the state to give them something they do not yet have—namely, legal parent status as to a new entrant to the human community and all the legal rights that go with it. Parents who seek conferral of custody rights on them as opposed to another parent, or as opposed to the state (when a child is in foster care) or a non-parent guardian, are also asking for something they do not currently have. Refusing these requests looks less like the state's imposing a cost on people than does taking away legal parent status in a termination of parental rights proceeding or taking custody away from a parent in a domestic relations or child protection proceeding.

Even with respect to state decisions taking away an existing legal status or disrupting a parent's relationship with a child, it is inconsistent with our views of analogous decisions in other contexts to characterize the decisions as punishment. For instance, in adults' decisions about the relationships they will form or dissolve with other adults, we generally do not characterize as punishment one person's deciding that he does not want the relationship. If one adult declined an invitation by another adult to marry, because the other lived in a neighborhood with very low life quality and was unwilling to move, we would not characterize that decision as punishment. The notion of punishment entails an intention to cause suffering, whereas in such a case any suffering is incidental and unintended. The same would be true if two individuals were already in a relationship such as a marriage and at some point a disagreement about where they would live became severe enough that one chose to exit the relationship. We would not say the one who chose to exit was "punishing" the other, unless her intent was just to inflict pain on the other as a consequence for his insistence on living in a bad place; we would instead say she is simply doing what she thinks best for herself.

The state, acting as an agent for the child, pursuant to its *parens patriae* responsibility, would simply be making the same sort of decisions about relationship formation and dissolution on behalf of an individual child. The state, in terminating parental rights or taking custody away from a parent, is not aiming to inflict suffering on the parent; it is aiming, rather, just to do what is best for the child. The law requires persons to do many things as conditions for becoming or remaining parents and custodians, such as having a home somewhere, securing medical care, getting a child to school, providing clothing and food to children, and dissociating from certain other individuals,[52] and those conditions are not deemed punitive.

Further, denying adults parentage or custody based on unchosen circumstances is not unfair. There are many things outside the control of parents and would-be parents on the basis of which the state denies them custody or parental status, and this is generally not considered unfair—for example, mental illness and mental or physical disability. Advocates for some such adults do sometimes object to the state's counting those characteristics or circumstances against those who seek custody of children—in particular, advocates for parents with physical disabilities and for domestic violence victims. Advocates for persons with disabilities, though, have generally not argued that the state must ignore any disabilities. Rather, they have argued the state has a moral and constitutional responsibility first to provide assistance that would compensate for the disability. Likewise, scholars who object to removal of children from domestic violence victims do not argue that witnessing domestic violence against a parent is not bad for children, nor that the state should be oblivious to it. Rather, they argue that the state should do more to assist the unfortunate parent. Some do maintain that it is always wrong to impose the cost of separation from children on women just because of conduct by someone else, but they provide no response to the reasoning above—in particular, the point that state decisions about child custody cannot permissibly be based on anything other than the child's best interests, and the point that the state routinely and without objection imposes costs on parents for several others things beyond parents' control. Similarly, one might maintain that my proposals are fair to parents only if coupled with substantial relocation assistance, greater than what currently exists. I believe a strong argument could be made for the state's having a moral duty to children to assist parents financially in moving, an argument that rests on an assumption of the state's partial responsibility for the children's predicaments. But the fact that governments generally do not provide relocation assistance following eminent domain or condemnation actions suggests popular morality does not ascribe a right to people to government relocation assistance whenever the government requires them to move.

Finally, it bears mention that the major normative premise of the unfairness objection, that people should not suffer because of the choices of others, applies even more clearly to the current plight of children in unfit communities and so bolsters the argument that children have a right not to live in such places. Children should not have to bear the enormous cost of growing up in conditions akin to a war zone that arises from choices parents make using their state-conferred power over children's lives. Forcing children to live in hellish places would seem more clearly unfair than forcing parents to move out of hellish places, with or without state assistance.

Disparate impact on persons who are poor or of minority race

Related to the first objection above is a group-focused unfairness complaint. The reforms I propose would fall most heavily on poor and minority race people. Concentration of racial minorities in blighted areas is in significant part a result of racist government policies and racist practices of private businesses and individuals, so it will seem to some like piling one injustice on top of another for historically subordinated groups. This is similar to the complaint often leveled against state child-protection interventions more generally, and against other government attempts to address rampant disorder in blighted urban areas.

The disparate impact complaint is not very strong with my proposals nor with already-deployed strategies, including intensified policing and other disorder-relocation programs. These aim to improve safety and quality of life more generally in poor, minority-race communities, and simply reflect the reality that within those communities there are very high rates of both victims and perpetrators of crime and other dysfunctional behavior. My proposals are aimed at helping children who are or would begin living in poverty absent the reforms, and these children are disproportionately of minority race. Thus, if you focus on certain groups of *adults*, you will see an adverse disparate impact, to the extent the reforms result in coercing some to disrupt their lives or denying some parent status or custody. If instead you focus on children, you will see an effort to alleviate the existing negative disparate impact occasioned by the state's general empowerment of parents to choose any residential area they want, which disproportionately causes black children to live in destructive environments. Further, I have suggested parents actually benefit themselves when their children's welfare is advanced, even if the parents do not see the benefit and feel they are suffering in the process, so it is unclear even adults are, on the whole, made worse off.

The objection fails also because there is little to commend a moral premise (and no doctrinal support for a constitutional argument) that people are entitled not to have the state adopt policies whose cost falls most heavily on a group to which they belong, when the policies do not reflect an aim of causing that group suffering and instead reflect entirely legitimate government aims. There are innumerable examples of other government policies that have a disparate impact but do not lead to this sort of group-based unfairness complaint. Tax laws aim to encourage activities the government values and discourage activities the government disvalues, and as such have a negative disparate impact on groups engaged in activities the government does not value. Even when similar disparate impact complaints do arise in other contexts—for example, in connection with bans on activities most likely to be engaged in by persons who are poor, such as prostitution and shoplifting—they do not carry the day.

Further, we generally accept that certain types of private choices (e.g., partner selection) in the aggregate have a disparate impact on historically subordinated groups (e.g., persons who are poor, disabled, mentally ill), but that those choices must nevertheless be accepted. As argued above, state best-interests decision-making about children's relationships should be viewed as substituting for self-determining relationship choices private individuals ordinarily make for themselves, warranted only by children's need for a surrogate decision-maker. No one would suggest the state should force, or even encourage, any adults to partner or live with poor people. It would treat children instru-mentally to allow sympathy for unfortunate adults to justify sacrificing the children's welfare, by giving those adults parental status or custody as a kind of compensation for their misfortunes, ignoring the welfare costs for the children. It is a basic premise of our shared morality that we should not treat any persons as instruments for others' gratifica-tion. Children, it seems necessary occasionally to remind people, are persons.

The reforms would harm the very persons they aim to benefit

Both advocates for persons with disabilities and scholars opposed to removals of chil-dren from domestic violence victims also argue that removal from parental custody does more harm to children than good, even if there are problems with parental custody. At least in most cases, they argue, the best outcome for the child will be to maintain paren-tal custody despite the costs for a child that a disability or witnessing abuse of their parent might entail. One might argue, similarly, that even if state decision-making about children's legal relationships and residences is a proxy decision for the children in which nothing matters except what is best for the children, that assessment must be a comprehensive one, weighing the costs and benefits as to each of several imperfect alternatives. Further, although bad neighborhoods are a problem for children, separating children from parents just for that reason will typically not serve children's overall well-being. Encouraging parents to move out and offering them assistance to do so is one thing, but removing children from their custody if they decline is quite another, and likely to be, on the whole, bad for the children. Even if the parents are being irrational and selfish, that does not make TPR in a child's best interests.

I would first note that this objection is inapposite to my proposal for revising domestic relations and child protection laws, which would simply make neighborhood quality one of many factors in an overall best-interests assessment, to be balanced against other child welfare considerations. Moreover, neighborhood assessment would take into account any existing positive aspects, such as supportive social networks.

The zoning proposal, though, could entail denial or disruption of parent–child rela-tionships, when adults refuse to move out of unfit communities. However, an objec-tion to the zoning proposal based on the costs of separating children from parents has substantial purchase only in contexts where certain adults have an established and healthy social parent–child relationship with their children. It has some but very little purchase in the context of state decision-making as to who will be a newborn baby's legal parents, because then there is not the concern about severing an existing attach-ment, and there is ample supply of adoptive parents for newborns. The biological con-nection is a relevant and significant consideration in assessing the overall long-term welfare of a child, but it is only one among many and by any objective measure less significant than a child's interests in basic health and safety. An argument based on costs of separating children from parents also has little purchase in situations where custodial parents' relationship with a child is attenuated for other reasons, such as maltreatment or long absences, and parental refusal to move with the child might evidence such attenuation.

The greatest concern would relate to removal of children old enough to have some attachment to parents who have not maltreated them, yet who for some reason refuse to move out of a neighborhood deemed unfit for children. One way to address this concern might be to take the stronger step of simply ordering the parents to move by issuing an order to vacate. Many local governments have substantial experience with such orders addressed to entire households.[53] Alternatively, the state might infer that parents who place more importance on staying in a current home and maintaining connections to local residents than on maintaining custody of their children are indifferent or marginal parents, even though they would not otherwise be deemed to have maltreated the children. It might treat the decision to stay behind as itself a form of neglect, just as child protection agencies do when parents choose to continue living with another adult who has abused their child, regardless of the reason. In "failure to protect" cases, a refusal to change one's living situation for the sake of the child signals an unwillingness to provide adequately for the child, even if reasons for staying are benign, and failure to protect alone can be a sufficient basis for removing a child from parental custody and ultimately terminating parental rights. The situation would be no different conceptually from one in which a parent left a home shared with a child in a good neighborhood, moved by herself to a blighted neighborhood, and refused to return to be with the child because she had grown accustomed to the new surroundings and formed new social connections.

Even with respect to parents who would be willing—delighted even—to accept subsidies and services that facilitate relocation with their children, some might object that making relocation mandatory forcibly divorces parents from supportive social networks.[54] As noted above, however, though neighborhood assessment should take into account such networks, there is substantial evidence that today social networks in blighted urban neighborhoods are quite weak, whereas relocated families in MTO and other voucher programs have been eventually able to enter into stronger networks in the better neighborhoods to which they move.[55] Residents in low-poverty neighborhoods are often initially resistant to entry of voucher users and suspicious of them when they first arrive, but typically they soon after welcome relocated families into their community.[56] And of course, parents would still be able to visit and help their own parents or grandparents living back in the old neighborhood, albeit to a lesser degree. Liberals who support busing children five days a week, from inner-city areas to suburbs, ought to accept the idea that parents forced to relocate might have to get on a bus to see people in the old neighborhood, or might have to ask another family member or friend to bring elderly extended family members out to see the children.

And, of course, some will argue for money solutions that make everyone in urban ghettos happier and better off. I repeat: There's no money, they don't work, children can't wait. Liberals need to justify the state's empowering parents *today* to force a child to live in any of the life-destroying neighborhoods that exist *today*. True, no such neighborhoods should exist. But they do.

Effect on community

It is plausible to suppose the reforms I propose would lead to further deterioration of bad neighborhoods, devolution into complete chaos and rampant violence among the adults who remain, especially if resources are shifted from law enforcement to help pay for relocating children. On the other hand, some might speculate that making people leave one bad place will just result in transplantation of the blight to another place, as with urban renewal.

Emptying the worst neighborhoods of children would likely result in withdrawal of government-provided services and programs, including schools, that create jobs and infuse wealth; reduce already depressed property values; and rob the communities of any vibrancy and civic pride that might now exist. To declare a neighborhood unfit for children is like condemning and evacuating a building, leaving it to crumble, one might argue. However, to conclude from this concern that the state should continue to ignore the impact of community dysfunction on children's welfare when making decisions about the children's lives, one would need to add a further, normative premise along the lines of "the state should not sacrifice the interests of adults who might remain in a community after the children are removed, in order to protect the interests of children." That premise is not at all plausible, for at least two reasons.

First, even if a balancing of adults' and children's interests were appropriate, the state should choose in this context to protect children's interests, because they are clearly weightier. Children's fundamental developmental interests, and indeed survival, are at stake. In contrast, the marginal effect of my proposal on the lives of adults who would remain in condemned neighborhoods would be relatively small. When schools and other government services and programs for children close, some will lose jobs, but they can look for work elsewhere, with competition for the jobs reduced by the exit of many parents. Losses in property values are more likely to be felt by absentee landlords than by residents; in fact, rents might drop for remaining residents.[57] Loss of any existing vitality and pride would inflict just a psychological cost that is modest in comparison with the gain in psychological wellbeing for children. And those who cannot tolerate increased levels of disorder can choose to leave.

Second, such a balancing is not appropriate. Again, when the state presumes to make such profound decisions about the intimate lives of private individuals, which it can justifiably do only because some private individuals are incapable of making the decisions themselves, it must aim to match as closely as possible the decision-making the individuals themselves would do if able. There is no justification for injecting others' interests into the decision calculus. Adults are entitled to, and generally do, decide where they will live without compromising their self-regarding interests to bolster struggling communities. Young children should have an equivalent legal right, protecting their interests rather than their choices, effectuated by the state as surrogate, to exit and stay out of communities unfit for children. They should not be held hostage in horrible neighborhoods to guard against the danger of further deterioration.

Lastly, further community disintegration would not necessarily be the ultimate consequence of facilitating children's exit from currently dysfunctional communities. A public declaration that a community is unfit for children and that the state will pursue a policy of making the community childless might trigger sufficient sympathy for the adults living in that community to generate a combination of (a) more public support for revitalization than has ever before existed and (b) more motivation than ever before among adults living in such a community, including the de facto leaders (who likely have offspring in the neighborhood), to establish sufficient order to get the "no-child" designation lifted. Certainly all the proposals would call public attention to a situation unjust to the children and arguably to the adults as well. More realistically (though still highly speculative), the rezoning might discourage pregnancy among adolescents more effectively than anything else the state can do; teens are more worried than any other age cohort about maintaining peer relationships, and awareness that having a baby means you must move away might make girls and their boyfriends think more seriously about avoiding pregnancy.

As for the fatalistic prediction that the state cannot eliminate problems by moving people, because the problems will move with them, that is much more plausible with respect to state decisions to order *all* residents of an area to evacuate.[58] My "no–child zone" proposal is superior to an all–out condemnation of a neighborhood from a child welfare and public health perspective because it would separate children and their custodial parents (assuming nearly all parents would choose to move) from other residents in unfit communities—in particular, those creating the dangers to children's welfare. It would cause children to grow up in different places with very different influences from what they now experience, leaving as far behind as possible the bulk of those who perpetuate the dysfunction by operating the drug trade and engaging in violence. Of course, some custodial parents are involved in illegal activities, but relocating them could end that involvement. Some people who relocate might retain ties to the inner city, at least for a while, and that might be more likely with people who are coerced into moving than has been the case with people who voluntarily choose to move. This is a fear of receiving communities. But experience with existing programs reveals an eventual shift in focus by parents and children, as they become accepted into, accustomed to, and appreciative of their safer and healthier new environments.[59]

Infringement of adults' constitutional rights

Lastly, let us consider potential constitutional challenges. I noted in the first part of this chapter the civil–liberties objections to other regulatory approaches to addressing inner-city disorder. Courts generally uphold programs that simply condition public benefits on individuals' willingness to go to a different place, as with campuses for the homeless.[60] My proposal is like that insofar as it does not entail directly ordering any adults to move out of blighted neighborhoods, but rather makes such a move a condition for enjoying the benefit of state–conferred legal–parent status.

FREEDOM IN CHOICE OF RESIDENTIAL LOCATION

The freedom to choose where one lives is, as an empirical matter, an important liberty. One strand of judicial doctrine establishes a right to interstate travel under the Equal Protection Clause and Privileges and Immunities Clause. Most cases involve discrimination in conferring government benefits based on length of residence in a particular location (which states and localities have done to discourage poor people from moving in).[61] My proposals entail no discrimination based on length of residency nor any inherent inter–state dimension. There is some discrimination, based on parental status or parental aspiration, but those persons are obviously not similarly situated to people who are not parents or seeking parental status, in terms of the basic child–welfare aim of the reforms, to which my proposal is clearly rationally related.

Some lower courts have found in the Federal Constitution's Fourteenth Amendment Due Process Clause a fundamental right to freedom of *intra*-state travel. One such court addressed a city's excluding persons convicted of drug crimes from residing in, or even entering, certain "drug zones." The Court of Appeals for the Sixth Circuit (covering Michigan, Ohio, Tennessee, and Kentucky) acknowledged that "the City's interest in enacting the Ordinance—to enhance the quality of life in drug-plagued neighborhoods and to protect the health, safety, and welfare of citizens in those areas—represents a compelling government interest," but found the ordinance not sufficiently narrowly tailored to address the problem of drug crime recidivism, and so invalidated the ordinance.[62] That decision might support application of strict scrutiny to my proposals.

The few other courts recognizing such a right, though, have applied less stringent intermediate scrutiny or rational basis review, and most lower courts have declined to recognize constitutional protection of free intrastate travel.[63] The Eighth Circuit, addressing a challenge to a law prohibiting sex offenders from living near schools, found it unnecessary to decide whether there is such a constitutional right, because it determined that the law did not limit anyone's freedom to travel throughout the state, implicitly treating a prohibition on living in a particular place as not restricting one's freedom to travel to that place. Other federal courts consistently uphold restrictions on where sex offenders live, which serve the same broader purpose as my proposals—separating children from unrelated adults who would endanger them by living in the same neighborhoods. Convicted sex offenders have challenged these restrictions not only on the basis of a right to travel but also on the grounds that the restrictions infringed a right of intimate association by impacting their family lives—either forcing other family members also to abide by the restrictions or forcing a family to split up into different residences. Courts have nonetheless generally upheld the restrictions, finding that such restrictions do not infringe a fundamental right and serve sufficiently well the legitimate state interest of protecting children from abuse.

Thus, there is some support at the federal appellate level for attributing a fundamental constitutional right to freedom of intrastate travel and for finding that laws excluding people from particular places infringe that right, but that support is slim and even courts recognizing the right uphold most state laws and local ordinances restricting people's residential choices. It should certainly be relevant that my proposal would not exclude anyone from any city altogether, but would simply, like condemnation actions, require some people to move out of particular neighborhoods, and it would not preclude parents from entering the no-child zones to visit.

Perhaps the most relevant group of lower court decisions under the right to travel umbrella addresses constitutional objections by custodial parents who wish to relocate and who are told they will lose custody to the other parent if they do. One state supreme court has held that such an order violated a custodial parent's constitutional right to travel, but most state appellate courts have held that the best interests of the child are sufficient justification for burdening the custodial parent's exercise of the right to travel.[64]

The closest doctrinal fit for a Fourteenth Amendment challenge to the reforms at issue here, though, would appear to be the substantive due process analysis of land use regulations that limit who can live together in particular localities. The Supreme Court has not established a fundamental right to live where one wishes, but it has struck down a regulation that limited what types of family relationships people are permitted to have in a particular residential area. In *Moore v. City of East Cleveland* (1977) the Court invalidated a local ordinance prohibiting occupancy of a dwelling by persons who did not form a traditional unitary family, when a woman caring for two grandchildren was charged with violating the ordinance because she also had an uncle and cousin of the children living in her house. The plurality opinion (i.e., endorsed by less than a majority) noted that, whereas due process challenges to land use regulation generally trigger only rational basis review (requiring the state to show simply that the regulation is a rational means of serving some legitimate state interest), when a land use regulation has the effect of interfering with family life, a court should apply heightened scrutiny. The plurality then found that the ordinance was not closely related to a compelling state interest, having as its principal ostensible aim the relatively unimportant one of avoiding excessive car traffic in a neighborhood.

An outright ban on children living in unfit communities bears resemblance to the zoning ordinance at issue in *Moore*. It would directly aim at, rather than having the incidental effect of, precluding certain family configurations in certain places. A court might therefore apply heightened scrutiny to such a ban. My proposals for reforming domestic relations and child protection law also directly target family life, but they do not amount to an outright ban on any collection of individuals residing together; they simply make an adult's residential location one factor in a decision as to whether she can share her home with a child. A threshold question would therefore be whether simply making a person's location a relevant consideration burdens the right to live with family where one wishes so much as to constitute an infringement of fundamental liberty rights. Courts would likely answer that question negatively, considering the many protected liberties whose exercise routinely affects custody decisions between parents, but I will assume for the sake of the analysis further below that an infringement would be found, thereby forcing the state to show that considering location in decisions about children's family life is necessary to serve a compelling state interest.

In sum, courts have not been especially protective of individuals' desires to live in particular places, so there is no clear basis or especially strong support for an objection based on a supposed constitutional right to live wherever one wants and to do so without the state imposing costs based on the place one chooses. But because the laws impact family life, courts might well apply heightened scrutiny. I consider below, after discussing other plausible rights claims, whether my proposals could survive such scrutiny.

PARENTAL RIGHTS

Chapter 4 discussed the constitutional rights of biological parents to become legal parents to a child and explained why fitness to parent is a third requirement for biological parents to receive constitutional protection. In the current context, we are concerned with biological parents who are not inherently unfit but living in a neighborhood terribly unsuitable for children. If the state were to say (as it should) that making a child live in a horrible neighborhood constitutes maltreatment, as it does with making a child live in a horrible home environment, then that choice could be deemed to make a birth parent unfit, in which case a birth parent intent on taking a newborn to live in such neighborhood would receive no constitutional guarantee of becoming a legal parent.

Here, though, I will assume biological parents have already been vested with legal parent status, and the pertinent constitutional question is therefore whether they possess a Fourteenth Amendment substantive due process to raise their child where they see fit. A related question is whether they would receive constitutional protection against termination of their parental status, but the answer to that really hinges on the answer to the prior one of a right to choose the residential location of one's child. This is part of the reason why the Supreme Court has never presumed to dictate substantive rules for TPR but rather has only afforded legal parents certain procedural protections in connection with a TPR proceeding.

The Court has consistently held that legal parents receive some constitutional protection of their parenting actions and choices under the Due Process Clause. In cases not also involving a religious free-exercise claim, the Court has appeared to apply rational basis review.[65] In its most recent decision, *Troxel v. Granville*, the plurality opinion seemed to treat a parental substantive due process right simpliciter as a fairly weak right, requiring only that the state accord some presumption or deference to legal parents' views of the child's best interests when a third party demands visitation with a child.[66] The Court did not reject the best-interests test as a basis for overriding parental wishes. So parents would receive some constitutional protection for residential choices, but not very strong protection.

If a court would apply merely rational basis review, simply starting with a modest presumption that parents' residential choice is in their child's best interests, it should be easy for a state or municipality to defend any of the proposals in this chapter. These proposals have the aim and effect of causing some children to live in decent communities rather than neighborhoods that endanger their welfare, and avoiding dangers to children's welfare is clearly a legitimate state interest. If children are living in hellish surroundings because of parental choice, then, as with parents found living under a bridge with children, the presumption of their acting in a child's best interests should be easily overcome. If they are not there because of choice, the constitutional right to make parenting choices would not even come into play.

If the proposals advanced here would instead be subjected to strict scrutiny, a court would demand a showing that they are necessary to serve a compelling state interest. The Supreme Court has consistently treated protection of children's health and safety as a compelling state interest, even in cases where the only interest of children at stake was an interest in somewhat better education. In the case of unfit communities, not only children's educational interest, but their very survival is at stake. The real challenge for the government would be to show there is no less intrusive way of effectively protecting the children. With respect to the proposal for declaring communities unfit and prohibiting residence by children in them, complaining parties might assert that states should be required to eliminate the community dysfunctions that pervade children's lives in the nation's worst neighborhoods, rather than aiming to evacuate children from those places. But no court is going to hold that the state may not limit a parent's harmful choices when it might be theoretically possible for the state to transform the world in such a way that the choices do not result in harm. Imagine in the affirmative action cases, for example, if the Court said Texas or some other state must, rather than considering race in admissions to universities, transform social circumstances in the state so that opportunities throughout life are equal for people of all races. Community dysfunction in the worst urban areas runs so deep, and arises to a large extent from private conduct the state cannot completely control, that no amount of money is going to make it functional and suitable for children, certainly not overnight. So when an individual parent challenges her coerced relocation, and the state says "we are protecting your child," she will get nowhere by retorting "change my community instead." And it is hard to imagine a third way of sparing that child from the harm of growing up in that community. Significantly, courts have not required states or localities to find ways of eliminating blight without moving people out when they condemn areas and declare them unsuitable for any human habitation. And in the analogous context of declaring homes unfit, states now routinely dictate that certain homes must be child-free, because of the adults who live there and the conditions those adults create, and that practice is not deemed constitutionally problematic, and it would be much more feasible for the state itself to improve conditions within individual homes than in entire communities. In addition, courts in child protection proceedings are increasingly ordering an abusive parent out of the house so the child can remain, thereby denying that parent both the freedom to live wherever he wishes and custody of his child, for the sake of protecting the child's welfare.

What a court might require the state to do, when it orders evacuation of children from unfit communities or when it threatens to deny legal parent status or custody to someone, is to provide adequate relocation assistance. As to any parents who would be willing to relocate if they had the resources, but who are truly unable to afford to do so, providing relocation assistance is clearly a preferable and perhaps constitutionally man- datory alternative to severing the parents' connection with children. Thus, a potential strategy for forcing states to provide greater funding for relocation programs than they currently do might actually be to first advance a constitutional claim on behalf of chil- dren, challenging state laws that cause them to live in horrible neighborhoods, and then, when the state commands that children may not live in such places, to advance a constitutional claim by parents against the state's effectively forcing them to relocate without providing the necessary assistance for them to do so.

In sum, then, adults adversely affected as a result of the legal system considering the quality of the community they live in when determining parentage or custody of a child cannot plausibly object that they are being unfairly punished, that doing so would have an unjustifiable impact on an historically subordinate group or on a community, that doing so would not in fact help children, or that their constitutional rights are being violated. This is true also of zoning the worst residential areas adult-only, because evacuating children from those places is the only realistic way of serving the state's compelling aim—and moral and constitutional obligation—to avoid forcing children to live in terribly unsafe and unhealthy environments. Adversely affected persons might have a valid complaint against a society and an economic system that tolerates great dis- parities in wealth and horrible living conditions for some, and that does too little to help people overcome damaging childhoods, but that complaint does not warrant forcing the next generation to be subjected to the same horrible living conditions and damaged in the same ways. At most, those adults might have a constitutional right to state assistance in relocating.

Conclusion

Growing up in a dangerous and unhealthy neighborhood is neither inevitable nor excusable for any child. For many, it is difficult to see that children's presence in such places is a contingent fact, representing a policy choice on the state's part. But it is a choice and requires defense, given that children have a presumptive moral and constitu- tional right against the state's placing them into relationships with, and the custody of, adults who live in such places. The state could do otherwise, and I have proposed reforms by which the state could ensure children do not grow up in such places. The weakness of the objections to those proposals suggests that the current state of affairs is in fact indefensible.

Implementing the proposed changes to domestic relations and child protection law would not pose significant practical difficulties or public cost. When children are already in the child protective system or already the subject of other court proceedings because of a dispute between legal parents, it is a simple matter to add neighborhood quality to the factors informing decisions. In child-protection cases, this might result in more children being placed into families with adults who are not biological parents or relatives, so might increase foster care costs to an uncertain degree. In disputes between parents or between two applicants for adoption, taking into account neighborhood quality imposes no additional cost on the state other than some additional evidence taking.

The more difficult component of the reforms, obviously, is mandating relocations. Moving can certainly be arduous for adults and children, especially if going to an entirely new community. Policing exclusion of children could be difficult; a parent could keep a child hidden away in an apartment to avoid detection. But as a neighborhood becomes near-childless, perhaps few parents would want to remain in them anyway and a child's presence would be more conspicuous to neighbors, who might report violations. Some transplanted youths might seek to return, maintain or develop gang and drug-trade involvement, or bring behavioral problems to the new location. But policing against return would be little different from the enforcement of curfews police now do, and any concerns regarding older children will arise only when a neighborhood is first declared unfit, because any relocations later in time should only be of newborns. Further, some special attention should be paid, by a different office in the local social services department, to non-parent adults left behind who have been dependent for care on those who leave and who might now need the state to provide transportation or alternative caregivers.

Further complexity arises at the administrative level. Given neighborhood dynamism, governing regulations would need to account for change in community conditions over time, positive or negative, and guard against repeated changes in a neighborhood's status in order to create some stability. That should be fairly simple, though. A positive change in status, it is worth noting, could be an occasion for a great public celebration, which in turn could recommit residents to creating the best possible community environment for children and inspire other dysfunction-plagued communities. Additionally, though, the power to declare neighborhoods unfit is one susceptible to abuse for reasons of political strategy, personal gain by politicians, and race- or class-based prejudice. Residents would need to have effective recourse to administrative or judicial proceedings to participate in or challenge zoning decisions, but that is generally already true today.

The practical complexities, potential costs, and political obstacles to no-child zoning have repeatedly tempted me to say "forget that idea," but I keep coming back to this: It is a horrible injustice to children for us to force them to grow up in this country's worst neighborhoods, and they are entitled to force us to FIGURE IT OUT, and to GET THEM OUT at the earliest possible time. I hope some readers more knowledgeable about housing and urban policy than I, rather than quickly dismissing and forgetting the idea, will accept as an intellectual challenge—a thought experiment—to try to figure out how to use no-child zoning or something like it to give these children, all of them, a decent chance at a decent life.

Notes

1 See Cambria (2016).
2 See Wogan (2015); Reynolds and Rohlin (2015, 1–15) (discussing the literature and results of the authors' study); Rich and Stoker (2010, 775–96); see also Olsen and Ludwig (2013, 208) (stating that President Johnson's Model Cities program "seems to have had no significant long-term impact"); Turner *et al.* (2009, 4) ("The Urban Renewal policies of the 1950s and '60s, which were meant to revitalize downtown areas, further exacerbated the problem of racial concentration").

3 See, for example, Elliott *et al.* (2006, 294, 297); Smith and Fong (2004, 216–18); Gonzalez (2011).

4 See generally Li (2016); Turner *et al.* (2009, 4) ("While Urban Renewal projects effectively removed urban slums and created new business districts, little of the private housing for blacks was restored. With the acquiescence of the federal government, local governments and private developers displaced former minority slum dwellers to public housing in already-segregated neighborhoods, further exacerbating patterns of racial segregation and creating pockets of severe poverty").

5 See Crouch and Moskop (2014).

6 For example, Siegel-Hawley (2015).

7 See Dwyer (2002).

8 See Schneider (2017, 21); St. John *et al.* (2015, 128–9, 142–4).

9 See Pilutik (2013).

10 Garnett (2010).

11 See Chetty *et al.* (2016, 855–902); Turner *et al.* (2009, 80–2); Curley (2007, 73) (asserting that MTO, "was successful in dramatically improving housing and neighborhood conditions for families," who generally integrated into a new social network rather than recreating the old one in a new place); Kingsley (2009, 266–7); Rosenbaum *et al.* (2005, 156–8). One possible exception is that a greater percentage (~7 percent) of relocated adolescent boys in the Moving to Opportunity program manifested emotional and behavioral disorders, relative to a control group that was not offered relocation vouchers. See Kessler *et al.* (2014, 937–47). But it is unknown whether the relocation caused the disorders, and they occurred for a rather small percentage of the youths.

12 Rubinowitz and Rosenbaum (2002).

13 See Chyn (2016).

14 Popkin (2016, 51, 53, 57).

15 Popkin (2016, 74).

16 See, for example, Jonsson (2016) (quoting Harvard sociologist Robert Sampson, who has himself documented the fateful effects of neighborhood environment on children, as saying "The problem with [focusing on moving people out of bad neighborhoods] is that people don't necessarily want to leave their communities ... That means we have to provide opportunities for people in the places [they] live").

17 Hochschild (2003); see also Jonsson (2016) (quoting the director of the Center for the Study of Southern Culture as saying "I reject this whole idea of ... 'What's wrong with those people—why don't they move from lowest to the middle to the top?'... Any type of explanation that starts to sound like the problem is internal to the group itself just runs into all sorts of historical and ethical objections").

18 Cf. Appelbaum (2015) (reporting the assessment of a mother who relocated to a nice suburban area under a housing-subsidy program that aims to manipulate residents of the worst neighborhoods in Dallas to move to much more affluent neighborhoods, who acknowledged the costs of moving, such as teenagers' struggles to fit into a new peer group, but said such costs "are nothing compared with the feeling that she and her family are now safe").

19 Census tracts are "smaller and more socially homogeneous [relative to 'neighborhoods'] areas of roughly three thousand to five thousand residents; their boundaries are usually drawn to take into account major streets, parks, and other geographical features." Sampson (2000, 207).

20 See Edin and Nelson (2013, 14); Edin and Kefalas (2005, 14).

21 To a large extent, these are simply the obverse of conditions I have identified as characterizing harmful community environments—for example, ample adult role models; employment opportunities; neighbors comfortable being outdoors where they interact, create support networks, and keep an eye on other parents' children; good schools with capable and caring teachers; and good low-cost medical facilities. Others include the existence of a nurse–family partnership program and good, affordable daycare. See Garbarino *et al.* (2005, 308–11); Sampson (2000, 211–12, 214–15).

22 See Kurre (2003, 109).

23 Citizen's Committee for Children of New York (2016); see also Turner *et al.* (2009, 86).

24 See, for example, Turner *et al.* (2009, 87) (noting that some applicants for housing vouchers must wait years); Tegeler (2015, 210–11) (noting that demand for relocation assistance currently far exceeds supply).

25 Hartman and Squires (2010, 5).
26 In some places, litigation has been brought to require changes to or expansion of government programs of relocation assistance. See Shaw (2008) (discussing relocation in the Chicago area); Siegel (2006) (discussing litigation over housing subsidy programs in Baltimore).
27 See Sard and Rice (2014).
28 Sard and Rice (2014, 6); Turner *et al.* (2009, 87).
29 See Sard and Rice (2014).
30 Turner *et al.* (2009, 17); Sard and Rice (2014, 84); O'Neil (2008, 121–2).
31 Current federal regulations governing federally-funding housing voucher programs prohibit discrimination against families with children but do not require giving them priority. 24 C.F.R. 982.202(b). They give local public housing agencies some discretion in setting priorities, and at least three do now give preference to families with children—Cedar Rapids, Iowa; DuPage County, Illinois; and Southeastern Minnesota.
32 See, for example, Va. Code Ann. § 15.2–931 (2009) ("It has been and is continuing to be the policy of the Commonwealth to authorize each locality … to prevent blight and other environmental degradation…"); Va. Code Ann. § 36–49 (2009) (providing provisions for the adoption of redevelopment plans to address blighted areas); 35 Pa. Cons. Stat. §§ 1701–1719.2 (2008) (Pennsylvania's Urban Redevelopment Law, the purpose of which is the clearance, reconstruction, and rehabilitation of blighted areas); N.J. Stat. Ann. § 40A:12A-5 (West 2009) (authorizing evacuation of persons from areas deemed in need of redevelopment, identified on the basis of considerations such as: "The generality of buildings are substandard, unsafe, unsanitary, dilapidated, or obsolescent, or possess any of such characteristics, or are so lacking in light, air, or space, as to be conducive to unwholesome living or working conditions," "[t]he discontinuance of the use of buildings previously used for commercial, manufacturing, or industrial purposes; the abandonment of such buildings; or the same being allowed to fall into so great a state of disrepair as to be untenantable," and "[a]reas with buildings or improvements which, by reason of dilapidation, obsolescence, overcrowding, faulty arrangement or design, lack of ventilation, light and sanitary facilities, excessive land coverage, deleterious land use or obsolete layout, or any combination of these or other factors, are detrimental to the safety, health, morals, or welfare of the community"). Cf. Kelo v. City of New London, 545 U.S. 469, 473 (2005) (addressing takings of property following state's declaration that New London was a "distressed municipality").
33 See, for example, N.C. Gen. Stat. Ann. § 160A-503(a) (2010) (defining "blighted parcel" to include properties whose existence contributes to juvenile delinquency and crime or is "detrimental to the public health, safety, morals, or welfare"); Ga. Code Ann. § 22–1-1(1) (2017) (defining blight by reference to conditions that include repeated illegal activity and being "conducive to ill health, transmission of disease, infant mortality, or crime"); Ala. Code § 24–2-1 (2006).
34 See Appelbaum (2015).
35 See, for example, Zezima (2008) (discussing creation of "safe zones" in New Bedford, Massachusetts where sex offenders are not permitted to enter, including public libraries).
36 See Cisneros *et al.* (2009, 150–75); Rosenbaum *et al.* (2005, 150–75). Federal law authorizing housing subsidy programs is found at 42 U.S.C.A. § 1437f (West 2009). Cf. Federal Uniform Relocation Assistance Act, 42 U.S.C. § 4601–55 (2006) (requiring relocation assistance to property owners and tenants when federal agencies or state and local governments using federal money condemn properties).
37 See Rosenbaum *et al.* (2005, 150–75); Bebow and Olivo (2005); Korte (2008, A1).
38 Korte (2008) (noting resistance to entry of housing voucher holders in large numbers into middle-class neighborhoods); Goering (2005, 127–49); Rosenbaum *et al.* (2005, 150–75).
39 See 42 U.S.C.A. § 1437f(x).
40 See, for example, Kneebone and Raphael (2011, 14) ("[W]e find very little evidence that the decentralization of poverty and minority households has contributed to higher crime in distant suburbs. Our results clearly indicate that demographic changes in the nation's suburbs, if anything, lower crime rates all else held equal").
41 See Chetty (2016, 856, 858).
42 See, for example, Lewis-McCoy (2014).
43 Olsen (1993).

44 Cf. DeShaney v. Winnebago Cty. Dep't Soc. Servs., 489 U.S. 189 (1989).

45 See, for example, Nicini v. Morra, 212 F.3d 798, 809–12 (3d Cir. 2000) (adopting a "delib-erate indifference" standard to selection of foster parents and citing decisions of other courts applying similar standard); Kenny A. v. Perdue, No. 1:02-CV-1686-MHS, 2004 WL 5503780, at *3–4 (N.D. Ga. Dec. 13, 2004) (holding that children have a substantive due process right to the state's selecting foster parents on the basis of a "professional judgment").

46 See, for example, Masulli Reyes et al. (2014) ("Yvonne Brooks is sickened by the ongoing bloodshed in her East Side neighborhood. But Wilmington is her home …").

47 See Kurre (2003, 109); Sherman (2006).

48 See Desmond (2016, 3).

49 On the benefits of mixed-race communities, see Burch (2014, 223–47) (reporting on a study finding that incarceration of blacks in highly-segregated counties in North Carolina was twice that of blacks in more integrated counties, after controlling for income and rates of crime, poverty, unemployment, homeownership, and other factors); Turner et al. (2009, Ch. 2).

50 See Department of Housing & Urban Development (2015).

51 Luo et al. (2010, 10) (explaining the enormous growth of temporary employment in counties which were at the lowest levels of temporary employment).

52 See, for example, McMillan (2012, 134) ("Family Treatment Court clients were routinely required to choose between their partner and their children … CWS workers' standard response was, 'You're right, we can't tell you who to be friends with. We can, however, decline to return your children if we feel the environment you provide for them is unsafe.'")

53 See Schultz (2005, 212).

54 This is the primary explanation for the low rate among housing voucher recipients of exit out of high-poverty areas; people wish to retain their social and support networks. See Skobba and Goetz (2013).

55 See, for example, Smith and Fong (2004, 57ff, 214–18) (discussing the destructive effect of pervasive crime on social networks in impoverished neighborhoods); Varady and Walker (2003, 26).

56 See, for example, Rosenbaum et al. (2005, 158).

57 Landlords, incidentally, could not demand compensation for this loss of value, because the zoning would not deprive the properties of all value and would not substantially defeat any reasonable investment-backed expectation). Cf. Murr v. Wisconsin, 137 S.Ct. 1933, 1942–1943 (discussing "guidelines" for addressing claims of "regulatory takings").

58 See Curley (2007, 71, 85) (discussing this problem with respect to the component of the federal Hope VI program that involves rebuilding housing projects).

59 Rosenbaum et al. (2005, 161–70); Kingsley (2009, 266).

60 See Garnett (2005, 1125–6).

61 See Schragger (2016, 107).

62 Johnson v. City of Cincinnati, 310 F.3d 484, 493 (6th Cir. 2002). The court reaffirmed that analysis and holding in Cole v. City of Memphis, 839 F.3d 530, 537 (6th Cir. 2016), cert. denied sub nom. City of Memphis, Tenn. v. Cole, 137 S. Ct. 2220 (2017), while also holding that intermediate scrutiny would apply to more modest restrictions on presence in certain places, such as a curfew.

63 See Doe v. Miller, 405 F.3d 700, 712–13 (8th Cir. 2005) (citing cases).

64 See, for example, Baxendale v. Raich, 878 N.E.2d 1252, 1259 (Ind. 2008) (holding that order changing custody to father if mother moves to another state did not violate mother's right to travel because the burden on her relationship with her children was modest and was justified by the children's best interests) (citing similar decisions in other states).

65 See Meyer (2006, 141–2). A clergy member whose ministry is in the ghetto might also have a free exercise claim. Wisconsin v. Yoder, 406 U.S. 205 (1972) applied strict scrutiny to a parental free exercise claim, but it is unclear whether that is still good law after Employment Div. v. Smith 494 U.S. 872 (1990), and, if so, to what extent it applies to groups other than the Amish. In any event, the Supreme Court's decision in favor of Amish parents rested on a conclusion that this would result in no detriment to the children at all. In two other parental free exercise cases, the Court decided against the parents, because it perceived risk of harm. See Dwyer (2011).

66 Cf. Troxel v. Granville, 530 U.S. 57 (2000).

Bibliography

Appelbaum, Binyamin. "Vouchers Help Families Move Far from Public Housing." *New York Times*, July 7, 2015, sec. Economy.

Bebow, John and Antonio Olivo. "CHA Moves Tenants Out—But Not Up: Ex-Residents Still Live in Struggling, Segregated Areas." *Chicago Tribune*, February 27, 2005.

Burch, Traci. "The Old Jim Crow: Racial Residential Segregation and Neighborhood Imprisonment." *Law & Policy* 36(3) (2014): 223–55.

Cambria, Nancy. "The Crisis within: How Toxic Stress and Trauma Endanger Our Children." *St. Louis Post-Dispatch*, February 21, 2016, sec. The Crisis.

Chetty, Raj, John N. Friedman, and Jonah E. Rockoff. "Measuring the Impacts of Teachers II: Teacher Value-Added and Student Outcomes in Adulthood," *American Economic Review* 104(9) (2014): 2633–79.

Chetty, Raj, Nathaniel Hendren, and Lawrence F. Katz. "The Effects of Exposure to Better Neighborhoods on Children: New Evidence from the Moving to Opportunity Project," *American Economic Review* 106(4) (2016): 855–902.

Chyn, Eric. Working Paper: "Moved to Opportunity: The Long-Run Effect of Public Housing Demolition on Labor Market Outcomes of Children" (2016).

Cisneros, Henry G. and Lora Engdahl (eds.). *From Despair to Hope: Hope VI and the New Promise of Public Housing in America's Cities*. Washington, DC: Brookings Institution Press, 2009.

Citizens' Committee for Children of New York. *Citizen's Committee for Children of New York: Community Risk Ranking: Child Well-Being in New York City's 59 Community Districts*. New York: Citizens' Committee for Children of New York, Inc., 2016.

"Creating Options," Commentary in Owen Fiss, *A Way Out: America's Ghettos and the Legacy of Racism*. Princeton, NJ: Princeton University Press, 2003, 68–73.

Crouch, Elisa and Walker Moskop. "Poverty and Academic Struggle Go Hand-in-Hand." *St. Louis Post-Dispatch*, May 17, 2014, sec. Education.

Curley, Alexandra M. "Children and the State: Dispersing the Poor: New Directions in Public Housing Policy, in Child Poverty in America Today." Chap. 5, In *Child Poverty in America Today*, edited by Barbara A. Arrighi and David J. Maume, Vol. 4, 73. Westport, CT: Praeger, 2007.

Department of Housing & Urban Development, "Housing Choice Voucher Program: Streamlining the Portability Process," 24 CFR Part 982 (2015).

Desmond, Matthew. *Evicted: Profit and Poverty in the American City*. New York: Crown, 2016.

Dwyer, James G. *Vouchers within Reason: A Child-Centered Approach to Education Reform*. Ithaca, NY: Cornell University Press, 2002.

Dwyer, James G. "A Constitutional Birthright: The State, Parentage, and the Rights of Newborn Persons," *UCLA Law Review* 56 (2009): 755–835.

Dwyer, James G. "The Good, the Bad, and the Ugly of Employment Division v. Smith for Family Law," *Cardozo Law Review* 23(5) (2011): 1781–90.

Edin, Kathryn and Maria Kefalas. *Promises I Can Keep: Why Poor Women Put Motherhood Before Marriage*. Berkeley, CA: University of California Press, 2005.

Edin, Kathryn and Timothy J. Nelson. *Doing the Best I Can: Fatherhood in the Inner City*. CA: University of California Press, 2013.

Elliott, Delbert S. *et al. Good Kids from Bad Neighborhoods: Successful Development in Social Context*. New York: Cambridge University Press, 2006.

Garbarino, James, Catherine P. Bradshaw, and Kathleen Kostelny. "Neighborhood and Community Influences on Parenting." In *Parenting: An Ecological Perspective*, edited by Tom Luster and Lynn Okagaki. 2nd ed. New York: Routledge, 2005.

Garnett, Nicole Stelle. "Relocating Disorder." *Virginia Law Review* 91(5) (2005): 1075–134.

Garnett, Nicole Stelle. *Ordering the City: Land Use, Policing, and the Restoration of Urban America*. New Haven, CT: Yale University Press, 2010.

Goering, John. "Expanding Housing Choice and Integrating Neighborhoods: The MTO Experiment." Chap. 6, In *The Geography of Opportunity: Race and Housing Choice in Metropolitan America*, edited by Xavier de Souza Briggs, 127. Washington, DC: The Brookings Institution, 2005.

Gonzalez, David. "In the South Bronx, Blight Returns to a Rehabilitated Block." *New York Times*, January 6, 2011, sec. NY/Region.

Hartman, Chester and Gregory D. Squires. "Integration Exhaustion, Race Fatigue, and the American Dream." In *The Integration Debate: Competing Futures for American Cities*, edited by C. Hartman and G.D. Squires, 1–8. New York: Routledge, 2010.

Henriquez, Sandra B. Department of Housing & Urban Development, "Public Housing and Section 8 Program: Housing Choice Voucher Program: Streamlining the Portability Process," 24 CFR Part 982 (2015): 18731–8.

Hochschild, Jennifer. "Creating Options." In *A Way Out: America's Ghettos and the Legacy of Racism*, edited by Joshua Cohen *et al*. Princeton, NJ: Princeton University Press, 2003.

Jonsson, Patrik. "In Poor Neighborhoods, Is It Better to Fix Up Or Move Out?" *The Christian Science Monitor* (April 4, 2016).

Kessler, Ronald C., Greg J. Duncan, and Lisa A. Gennetian. "Associations of Housing Mobility Interventions for Children in High-Poverty Neighborhoods with Subsequent Mental Disorders during Adolescence," *Jama* 311(9) (2014): 937–48.

Kingsley, G. Thomas. "Taking Advantage of What We Have Learned." In *From Despair to Hope: Hope VI and the New Promise of Public Housing in America's Cities*, edited by Henry G. Cisneros, Lora Engdahl and Kurt L. Schmoke, 266–7. Washington, DC: Brookings Institution Press, 2009.

Kneebone, Elizabeth and Steven Raphael. *City and Suburban Crime Trends in Metropolitan America*. Washington, DC: Brookings, 2011.

Korte, Gregory. "Subsidized Housing Redefining Suburbia." *Cincinnati Enquirer*, September 14, 2008.

Kurre, James A. "Is the Cost of Living Less in Rural Areas?" *International Regional Science Review* 26(1) (January 1, 2003): 86–109.

Lewis-McCoy, R. L'Heureux. *Inequality in the Promised Land: Race, Resources, and Suburban Schooling*. Stanford, CA: Stanford University Press, 2014.

Li, Bethany. "Now is the Time! Challenging Resegregation and Displacement in the Age of Hypergentrification," *Fordham Law Review* 85(3) (2016): 1189–242.

Luo, Tian, Amar Mann, and Richard Holden. "Temporary Help: The Expanding Role of Temporary Help Services from 1990 to 2008," *Monthly Labor Review* (August 2010): 3–16.

Masulli Reyes, Jessica *et al*. "Wilmington Suspects Get Younger, But Their Guns Are More Powerful," *Delaware Online* (2014).

McMillan, Heidee. *Therapeutic Justice and Addicted Parents: A Family Treatment Court Evaluation Lfb Scholarly Pub LLC* (2012).

Meyer, David D. "Parenthood in a Time of Transition: Tensions between Legal, Biological, and Social Conceptions of Parenthood," *The American Journal of Comparative Law* 54 (2006): 125–44.

Olsen, Edgar O. and Jens Ludwig. "Performance and Legacy of Housing Policies." In *Legacies of the War on Poverty*, edited by Martha J. Bailey and Sheldon Danziger, 208. New York: Russel Sage Foundation, 2013.

Olsen, Francis. "Feminist Critiques of the Public/Private Distinction," *Constitutional Commentary* 10 (1993): 319–27.

O'Neil, Jennifer L. "Housing Mobility Counseling." In *Public Housing and the Legacy of Segregation*, edited by Margery Austin Turner, Susan J. Popkin, and Lynette Rawlings. Washington, DC: Urban Institute Press, 2008.

Pilutik, Scott. "Frisk Assessment: Mayor Bloomberg's Efficiency Arguments about Stop-and-Frisk Are Wrong, as Well as Irrelevant." *Slate* (August 19, 2013).

Popkin, Susan J. *No Simple Solutions: Transforming Public Housing in Chicago*. Lanham, MD: Rowman & Littlefield, 2016.

Reynolds, Curtis Lockwood and Shawn M. Rohlin. "The Effects of Location-based Tax Policies on the Distribution of Household Income: Evidence from the Federal Empowerment Zone Program," *Journal of Urban Economics* 88(C) (2015): 1–15.

Rich, Michael J. and Robert P. Stoker. "Rethinking Empowerment: Evidence from Local Empowerment Zone Programs," *Urban Affairs Review* 45 (2010): 775–96.

Rosenbaum, James, Stefanie DeLuca, and Tammy Tuck. "New Capabilities in New Places: Low-Income Black Families in Suburbia." In *The Geography of Opportunity: Race and Housing Choice in Metropolitan America*, edited by Xavier de Souza Briggs, 150–75. Washington, DC: Brookings Institution Press, 2005.

Rubinowitz, Leonard and James E. Rosenbaum *Crossing the Class and Color Lines: From Public Housing to White Suburbia*. Chicago, IL: University of Chicago Press, 2002.

Sampson, Robert. "The Neighborhood Context of Investing in Children: Facilitating Mechanisms and Undermining Risks." In *Securing the Future: Investing in Children from Birth to College*, edited by Danziger, Sheldon and Jane Waldfogel, 205–7, 2000.

Sard, Barbara and Douglas Rice. *Creating Opportunity for Children: How Housing Location can make a Difference*. Washington, DC: Center on Budget and Policy Priorities, 2014.

Schneider, Jack. *Beyond Test Scores: A Better Way to Measure School Quality*. Cambridge, MA: Harvard University Press, 2017.

Schragger, Richard. *City Power: Urban Governance in a Global Age*. 1st ed. New York: Oxford University Press, 2016.

Schultz, David. "What's Yours Can Be Mine: Are There Any Private Takings After Kelo v. City of New London, *UCLA Journal of Environmental Law and Policy* 24(1) (2005): 195–234.

Shaw, Bob. "The War Over Affordable Housing." *Pioneer Press*, June 28, 2008, sec. News.

Sherman, Jennifer. "Coping with Rural Poverty: Economic Survival and Moral Capital in Rural America," *Social Forces* 85(2) (2006): 891–913.

Siegel, Eric. "U.S. Judge Is Asked to Order Housing for Poor in Suburbs." *Baltimore Sun*, March 21, 2006.

Siegel-Hawley, Genevieve. "Tearing Down Fences: School Boundary Lines and Equal Educational Opportunity in the Twenty-First Century." In *The Enduring Legacy of Rodriguez: Creating New Pathways to Equal Educational Opportunity*, edited by Charles J. Ogletree and Kimberly J. Robinson, 183–99. Cambridge, MA: Harvard Education Press, 2015.

Skobba, Kimberly and Edward Goetz. "Mobility Decisions of very Law-Income Households," *Cityscape: A Journal of Policy Development and Research* 15(2) (2013): 155–61.

Smith, Margaret G. and Rowena Fong. *The Children of Neglect: When No One Cares*, 216–17. New York: Brunner-Routledge, 2004.

St. John, Edward P., Victoria J. Milazzo Bigelow, Kim Callahan Lijana, and Johanna C. Massé. *Left Behind: Urban High Schools and the Failure of Market Reform*. Baltimore, MD: John Hopkins University Press, 2015.

Tegeler, Philip D. "The Persistence of Segregation in Government Housing Programs." Chap. 9. In *The Geography of Opportunity: Race and Housing Choice in Metropolitan America*, edited by Xavier de Souza Briggs, 197–210–11. Washington, DC: The Brookings Institution, 2015.

Turner, Margery Austin, Susan J. Popkin, and Lynette Rawlings. *Public Housing and the Legacy of Segregation*. Washington, DC: The Urban Institute Press, 2009.

Varady, David P. and Carole C. Walker. "Housing Vouchers and Residential Mobility," *Journal of Planning Literature* 18(1) (August 1, 2003): 17–26.

Wogan, J.B. "Obama Tries to End the Cycle of Broken Poverty Promises." *Governing* (July 2015).

Zezima, Katie. "After Rape, Calls to Limit Where Sex Offenders Go." *New York Times*, February 18, 2008.

Part III

Liberal supports for the cycle

In addition to insisting endlessly that government should spend more on anti-poverty programs, and in addition to opposing any child-welfare focused measures that might occasion additional suffering or loss of liberty for poor adults, adult-centered liberals endorse their own set of supposed child-welfare policies that are, in reality, aimed at protecting parents and communities but, in practice, detrimental to children. Liberals' opposition to child-centered reforms and promotion of adult-centered policies collectively operate to ensure another generation will suffer the same fate as the adults whom liberals strive to protect, and therefore also to perpetuate community pathology. Liberals have often convinced legislatures, by misusing social science, to adopt all sorts of programs aimed at avoiding separating children from parents, programs that, one after another, show little or no signs of success but make liberals feel better because they can say that they are trying. There is no end to the experimental programs ACLs promote with the false hope that the magical formula for fixing damaged parents has finally been discovered. Liberals never admit that their policy positions and pet programs protect parents at the expense of children, but instead implausibly deny any conflict of interests exists between children and their birth parents or communities, defending this view, if they even acknowledge the potential for conflict, with illogical arguments and unsupportable empirical claims.

Chapter 6

Liberals' search for the Holy Grail

It is common to characterize the modern history of child-protection policy as a swinging pendulum, as if a single force were aimlessly swaying back and forth, never finding the right position, going too far in one direction then too far in another. It might better be characterized as a contest between opposing forces, a soccer game perhaps. On one side are the defenders of poor and minority-race parents and communities, trying to kick the policy ball from many different angles toward the goal of universal biological-parent success within thriving communities. On the other side is a varied group with varied motivations whose shared goal is to prevent damage to children early in life from maltreatment or community dysfunction. Some on the Child Saver side are advocates for children, others might be primarily concerned to reduce the many social costs caused by child maltreatment and the inter-generational cycle (foster care, policing, medical care, ineffectual public schools, etc.).

The ball actually never gets too far from midfield. When the Child Savers have some success, the Adult Protectors get riled up about the disparate impact child saving is having on poor minority-race parents and communities, as children are removed from them at a higher rate, and they push back with insistence that this adult suffering is unnecessary and the policies are hurting children too and the system is broken and there is a promising new pilot program that sympathetic social scientists will show to be the solution that makes everyone happy and free. When the Parent Protectors' pet programs prove unsuccessful and more children suffer maltreatment and impermanence, the Child Savers persuade policy makers to legislate a more hard-nosed approach, intensifying the state response to signs of parental dysfunction, tightening timelines for rehabilitation, moving more children more quickly to different families in different communities. But this has a disparate impact, and liberal policy makers back down again when charged with racism, upper-class arrogance, imperialism, genocide, and so forth. And once again the Parent Protectors have a very promising pilot program, and gullible legislators are persuaded by bad research that this new approach is the one that will 'heal families' and save the government a lot of money. This chapter surveys the history of ACLs' empty promises to protect children while also (and primarily) protecting parents and communities.

I should preface description of this string of failed initiatives by reminding that what ACLs *most* want (in theory) is massive spending on anti-poverty programs.[1] I support that myself. Short of that, we liberals would be happy to see far greater investment of public resources in day care, nurse–family partnerships, paid parental leave, health care, etc. But there is no more money, so the following constitute ACLs' ever-evolving alternative strategy for protecting dysfunctional parents.

The magic pill for reducing maltreatment rates

The prevailing liberal attitude toward child maltreatment entails an unshakable belief that the disproportionate rate of minority-race parents in reports, findings, and removals is a reflection of bias on the part of mandatory reporters and CPS, as well as a conviction that the proper response to any maltreatment charges against poor people that are genuine is to offer assistance for as long as the parents keep trying. The first aspect of this liberal view has led to calls for retraining of CPS workers, the content of which is mysterious and undoubtedly varied but the clear aim of which is to leave in parental custody more black children reported as abused or neglected. The second aspect has led to a succession of policy initiatives that has included: Intensive Family Preservation Services, Family Drug Courts, and Differential Response.

The race–disproportionality debacle

A long-standing complaint on the Left has been that black children, though only 14 percent of the child population in the US, compose a quarter to a third of the child foster care population.[2] For many years, up until 2011, the topic was a subject of great debate in the child-welfare policy arena and an impetus to agency reform in many jurisdictions. Liberal advocates for minority-race adults insisted disproportionate foster care rates—the "Containment of Children of Color"[3]— reflected racial bias, and that the lives of many black children would go far better if we could simply eliminate that bias. Annette Appell, for example, wrote in 1997:

> Nationwide, juvenile courts and child protection agencies target hundreds of thousands of mothers who are disproportionately poor and of color, even though child abuse and neglect is not confined to any social class or race. The protective systems … specifically identify and treat these mothers based largely on race, class, and gender…. [An] "othering" of poor families, particularly when they are of color, makes it easy for the dominant culture to devalue them: to view them as dysfunctional and not families at all. Just as these families are not families, these mothers are not really mothers. They deviate from the normative notions of mother and womanhood and are defined as bad. The result is an often punitive, rather than empowering, system focused more on mothers than on their children.[4]

In addition to harming individual parents and children, ACLs charged, the race-bias-driven mass removal of black children from parental custody was destroying "the black family" and "the black community,"[5] which of course leads to "situating" the phenomenon within the usual historical "narrative" that starts with slavery.[6] Many also falsely charge that children are in greater danger in foster care than at home with parents who have been reported for maltreatment,[7] when in fact the reported maltreatment rate for foster care (0.27 percent) is much lower *even than the rate for the general population* (around 1 percent, and 1.5 percent for black children),[8] despite the routine contact foster parents have with CPS caseworkers.

This bias complaint always rang false to those most familiar with the etiology of child maltreatment. They know it occurs disproportionately among the poor, both because poverty entails stress and lack of resources and because certain personal characteristics that cause people to be in poverty also tend to cause them to abuse or neglect their children.[9] And they know poverty—especially deep and concentrated poverty—is more prevalent among black Americans than among whites. It also rang false because case-workers in any given CPS office are typically of the same race as the population they serve. I have observed this in visiting many CPS offices, and what little published information there is about the workforce of CPS offices in large cities confirms that case workers generally match demographically the poorer part of the population they serve.[10] We know that students in social work degree programs in American universities are disproportionately black and overwhelmingly female; less than half are white, and white graduates are more likely to take positions in social-work fields other than child protection, such as school counseling, elder care, and direct provision of family ser-vices.[11] Thus, it seems most case workers in a CPS office serving a poor urban black population, deciding whether to investigate black families, and conducting investiga-tions, substantiating reports of maltreatment, and sometimes removing black children, are themselves black—and specifically, black women, likely to be mothers themselves—and from the city where they work. Further, as previously noted, CPS caseworkers are in general quite protective of parents in the communities they serve, viewing parents who come into the system as their clients, more so than the children who have been maltreated. So the assertion that CPS employees were "othering" poor black parents is odd, and of course unsupported with evidence; it was an invalid inference from the simple fact of race disproportionality in foster care by liberals inclined to fashion policy on the basis of ideology rather than fact.

Those who insisted racial bias was at the root of foster-care race disproportionality thought they had hard evidence when, in 1996, the federal government published a report called the National Incidence Study (NIS) claiming to have found there is no signi-ficant difference in actual rates of child maltreatment as between black and white parents. The NIS is a congressionally mandated, periodic effort to assess actual incidence of child abuse and neglect based on information gathered from multiple sources other than CPS records, such as surveys of residents in different communities and in different demographic groups. CPS records cannot be relied on, precisely because of the alleged bias in every step of the CPS process, so the NIS looks to outside sources and is generally deemed reli-able. The 1996 report analyzed the third iteration of the study, "NIS-3."

It turned out, however, that NIS-3 data did not in fact show similar maltreatment rates across races. To the contrary, the data suggested much higher maltreatment rates among blacks, but the sample size was simply not large enough to deem the results significant in a scientific sense.[12] The authors of the report, however, instead of saying "we have not proven that there is," said "we have found that there is not," which was false, as they must have known.[13]

Based on the NIS-3 authors' claim, and despite serious critiques of their methodol-ogy and reasoning, "powerful foundations, non-profit organizations, and academics" joined in a "Racial Disproportionality Movement" aimed at reducing the rate at which black children are placed in foster care and increasing the rate at which those removed return to parents' custody.[14] Many of these players, including the Casey Family Pro-grams that have been providing "almost all the private funds available in the child welfare area for both advocacy and research,"[15] have been fighting for decades an ideologically-driven battle to diminish CPS involvement in family life and correspond-ingly enlarge parental and community sovereignty over children (especially black chil-dren). They have opposed non-relative foster care, trans-racial adoption, and shortened timelines for parental rehabilitation.[16] Charging the child-welfare system with racial bias became their "new vehicle with which to refight the ASFA and MEPA [Multi-Ethnic Placement Act] battles that they lost, and to promote the alternative policies they have for years been advocating" such as Intensive Family Preservation Services and Differential Response (discussed below), which are parent-happiness-focused and have not benefitted children.[17]

These liberal actors, dominant in the child welfare arena, have thus demanded that state governments adopt, as an explicit goal, reducing the number of black children in foster care—not, improving black children's wellbeing, but simply more black children remaining in parental custody after maltreatment reports or returning quickly after removal to the custody of parents who abused or neglected them. As will be seen repeatedly in this chapter, ACLs' goal is simply black parents' having possession of children. And the Casey foundation funds research aimed at showing that various pet projects serve that goal, which Casey-funded researchers routinely mischaracterize as a "child welfare outcome." Proponents of this goal urged the federal government to condition states' receipt of certain federal funds on their having everyone in the child welfare system undergo "anti-racism training so that they will recognize the truth that the system is functioning in a racially discriminatory way."[18]

There is nothing inherently bad about instruction to counteract any racial bias, but the message social workers in urban areas (who are predominantly of minority race) were likely to receive, especially if no bias has actually been found, was simply that they should be more hesitant to place or keep any black child in foster care, implicitly requiring more serious maltreatment than they do with white children. The training still being provided by one national organization that worked with numerous local courts and agencies includes:

> a multi-year training initiative that focuses on historical trauma as experienced by African-American, Native American, and Native Hawaiian families. In addition to providing resources such as *The New Jim Crow: Mass Incarceration in the Age of Color-blindness* to Safe Babies Teams, we are conducting training focused on increasing awareness of the history of racism, current structural racism, and how disparate treatment of color affects their experience of the child welfare system.[19]

Apart from the last item—an understanding of how minority-race parents experience the system (which minority-race social workers probably already had)—it is difficult to see how any of that would enhance the work of keeping babies safe; indeed, it would seem to do the opposite, by making each baby simply another data point in the "historical narrative" of the "destruction of the black family." Such training would also send the message that bias is *the* problem and that is where attention should be focused, when in fact it was not a problem at all as far as the evidence ultimately showed. But dare to disagree with the Movement's protagonists and "you are by definition racist in your thinking and in need of anti-racism training" yourself.[20]

In 2010, however, the next National Incidence Study came out, NIS-4. With a larger sample size than the NIS-3 had, it showed definitively that actual maltreatment rates are much higher among African-Americans than among whites and correspond to the different rates of foster-care placement.[21] Other research has found no difference in decision-making between black and white CPS workers dealing with black families.[22] NIS-4, along with the published criticisms of the NIS-3 authors' unwarranted claims, largely put the Race Disproportionality Movement to rest.[23] ACLs, however, have continued repeating those false claims despite NIS-4, to serve their adult-protective aims.[24] They simply do not want attention to focus on the reality that a great number of black children are suffering because of what black parents do to them, most likely because they fear that would lead many people to vilify black parents or they might have to endorse policies that separate more black children from black parents.

NIS-4 also confirmed that the correlation between maltreatment and socio-economic status explains race disproportionality in foster care; the study revealed little or no difference in rates of actual maltreatment between black children in low-income households and white children in low-income households.[25] Relatedly, it showed a trend of decreased maltreatment among white children but steady or worse rates among black children, attributable to "the enlarged gap between Black and White children in economic well-being" since the prior NIS study.[26] Given that the recession hit African-Americans harder than whites in this country, one might expect the disproportionality in foster care to have grown since 2006—the year for which data for the NIS-4 was gathered. In fact, however, the percentage of children in foster care who are black fell significantly between 2006 and 2015, from 32 percent to 24 percent.[27] One hopes this means, counter-intuitively, that rates of actual maltreatment warranting removal have declined for black children during those years, rather than that efforts to "retrain" CPS workers to leave black children home after maltreatment or return them more quickly after removal have left black children in danger of repeated maltreatment.

Importantly, reliance on bad science was not the only flaw in the outlook and claims of the Race Disproportionality Movement. In addition, those charging racial bias made elementary mistakes of logic in reasoning to a platform of less "intervention" (i.e., greater legal empowerment of adults) in black families. They leapt from the (false) supposition that rates of maltreatment are the same across races to the conclusion that disproportionate removal of black children must constitute a wrong to "blacks." But to establish that, they would also need to show that many of the removals were improper—that is, not necessary to protect the welfare of children, which they have never done. The mere fact of disproportionate removal in no way establishes that. It could instead be that race disproportionality in foster care occurred despite the (falsely) supposed equality in rates of actual maltreatment because there were not enough removals of white children. In that case, the "harm" of the disparate racial impact would have been to white children, not black adults. This logical error clearly reflects the adult-centered outlook of ACLs. And the latter possibility—that there are few improper removals and should simply be more removals of white children—is far more likely, given the frequently-observed excessive caseloads CPS workers carry, the shortage of approved foster care placements, and the adult-focused outlook that pervades the "child-protective" system.[28] When child welfare systems and courts are "drowning" in founded maltreatment reports, CPS agencies are grossly under-staffed, and children are sleeping in CPS offices because there are no foster-care placements available for them, it is safe to assume CPS employees are not out looking for more "clients."[29] They have to err on the side of deeming reports unfounded and removal unwarranted if they are not to drown in case files. Thus, studies have consistently shown across-the-board under-intervention.[30] If removals are generally warranted, black parents cannot legitimately complain about losing custody; "Those white parents get to abuse their children, so why can't I?" is not a compelling moral claim.

Consider by way of analogy the similar race-disproportionality in domestic violence interventions.[31] Rates of police response to partner violence are also higher among blacks than among whites, presumably for the same reason—that is, higher rates of poverty and personal problems associated with poverty translate into more dysfunctional intimate relationships. Yet liberals do not react to this reality by urging that police be trained to intervene less in partner violence situations where the alleged perpetrator is black, and they would not do so even if it were the case that race-based attitudes cause police to under-intervene when alleged perpetrators are white. Imagine a liberal state governor giving this press statement:

> We need to stop separating black men from their women just because they have not been model partners. What looks like partner abuse might simply reflect cultural differences, and police need to be trained to be sensitive to that. Further, any actually sub-optimal behavior reflects poverty, mental health problems, and the frustration of living in a pervasively racist society. So instead of destroying black families by imposing stay-away order on "bad husbands" and "bad boyfriends," we should raise taxes and invest in schools, jobs, counseling, and relationship education. Black men should not suffer for the legislature's failure to do this. I am therefore declaring that the executive branch and its agencies will no longer enforce criminal domestic violence laws except in cases of severe physical injury or death, and I call on the legislature to amend civil domestic violence laws so that court-ordered separation of intimate partners from each other will in every case be a last resort, adopted only after social service agencies have first made every effort to reform the alleged abuser, and so that when separation is absolutely necessary then agencies effect reunification as soon as possible, especially with struggling black partners.

How would liberals react to that statement? When victims of family violence are adult females, liberals are uniformly and intensely victim-focused and display no sympathy for the perpetrators and their personal struggles, let alone ascribing to the perpetrators any right to state assistance in preserving their relationships with the victims. Liberals do not find ways to argue that non-intervention or a lighter touch would actually be better for victims as well as perpetrators; that kind of talk is reminiscent of the oppressive coverture regime that denied women full personhood. And liberals do not bemoan the impact on minority communities of breaking up (by means of no-contact orders) intimate partnerships. Whatever an adult victim of domestic abuse needs, she should get, period. But when the victims are children, feminist scholars and other liberals become intensely perpetrator-focused, brimming over with sympathy, accusing the state of having too little understanding of the personal and societal histories that led up to this maltreatment moment, of being too judgmental and too quick to act, of not doing everything possible to salvage the relationship (even if little or no relationship yet exists), and using all their powers of imagination to think of ways in which protecting perpetrators from suffering is also good for victims.

Family preservation extremism

In addition to creating a major distraction with the Racial Disproportionality Movement, liberals have promoted one innovative program after another whose singular objective, and sole measure of success, has been ensuring as many children as possible are in the custody of their biological parents (a measure quite different from improved child welfare). The Edna McConnell Clark Foundation and the Annie E. Casey

Foundation have fueled these other movements by funding pilot projects and, most troublingly, their own studies of those projects. By funding the studies, these foundations control who conducts the research and by what measure the researchers determine success. With positive research reports and lots of money in hand, they have enlisted the media in promoting their projects and have persuaded policy makers to enact supportive legislation or new agency guidelines. But one after another, "these reform initiatives have largely collapsed as the research has been found flawed and as the risks to children have become obvious."[32]

Intensive family preservation services

First was IFPS, an approach to responding to maltreatment reports many states adopted from the 1970s through the 1990s. Bartholet explains:

> The basic idea was to define children who are identified as abused and neglected as being "at risk of removal" to foster care, with the goal of keeping as many as possible at home. The means was to provide social worker support services on an intensive basis for roughly six weeks based on the absurd notion that child maltreatment was typically a short-term crisis. The research evaluating IFPS focused not on how well or badly the program served child interests, but instead on whether IFPS succeeded in its goal of keeping children at home, thus saving the state money through the reduction of foster care costs.[33]

Children who need to be removed from parental custody because of maltreatment are at greatly heightened risk of serious harm if returned to parents, for reasons that cannot be eliminated in six weeks.[34]

Richard Gelles attributes the IFPS movement's political success to the Clark and Casey Foundations:

> [T]he expansion of the concept of family preservation and the growing support for the programs … could not have been achieved without the support, financial and otherwise, of two large and influential foundations. The Edna McConnell Clark Foundation … and the Annie E. Casey Foundation … played crucial roles in the selling, or overselling, of family preservation. Both foundations marketed family preservation with a near-religious zeal and substantial financial support. They funded start-up and demonstration programs and then promoted them. [They] became the official repositories of expertise and data on family preservation. State, local, and federal agencies and officials … relied on the two foundations for their evaluation data…. When the believers are foundations who can invest millions of dollars each year in touting the programs and when the critics are academics who merely publish their research results in scholarly journals, the outcome is entirely predictable. State and local agency heads, legislators and legislative aides, governors and presidential administrations were told about the unqualified successes of family preservation and the tremendous cost savings. The skeptics and critics were either unknown or cast as merely academic gadflies.[35]

After many years during which IFPS spread around the country, child welfare experts began "to focus on the flaw at the heart of the research, namely that it paid no attention to child interests." Indeed, they found that "IFPS failed even to succeed in its family preservation goal." And so ultimately "the program was seriously discredited and largely abandoned."[36]

Family drug courts

Family drug courts (FDCs) are spinoffs from juvenile courts, to which are referred some maltreatment cases in which parental substance abuse was a factor. Approximately three quarters of all substantiated maltreatment is associated with parental substance abuse, and most of those parents have quite long-term addictions.[37] As noted in Chapter 2, treatment success rates for addiction in general are less than 20 percent, and the threat of TPR with addicted parents was not producing better results.[38] In addition, a substantial percentage of reunifications with substance-abusing parents are failures; CPS has to remove the children again because maltreatment recurs—13 percent within one year, 17 percent within two years. Further, though participants and observers generally overlook these additional bad-outcomes: (a) as a general matter, most maltreatment goes undetected, so probably an even greater percentage of reunified children should be removed again but are not; (b) a substantial portion of parents who reunify resume drug use and end up in jail or prison, resulting in separations unlikely to be reflected in re-entry rates (CPS does not get alerted whenever an arrestee is a parent, so children typically simply go to live with a relative); (c) many other parents subsequently abandon the children for lengthy periods, leaving them with relatives or friends (again, no CPS involvement); and (d) a small number of parents kill their child after reunification. On the whole, then, the rate of fairy-tale outcomes for children who enter foster care because of substance-abusing parents (permanent reunification without subsequent maltreatment or separation) with the traditional juvenile court process has been miniscule.

Rather than conclude from this that TPRs should be expedited in a lot more cases—in particular, with newborns—some liberal judges decided in the late 1980s and early 1990s to try to spare more parents from the agony of TPRs by creating a different kind of court dedicated to this particular phenomenon of parental substance abuse. One reason for thinking this would produce better outcomes was that specializing would translate into expertise and efficiency, as it had for criminal drug courts. Judges would read all the medical and social science literature on substance abuse and substance abusers and then be better able to predict addicts' behavior and know what incentives have the best chance of changing behaviors. Another rationale was that a special court could adopt a different approach suitable for this population—assembling an optimal package of service providers, a multi-disciplinary team providing "wrap-around," and a therapeutic orientation. An underlying assumption was that parents with deep-seated problems would respond better to a softer approach—more empathic, nurturing, and supportive rather than adversarial. The judge is not a disinterested adjudicator but more like a coach and social worker, urging and encouraging, rewarding or admonishing the parent, and making sure she gets everything she needs to give it her best shot.[39]

All that sounds great; if anything can work, maybe that approach is it. When I first looked at FDCs, though, two concerns immediately arose. First, when the judge, whose only role should be surrogate decision-maker for the child, has decided she will instead be the mother's coach, in a milieu where everyone—including GALs and CPS workers—is expected to get with the therapeutic program, no one in the room will be primarily striving to do what is best for the child; no one involved is really an advocate or proxy for the child. One researcher explains:

> The court must operate within an ethic of caring, instead of an objective set of rules.... Pursuant to the theory of therapeutic jurisprudence, the court functions as an agent of therapeutic change and the role of the members of the drug court may be more akin to the relationship between psychotherapist and patient than the traditional role of judge and defendant.[40]

Undoubtedly some personnel involved have concern for the child, but the child is not the "patient" and most of the personnel never see the child; everyone's focus is a good outcome for the parent (whom they all see very often), and they likely just hope to avoid doing something really bad to the child.[41]

This concern first arose for me when I observed an FDC in Richmond, VA. The judge had developed a close relationship with the mothers that came before her, to the point that she was coming down off the bench in most hearings to hug the mothers. Can you imagine a judge today doing that with a man who abuses his wife because of his alcoholism, giving him a high five when he improves, hugging him in consolation when he falls back on the bottle and the judge must, with great reluctance, extend a stay-away order? If that did routinely occur, would it raise any concerns among advocates for domestic violence victims?

FDC judges thus appear to have taken over a role CPS case workers traditionally carried out—meeting regularly with parents to see how they are doing, give them recommendations and encouragement, coordinating all the services they need.[42] Why, one wonders, is a judge needed to fill this role? And if a judge is needed, why use the juvenile court judge, whose primary focus should be the child's welfare? So now many children in foster care have both CPS workers and judges allied with parents, equating their own professional success with the parents' success in recovering custody—not with positive welfare outcomes for the children.

As a result, there are probably few or no cases in which FDC judges seriously consider terminating parental rights before the ASFA 15-month timeline forces them to consider it, so long as parents are still seeking return of their children. They wait for the legal deadlines or parental indifference to force the issue, rather than ever taking the initiative to consider pulling the plug as soon as the cost-benefit analysis for the child dictates doing so. In effect, then, they never have to take responsibility for disappointing a parent; they can always say "the law forces me to do this now." No courage required. And even when the ASFA timeline compels consideration of TPR, FDC judges are likely to reject it if they hold on to any hope for a parent's recovery; the 15/22 rule does not mandate TPR, it only mandates consideration.

My second concern was that the literature touting FDCs uniformly defines success in terms of—as usual—parents having possession of their children, not in terms of ensuring children's developmental needs are met. Many FDC proponents have acknowledged that the impetus for proliferation of these courts in the late 1990s was the then-new ASFA 15/22 timeline, which "exerted particular pressure on families with parental SUD because of the intractable nature of substance use disorders and the amount of time typically required for treatment access and necessary prolonged, service duration and intensity."[43] As noted in Chapter 2, advocates for women and for poor people raised a hue and cry that this timeline was too short for substance abusers; overcoming an addiction takes a long time, so the 15/22 rule was perceived as a terrible further injustice to parents who had been driven to drugs by poverty, domestic violence, their own traumatic upbringing, etc. (even though it only requires *consideration* of TPR).

There are now roughly four hundred FDCs nationwide. Importantly, for interpreting the research, they typically do not take all substance-abusing parents in the system. A juvenile court judge or administrator must refer parents from the regular juvenile court to the FDC docket, and they screen out parents they deem not suitable for FDC, based either on a subjective judgment of unlikelihood of success or, more commonly, on objective exclusionary criteria such as diagnosed mental illness, more serious maltreatment, and criminal record. Further, when a parent first appears in FDC, the judge gages level of commitment; she explains what the program entails and asks the parent if she or he truly is ready to commit wholeheartedly to the program and try to change. If the parent says no, or if the judge doubts her devotion to recovering sobriety and the child, the parent is sent back to a regular juvenile court docket. Moreover, a substantial percentage accepted into the program fail to complete. So any study that looks at FDC graduates, or even all who initiated services in the FDC program, is examining a very select subset, and the results cannot by any means be generalized to all substance-abusing CPS-involved parents.

For parents who remain, the FDC program entails immediate assessment of addiction severity, faster enrollment in a treatment program, appointment of a social worker to oversee and orchestrate services, a more robust package of services (requiring parents to devote a great deal of time), frequent random drug/alcohol testing, and frequent appearances in court. The judge communicates that she will be a partner in the struggle, gets to know "her mothers" well, and administers graduated rewards for compliance with the program, compassionate warnings about what the judge will be forced to do if the parent does not comply. Typical requirements for "graduation" from an FDC are

> to participate for at least 1 year, demonstrate a specified minimum period of continuous sobriety (usually at least 3 months), a stable living situation, and a substantial continuous period of time during which the participant is meeting his or her obligations to his or her children.[44]

Graduation should result in the ultimate reward: return of the child.

There have now been dozens of studies of family drug courts. Most do not appear in peer-reviewed journals and receive a lot of criticism for their "lack of rigorous study designs, small sample sizes, absence of comparison groups or use of inappropriate comparison groups, inclusion of only program graduates in the outcome data, and lack of appropriate statistical controls when calculating results."[45] I would add that they uniformly ask wrong questions and omit right questions. As with studies of other adult-centered interventions, the ultimate question these studies all aim to answer is "do the mothers recover possession of their offspring?"[46] And researchers uniformly mischaracterize this as a "child welfare outcome" question; in fact, study after study characterizes "child welfare outcomes" as entailing *only or primarily* whether reunification occurred.

Reunification per se is emphatically not a child-welfare outcome, *at all*. If it were, the system would simply return all children to parents immediately after removal and declare victory. Reunification *could* serve as a proxy for child welfare *if* the standard for reunifying were that it is in the best-interests of the child, all things considered, and courts rigorously applied it. But that is generally not the standard for reunification; it is rather safety or "corrected the conditions that led to removal."[47] A child might be physically safe but suffer psychologically, emotionally, and developmentally in a parent's home and not have special needs met (e.g., arising from in utero exposure). In addition, the prevailing standard for and approach to ordering reunification leaves entirely out of the equation how time in foster care has changed the child's situation—in particular, whether the child has attached to the foster parents, which is what an advocate for children would expect and want for any child placed immediately after birth with foster parents and remaining with them for 15 months or more. If the child does not attach securely to the foster parents in that situation, he or she is highly unlikely ever to have a secure attachment to anyone. The reunification standard also leaves out whether it is a bad time for the child developmentally to be suddenly changing home environment. So judges will blithely destroy existing attachment relationships with foster parents, or disrupt any recovery process the child might be going through, because all that matters to them is whether a parent did what she was asked to do and therefore deserves custody of her child. Also legally irrelevant is whether it would be extremely difficult now for the child to form a secure attachment with the birth parents.

A few studies have looked at length of time in foster care and assume shorter is better. But short foster care duration is also not actually a child welfare outcome. If it were, CPS would return children a day after removal and declare victory. The one measure some studies apply that is a child welfare outcome is rate of maltreatment recurrence. But many studies do not. Entirely lacking are longitudinal studies examining mental health, behavioral, educational, employment, or other outcomes for children of FDC participants.[48] FDCs have now been around for nearly 30 years, and if courts have social security numbers for family members in past cases, and if confidentiality laws permit, those numbers might be used to locate many of them or compare with public records. But some institution interested in the children's wellbeing would have to fund that research.

An additional conceptual problem with all the studies is that their sole measure of whether FDCs are good from a policy standpoint is whether they increase rates of reunification relative to the more traditional court process in maltreatment cases. No one attempts to compare the fate of children whose parents become FDC "patients" with children immediately placed for adoption when found to be maltreated or at high risk because of parental substance abuse. Perhaps this happens too rarely to present a sizeable enough comparison group, but it seems no FDC proponents or researchers even recognize this as a pertinent question. In other words, no one asks: "What is the best decision for this child just reported as maltreated or in danger?" The only question asked is: "Is FDC better for parents than the miserable rate of success the traditional juvenile court has?"

As a result, no one ever asks what is a minimally acceptable level of reunification-without-reentry—that is, a criterion for deciding whether states should continue this FDC experiment instead of doing more fast-track TPRs and placing children for adoption. The background, unstated assumption is that, no matter what, the objective must always be for as many parents as possible to recover possession of their offspring, so courts and agencies should undertake prolonged rehabilitation efforts in every case.[49] So if the permanent reunification rate for substance-abusing parents on the whole increases from 15 percent to 18 percent, that proves the efficacy of FDCs (a 20 percent improvement!). (In reality, though, no one asks whether the rate for substance-abusing parents on the whole has improved; they only try to figure out whether certain FDCs increase the likelihood of success for the select subset of parents who are invited to participate in them and accept.)

So what do the studies show? I describe them in detail in an Appendix. On the whole, they create a mixed and fuzzy picture.[50] Most show FDC parents (who, recall, are a select subset of all substance-abusing parents) recover possession of their offspring, and avoid TPR (for the moment), at a higher rate than as-comparable-as-possible (so also a select subset) non-FDC parents.[51] (Snohomish, Washington—68.5 percent versus 62 percent; Tulsa—30 percent versus 15 percent within 500 days, 61 percent versus 25 percent within 1000 days; Sacramento—42 percent versus 27 percent; unnamed "large western city"—40 percent versus 18 percent; Hillsborough County, FL—53 percent versus 42 percent; "three western sites"—70 percent versus 40 percent). A study of the FDC in Pima County, AZ is especially interesting because that court, at least when the study was done, apparently had no exclusionary criteria, so the only difference between FDC parents and those who received the traditional process was that the former chose to participate and the latter declined. The study found that although nearly every FDC parent entered treatment, only half finished. They reunified with their children,[52] but half of the children who reunified were again later removed and placed again in foster care. Thus, even if one overestimates "success" by calling a success any case in which a parent recovers possession of her child and the child does not later return to foster care (thus ignoring cases in which subsequent maltreatment was undetected; cases in which parents later were arrested and went to jail or prison, or abandoned or killed the child; and other cases in which reunification was not in the child's best interests in the long run—e.g., because it involved traumatic separation from foster-care attachment figures), the success rate of this unusual program that took all comers was just 25 percent—much less than most of the studied programs that screened out unpromising parents.

Some studies also examine delayed impermanence. Some of those show children of FDC parents spend less time in foster care and achieve some form of permanence faster than children of comparable non-FDC parents. (For example, Snohomish, Washington—393 days for FDC versus 848 days for non-FDC). Many others, however, show the opposite—that is, that FDCs tend to drag out the rehabilitation process, most likely because the judge, having bonded with "her mothers," finds it extraordinarily difficult to pull the TPR trigger.[53] (For example, Hillsborough, FL—"FDTC participants 27–29 percent longer to achieve permanency than non-FDTC participants"; "three western sites"—288 days versus 228 days.) As for maltreatment recurrence after reunification, the few studies that looked at it showed disparate results.[54] (Sacramento—"22.9 percent of the 362 DDC children who reunified within 24 months experienced reentry into care compared to 10.6 percent of the comparison group children"; Hillsborough, FL—2 percent (FDC) versus 12 percent (non-FDC) re-entry within a year after reunification; "large western city"—38 percent of FDC parents investigated again for maltreatment within short time after reunification, 54 percent of control group).

As noted, an additional huge part of the permanency picture for children of substance-abusing parents, which almost no researchers even consider, is the likelihood of parents separating from children again after reunification for reasons *other than* another CPS removal—in particular, incarceration or abandonment. Two studies that did look at this phenomenon found *rates of new criminal arrests for FDC participants of 40 percent and 54 percent*. For comparison groups, it was 63 percent and 67 percent.[55] In addition, many parents give up on child rearing after reunification, leave the child with a relative (typically grandma), and disappear. And any infants returned in their first half

year of life to the custody of a parent with an addiction problem are at greatly heightened risk of death from accident (e.g., mom gets high and falls asleep on the baby) or
intentional conduct (e.g., shaking).[56] None of those failures register in the studies,
because they do not result in "re-entry," and FDCs' advocates never talk about them.
Don't ask, don't tell.

Thus, the long-run story for the vast majority of children put in limbo while FDC
judges try to work magic is likely quite bleak. Moreover, no study shows with any confidence that it is any better for any children *because of the FDC* than normal court proceedings following a child protective removal. Advocates who claim that their
effectiveness has been proven are wrong. All comparative studies are infected with
selection bias—in particular, nearly all fail to control for the subjective element in
judges' selecting parents to participate and the significance of parents' declining an offer
to enter the program.

What the studies *do* suggest is that we have some idea of which substance-abusing
parents are more likely to succeed than others in getting their addiction under control
and otherwise making themselves prepared to take care of a child properly. We could
use that to do triage. And that could serve as a partial basis for having a conversation
about what likelihood of recovery within what time frame is sufficiently good to make
it a good gamble to take on behalf of a child, taking into account a child's differing
time-related developmental needs at different ages, and the nature of a child's existing
relationship with a parent. But almost no one in the field of child maltreatment wants
to do triage or have that conversation; the "must try to save every parent" mentality is
pervasive and controlling.[57]

Related to the possibility of triage, notably absent from the studies is mention of what
happens with the parents screened out of the FDC because their cases were too severe,
or rejected by the FDC judge because they displayed too little motivation to change.
You might suppose those parents—that is, those thought least likely to succeed with the
Cadillac program—would be immediately moved to TPRs. If they are unpromising in
FDC, then they stand little or no chance in regular juvenile court, right? But it seems
instead they simply remain on the regular juvenile court docket, going through the
motions, *where they might end up in the control group!* They might actually be given even
longer than FDC parents to demonstrate a safe home environment or correction of the
conditions that led to removal, simply because their progress is slower or non-existent
yet caseworkers do not want to give up on them (recall the huge disparity in time-to-
permanence for the non-FDC group in Snohomish). Thus, their children are subjected
to impermanence even longer, without regard to their age at time of entry into foster
care. How is this possible? Because the child protection system in too many jurisdictions
is not about child welfare; it is about trying to fix deeply-damaged parents, even when
the system itself identifies them as more or less hopeless.

The FDC model makes most sense in cases involving older children who have an
established, positive relationship with the struggling parents. In those cases, it is usually
best for the child that the state make substantial efforts to rehabilitate parents, even if it
will take a couple of years to know whether the parents can succeed. Older children
typically have a substantial psychological stake in continuation of the relationship,
despite the abuse or neglect it has entailed; they are less likely to bond with foster
parents than are younger children; and adoption is generally not a realistic option for
them. As such, the better able courts are to pursue the objective of rehabilitation, the
more likely is a good outcome for those older children.

Rules for transfer to an FDC, however, do not differentiate among cases based on the age of the child, and cases involving babies actually predominate in many FDCs. A study of three FDCs in large cities found that in 63 percent of the courts' cases the child at issue was not even born yet.[58] A quarter of the parents had previously had rights terminated as to one or more other children,[59] so the court could have terminated rights as to the newborn immediately if they found that to be in the child's best interests. And it most likely *would have been* in the newborns' best interests to do an immediate TPR in nearly all of those cases, but this never occurred, in part because of the false hope occasioned by this new pet project of the Left, coupled with liberal judges' and liberal CPS workers' tremendous sympathy for the parents. What likely happened instead with most of those babies was that they were placed at birth with foster parents, staying with them for 15 or more months and developing an attachment, then yanked out for "reunification," disrupting the attachment, then separated from their mothers again because of maltreatment, abandonment, or mom's getting sent to jail or prison, and went again to foster care (maybe the same foster parents, maybe not) or got left with relatives. Destructive chaos.

Normatively, we might ask by what authority judges arrogate to themselves the power to redefine the goals of a child protection proceeding or to transform a child protection proceeding into a parent–rehabilitation proceeding. If a state's legislature has declared that the primary or controlling aim of legal proceedings arising from parental unfitness is to serve the welfare of children,[60] how can the federal Office of Justice Programs or any individual judge presume to say the goal is something else? If specialized domestic violence judges got together and declared that henceforth the goal of domestic violence proceedings would be to keep couples together, the public would surely demand to know the source of their power to define the aims of those proceedings. It is so easy for governmental actors to get away with extraordinary things when the only persons prejudiced thereby are children.

As Chapter 4 explained, what should happen with newborns whose birth parent has a substance abuse problem (or a history of child maltreatment or violent crime, or is incarcerated) is an assessment of the prospects for that parent to become an adequate and permanent custodian for the child within six months.[61] That assessment would take into account mental health diagnosis (some mental illnesses are much harder to treat than others), drug of choice (some are more addictive and dangerous than others),[62] maltreatment history, previous rehabilitation efforts, prior TPRs, criminal history, positive opportunities (e.g., for employment and better housing), family support, and additional stressors (e.g., other children in foster care, chronic victimization by partners, coresidence with other substance abusers).[63] If the prognosis is too poor for it to be a sensible gamble for the child, the state should terminate the child's legal tie to that birth parent immediately and effect an adoptive placement. If there is substantial chance for reform by six months, then the state should place the newborn in a pre-adoptive foster home and engage in concurrent planning. Then, at the six month mark, the state's options should be limited to (a) placement in the birth parent's custody, if that is safe and likely to be permanent, (b) a short time extension if there is good cause from a child-centered perspective, or (c) TPR. Sadly, a six-month timeline would likely mean most serious drug users lose their legal tie to their offspring right after the child is born; it is exceedingly rare for addicts to attain lasting sobriety within six months.[64] ACLs' instinctive reaction to that fact is to say "but that's not fair, you are not giving parents a realistic amount of time." But children's timelines cannot tolerate extension of impermanence into the crucial attachment period; they need good and permanent caregivers to be in place before it begins. And they are entitled to have their timeline control.

What the child welfare system needs to develop, in short, is a triage response to substance abuse among parents of newborns, driven by children's developmental needs and timeline, using research-based protocols to identify the most hopeful cases and concentrate resources on them, while quickly seeking alternative caregivers for children in the other cases. Morally groundless notions of fairness to parents should not be part of the equation.

Differential response

The latest liberal bandwagon in CPS practice is to create a two-track system for responding to maltreatment reports and relegate most to a "soft-touch," no-coercion track. When someone calls the CPS hotline, report handlers first determine whether a report is valid, which means the conduct described satisfies the statutory definitions of abuse or neglect. If a neighbor calls the hotline simply because children are being noisy or have dirty clothes or a parent yelled at a child, the operator ticks off the "invalid" box and CPS does nothing. If, on the other hand, someone reports serious injury to a child or describes conditions presenting imminent danger of substantial harm, the report would be "valid." The traditional reaction to valid reports is to conduct an investigation to determine whether the report is also "founded," meaning the investigator collected sufficient evidence to substantiate the charge. If not, the case is closed. If substantiated, CPS creates a record of that so if there is recurrence of maltreatment CPS can document the prior incident to assist its own decision-making and that of a court. A substantiation is also necessary for CPS to secure a court order authorizing removal of a child in danger of harm. Everyone in the child welfare field recognizes that removing a child from his or her home is likely to cause at least anxiety, even if he or she immediately goes to the home of another parent or a well-known relative, and in some cases is deeply upsetting. Agencies have always had a variety of responses to maltreatment reports at their disposal, once they determined that a report was founded, and even under the traditional approach have placed only a minority of children with a founded maltreatment report in foster care.[65] But they examined the family situation in some depth, created a record, and had a basis for inducing parents to accept assistance, services, and monitoring aimed at preventing recurrence of abuse or neglect.

Under the new "differential response" policy (DR), the CPS reaction to a valid report is instead first to determine whether it should go on an investigation track (the traditional response) or instead, if the screener deems it a "low-risk" situation, on an "assessment" track. With the latter, there is no involuntary subjection to examination of the children and home, no formal agency finding of maltreatment, no determination of who was responsible for any harm to children, and no coercion to accept services or assistance. Caseworkers give parents a call, or stop by and ring the doorbell, to ask whether the parents' would like to discuss how CPS can help them. Parents' declining, in and of itself, cannot be a basis for switching the case to the traditional, investigation track. If parents refuse what is offered, or refuse even to talk to the caseworker, CPS caseworkers must close the case and do nothing further. As Claire Houston observes, this is reminiscent of the way police used to respond to domestic violence calls, asking the husband if he needs any help, maybe offering information about anger management classes, but avoiding any intrusive questioning or alienating coercion.[66]

Most parents are initially receptive, but a substantial minority rebuff CPS's overtures at the outset. For those who open the door, CPS provides financial assistance, such as rent subsidies and appliances for the home, and it also offers services such as counseling, childcare, and transportation, which parents are free to take or refuse. Many take the assistance but refuse the services. A major concern is that parents whose children are, among those put on the assessment track, suffering the more serious maltreatment or at greater risk of maltreatment are those most likely to be among the half of parents who either refuse at the outset to have any communication or contact or sever contact after receiving the financial assistance. The immediate consequence of DR, then, is in effect to screen out another large portion of maltreatment reports; for parents who refuse all participation, the only difference relative to invalidation of a report is that CPS has made the parents aware that someone reported them. This might cause some to improve their parenting, and with truly low-risk situations that might be enough to eliminate any cause for concern. (Though liberals have complained even about such "implicit warnings" as unjustified coercion.)[67] But it will undoubtedly cause others simply to be more secretive and reclusive, and to ensure their children do not reveal any problems at home. The latter group might never show up again on anyone's radar, yet the children are at pronounced risk. And if any of these parents are reported again for maltreatment, because there was no finding the first time, CPS will view them as having no verified maltreatment history, which might cause them again to deem these parents low risk and put them on the AR track.[68]

The assumptions underlying DR are that the bulk of maltreatment reports involve low risk of harm to children and reflect simply temporary struggles of parents in poverty who only need a little help (the same assumption underlying Intensive Family Preservation Services), and that those parents are more likely to be receptive to help if it is presented in a non-threatening, non-coercive way (an assumption also underlying Family Drug Courts). For policy makers with an eye on the budget, and for caseworkers buried in paperwork, DR is very attractive because the alternative track requires much less agency employee time and keeps cases out of court.[69] Caseworkers also like that they spend less time acting as investigators, which is typically not what they had in mind when starting a career in social work. Between 2009 and 2012, the number of abuse and neglect petitions filed in the Richmond, Virginia Juvenile and Domestic Relations Court dropped from 284 for the year to 76.[70] And ACLs endorse DR because it reduces the coercion and "surveillance of African-American family life," which to their mind is what actually "erode[s] the dreams of the child for a future,"[71] and it frees up the time of parents reported for maltreatment for "working to achieve political and economic progress."[72]

Federal legislation has pushed states to adopt DR. The 2010 reauthorization of the Child Abuse and Prevention Treatment Act (CAPTA), through which states receive roughly half their funding for child protection, required states henceforth to include in their child protection process "differential response in triage procedures for the appropriate referral of a child not at risk of imminent harm to a community organization or voluntary preventive service." Behind this federal legislation, once again, stands the behemoth Casey Family Programs foundation, ideologically committed to drastic reduction of the foster care population, which envisioned that most maltreatment reports would be diverted to the no-investigation track under DR, and that any additional money needed to cover the financial assistance being offered to families would come out of foster-care funding streams.[73]

Half the states in the US have now adopted DR, and local agencies are diverting up to 80 percent of all CPS reports to the alternate, no-investigation track (with no observed difference in rates across races).[74] These states can easily declare victory in the short run; the number of founded maltreatment reports instantly drops precipitously, simply because CPS is no longer determining in the majority of cases whether a report is founded or not. But once again, the proper question to be asking is whether child wellbeing has been improved. It is not in this instance whether there are fewer founded reports, and it is never whether more reported children are remaining at home. We need to know whether children are safe and receiving adequate care, and that is difficult to determine when the only indicator researched is subsequent re-reporting. Research done on child protection in jurisdictions without DR suggests DR would put children at great risk of prolonged maltreatment. Elizabeth Bartholet explains:

> Research shows that children on the traditional CPS track are at enormous risk of repeat maltreatment by their parents. If kept at home, most will continue to be abused and neglected. If removed to foster care and then returned home, most will be again abused and neglected. The large majority of the CPS caseload that DR is designed to move to the voluntary track are not minor "dirty house" or "mere poverty" cases, as advocates often contend. CPS legislation is designed to protect poor parents from state intervention based on circumstances beyond the parents' control. The cases in which CPS intervenes generally involve serious drug and/or alcohol abuse, forms of "neglect" that are known to destroy kids' chances for normal development, and situations where serious violence exists but is simply not obvious.... Research reveals that while it is hard for parents to free themselves from drug and alcohol addiction, coercive pressure to engage in treatment does sometimes work. Polite requests to engage in treatment on a purely voluntary basis are not likely to work better or, indeed, as well.[75]

DR's underlying premise that most valid reports to CPS reflect low-risk situations for children is implausible. As discussed earlier, we know actual rates of abuse and neglect far exceed rates of reporting—that is, that most child maltreatment goes undetected, or unreported by those who observe it. We know that even before DR, most valid reports were deemed "unfounded" simply because it is generally difficult to document what happened and who was responsible in child maltreatment cases, given that the victim is most often a small child and the conduct occurs inside a home. We know that the vast majority of valid reports concern parents who have serious problems—in particular, mental illness and substance abuse.[76] And these reports are not coming from roving bands of government agents looking for children to sweep up; they are coming from members of the community in which the parents live, who are sufficiently disturbed by a child's situation to override the general aversion most people have to getting involved in other people's problems and the practical difficulties of figuring out who to call.

We also know that child fatalities occur disproportionately to children whose caregivers were previously reported for maltreatment,[77] and that most child fatalities result from neglect rather than abuse, "including starvation, inadequate medical care, unsafe co-sleeping, or drowning in the bathtub," belying the assertion of some that neglect cases do not warrant serious CPS attention.[78] We know that a substantial portion of parents reported once for maltreatment will be reported again if the child remains in their custody.[79] Emily Putnam-Hornstein and colleagues found in a study in California that among children reported for maltreatment before turning one, 82 percent remained in their parents' home and 61 percent of those who remained were re-reported for maltreatment within five years. Significantly: "Infants whose initial allegation was not investigated had re-reporting rates that were equal to or higher than other infants remaining in the home without services."[80] And, in contrast, we know rates of abuse and neglect in foster care are miniscule by comparison—one quarter of a percent annually[81]—and that "foster care removal generally serves children's best interests in terms of such factors as risk of violence to children, child "risk behaviors," child quality of life, and other measures of safety and well-being."[82]

So what have we learned about the actual effects of DR? First, although CPS is supposed to assign only "low risk" reports to the assessment, or "Alternative Response," track, in practice it is relegating a great number of high-risk reports to the no-investigation track.[83] Second, about half of parents put on the AR track either rebuff CPS's initial overtures or sever contact before completing parenting-improvement services. Third, and most importantly, on the one indicator of child wellbeing researchers have looked at—re-reporting for maltreatment—there is a high rate for parents put on the AR track—on average, about half of all cases. Thus, at least that many children continued to be subject to prolonged abuse and/or neglect because CPS backed off the previous time (and probably a much greater number than those re-reported, because we know most maltreatment is not reported, and, as noted, CPS's first contact likely causes relatively dangerous parents to become more secretive and reclusive).[84] Indeed, in a study of Illinois' DR implementation, there was a higher rate of re-reporting among (supposedly low risk) AR cases than among (high risk) traditional response cases. As investigative journalist Daniel Heimpel, who specializes in child welfare, put it: "children whose parents had benefitted from twice as much social work time, $400 stipends and a philosophy that stresses family strengths were more likely to be reported for child maltreatment and become victims of substantiated abuse or neglect."[85] Other studies show similar re-reporting rates between AR and investigation-track parents, but one should expect to see much lower rates with AR parents if they are actually lower-risk.

Fourth, AR cases rarely get switched to the investigation track, consistent with the common-sense prediction that the most worrisome parents will simply refuse to answer the door. An audit in Richmond, Virginia found caseworkers were walking away even after observing signs of more serious harm:

> As part of a statewide shift to reducing the number of children in foster care, the department "decided to apply the philosophy of keeping vulnerable children, assisted by the Child Protective Services, in their homes," ... [but] the city "went too far in its quest to reduce the number of removals..." This included leaving children with caregivers who were addicted to drugs and faced "ongoing psychiatric challenges," those with history of abuse and homelessness and those who "lacked the cognitive skills to care for their children." The report documents cases in which children were left with their caregivers even though there was evidence that they were beaten, burned, wearing clothing that smelled like "sewage" and lacked medical care for serious conditions.[86]

Richard Barth, "a highly respected child welfare expert, says that unless AR cases are referred back 'a substantial amount of the time (25% perhaps), then the system isn't working.'"[87] Fifth, the soft touch does not seem to produce greater parent cooperation.

A three-site study sponsored by the Children's Bureau (the federal child-welfare agency oversight office) found that parents on the investigation track had "more positive engagement attributes (such as being cooperative, receptive to help, and engaged)" than parents on the AR track.[88]

However, many of the reports issued by Casey-supported research teams, which have been lambasted by independent researchers as advocacy disguised as science, with severe methodological flaws and unsupported conclusions,[89] has focused on parent happiness as the primary measure of success. They find precisely what one would expect—that is, that parents for whom all was voluntary, who were offered uncondi-tioned financial assistance, and who did not slam the door in the CPS caseworker's face (and so could be asked) were on average happier with how their case was handled than parents who were investigated, found to be maltreating, and pressured into accepting help.[90] The adult-focused bias could not be clearer. Plus, AR greatly reduces investiga-tion costs. So it is a win-win situation for the state and parents. Children, as usual, are the losers with this parent-focused experiment.

All that said, differentiating reports based on risk, so that agency resources can be used most efficiently and unnecessary disruption of family life can be avoided, makes perfect sense. As noted in discussion of Birth Match, agencies are beginning to use pre-dictive analytics to make handling of valid maltreatment reports a rational, deliberate process, with objective and evidence-based standards of risk applied consistently, rather than ad hoc decision-making based on subjective judgments of risk skewed by institu-tional interests. Until DR is rationalized in that way, it is endangering children for the sake of parental happiness.

Fighting back against the carceral state by imprisoning babies

Mass incarceration has massively impacted inner-city black families. Most liberals believe much incarceration is unnecessary to protect the community, and we wish our government would find more humane ways of dealing with people whose lives have driven them to conduct we criminalize. Nevertheless, there are millions of parents in prison who are serving lengthy sentences that make it impossible for them to be home caring for a child, and most of these parents are deeply damaged people who would be unwilling or unable anyway to provide children with the care they need. That is a simple fact, not going to change any time soon, for black children in poor urban areas. An advocate for children responds to this reality by thinking about all the possible choices and actions the state could take regarding the children and urging our govern-ment to pursue the best of those.

ACLs, however, see the parents' separation from their children as a further injustice that our racist society inflicts on poor black people, and they categorically reject the idea that the incarceration is a reason to end a legal parent–child relationship or even keep parent and child separated. I have already noted the vociferous complaints about application of the 15/22 rule, requiring a petition for TPR, to incarcerated parents, which rest above all on perceived unfairness to the parents; they are unable to do any-thing for the child, because the state put them in prison, so how can they be blamed for not regaining custody in 15 months? In their adult-centered outlook, child protection law is about punishing parents for blameworthy conduct.[91] And, as always, after taking their adult-protective position, they flail about trying to find some basis for suggesting their position is also better for children, typically by making extravagant claims about how essential it is for children to remain in a relationship with their biological parents (even if only to visit them through a glass partition once a year) and be part of "their community" (however dysfunctional), regardless of what age they are or whether they have any existing bond with their biological parents.

In addition to opposing TPR based on incarceration, ACLs have also contrived another pet program that actually unites children with incarcerated parents. Children in the community have always generally been able in theory to visit parents in prison, but there are many practical obstacles to this and anyway research suggests that visitation in its usual form (through a glass wall in a regular prison visitation room) makes the children worse off psychologically and emotionally.[92] So advocates for female prisoners want the children actually living in the prison. Perhaps better than any other program or position I have discussed in this book, prison nurseries epitomize the social-welfare Left's adult-centered ideological orientation to family and community dysfunction and their cynical attitude toward scientific evidence.

In the mid-twentieth century about 20 states had prison nurseries. All but one closed them in the 1960s and 1970s when children's rights became something people talked about and government agencies started getting sued more often when people in their institutions got hurt. New York's was the only program to survive this re-examination. But starting 20 years ago, advocates for women prisoners started successfully pushing for their reincarnation, and today about ten states have them. They primarily house babies born while the mothers are incarcerated, though at least one program entails putting babies born prior to the mother's incarceration into the prison with her. In New York today, a person might spend the first 12 to 18 months of his or her life behind bars, and this is far more likely to occur if that baby is black. In Washington State, a person might live in prison from birth to his or her third birthday.[93] This occurs with no legal process, no appointment of an advocate for the child, and no competent determination that living in prison is in the baby's best interests; if an inmate qualifies under program rules (which typically exclude violent offenders) and prison officials think the baby will be safe, then the inmate is deemed entitled to have the state place the baby in the prison. The patent violation of both children's constitutional procedural rights and federal laws prohibiting housing of minors in adult prisons does not even register as a concern for prison officials or state legislators. The ACLU should be up in arms, but has been silent.

The vast majority of Americans have never heard of this phenomenon. When I mention it to non-academics, they are appalled. When I mention it to liberal feminist academics, they say "of course, the baby should be with its mother," without even inquiring "so what are conditions like, are the babies safe, how is the decision made to place them in prison, how long do they stay, have there been any studies on how that affects the child?" So who is promoting this? As with IFPS, race-sensitivity training for CPS caseworkers, and DR, it was not the idea of advocates for children. In this instance, it was the idea of advocates for incarcerated women, who observed how inmates suffer from being separated from a newborn child after birth. These advocates are always seeking ways to reduce the suffering women prisoners experience, regularly complaining to human-rights organizations about conditions in the prisons, and this was another way to do that—have the state put the inmates' babies in the prison too.

They have had to convince prison officials and legislatures, however, to authorize and fund new programs. They do this by touting studies regarding recidivism, purporting to show prison nurseries make inmates less likely to reoffend after release, even though they know the studies are flawed,[94] and by making completely unsupported claims about benefits for the children. There was actually no research 20 years ago to support advocates' claims that being imprisoned with their birth mothers would be good for the children. What little research had been done at that time on babies and infants living in prisons showed negative effects. So proponents for prison nurseries instead appealed to liberal legislators' heartstrings, invoking the adage that a baby should be with his or her mother and (accurately) describing the tragic lives these women have had. They hoodwinked prison officials and conservative state legislators into believing prison nurseries are an effective crime-reduction strategy.[95] Some claimed it was cost-saving, based on the absolutely false premise that the alternative for babies born to prison inmates is to go into foster care (this almost never happens; as long as some relative is willing to take the baby, CPS does not even get involved).[96]

In 2010, the first longitudinal study of prison babies was reported. The authors were Columbia University nursing school faculty and students who were providing services to the mothers in the prison nursery at Bedford Hills Maximum Security Prison (and who therefore appeared to have a conflict of interests with the human research subjects—i.e., the infants). The authors' report makes it difficult to perceive the bad outcomes, but I was able, with some digging and piecing together, to figure out that the ideal that advocates hypothesize—that the child securely attaches to the incarcerated mother and then remains with her for the rest of childhood—is realized for only about 10 percent of these children. The secure attachment rate overall was probably around 20 percent, which is lower than that for children who bounce around among caregivers in the community while their mothers are in prison. Moreover, the rate of mother–child separation, either during the prison–nursery stay (because mom changed her mind or committed a rule infraction) or after the mother's release (because mother abandoned or maltreated the child or because mother returned to prison) was very high, well over 50 percent.

The authors of the report, however, intent on telling a success story, painted a grossly distorted picture of prison–nursery effects by discussing only one aspect of outcomes (signs of secure attachment to mother at the one-year mark) for a small subcategory of all the children whom the state placed in the prison (30 out of the 100 initially in the study). The authors and other advocates for women in prison since then have pushed for expansion of prison–nurseries on the basis of this grossly distorted picture, making wildly false claims that the programs produce child–welfare outcomes comparable to that for the general population. The fact that the vast majority of children actually failed to form a secure attachment or suffered attachment disruption because their mothers later left them simply did not fit in with the story the researchers/advocates wanted to tell, and so they excluded it, and other advocates manifest zero interest in the fate of those children.

Should incarcerated criminals become parents with custody of children? In the adoption context, the answer is clearly no. If an adoption agency received an application from a prison inmate, it would unhesitatingly throw the application in the trash, probably in shock that such a person would think themselves suitable. The agency would do this even if the prison in which the applicant lived had created a special unit for child rearing. In fact, the agency would reject an application by that person even long after he or she left prison. This seems appropriate to me, and I presume to everyone else in the world. Of course there can be exceptions, but no one would think it justifiable to gamble on that slight possibility with a child.

So what must be at work in the minds of liberals who instinctively support prison nurseries, and who are deaf to empirical noise about bad child-welfare outcomes for children whom the state forces to live in prisons, is one or more assumptions tied to the fact of biological motherhood. One such assumption is that a birth mother owns her child, the fruits of her labors, a moral assumption no serious ethical theorist today would defend. Another is that the only alternatives to imprisoning the newborn are temporary custody with relatives in the community, which they correctly note results in bad outcomes for children, or foster care. Advocates for women prisoners will not even acknowledge a third, readily-available, and very positive alternative—adoption. They oppose even giving pregnant inmates information about the availability of adoptive parents, in case some women might want to choose that. Another assumption likely at work for many is that being raised by a biological parent, and in the community to which the biological parents belong (however dysfunctional), is of utmost importance to human welfare, more important than secure attachment or safety or any other aspect of human wellbeing, an assumption ample evidence shows to be false. (One hears the same sort of unfounded claims about child welfare from defenders of the Indian Child Welfare Act, which treats children with the slightest genetic connection to a Native American tribe as a tribal resource and "needing" to be connected to "their culture.") But it is unlikely that proponents of prison nurseries actually give much thought to children's welfare.

What exactly is wrong with prison nurseries? Why don't they produce good outcomes for many children? Above all is the reality of the life trajectories of the vast majority of women who go to prison. In ACLs' imagination, incarcerated women are normally constituted individuals who one day made a silly little mistake, perhaps because an abusive boyfriend coerced or tricked her into doing it, or got caught once using drugs, and ended up with a two-year prison sentence. That is delusional. Women in prison are overwhelmingly deeply-damaged people who come from dysfunctional families in dysfunctional neighborhoods where they had dysfunctional relationships and who suffer from serious mental health problems and/or addictions, who committed either a very serious offense or multiple lesser offenses, and who will return to the same dysfunctional family and neighborhood and relationships upon exiting prison.[97] They themselves will tell you that: "we're all sick and broken when we enter these gates, or we wouldn't be here."[98] They are the end product of the process I described in Chapter 2. These women are simply not good prospects for parenthood. Adoption agencies would reject them as potential parents not because the agencies want to further punish the women for their crimes, but because these women are at extremely high risk of maltreating and abandoning any child whom the state places into a family relationship with them. A high percentage of them had already lost custody of other children because of maltreatment before becoming involved in the criminal justice system.[99] They are damaged, they will return to the environment that led them to crime, and their life struggles will be multiplied by the fact of having a prison record; employers, landlords, and some family members will not want to deal with them—in fact, might be legally prohibited from interacting with them.

In addition to the immense struggles incarcerated women would face to establish a healthy home for an infant or toddler after release, there is the reality of life for a baby in a prison. Advocates for female prisoners routinely portray that life—including that for inmates in a prison nursery—as stressful, hostile, and stultifying.[100] Guards wield extraordinary power over them and use it to coerce, abuse, and severely regulate. Daily life is regimented, inflexible, unbending to a child's needs—for example, with nursing allowed only at scheduled times. Numerous reports have been issued in recent years about the long-term adverse consequences of caregiver stress in early childhood.[101] Moreover, there is very little of the stimulation, the new experiences, children need for healthy brain development. Readers who find the idea of prison nurseries benign should imagine bringing their own child or grandchild or niece or nephew every day to a women's prison and dropping off him or her for daycare in the prison nursery. (Most of the mothers, incidentally, must go to jobs in the prison during the day and leave their children in the care of other inmates.) What reservations would you have about that? Think about the experiences your child, grandchild, etc. has or had in infancy—the walks, the interactions with new people and with animals on a daily basis, the stores, the museums, the playgrounds, the trees, the ocean waves, the homes of relatives and friends, and on and on. One former Bedford Hills inmate told a reporter that after she and her toddler left the prison, the child was terrified by the sight of blowing leaves.

Thus, we, the adult citizens whom state legislators represent, are choosing to put newborn children into prisons, with little prospect for good outcomes, and almost no one expresses any qualms about this. Our national government is encouraging it. Liberal media outlets and reporters have been quite intrigued by prison nurseries, but mostly create supportively slanted presentations highlighting the voices of advocates for incarcerated women. I have been asked numerous times for interviews with newspaper and magazine writers, and to appear on television and radio programs, simply because I am the only academic or lawyer they can find who is challenging the practice.

Ironically, one organization opposing the practice of housing babies in prisons (though without challenging it in any concrete way) is the Women Prisoners Association, which advocates instead for community-based supervised housing for mother–child dyads.[102] I, too, would support placement of babies with their birth mothers in a home-like (but secure) facility in a community environment, with infants having opportunities for regular outings, provided (a) participation were limited to mothers with strong prospects for being good, permanent caretakers, and (b) mothers were required to remain in the facility for three years regardless of how much of their sentenced time they had left to serve. The latter condition would incidentally provide a test of commitment for mothers who have much less than three years left to serve (as well as a test for their advocates, to see whether they truly care about positive outcomes for the children).

None of the foregoing can put a dent in the determination of prison-nursery proponents. They see or imagine poor women who have had miserable lives either being made happier by having a baby with them or else being emotionally devastated by giving birth and then returning alone to a prison cell, and that is all that matters to them. You can point out that the recidivism claim is unfounded, but they will keep making it. You can point out that the vast majority of the children ultimately end up separated from their mothers, but they will respond with "well, at least they had a chance" or "at least they didn't end up in foster care" or "that's because the state doesn't provide the support these women need when they exit prison." Because neither reduced recidivism nor child welfare is actually the objective for these liberals; their sole aim is alleviating the suffering and improving the life prospects of poor women, and they are simply using children to accomplish that.[103]

With both drug courts and prison nurseries, most liberals do not see that they are supporting policies and practices that inflict on infants the same damage their clients incurred as children. And that no one would seriously propose doing anything comparable to any group of adults. Imagine if someone proposed that before an abused wife could sever her relationship with her abuser, she had to give him two years to see if a specialty court with wrap-around services could turn him around. Advocates for women would be outraged. Or if someone proposed putting in prison elderly relatives of inmates—for example, their parent who needs constant care, arguing this would reduce criminal recidivism and be better for those relatives than remaining in the community with other relatives or in a care facility. Advocates for the elderly would vehemently protest. There is thus among most liberals an implicit denigration of this most vulnerable population—newborn children—by people who ordinarily show great solicitude for vulnerable populations. In the next chapter, I delve deeper into the explanation for that.

Summary

Liberals justly pride themselves on being compassionate and respectful toward the worst-off in our society. When members within the worst-off families have unified interests, liberals' concern genuinely extends to children as well as parents. But when the interests of children and parents conflict, because parents are not able to care for the children even if they receive what assistance child welfare agencies have to offer, liberals' sympathies and protective impulses run primarily to the adults. They then manifest a fanatical commitment to the dogma that every parent is fixable and deserves endless opportunity to prove it. They flail about searching for the magical program of rehabilitation that will make involuntary TPR a bad collective memory. They deny any conflict of interests exists, insisting that so long as there is any chance of parents reforming, then it is good for children to wait. They project onto children profound needs children do not actually have, discounting or ignoring needs children actually have, viewing permanency planning through an adult-timeline lens. They accuse anyone who disagrees with them of being callous, racist, classist, judgmental, genocidal, imperialist child stealers. But they fail to see their own callous indifference to the needs of children, especially black children, and their responsibility for those children becoming damaged persons themselves, because they (liberals) oppose the reforms necessary to prevent that from happening.

Notes

1 See, for example, Wakefield and Wildeman (2014, 162).
2 *Foster Care Statistics 2015* (Children's Bureau, 2017).
3 Williams (2015, 302).
4 Appell (1997, 578–9). See also Dixon (2008, 109) (contending that white middle class case workers fail to appreciate cultural differences, hold racist assumptions about the deficiency of blacks as parents, and have less respect for black families' integrity and privacy than they have for white families).
5 See, for example, White (2006).
6 See, for example, Dixon (2008, 111) ("The dogma that supported four centuries of chattel slavery has proven to be a continuing presence that affects major facets of life for many African-Americans").
7 See, for example, Murray and Luker (2015, 323) (asserting that a research time had "found that forty-nine percent of female adolescents in foster care reported forced sex," and citing a study that actually made no finding as to the percentage of girls forced to have sex by a member of a foster-care household (as opposed to, for example, having come into foster

care because they were sexually abused in their parents' household, or being raped after leaving foster care); Cooper (2013, 218–19) ("Once in foster care, however, children face heightened risk for abuse and neglect within the system itself and generally suffer poorer outcomes and prospects, as studies and current events repeatedly demonstrate. What this means, therefore, is that African American and Native American children, especially those who are poor, are disproportionately more likely to enter foster care, where they are at high risk of secondary harm by the system itself").

8 See *Child Welfare Outcomes 2010–2014: Report to Congress*, 3; Child Trends Data Bank, *Child Maltreatment: Indicators of Wellbeing* (2016).

9 See, for example, Smith and Fong (2004, 47–52).

10 See, for example, Baeder (2013) (noting that in Los Angeles County, where 8 percent of children are black: "Of the 3,179 county social workers who make up the county's front-line staff, 907 [~30%] are black. The largest number of social workers, 1,390, are Hispanic. About 590 are white. Some 280 are Asian or Filipino. And 10 are American Indian."); Silver (2015, 8) (noting that most case managers for youth in a supervised independent living program were black women).

11 Council on Social Work Education (2016, 22) (showing that one quarter of full-time students, and one third of part-time students, for social work as a whole, were black).

12 See Drake and Jonson-Reid (2011, 16–20).

13 See Drake and Jonson-Reid (2011, 17) (quoting the final report as saying "The NIS findings suggest … that the differential representation of minorities in the child welfare population does not derive from inherent differences in the rates at which they are abused or neglected."); Bartholet (2016, 729). ("Independent research eventually demonstrated that the claim at the heart of the Racial Disproportionality movement was a lie. The NIS-3 study's own data, hidden in a later-published appendix, showed that black children were victimized by maltreatment at much higher rates than white children, and indeed at rates that roughly matched their removal rates.)

14 Elizabeth Bartholet (2009), 873–4.

15 Bartholet (2009, 879).

16 See, for example, Dixon (2008).

17 Bartholet (2009, 873).

18 Bartholet (2009, 876). See also American Bar Association House of Delegates (2008) (urging that all "child welfare agencies, dependency courts and judges, government, parents' and children's attorneys, guardians ad litem and court-appointed special advocates to receive training on cultural competencies, institutional biases, and avoidance of disparate treatment of racial and ethnic minority children and families").

19 Zero to Three (2014).

20 Zero to Three (2014).

21 Sedlak, McPherson, and Das (2010a); Bartholet (2012, 1325–7, 1339–40). See also *The National Incidence Study (NIS): Statistics* (2013); Sedlak, McPherson, and Das (2010b, 4).

22 See Font, Berger, and Slack (2012).

23 See Dettlaff (2014, 149–68).

24 See, for example, Beniwal (2017, 1043) ("some studies indicate that there is no difference in the overall maltreatment rate between black children and white children. Still others suggest that the maltreatment rates for black children are actually lower than that of white children" and citing sources basing their claims on NIS-3); Williams (2015, 302); Murray and Luker (2015, 322–3); Cooper (2013, 252) (asserting: "Well documented in foster care, unintentional bias affects all of the system's players." and in support citing only articles from 1997 and 2007 that relied on the NIS-3 reporters' false claims, and the fact that there are "many conferences, some annual, which address this issue"); Roberts (2012, 1486) ("it takes more risk of maltreatment for a white child to be placed in foster care compared to the risk for a black child"); Whittico (2015, 427–9); Williams (2015, 302–4); Federle (2014, 706) (conceding that "[t]he most recent estimates of the incidences of abuse and neglect in the United States found statistically significant racial differences in the rates of maltreatment") and Federle (2014, 711) (but nevertheless charging: "The disproportionate representation of African American children in the child welfare system, for example, is … evidence of systemic and institutionalized racism").

25 Sedlak, McPherson, and Das (2010b, 1). In middle- and upper-income households, black children were still at somewhat higher risk than white children at the same SES level, but the rates for all racial groups were much lower than in low-income households. *Idem*, at 14–15.

26 Sedlak, McPherson, and Das (2010b, 1).

27 Children's Bureau, 2017, 9).

28 See, for example, Zullo (2013) ("between 2011 and 2013, turnover in [Richmond, VA] Child Protective Services more than doubled and average caseloads increased to 46 active cases per month, nearly four times the standard set by the Child Welfare League of America").

29 See Kwiatkowski (2017).

30 See Bartholet (2009, 910–11); Bartholet (2012, 1334, 1354–5).

31 Cf. Washington (2012). ("Victims and perpetrators of domestic violence in Norfolk were overwhelmingly African American").

32 Bartholet (2015, 578–9).

33 Bartholet (2015, 582).

34 See Dexheimer and Ball (2015), ("Each prior removal of a child increased the odds of death by a multiple of 14. In short, 'a prior removal just skyrocketed a kid's risk of dying,'" quoting Albert Blackmon, a data scientist for the North Carolina-based SAS Institute, who studied the family histories in 779 child maltreatment-caused fatalities).

35 Gelles (1996, 133–5).

36 Bartholet (2015, 582).

37 See Barth and Brooks (2000), 23.

38 See Brook, Akin, Lloyd, and Yan (2015, 36); Marlowe and Carey (2012, 1) ("more than 60% of parents in dependency cases do not comply adequately with substance abuse treatment conditions and more than 80% fail to complete treatment"); Choi, Huang, and Ryan (2012) (reporting on a demonstration program in Illinois, in an urban area with a predominantly African-American population (78 percent), that provided assessment, services, and a "Recovery Coach" to mothers in a regular juvenile court, finding that 27 percent of mothers regained custody of their children, and noting that a prior study had found "only 22% of mothers successfully completed all required levels of care including detoxification, residential inpatient, intensive outpatient, outpatient, recovery home, and support group," and another that found "only 23.4% of parents completed all recommended substance abuse treatments including inpatient, partial hospitalization, intensive outpatient, and outpatient treatment programs.") These studies look at parents who enter treatment, so exclude those who refuse or simply never show up to initial sessions or intake. Thus, the rate of reunification for all substance-abusing parents from whom children are removed and who go through the traditional juvenile-court process is likely below 20 percent.

39 For example, Oetjen, Cohen, Tribble, and Suthahar (2003, 6) (stating that the judge aims to establish a "rehabilitative relationship" and "consciously therapeutic rapport" with parents), 8 (stating that the FDC favors a "non-adversarial approach").

40 Choi (2012, 450–1).

41 Cf. Haack, Alemi, Nemes, and Cohen (2005, 19) (stating that the parent is "the party" before the court, and that the federal government's Office of Justice Programs, which has overseen the development of FDCs, has "identified the goals of FDC as to help the parent to become emotionally, financially, and personally self-sufficient and to develop parenting and coping skills adequate for serving as an effective parent on a day-to-day basis."); Oetjen, Cohen, Tribble and Suthahar (2003, 3) (stating that "parents are the 'clients'" in FDCs).

42 Cf. Haack, Alemi, Nemes, and Cohen (2005) ("The distinction between judicial activity and substance abuse treatment blurs …").

43 See Brook, Akin, Lloyd, Johnson-Motoyama, and Yan (2016, 24). See also Haack, Alemi, Nemes, and Cohen (2005, 18) ("Family Drug Courts were developed in part as the judiciary's response to ASFA's stringent time lines. It was an attempt to recognize and accommodate the chronic relapsing nature of substance abuse and the co-morbid conditions that accompany it").

44 Choi (2012, 448).

45 Office of Juvenile Justice and Delinquency Prevention, "Literature Review: Family Drug Courts" (2016). See also Brook *et al.* (2015, 37) ("Much previous research on FDCs is limited in rigor").

46 See, for example, Dakof, Cohen, and Duarte (2009, 13) ("Family/dependency drug courts were established to assist courts and child welfare agencies in their efforts to help parents overcome their drug dependency so they can provide a healthy and safe environment for their children and avoid losing their parental rights"). See also *idem* at 12 (stating that drug courts "with their emphasis on recovery and personal transformation in lieu of punishment, embody the principles of therapeutic jurisprudence").

47 See 42 U.S.C.A. § 675A (requiring states, following removal of a child, to develop a "plan for assuring that the child receives safe and proper care and that services are provided to the parents, child, and foster parents in order to improve the conditions in the parents' home, facilitate return of the child to his own safe home…"

48 Cosden and Koch (2015), looked at children who reunified with FDC parents and asked whether they had improved on certain measures from initial removal to time of reunification (finding that 14 percent to 34 percent of them had improved to some significant degree while in foster care on seven measures—gross motor, fine motor, communication, personal-social, internalizing, externalizing, and problem solving). They did not follow up with the children after return to parents.

49 Cf. Brook *et al.* (2015, 37) (characterizing the aim of FDCs as "balancing the rights and needs of parents and children").

50 See Gifford, Eldred, Vernerey, and Sloan (2014, 1661) (summarizing studies); Marlowe and Carey (2012, 8–9) (presenting a tabular summary of those prior to 2012.)

51 van Wormer and Hsieh (2016, 52–3).

52 There was actually a higher treatment-completion rate among those who refused to participate in the FDC. Ashford (2004, 34).

53 Chuang, Moore, Barrett, and Young (2012, 1897) (stating that four of five previous studies "found either no impact on time to permanency or a significant increase in time to permanency due to FDTC participation"); Gifford, Eldred, Vernerey, and Sloan (2014, 1661).

54 See Gifford, Eldred, Vernerey, and Sloan (2014, 1661).

55 See Marlowe and Carey (2012, 3). The overlap with reunification is not indicated.

56 See Putnam-Hornstein, Schneiderman, Cleves, Magruder, and Krous (2014).

57 Cf. Brook, Akin, Lloyd, Johnson-Motoyama, and Yan (2016) (comparing cost to state for FDTC cases versus comparison-group cases but not even mentioning the (presumably drastically lower) cost of cases as to which CPS seeks immediate TPR).

58 Haack, Alemi, Nemes, and Cohen (2005, 20). Most of these parents have older children as well, though; overall, three quarters of cases before those FDCs involved two or more children. *Idem*, 21.

59 Haack, Alemi, Nemes, and Cohen (2005, 21).

60 See, for example, Florida Statutes 39.001 ("(1) The purposes of this chapter are: (a) To provide for the care, safety, and protection of children in an environment that fosters healthy social, emotional, intellectual, and physical development; to ensure secure and safe custody; to promote the health and well-being of all children under the state's care; and to prevent the occurrence of child abuse, neglect, and abandonment…. (b) 1. The health and safety of the children served shall be of paramount concern."); [south Carolina Code].

61 See Child Welfare Information Gateway (2017).

62 Cocaine appears still to be the most common. See Dakof, Cohen, and Duarte (2009, 18).

63 Most FDC parents are high school dropouts living on welfare and have no partner to assist with parenting. Dakof, Cohen, and Duarte (2009, 18), cf. Haack, Alemi, Nemes, and Cohen (2005), at 21 (stating that 80 percent of FDC cases involve an allegation of domestic violence).

64 See, for example, Huang and Ryan (2011), § 3.2; Oliveros and Kaufman (2011, 30) (describing research finding "recovery coaches" increase reunification rates only from 13 percent to 18 percent); *idem*, at 33–4 (summarizing studies showing that FDCs increase reunification rates substantially but with average stay in foster care still over a year, and that FDCs also double the rate of renewed maltreatment and return to foster care); Budde and Harden (2003) (finding that in Illinois only 14 percent of substance exposed infants achieved reunification within 7 years).

65 See Hughes, Rycus, Saunders-Adams, Hughes, and Hughes (2013, 504–6) (characterizing as grossly overstated the frequent complaint that CPS is "inflexible," "legalistic," and "threatening"); Kohl (2007, 5) (stating that in the overwhelming majority of cases that come to CPS attention, the child is kept at home with a biological parent or another caregiver, even if parents do not receive services).
66 Houston (2017).
67 See, for example, Gupta-Kagan (2014, 900).
68 Cf. Steffen *et al.* (2012) ("Of the 72 children who have died since 2007 after their families or caregivers came to the attention of social services, 13 had every call made to child welfare workers screened out, or left unassigned and uninvestigated."); Meinig and Dowd (2005) (noting instance in which a mother had two prior reports alleging substance-abuse related neglect, but the caseworker assigned the third report noted "No prior history with CPS").
69 See, for example, Zullo (2012) (reporting that "a social services deputy director accused in one of the letters of taking 'drastic measures to ensure that children remain in abusive homes,' is on administrative leave").
70 Zullo (2012).
71 Williams (2015, 303).
72 Williams (2015, 305).
73 Bartholet 2015, 576–7, 591–2); Heimpel (2014a) (quoting Eric Fenner, the managing director at Casey Family Programs, who stated that they had "goals of 70 percent").
74 See Hughes, Rycus, Saunders-Adams, Hughes, and Hughes (2013, 497) ("One research study identified that the percentage of families assigned to the alternative track in different counties ranged from 19% to 70% … Other state exhibited differences in the percentages … with 47% in Minnesota, 61% in Virginia, and 71% in Missouri."); Janczewski and Mersky (2016, 124) (on percentage of AR cases); *idem*, 128 (finding no difference in treatment between whites and African-Americans.); Virginia Child Protective Services (2016), "CPS Accountability Referrals Type Of Abuse Annual Report: Report Period: 7/1/2015 to 6/30/2016—Statewide Data" (showing 20,090 valid reports investigated and 44,664 valid reports diverted to "family assessment"); Kyte, Trocmé, and Chamberland (2013, 129) (stating that approximately 60 to 80 percent of cases are diverted to a DR track in many states).
75 Bartholet (2015, 579).
76 See Vaughan-Eden and Vandervort (2013, 551) ("the vast majority of families who come to the attention of CPS are quite dysfunctional. Many are overtly pathological and either unable or unwilling to make the changes necessary to provide for their children's physical and emotional safety and/or to provide a minimal level of responsible care").
77 Commission to Eliminate Child Abuse and Neglect Fatalities (2016, 43–4).
78 See Commission to Eliminate Child Abuse and Neglect Fatalities (2016, 18).
79 See Bartholet (2015, 596) (citing Nancy Peddle *et al.*, 2002 (finding a one-third rate of re-reporting within 12 months)).
80 Putnam-Hornstein, Simon, Eastman, and Magruder (2014).
81 *Child Welfare Outcomes 2010–2014: Report to Congress* (2017, 3).
82 Mersky and Janczewski (2013, 369) ("research has shown that crime and its earlier behavioral correlates do not vary as a function of placement status…. Moreover, some evidence suggests that out-of-home placement actually reduces the risk of juvenile arrest or incarceration for racial and ethnic minority youth"); *idem*, 373–4 (finding long-term outcomes for former foster-care youths similar or better to youths who remained in the home after a maltreatment report, even though the households of the non-removed youths presumably presented lesser dangers than the homes from which foster-care youth were removed); Bartholet (2015, 597); Berrick (2008, 108–17); and Taussig, Clyman, and Landsverk (2001, 6) ("There was, and continues to be, a pervasive belief that reunification is best for children, despite the lack of research to support this assertion…. Studies that have interviewed current and former foster children report that the youth generally had positive feelings about being placed in foster care. Most youth thought it was in their best interest and reported that things would have gotten worse at home without child welfare intervention").
83 Bartholet (2015 602–3) ("One California DR study found that almost half of the AR sample cases analyzed in the program were either 'high risk' or 'very high risk' … Even the advocacy

research that purports to find DR successful documents the serious risk characterizing many cases on the AR track. A 2010 Ohio study found that almost half of the AR cases had at least one past report of abuse and neglect, and almost 15% had four or more prior reports. A recent Colorado study noted that 76% of the AR cases were medium risk and 10% were high risk."); Steffen *et al.* (2012) ("in 2011 there were 7,039 third referrals of abuse or neglect that should have automatically been investigated under the policy. Fewer than half—47 percent—were investigated").

84 Bartholet (2015, 603) ("The California study noted above reveals a one-third re-report rate within the brief nine-month AR treatment period. Even the lead authors of the early advocacy research supporting DR, Tony Loman and Gary Siegel, note the "high rates of recidivism." Their 2014 Ohio Report shows that roughly half of all AR families received at least one subsequent family risk assessment. Their 2004 Minnesota Report says the overall re-report rate is about one in three families during a relatively short tracking period of two to three years. It predicts that long-term rates would rise to something like the general CPS recurrence rate of 65%. In an interview, Tony Loman indicated that typically in his DR research, he found an unduly high re-report rate, noting that in the Missouri DR program, the rate was 50% to 60% after five to seven years").

85 Heimpel (2014b).

86 Zullo (2013).

87 Bartholet (2015, 603–4).

88 Children's Bureau, "Issue Brief: Differential Response to Reports of Child Abuse and Neglect" (Child Welfare Information Gateway, 2014).

89 See Bartholet (2015, 620–5).

90 See Bartholet (2015, 615–16).

91 See, for example, Dice, Claussen, Katz, and Cohen (2004, 1) (asserting, without supporting citation, that the non-FDC court process for responding to child maltreatment and endangerment is punitive).

92 Dallaire, Zeman, and Thrash (2015, 23–4, 35).

93 For fuller description of the programs and governing laws and policies, and for citations to the research relied on below, see Dwyer (2014).

94 See, for example, Goshin and Byrne (2009, 276) (characterizing the recidivism studies as "specious," but shortly thereafter stating: "Decreased recidivism after release from a nursery program is currently the positive outcome with the most empirical support…. Decreased maternal recidivism is an undoubtedly positive outcome for children as well as their mothers"). See also Goshin and Byrne (2009, 289) ("The evidence linking prison nursery participation to large reductions in recidivism makes them politically viable.") The problem with most of the studies, specifically, is that they compare recidivism rates for the entire prison population, or for the entire prison population minus the women in the prison nurseries, to the recidivism rate for inmates who *passed the screening process* for entering the prison nursery program *and who remained there until their release*. Because the prisons screen out from the nursery programs more serious offenders, and because a significant portion of women who enter the prison nurseries drop out before release because they lose interest or commit a rule infraction, the comparison is illicit. The women who complete the prison nursery programs have background characteristics significantly different from those of the rest of the prison population, characteristics that make them less likely to reoffend anyways. That is a good thing for the program, but it belies any claims that a lower rate of recidivism among the nursery-program completers is *because of being in the program*. It is equally possible that the nursery-program had no effect on the recidivism for that select group or that it actually increased recidivism among them—for example, if it distracted them from working on their underlying mental health, addiction, and family problems.

95 Some proponents also point out that prison nurseries are common in other countries, but I do not know whether that convinces anyone in the US to think they are a good idea. See, for example, Yager (2015, 67). The reality is that developing countries have no foster care or adoption systems, so children born to prison inmates whose relatives do not want them literally have no other way to survive except to go into prison, and the governments of those countries express dismay that this is happening to children, are embarrassed by it, and have laws strongly discouraging it. For example, in Cambodia, state officials must try to

identify alternatives, and the law speaks of a child's right to be separated from imprisoned parents. The African Charter on Rights & Welfare of Children commits state parties to try to ensure that children are not imprisoned with their mothers. And a woman in Nepal was named one of the "Top Heroes of 2012" by CNN for trying to get small children out of prisons and into the community, even though the only apparent alternative is an institutional setting. Other western nations that have prison nurseries generally have less prison-like prisons, house a population that comes from less toxic backgrounds, and, in any event, are governed by people who are just as adult-focused as are Americans; putting babies in prison is viewed as the mothers' right.

96 See, for example, Yager (2015, 69) (quoting a prison-nursery advocate on the University of Nebraska criminal-justice faculty as claiming that Nebraska's prison nursery program "would pay for itself over time" because its costs "total about 40 percent less each year than foster care for the babies who would otherwise end up there").

97 Cf. Baradaran (2013, 175) (stating: "Typically, no one calls the police when drugs are sold or used" and "police choose to apprehend only about 10% of drug users"); Yager (2015, 69) (noting that more than half of the mothers in the Nebraska prison nursery reported that their own mothers had been incarcerated).

98 Mothers of Bedford Hills (Covey Productions Apr. 2011) (documentary film).

99 See Goshin (2015, 479) (citing studies).

100 See, for example, Ocen (2011) ("the disablement experience by Black women is exacerbated by the sexual abuse, medical neglect, and solitary confinement that are rampant in prisons").

101 See, for example, McLaughlin, Sheridan, Tibu, Fox, Zeanah, and Nelson (2015); Mueller et al. (2010, 337) (noting "risk for later psychopathology, including anxiety, depression, post-traumatic stress disorder, substance abuse, and psychosis").

102 See Women's Prison Association (2009).

103 See, for example, Yager (2015, 66) (reporting that the manager of one prison nursery stated "The long-term goal is that women leave better than when they came in").

Bibliography

American Bar Association House of Delegates. *Reducing Racial Disparities in the Child Welfare System*. American Bar Association House of Delegates, 2008.

Appell, Annette R. "Protecting Children or Punishing Mothers: Gender, Race, and Class in the Child Protection System," *South Carolina Law Review* 48 (1997): 577–613.

Ashford, José B. "Treating Substance-Abusing Parents: A Study of the Pima County Family Drug Court Approach," *Juvenile & Family Court Journal* 55 (2004): 27–37.

Baeder, Ben. "Studies: Disproportionate Number of Black Children Wind Up in L.A. Foster Care." *Los Angeles Daily News*. March 23, 2013.

Baradaran, Shima. "Race, Prediction, and Discretion," *The George Washington Law Review* 81(1) (2013): 157–222.

Barth, Richard and Devon Books. "Outcomes of Drug-Exposed Children Eight Years Posta-doption." In *Adoption and Prenatal Alcohol and Drug Exposure: Research, Policy and Practice*, edited by R.P. Barth, M. Freundlich, and D. Brodzinsky. Washington, DC: Child Welfare League of America (2000): 23–58.

Brooks, Devon and Richard P. Barth. "Characteristics and Outcomes of Drug-Exposed and Non Drug-Exposed Children in Kinship and Non-Relative Foster Care," *Children and Youth Services* Review 20(6) (1998): 475–501.

Bartholet, Elizabeth. "The Racial Disproportionality Movement in Child Welfare: False Facts and Dangerous Directions," *Arizona Law Review* 51 (2009): 871–932.

Bartholet, Elizabeth. "Creating a Child-Friendly Child Welfare System: Effective Early Intervention to Prevent Maltreatment and Protect Victimized Children," *Buffalo Law Review* 60 (2012): 1321–72.

Bartholet, Elizabeth. "Differential Response: A Dangerous Experiment in Child Welfare," *Florida State University Law Review* 42 (2015): 573–643.

Bartholet, Elizabeth. "Thoughts on the Liberal Dilemma in Child Welfare Reform," *William & Mary Bill of Rights Journal* 24 (2016): 725–32.

Beniwal, Rakesh. "Implicit Bias in Child Welfare: Overcoming Intent," *Connecticut Law Review* 49(3) (2017): 1021–67.

Berrick, Jill Duerr. *Take Me Home*. New York: Oxford University Press, 2008.

Brook, Jody, Becci A. Akin, Margaret H. Lloyd, and Yueqi Yan. "Family Drug Court, Targeted Parent Training and Family Reunification: Did This Enhanced Service Strategy Make a Difference?" *Juvenile & Family Court Journal* 66(2) (2015): 35–52.

Brook, Jody, Becci A. Akin, Margaret H. Lloyd, Michelle Johnson-Motoyama, and Yueqi Yan. "Family Drug Treatment Courts as Comprehensive Service Models: Cost Considerations," *Juvenile & Family Court Journal* 67(3) (2016): 23–43.

Budde, Stephen and A. Harden. "Substance Exposed Infants in Illinois (1998–2001): Trends in Caseloads, Placement, and Subsequent Maltreatment." Chicago, IL: Chapin Hall Center for Children, 2003.

Child Trends Data Bank. *Child Maltreatment: Indicators of Wellbeing*. Bethesda, MD: Child Trends Data Bank, 2016.

Child Welfare Information Gateway. *Issue Brief: Differential Response to Reports of Child Abuse and Neglect*. Washington, DC: Child Welfare Information Gateway, Children's Bureau, 2014.

Child Welfare Information Gateway. *Structured Decision-Making*. Washington, DC: Child Welfare Information Gateway, Children's Bureau, Administration for Children & Families, US Department of Health & Human Services. 2017.

Child Welfare Outcomes 2010–2014: Report to Congress. Washington, DC: Children's Bureau, Administration for Children & Families, US Department of Health & Human Services, 2017.

Children's Bureau. *Foster Care Statistics 2015: Numbers and Trends March 2017*. Washington, DC: Child Welfare Information Gateway, Children's Bureau/ACYF/ACF/HHS, 2017.

Choi, Sam, Hui Huang, and Joseph P. Ryan. "Substance Abuse Treatment Completion in Child Welfare: Does Substance Abuse Treatment Completion Matter in the Decision to Reunify Families?" *Children and Youth Services Review* 34(9) (2012): 1639–45.

Choi, Sam. "Family Drug Courts in Child Welfare," *Child and Adolescent Social Work Journal* 29(6) (2012): 447–61.

Chuang, Emmeline, Kathleen Moore, Blake Barrett, and M. Scott Young. "Effect of an Integrated Family Dependency Treatment Court on Child Welfare Reunification, Time to Permanency and Re-entry Rates," *Children and Youth Services Review* 34(9) (2012): 1896–902.

Commission to Eliminate Child Abuse and Neglect Fatalities. *Within Our Reach: A National Strategy to Eliminate Child Abuse and Neglect Fatalities*. Washington, DC: Commission to Eliminate Child Abuse and Neglect Fatalities, Children's Bureau, Administration for Children & Families, US Department of Health & Human Services, 2016.

Cooper, Tanya Asim. "Racial Bias in American Foster Care: The National Debate," *Marquette Law Review* 97(2) (2013): 215–77.

Cosden, Merith and Lauren M. Koch. "Changes in Adult, Child, and Family Functioning among Participants in a Family Treatment Drug Court," *Child Welfare* 94(5) (2015): 89–106.

Council on Social Work Education. *2015 Annual Statistics on Social Work Education in the United States*. Council on Social Work Education, 2016.

Dakof, Gayle A., Jeri B. Cohen, and Eliette Duarte. "Increasing Family Reunification for Substance-Abusing Mothers and their Children: Comparing Two Drug Court Interventions in Miami," *Juvenile and Family Court Journal* 60 (2009): 11–23.

Dallaire, Danielle, Janice Zeman, and Todd Thrash. "Differential Effects of Type of Children's Contact with Their Jailed Mothers and Children's Behavior Problems." In *Children's Contact with Incarcerated Parents: Implications for Policy and Intervention*, edited by Julie Poehlmann-Tynan. Cham, Switzerland: Springer International Publishing, 2015: 23–38.

Dettlaff, Alan J. "The Evolving Understanding of Disproportionality and Disparities in Child Welfare." In *Handbook of Child Maltreatment*, edited by Jill E. Korbin and Richard D. Kingman. Dordrecht, the Netherlands: Springer, 2014: 149–68.

Dexheimer, Eric and Andea Ball. *State Moves toward Intervention before Tragedy Strikes. Missed Signs, Fatal Consequences: Part 3: Agency Has Faced Uphill Battle.* Statesman Investigates: Austin American-Statesman, 2015.

Dice, Jaime L., Angelika H. Claussen, Lynne F. Katz, and Jeri B. Cohen. "Parenting in Dependency Drug Court," *Juvenile and Family Court Journal* 55(3) (2004): 1–10.

Dixon, Jessica. "The African-American Child Welfare Act: A Legal Redress for African-American Disproportionality in Child Protection Cases," *Berkeley Journal of African-American Law & Policy* 10(2) (2008): 449–535.

Drake, Brett and Melissa Jonson-Reid. "NIS Interpretations: Race and the National Incidence Studies of Child Abuse and Neglect," *Children and Youth Services Review* 33(1) (2011): 16–20.

Dwyer, James G. "Jailing Black Babies," *Utah Law Review* 465(3) (October 2014): 465–541.

Federle, Katherine Hunt. "The Violence of Paternalism," *Wake Forest Law Review* 49 (2014): 703–12.

Font, Sarah A., Lawrence M. Berger, and Kristen S. Slack. "Examining Racial Disproportionality in Child Protective Services Case Decisions," *Children and Youth Services Review* 34(11) (2012): 2188–200.

Gelles, Richard. *The Book of David: How Preserving Families Can Cost Children's Lives.* New York: Basic Books, 1996.

Gifford, Elizabeth Joanne, Lindsey Morgan Eldred, Allison Vernerey, and Frank Sloan. "How Does Family Drug Treatment Court Participation Affect Child Welfare Outcomes?" *Child Abuse & Neglect* 38(10) (2014): 1659–70.

Goshin, Lorie. "Ethnographic Assessment of an Alternative to Incarceration for Women with Minor Children," *American Journal of Orthopsychiatry* 85(5) (2015): 469–82.

Goshin, Lorie Smith and Mary Woods Byrne. "Converging Streams of Opportunity for Prison Nursery Programs in the United States," *Journal of Offender Rehabilitation* 48(4) (2009): 271–95.

Gupta-Kagan, Josh. "Toward a Public Health Legal Structure for Child Welfare," *Nebraska Law Review* 92(4) (2014): 897–965.

Haack, Mary, Farrokh Alemi, Susanna Nemes, and Jeri B. Cohen. "Experience with Family Drug Courts in Three Cities," *Substance Abuse* 25(4) (2005): 17–25.

Heimpel, Daniel. "Are Child Protection Quotas Endangering Minnesota Children?" *The Chronicle of Social Change.* September 22, 2014a.

Heimpel, Daniel. "Differential Response Dealt Heavy Blow," *The Chronicle of Social Change.* June 24, 2014b.

Houston, Claire. "What Ever Happened to the 'Child Maltreatment Revolution'?" *The Georgetown Journal of Gender and the Law* 19(1) (2017): 1–42.

Huang, Hui and Joseph P. Ryan. "Trying to Come Home: Substance Exposed Infants, Mothers, and Family Reunification," *Children and Youth Services Review* 33(2) (2011): 322–9.

Hughes, Ronald C., Judith S. Rycus, Stacey M. Saunders-Adams, Laura K. Hughes, and Kelli N. Hughes. "Issues in Differential Response," *Research on Social Work Practice* 23(5) (2013): 493–520.

Janczewski, Colleen E. and Joshua P. Mersky. "What's so Different about Differential Response?" *Children and Youth Services Review* 67 (2016): 123–32.

Kohl, Patricia L. *Unsuccessful In-Home Child Welfare Service Plans Following a Maltreatment Investigation: Racial and Ethnic Differences.* Casey-CSSP Alliance for Racial Equity in Child Welfare, 2007.

Kwiatkowski, Marisa. "Advocates Claim State's Child Welfare System is Drowning; DCS Director: Kids will Die under Holcomb's Policies," *The Indianapolis Star,* December 20, 2017.

Kyte, Alicia, Nico Trocmé, and Claire Chamberland. "Evaluating Where We're at with Differential Response," *Child Abuse & Neglect* 37(2–3) (February–March 2013): 125–9.

Marlowe, Douglas B. and Shannon M. Carey. "Research Update on Family Drug Courts." National Association of Drug Court Professionals, 2012.

McLaughlin, Katie A., Margaret A. Sheridan, Florin Tibu, Nathan A. Fox, Charles H. Zeanah, and Charles A. Nelson. "Causal Effects of the Early Caregiving Environment on Development of Stress Response Systems in Children," *Proceedings of the National Academy of Sciences of the United States of America* 112(18) (2015): 5637–42.

Meinig, Mary and Patrick Dowd. "Justice and Raiden Robinson Fatalities Review." State of Washington Office of the Family and Children's Ombudsman, 2005.

Mersky, Joshua P. and Colleen Janczewski. "Adult Well-Being of Foster Care Alumni: Comparisons to Other Child Welfare Recipients and a Non-Child Welfare Sample in a High-Risk, Urban Setting," *Children and Youth Services Review* 35(3) (2013): 367–76.

Mothers of Bedford. Directed by Jenifer McShane. Covey Productions, 2011.

Mueller, Sven C., Francoise S. Maheu, Mary Dozier, Elizabeth Peloso, Darcy Mandell, Ellen Leibenluft, Daniel S. Pine, and Monique Ernst. "Early-Life Stress is Associated with Impairment in Cognitive Control in Adolescence: An fMRI study," *Neuropsychologia* 48(10) (2010): 3037–44.

Murray, Melissa and Kristin Luker. *Cases on Reproductive Rights and Justice*. St. Paul, MN: Foundation Press, 2015.

National Incidence Study (NIS): Statistics. Washington, DC: Child Welfare Information Gateway, Children's Bureau, Administration for Children & Families, US Department of Health & Human Services, 2013.

Ocen, Priscilla A. "Beyond Analogy: A Response to Surfacing Disability through a Critical Race Theoretical Paradigm," *Georgetown Journal of Law and Modern Critical Race Perspectives* 2 (2011): 255–6.

Oetjen, Cohen, Tribble and Suthahar. "Development of the Miami-Dade County Dependency Drug Court, Technical Assistance Brief." Permanency Planning for Children Department, National Council of Juvenile and Family Court Judges, 2003.

Office of Juvenile Justice and Delinquency Prevention. *Literature Review: Family Drug Courts*. Washington, DC: Office of Juvenile Justice and Delinquency Prevention, 2016.

Oliveros, Arazais and Joan Kaufman. "Addressing Substance Abuse Treatment Needs of Parents Involved with the Child Welfare System," *Child Welfare* 90(1) (2011): 25–41.

Peddle, Nancy, Ching-Tung Wang, Javier Díaz, and Robert Reid. *Current Trends in Child Abuse Prevention and Fatalities: The 2000 Fifty State Survey*. Chicago, IL: Prevent Child Abuse America, National Center on Child Abuse Prevention Research, 2002.

Putnam-Hornstein, Emily, James David Simon, Andrea Lane Eastman, and Joseph Magruder. "Risk of Re-Reporting among Infants Who Remain at Home Following Alleged Maltreatment," *Child Maltreatment* 20(2) (2014): 92–103.

Putnam-Hornstein, Emily, Janet U. Schneiderman, Mario A. Cleves, Joseph Magruder, and Henry F. Krous. "A Prospective Study of Sudden Unexpected Infant Death after Reported Maltreatment," *The Journal of Pediatrics* 164 (1) (2014): 142–8.

Roberts, Dorothy E. "The Community Dimension of State Child Protection," *Hofstra Law Review* 34 (2005): 23–37.

Roberts, Dorothy E. "Prison, Foster Care, and the Systemic Punishment of Black Mothers," *UCLA Law Review* 59 (2012): 1474–500.

Sedlak, Andrea J., Jane Mettenburg, Monica Basena, Ian Petta, Karla McPherson, Angela Greene, and Spencer Li. *Fourth National Incidence Study of Child Abuse and Neglect (NIS–4)*. Washington, DC: US Department of Health and Human Services, Administration for Children and Families, 2010a.

Sedlak, Andrea, Karla McPherson, and Barnali Das. *Fourth National Incidence Study of Child Abuse and Neglect (NIS–4): Supplementary Analysis of Race Differences in Child Maltreatment Rates in the NIS-4*. Washington, DC: Office of Planning, Research, and Evaluation (OPRE) and the Children's Bureau Administration for Children and Families (ACF), US Department of Health and Human Services (DHHS), 2010b.

Silver, Lauren J. *System Kids: Adolescent Mothers and the Politics of Regulation.* Durham, NC: The University of North Carolina Press, 2015.

Smith, Margaret G. and Rowena Fong. *The Children of Neglect: When no One Cares.* New York: Brunner-Routledge, 2004.

Steffen, Jordan *et al.* "Failed to Death/Screened out Tragic Calls," *The Denver Post.* November 13, 2012.

Taussig, Heather N., Robert B. Clyman, and John Landsverk. "Children Who Return Home from Foster Care: A 6-Year Prospective Study of Behavioral Health Outcomes in Adolescence," *Pediatrics* 108(1) (2001): 1–6.

Vaughan-Eden, Viola and Frank E. Vandervort. "Invited Commentary on 'Issues in Differential Response'," *Research on Social Work Practice* 23(5) (2013): 550–1.

Virginia Child Protective Service. *CPS Accountability Referrals Type of Abuse Annual Report: Report Period: 7/1/2015 to 6/30/2016—Statewide Data.* Virginia Child Protective Service, 2016.

Wakefield, Sara and Christopher Wildeman. *Children of the Prison Boom: Mass Incarceration and the Future of American Inequality (Studies in Crime and Public Policy).* New York: Oxford University Press, 2014.

Washington, Michelle. "Teamwork, Saving Lives." *The Virginia Pilot*, March 27, 2012.

White, Christina. "Federally Mandated Destruction of the Black Family: The Adoption and Safe Families Act," *Northwestern Journal of Law & Social Policy* 1(1) (2006): 303–31.

Whittico, Gloria Ann. "If 'Past is Prologue': Toward the Development of A New 'Freedom Suit' for the Remediation of Foster Care Disproportionalities among African-American Children," *Capital University Law Review* 43 (2015): 407–34.

Williams, Starla J. "Violence against Poor and Minority Women & the Containment of Children of Color: A Response to Dorothy E. Roberts," *Widener Law Journal* 24(289) (2015): 289–311.

Women's Prison Association. *Prison Nursery Programs a Growing Trend in Women's Prisons.* Corrections.com, 2009.

van Wormer, Jacqueline and Ming-Li Hsieh. "Healing Families: Outcomes from a Family Drug Treatment Court," *Juvenile & Family Court Journal* 67(2) (2016): 49–65.

Yager, Sarah. "Prison Born: What Becomes of Babies Born to Mothers Behind Bars?" *The Atlantic* (July/August 2015, 2015): 62–7.

Zero to Three. *The Safe Babies Court Team Approach: Championing Children, Encouraging Parents, Engaging Communities.* Washington, DC: Zero to Three: National Center for Infants, Toddlers, and Families, 2014.

Zullo, Robert. "Foster Care Policies Questioned; Critics Say Agency Puts Richmond Children at Risk." *Richmond Times Dispatch.* December 16, 2012.

Zullo, Robert. "Social Services Director Retires after Scathing Report." *Richmond Times-Dispatch.* May 9, 2013.

Chapter 7

Understanding and overcoming liberal resistance

The cumulative effect of the liberal opposition described in Chapters 3 to 5 and of ACLs' family- and community-preservation extremism described in Chapter 6 is to imprison children, predominantly children of minority race, in an inter-generational cycle of dysfunction associated with poverty. It perpetuates the practice of throwing babies in the river. At bottom, liberals are unwilling to separate children from or add new limits to the freedom of poor black adults, even in the great number of cases when that is what the children need in order to be spared from becoming damaged persons themselves, because their primary allegiance lies with parents and "the black community." As such, the predominant liberal family policy contributes to continued destruction of individual black lives, and to perpetuation of a "black underclass"; sympathy for adult victims of injustice causes liberals to create new victims of that injustice.

As discussed below, I believe the political reality is such that, if liberals would support it, we could enact legal reforms that would spare nearly all children from growing up in the custody of unfit parents or in foster care and from growing up in horrible neighborhoods. "No-Child Zones" might be too radical, but all the others seem to me within the realm of political possibility, and creative cause lawyering on behalf of children might overcome political resistance on some issues. If that is so, should liberals be faulted for refusing to accept and support them? If their refusal means the status quo persists, the inter-generational cycle rolls on, crushing one cohort of black children after another, is it fair to say liberals bear substantial responsibility for this tragic phenomenon? I think it is.

That is very disconcerting to me, but I think I understand it. I fall pretty far left on the political spectrum, a big fan of wealth redistribution and social welfare spending in pursuit of social justice. I complain about conservatives seeming selfish and a lack of communitarian concern for people mired in poverty, and I view adults today caught up in poverty and dysfunction as victims of an unjust economic system and, for those of minority race, pervasive racism and race stereotyping, about which conservatives seem not to care or even see.

But, at the same time, I recognize western society has never approximated my Rawlsian ideal of roughly equal distribution of resources and fair equality of opportunity for all, that now it is actually going in the opposite direction, that economic justice is not even on the national political agenda in any serious way. As an advocate for children, I need to recognize that and respond pragmatically. I need to find other ways to protect the wellbeing and rights of children born today to adults buried in the ills of impoverished communities. I cannot look an abused child in the face and explain that *we* placed him in the custody of a drug addict or a person with a history of chronic and serious child maltreatment because I felt sympathy for his birth parents, or claim that I am not to blame because I have always supported more spending on anti-poverty programs. I have no excuse to offer that child for what we, the adult members of society, have done to him, through the laws our elected representatives create and continually reaffirm. Why do so many other liberals not recognize this?

The liberal mindset

Ordinarily, liberals manifest great concern for the welfare of children, especially those born to poor and minority-race parents. Liberals claim to want the state to spend generously on them through programs such as TANF, WIC, school lunches, Head Start, subsidized daycare, free clinics, inner-city public school funding, special education funding, homeless shelters for parents with children, battered women shelters that accommodate children, housing subsidies, juvenile rehabilitation services, legal aid, and so on.[1] (Though, as suggested earlier, most do not actually want to have to sacrifice themselves in any significant way to pay for these programs.) Liberals support integration of public schools to equalize educational opportunity for children of all backgrounds, affirmative action admission of poor and minority-race young adults to colleges. More generally, they hold "a strong commitment to alleviating the impersonal forces that limit personal advancement,"[2] and they believe it a proper role of the state to effect these things. "Government is nothing more than the aggregate goodwill of citizens," for liberals, and the vehicle for fulfilling our shared responsibility.[3] It is also the master planner, making wise policy decisions about where best to invest public resources, and investing in children makes good economic sense.[4]

But these policies and programs are all ones as to which the interests of parents and children in poor and subordinated communities are wholly aligned. They are easy to endorse for people who place high value on equality and corrective justice, and who approach social justice issues with a group orientation (help "the poor," advance "racial minorities").[5] Difficulties arise when there is a conflict of interest between subgroups within a community about which one cares. It is hard even to acknowledge the conflict, because something might need to be done but there is nothing that can be done that serves both subgroups, so one, it seems, must choose whose interests to favor. That is a choice we never want to have to make. So when I organized a conference on this topic in 2015 at William & Mary, I entitled it "The Liberal Dilemma in Child Welfare Reform," to focus participants' attention on this basic element of the perennial struggle between the Child Savers and the Parent Protectors. Anyone who denies that any such dilemma exists for liberals in thinking about the inter-generational cycle is simply not seeing the world clearly. Anyone who sees it should be willing to have a conversation about it, to talk about what is the morally right way to resolve such a conflict of interests between adults and children, even though it is a difficult conversation.

Liberals actually have no difficulty in some other contexts acknowledging and resolving conflicts between subgroups in a favored population. The relatively high rate of domestic violence in poor black communities presents such a conflict, given that it is predominantly (though not entirely) a matter of men abusing women. Liberals (white ones, at least) unhesitatingly side with the subgroup in the weaker, more vulnerable position. Or perhaps it is more accurate to say race-orientation evaporates in white liberals' minds when they think about domestic violence in black communities; then it is gender that defines their group orientation. Whatever the precise explanation, the intense sympathy that liberals display for poor black men, when thinking about incarceration in the abstract or about parents losing custody of their children because of child maltreatment charges, entirely evaporates when those same men hit a woman. This is so even though exactly the same explanation can be given for why they hit a woman as for why they hit a child or hold up a liquor store, in terms of the injustice that has been heaped on these men their entire lives. The indifference to the fate of partner abusers is actually incongruent not only with the sympathy liberals display for child abusers, but also with another core premise of liberal thinking on display in the child maltreatment context—namely, belief that people are inherently good and infinitely malleable, so readily susceptible to improvement.[6] Yet indifferent they are; woman abusers of any race are not for liberal feminists lost souls who need services to restore the relationship, but rather criminals who should be punished and removed. Women are the victims, women are a group historically oppressed, side with the women.

So why not with children when they are victims? They, too, are an historically subordinated and mistreated group, and black children especially. It is difficult to think of a group more oppressed or less able to help or protect themselves than black children in urban ghettos.[7] Yet as we have seen, across a great number of issues relevant to the plight of black children born into areas of concentrated poverty, ACLs oppose every reform aimed at improving their plight that could increase the suffering or reduce the freedom of adults, and rationalize away the effects on children. Is it really a simple matter of adult-centeredness?

The very different context of religiously-motivated parenting suggests not. I began my career writing about conservative religious schooling and religious parental objections to medical care, in the same child-centered vein I bring to this topic: Parents have no right to deprive their children of autonomy-promoting and gender-equal education, parents have no right to make their sick or injured children suffer for the sake of the parents' religious conviction. The state violates the rights of children by bestowing such power on parents. I got plenty of pushback from conservative legal scholars and advocacy organizations, but I cannot recall any disagreement from liberals. And in the education context, I was defending interests of children that are relatively esoteric in comparison with those under discussion in this book. I was not talking about keeping children out of places where guns are being wildly shot or preventing them from being permanently neurologically damaged by toxic substances or parents' fists; I was talking about protecting girls from being instructed in a way that could alter their self-perception or aspirations, and about ensuring that these physically healthy children in strong two-parent families acquired critical thinking skills. But liberals were totally on board with the denial of freedom to parents that this would entail: Yes, impose regulations on those fundamentalist schools and homeschoolers. (This might not reflect child-centeredness so much as dislike of the parents.) True, the parental interest in those cases—ensure your children adopt your worldview—might also be more rarified than in the present context, which involves parental interests in having any relationship with a child and being free to choose where they live. But consider liberals' reaction to the cult dramas that arise occasionally.

In 2008, a CPS agency in Texas, accompanied by police and a SWAT team, entered the Yearning For Zion Ranch—a spin off from a fundamentalist Mormon community in Arizona and Utah—and removed 462 children en masse, because teenage girls were being pressured into spiritual polygamous marriages with much older men. As a court later noted, the "department did not present any evidence of danger to the physical health and safety" of the children, and indeed it had no evidence of problems other than underage coupling and teen pregnancy when it removed the children. CPS found the children well fed, wearing clean clothes, playing happily outside their well-maintained houses, no signs of substance abuse or violence. The children appeared to have strong relationships with their strongly self-disciplined mothers, and the teen mothers did not appear to be suffering.

One would be hard pressed to say life for children at YFZ was worse than for children in West Baltimore or East St. Louis. The opposite seems clearly true, as troubling as the YFZ environment was. One would also be hard pressed to find any liberals complaining about the en masse removal of children from that community, or about the criminal conviction of men for having sex with their 15-year old spiritual brides, or about the State's eventual evacuation and seizure of the property. Liberals pretty uniformly (not counting the ACLU as liberal) support busting up polygamist communities and saving children from that highly-regimented, life-limiting environment; the parents (or, at least, the fathers) be damned. Any suffering the adults in those communities might experience as a result of children being removed or their community being destroyed does not even register for liberals. But propose evacuating children from a community marked by complete disorder, where not only are 15-year-old girls getting pregnant—sometimes with much older men—because they see no other path in life, but some are having sex with several men a day to make money for a pimp or getting passed around the gang, where children cannot safely play outside, cannot safely stay indoors, cannot be sure they will get fed today, might not have a coat for winter, might need to carry a gun to school, might have to start running errands for the local drug dealer, etc., and ACLs will accuse you of plotting the most sinister atrocity imaginable. Why the seeming inconsistency?

Two final points of comparison might help narrow in on an answer. Dysfunction is also pervasive in Native American communities and in some rural white communities, posing similar conflicts of interest between adults and children.[8] The latter context liberals mostly ignore, at least those in the legal academy. There have been journalistic books written about "Hillbillies," and some studies on social service provision in rural communities, especially with the heroin epidemic tearing through them, but not much work with a normative bent that specifically mentions rural white poverty. In contrast, liberal academics in law schools and social science departments have had a lot to say about Native Americans, and ACLs line up in defense of adult interests in those communities just as they do with poor black communities, making similar types of arguments, calling for more money and pilot programs and to find their strengths, etc. In fact, they adamantly defend the Indian Child Welfare Act, one of whose many condemnable (from a child-advocacy perspective) features is that it forces infants—whose native American ancestry might be miniscule—to move out of strong, healthy communities *into* dysfunctional communities, and not for the sake of continuity of parenting but actually disrupting a good parent–child relationship that has been forming with adoptive parents and transferring them to someone else's custody, and not necessarily a biological parent. Why? Because these children are a "tribal resource." (This child-as-collective-asset mentality, incidentally, is evident in the international realm also, underlying concerted efforts by international organizations such as UNICEF, cheered by ACLs, to shut down international adoption, another practice ACLs' see as neo-colonialist exploitation, stealing a natural resource from poor countries (never mind that the children are nearly all in orphanages that drain national resources)[9]).

So on the one hand with liberals you have complete disregard for parental interests and community survival—and championing of children's interests—in the religious context, and on the other hand complete devotion to parental interests and community survival—and disregard for children's interests (or even personhood)—in the urban black and Native American contexts, with neutrality or much less interest in the white poverty context.[10] Obviously, race distinguishes the two sides—child-centered with the religious groups we think of as white (polygamists, fundamentalist Christians, Christian Scientists), adult-centered with the two minority-race groups. But so does politics—child-centered with the conservative groups, adult-centered with the two groups that have a liberal outlook. We liberals do not like the worldview from which we think these conservative groups operate, in part because liberals on average take a dimmer view of religion,[11] and in part because of the content we perceive in their beliefs—social and economic conservatism, sexism, and, with some groups, racism. We do not want those views to spread. But we do not exactly celebrate, or even endorse, any "worldview" in the black ghetto, or the attitudes children there acquire as they grow up. Should not liberals also want to stop the spread of the oppositional culture there, and the fatalism, and the devaluing of human life?

Also distinguishing the two sides is intentionality; adults in religious communities are deliberately choosing something harmful (in our view) for children and could (we think) do otherwise, whereas the harms children incur in impoverished communities seem unintended, inflicted by adults in spite of themselves, contrary to what we suppose they actually want, what they would do if they could better control themselves and their situation. This distinguishing feature might (along with a gender element) also help to explain fairly universal liberal support for prohibiting female genital mutilation, even though it is principally something associated with black parents (albeit recent voluntary African immigrants, not descendants of American slaves). I do not think liberals would want to lean too heavily on that explanation explicitly for their different stance on the two sides, because it undermines their claim that the state impinges on adults' autonomy when it coerces them, but this might nevertheless be in the back of their minds.

Ultimately, I think the overriding explanation is history and the ideological commitments it has created for the Left. Liberals simply cannot adopt positions they see as falling in step with the march of brutal European-American dominance and destruction of black and brown men's and women's bodies, minds, and spirits. We cannot be on that side of the master–slave narrative that runs through this nation's entire history, the side of pain-inflicting power. White guilt has not entirely exhausted itself. We want to apologize and be believed. We want to reach out and make amends. Or stand back and leave in peace. We want to be real neighbors to each other, colleagues. When a white judge steps down from the bench and hugs a black mother trying mightily to resist the tormenting pull of addiction, it is a profound gesture. "We are women, we are mothers. And but for a different history…"

Andrew Hacker's more cynical take a quarter century ago is probably as accurate today:

> white liberals want to be liked by black people, as if having their goodwill is a seal of approval…. Liberals hope that blacks will acknowledge that some whites … are not The Enemy but, rather, can be counted as friends and allies. For blacks to grant this, if only by bestowing a smile, serves to certify one's moral stature. [Liberals

choose the black candidate for any officer position in a professional or academic organization, and applaud longest for the black speaker.] This will, they hope, serve as some recompense for the wrongs their race has done to his.... [L]iberals stand in dread of black disfavor ... [whereas] the approval of blacks ... is taken as absolving them of racism.[12]

Hacker also suggested that liberals cannot stomach the idea that the Great Society was a failure, that we could not fix all social ills if we just spent more money (only today, one must, to avoid appearing paternalistic, emphasize "community control" rather than top-down transformation).[13]

In any event, I am essentially arguing that we have to do one more tragic thing to a large number of unfortunate adults in order to stop the march. The only way for a liberal to stomach that, I think, is to keep the eye focused on the newborn child and never forget that we are responsible for what happens next to him or her, in the world as it is. We will be the oppressor of that child if we continue to endorse laws that throw him or her in the river. How can anyone stomach that? So my plea to ACLs is simple: Stop the post-modern babble and speak to that child, plainly and realistically, on the basis of research-supported facts rather than ideology.

The conservative mindset

The pitch to conservatives is much easier, I think. We liberals tend to chalk up all disagreements over public spending to selfishness and greed on the part of conservatives, but political scientists remind us that most conservatives are not wealthy and most support huge spending on the military. They attribute disagreement instead to deep differences in moral outlook. According to George Lakoff: "The ultimate conservative agenda ... is moral, not financial."[14]

The conservative worldview sees human nature as inherently inclined toward degradation, yet supposes all autonomous persons can be expected to subjugate that part of themselves and live in a dignified, disciplined, self-sufficient manner on the basis of principle. Anyone who does that should be left alone, but those who threaten public disorder or become a burden on others because of their choices deserve no such deference, nor assistance. "Liberty has a purpose, which is human dignity. Freedom for its own sake is not necessarily valuable and often leads to results that are exactly the opposite."[15] Endless support for the military makes sense not only because it is necessary to provide an essential public good, and so fits in with a conservative conception of limited government, but also because for conservatives it embodies and models for the rest of society a moral ideal—the (Christian) soldier.[16] Solicitude for corporations also makes sense even for conservatives with little stake in them, because they are "self-disciplined, energetic, competent, and resourceful rather than self-indulgent, lazy, unskilled, and hapless."[17]

In the conservative worldview, then, parental status and plenary power over children's lives, and protection from government intrusion, are the entitlement of all who approximate that ideal of the moral person, regardless of the particular content of their conception of the good. Hence, conservatives of any faith defend the power of fundamentalist Christians completely to control their children's schooling. Some even voiced modest support for the YFZ patriarchs, insisting the state should have clear evidence of immoral conduct before breaking up families. Conservatives also have more solicitude than liberals for "faith-healing" parents.[18]

Conservatives are much less inclined to ascribe any entitlement to parents they view as having descended into abject degradation and as failing to instill any discipline or virtue in their offspring. They strongly disapprove of the social disorder and dependency that, in their view, bad child rearing by such parents is perennially causing.[19] (In *The America We Deserve*, Donald Trump recommended forcing teen mothers to live in supervised, privately-funded group homes as a condition for public assistance, and in his 2016 campaign he compared inner cities to "the wild west" and promised "law and order.") Further, conservatives tend to "dismiss rehabilitation as pointless";[20] they do not share liberals' view of personality as infinitely malleable, but rather believe people who are dragging down the rest of society need their incentive structure changed, by infliction of severe punishment. Their view of government control mirrors their view of parental control—strict imposition of external discipline on those who do not discipline themselves; "Rewards for obedience and punishments for disobedience are crucial to maintaining moral authority."[21] Naturally, we should not expect those whom we blame for incarcerating the dysfunctional poor to defend the parental rights of those people. (Recall Newt Gingrich's proposal to put children of welfare mothers in orphanages.)[22] Lakoff suggests that even if liberals could prove some rehabilitative program is cost-effective, many conservatives would not support it, because "[t]he issue isn't about money, it's about morality."[23]

Conversely, reforms targeted at just children (rather than by helping their parents), and aimed at giving the children a life more likely to make them good upstanding citizens, are appealing to conservatives, even if they would entail some expense. Of course, they would prefer not to have to spend time or money getting other people's offspring the "Strict Father" parenting they need, but the same is true of earthquake relief.[24] They will do it, not only for the self-protective reason of preventing more disorder in society, but also because there is a compassionate component to the conservative outlook that reacts to human misfortunate for which a person is not to blame, as in natural disasters.[25] In fact, we should expect them to be especially likely to support effective programs and policies aimed at helping children when they do *not* also help dysfunctional adults, because the latter is simply distasteful to conservatives. And so it makes perfect sense that the primary authors and promoters of the Adoption and Safe Families Act, which entailed some new funding as well as new rules, principally to support transfer of children to upstanding citizens (adoption applicants), were Republicans. Much of what I have proposed is an expansion and improved implementation of ASFA's aims.

To the extent additional public funding is required, my proposals, focused on children, should gain more support from conservatives than do pleas for more funding of services for dysfunctional adults. Conservatives are more likely to support targeted assistance that is directed to "groups with positive social constructions, such as children … than groups with negative social constructions, such as … drug addicts."[26] However, "it is politically imprudent to explicitly identify problems as 'urban' or 'city' problems."[27] As I noted in the Introduction, my proposals would apply universally and make no reference to race nor to poverty per se.

I have glossed over here questions about what or whom legislators really serve— ideals, voters, donors, etc. There are enough examples of Democrats and Republicans voting as these worldview descriptions would predict to suggest they are informative. And surveys of Trump voters reveal sufficient fear of increasing social disorder and inter-racial conflict to suggest inner-city violence and black oppositional culture are salient for many conservatives, so tackling the "urban thug problem" might be attractive to them. Their hostility to affirmative action also gives them reason to eliminate its underlying justification—that is, that blacks come from a more disadvantaged background.[28] For their part, perhaps liberals have had enough decades of declining support for anti-poverty programs and of watching the inter-generational cycle of dysfunction roll on, despite all their pilot programs, to consider the very different approach I and other advocates for children recommend. I hope that this book will have made some impression on them.

Notes

1 Gross (2013, 54).
2 See Marietta (2012, 52).
3 See Marietta (2012, 54–5).
4 See Lakoff (2002, 287) ("To pragmatic liberals, social programs are investments; to idealistic liberals, they are a matter of social duty").
5 Marietta (2012, 107) ("Multiculturalists emphasize a group orientation over an individualistic focus …").
6 See Marietta (2012, 57).
7 Cf., Marietta (2012, 57–8) ("[T]he central question of liberalism is the Oppression Problem. The heart of the matter and source of disagreement is Who is oppressed? Who is oppressed more? Who is oppressed the most?"). See also Lakoff (2002, 165) (including among the "liberal categories of moral action," "Helping those who cannot help themselves" and "Protecting those who cannot protect themselves."
8 See, for example, Mersky and Janczewski (2017, 485).
9 See Dwyer (2013, 238–41).
10 This divide, incidentally, plays out also in Supreme Court jurisprudence; liberal Justices have been more child-centered in religious parenting cases, such as Wisconsin v. Yoder, but highly parent-focused in cases involving poor parents trying to avoid a TPR—Santosky v. Kramer, 455 U.S. 745 (1982) and Lassiter v. Department of Social Services 452 U.S. 18 (1981).
11 See Gross (2013, 51, 161, 162).
12 Hacker (1992, 71–72, 76).
13 Hacker (1992, 74–75).
14 See Lakoff (2002, 196).
15 Marietta (2012, 21–22).
16 Lakoff (2002, 192–93).
17 Lakoff (2002, 172).
18 See, for example, Brown (2017).
19 See Lakoff (2002, 197) ("conservatives claim that violent crime has been the result of 'permissive' childrearing practices").
20 Marietta (2012, 23).
21 See Lakoff (2002, 163–4).
22 Lakoff (2002, 170–1, 185–6).
23 Lakoff (2002, 184).
24 Lakoff (2002, 162).
25 Lakoff (2002, 181).
26 Lawrence, Stoker, and Wolman (2010, 416). See also *idem*, 421–2 ("Specifying elderly people or children as recipients increased support by more than 20 percentage points each … whereas targeting to low-income single mothers decreased support by 4 percentage points and increased opposition by 5 points").
27. Lawrence, Stoker, and Wolman (2010, 427).
28 See Edsall (2017); Cox (2017).

Bibliography

Brown, Nathan. "Senators Outline 5 Options on Faith Healing." *Cherokee Tribune* February 10, 2017.

Cox, Daniel. "Beyond Economics: Fears of Cultural Displacement Pushed the White Working Class to Trump." *PRRI/The Atlantic Report*, May 9, 2017.

Dwyer, James G. "Inter-Country Adoption and the Special Rights Fallacy," *University of Pennsylvania Journal of International Law* 35 (2013): 189–267.

Edsall, Thomas B. "The Trump Voter Paradox." *New York Times*, September 28, 2017.

Gross, Neil. *Why Are Professors Liberal and Why Do Conservatives Care?* Cambridge, MA: Harvard University Press, 2013.

Hacker, Andrew. *Two Nations: Black and White, Separate, Hostile, Unequal.* New York: Scribner, 1992.

Lakoff, George. *Moral Politics: How Liberals and Conservatives Think.* 2nd ed. Chicago, IL: University of Chicago Press, 2002.

Lawrence, Eric, Robert Stoker, and Harold Wolman. "Crafting Urban Policy: The Conditions of Public Support for Urban Policy Initiatives," *Urban Affairs Review* 45 (3) (2010): 412–30.

Marietta, Morgan. *A Citizen's Guide to American Ideology: Conservatism and Liberalism in Contemporary Politics.* New York: Routledge, 2012.

Mersky, Joshua P. and Colleen E. Janczewski. "Racial and Ethnic Differences in the Prevalence of Adverse Childhood Experiences," *Child Abuse & Neglect* 76 (2017): 480–7.

Conclusion

We are imprisoning black children literally in prison nurseries, and we are imprisoning them figuratively by placing them into parent–child relationships and community environments that are confining, dangerous, and destructive. Prison nurseries epitomize a fundamental failing in the dominant liberal response to family and community dysfunction. That response reflects a commendable sympathy for the life-long disadvantage and deprivation that adults living in chronic poverty have suffered, and a wish to transform their lives, but also an adult-centered denial of the harm that the resulting policies and programs are inflicting on children. Adult-centered liberals are reproducing in another generation the very disadvantage and deprivation they lament, thereby perpetuating the subordination of black people in America.

I have laid out in this book many proposals for child-centered reforms aimed at ending the cycle, in urban areas of concentrated poverty especially, but really wherever it exists. I call on policy makers to deliberate about them, and I call on attorney advocates for children to identify appropriate opportunities for impact litigation challenging existing laws—for example, seeking an injunction against application of parentage laws to a child whose biological parents have a terrible history of child maltreatment. They should find procedural hooks for getting appointed as attorney or "next friend" to represent children and get the constitutional arguments I have laid out here and in prior writings heard by a court.

My proposals are sure to be shocking, individually or in combination, to many people. But answer this question truthfully: Would not implementing all of them largely stop the inter-generational cycle of dysfunction among poor African-Americans? We would protect more children from pre-natal damage; ensure every child has, before the critical period of attachment begins, a permanent caregiver sufficiently capable that the state should not ever have to disrupt the relationship; and make sure no child has to grow up in horrible, destructive neighborhoods. The black ghetto would become a thing of the past, and the stereotype it now feeds would dissolve. My proposals would accomplish this, whereas existing approaches certainly will not.

Crucially, Liberals must acknowledge this: I am not proposing a massive expansion of government power over private life. I have explained in this book repeatedly that the government is already exerting extraordinary power over the most fundamental aspects of children's private lives, and it is doing this in an adult-centered way that is inexcusably indifferent to the impact on children. Any true liberal should be horrified by what the state is now doing to children, far more concerned about that than about the incidental effects on adults of treating children with the moral respect they deserve.

I close by repeating this admonition: The proper approach to child welfare policy is to ask one child at a time, what is best and right for that child. We should not be deciding the fate of any child based on sympathy for other individuals, concern for survival of communities, or comprehensive plans for remaking society. We adults are not required to make decisions about our family relationships, such as whether to marry or divorce someone, based on such considerations. We have a right to do what is best for ourselves, and children should have an equivalent right to the state's making any such decisions for them with the sole aim of doing what is best for them. The intergenerational cycle is not an abstraction; it is one newborn child after another going to live with certain people in a certain home and neighborhood environment, as a result of laws that we create.

I ask anyone who has read to the end to imagine this book not written by me but rather by a black youth who got caught in the cycle, having gone through the stages from pre-birth exposure to harmful substances to abuse in the home and traumatization in the neighborhood to school failure and expulsion for misbehavior, then to early parenthood and involvement with criminal activity and arrest, now sitting in prison and writing this book. Would the message ring more true if expressed by that voice? If so, how would you respond to that person, who is damaged in ways he or she likely will never overcome, whose life prospects were thwarted, who is hopeless and angry? Would you tell him his ideas are all wrong? That, if only he better understood the history and the structural forces that created the world into which we placed him at birth, it would be clear we did the right thing?

Appendix

Family drug court research

It is essential in digesting the research to recall that FDC parents are not representative of substance-abusing parents in the system on the whole. FDCs take those who would be most likely to succeed even without special help[1]—namely, those who pass screening (excluding those least likely to reunify),[2] convincingly profess commitment to change, commence services, and, in some studies, graduate. They leave out parents with more complex problems—in particular, those with serious mental health problems, those who committed more serious forms of maltreatment with the child now before the court, those who have a more troubling maltreatment history with other children, and those likely headed to prison. They also leave out the many CPS-involved parents who are largely indifferent to the removal of their children and/or have no desire at present to stop their substance abuse.[3] The studies are therefore simply irrelevant to the highest risk parents.[4]

All these narrowing features of FDCs make it extremely difficult, if not impossible, to create a valid control group with which to compare the treatment group. The closest possible approach is to create in some court a pool of all who pass screening criteria, have the judge or administrator decide which ones who pass screening they will allow in the FDC program (e.g., based on evident commitment), and then randomly divide those parents into a treatment group that enters the FDC program and a comparison group that is put on the traditional track. Then compare outcomes for the two groups. This neutralizes the selections process on the court side, but it is imperfect because it does not neutralize the choice on the parent side,[5] so some selection bias remains.

In any event, nearly all studies that have been done are not based on random assignment. Rather, they do a retrospective study of parents who have been in an FDC program and, if they do any comparison, it is with a group of parents who went through the traditional court process. The best among these studies do "propensity matching," finding people in the non-FDC parent pool with some of the same relevant characteristics as parents in the treatment group (e.g., those who did or would have satisfied the screening requirements). The latter could be from the same jurisdiction, in which case the reason for those persons not being in the FDC program (their refusal, judges' subjective judgment) is likely to be a confounding variable, along with difference in disposition among judges in that jurisdiction (if the non-FDC parents get a different judge). Or they might be from another jurisdiction similar in character, but then you still have a confounding problem if actual FDC participants have passed not only screening but also the FDC judge's subjective assessment of their commitment and personal capacities, and in addition there could be other differences between jurisdictions (e.g., CPS has different rules, practices, or culture; judges have different attitudes).

In sum, no one can say with confidence that FDCs have been proven to cause any improvement on any measure relative to traditional juvenile courts. What should be done, but has not, is simply to look at *entire* parent populations in two time periods in jurisdictions that now have FDCs—years before adoption of the FDC and years after adoption—and compare overall outcomes in those two time periods. Though the time difference could be confounding, this might still provide the best sense of whether the FDC is actually causing different outcome rates or rather is simply putting those most likely to succeed in a different courtroom.

Lastly, I would speculate that the vast majority of studies are not conducted at randomly-selected sites, but rather are chosen because the researchers (predominantly liberal social scientists) have an impression that those sites are especially effective and will show good results. Even if a researcher is entirely objective, s/he would typically need a judge or program administrator to cooperate, and that is less likely with floundering programs; no one wants their failure on display. (At least one study, in North Carolina, was able to look at publicly-available data the government maintains, without enlisting the FDC personnel to assist them.) So on the whole, one might assume the studies that have been done represent the best possible cases for FDC advocacy. Casual observation outside a research context can create a bleaker depiction. For example, a reporter in Ohio sat in on the Franklin County Family Drug Court for a week and counted that nine out of the eleven parents who appeared that week in court had dropped out of treatment, failed a drug test, or otherwise fallen off the rails. Fewer than half of parents, she learned, graduate from the program.[6]

Snohomish, Washington

The most recent study took place in Washington State. The Snohomish County Family Drug Treatment Court has "an extensive referral and screening process, and once accepted parents must complete multiple services and programs before they can be considered for graduation."[7] The comparison group was in the same courthouse but on the traditional docket, excluded from the FDC for reasons not stated. (Were they not offered participation in the FDC because deemed not sufficiently motivated or capable?) Ninety percent of parents were white, so unlikely to be living in areas of concentrated deep poverty (in contrast to blacks, for whom dysfunction is largely limited to urban ghettos). Seventy-five percent of FDC parents completed treatment and 68.5 percent recovered their children. Among parents in the comparison group (who were matched by propensity scores with FDC parents, so this is not a figure for all parents in the system but rather that most promising subset) 52 percent completed treatment and 62 percent recovered their children. The more striking difference was in length of time in foster care—an average of 393 days for children of FDC parents and a whopping 848 days for children of comparison-group parents. Another striking difference was in TPR rates—30 percent for the comparison group versus 9 percent for FDC parents. The remaining 22 percent of parents in the FDC group were categorized as "permanency planning," which likely means guardianship with a relative of the parents.[8] As with all other studies, the authors give no indication of what the rates of reunification are for substance-abusing parents who were not included in the study; these are presumably far worse. And like the vast majority of other studies, this one did not inquire into the rate of children's subsequent suffering of maltreatment or re-entry into foster care after reunification, let alone any other measure of child wellbeing.

Tulsa, OK

An evaluation in Tulsa, Oklahoma examined an FDC that featured the Strengthening Families and Celebrating Families! parenting programs, which "focus on child development, attachment and bonding, discipline, child and family safety, and family organization."[9] The study used propensity score matching to generate a comparison group, but omitted a host of parental characteristics likely to be predictive of rehabilitation, such as age, employment status, education, which substance parents abused, whether a parent had a serious mental health problem, with whom a parent lived, and the nature of the neighborhood in which parents lived (i.e., concentrated poverty and crime versus mixed-income and safe).[10] The comparison between the groups is therefore meaningless. Notably, the percentage of African American parents was 50 percent higher in the comparison group than in the FDC group. As noted above, substance-abusing black parents are far more likely to be living in neighborhoods where drug abuse and other crimes are pervasive. It also appears that the FDC group was limited to those who graduated, so it excludes those who were offered but declined participation, those who agreed but did not show up, and those who began the program but dropped out or were kicked out. What is of some interest in the study report is that fewer than 15 percent of FDC children returned to parental custody in less than a year, and those 15 percent probably did not include many infants. So the vast majority of infants being experimented on would have stayed with foster parents well into the critical attachment period.[11] At the 500 day mark, when secure attachment either would have developed with foster parents or else the child most likely never will have a secure attachment to anyone, 70 percent of FDC children were still in out-of-home placement.[12] For the comparison group, over 90 percent of children were in out-of-home placement at the one year mark, and still over 85 percent at the 500 day mark. The good news for the comparison group of children is that they were very likely never to return to their parents, but rather much more likely to stay with their attachment figures permanently; at the 1000 day mark (nearly three years), only a quarter of comparison-group children had been "returned" (a misnomer for those placed in foster care at birth) to birth parents, whereas 61 percent of FDC children had been.[13] (So 31 percent were taken away from their caregivers after being with them from somewhere between 500 (15 months) and 1000 days (almost three years). And an unstated percentage of the total 61 percent who reunified (probably around a tenth), CPS would have had to take out of the home again because of maltreatment.) And remember that this 61 percent represents a reunification rate for a small subset of all substance-abusing parents in the child welfare system—parents who qualified, were selected, agreed to participate, and graduated.

Despite the study's severe selection bias and finding of extensive stays in foster care, and despite the program's destruction of attachment relationships for at least a third of FDC children, the authors declared victory for FDCs.[14] No one likes their work to be meaningless, and everyone wants FDCs to provide the magic bullet.

Sacramento, CA

Sacramento's is one of the more long-standing programs and has been the subject of a couple of studies. The most recent report explains that parents are excluded from the city's FDC based on types of substantiated allegations (e.g., sexual abuse), the parent's referral to another type of family court (i.e., the County has an Early Intervention Family Drug Court Program), or parental medical or mental health needs that exceed the scope of services provided by FDC. The FDC has five compliance measures: (1) drug tests; (2) attendance in substance abuse treatment; (3) attendance in meeting with their service coordinator; (4) attendance in support groups (e.g., 12-step programs); and (5) compliance with other requirements ordered by the court. Typically, the FDC program requires participants to complete six months of treatment, and it considers clients noncompliant if they are discharged from treatment prior to completion, fail to follow the guidelines of the treatment provider, have any unexcused absences from treatment, forge or alter treatment attendance slips, or leave a detox or residential facility without authorization. Participants receive an orientation to available support groups at intake and are required to attend a minimum of six support groups per bi-monthly reporting period unless a special circumstance warrants a reduction of meetings (e.g., young infant in care, multiple children under the age of 5, employment, or school obligations).[15]

A total of 673 parents participated in FDC between October 1, 2011, and September 30, 2013. Of these parents, 140 (over 20 percent) had missing or erroneous data on key variables and so were excluded (Why did they have missing or erroneous data? The researchers did not say.). Of the 533 parents remaining in the sample, 206 were included in these analyses. These parents had: (1) a child who was removed prior to or during FDC participation; (2) services information on all compliance measures; and (3) their case closed so determination of the child's permanency outcome was known. Primary substance use by FDC parents was: Alcohol 30 (14.6 percent), Cocaine/Crack 5 (2.4 percent), Marijuana/Hashish 45 (21.8 percent), Heroin/Other Opiates 19 (9.2 percent), Methamphetamine 82 (39.8 percent), Unknown/Not Reported 25 (12.1 percent). Just over half of the 206 parents (55.3 percent) were reunified with their child. After controlling for parent demographics and other compliance measures, the only compliance measures that were statistically associated with the likelihood of a child being reunified were negative drug tests and support group attendance.

An earlier study had results reported in 2007 and 2011. It compared families in maltreatment cases before the FDC was created that would have been invited (but it was unknowable whether they would have accepted), with families invited after the FDC was created who accepted the invitation.[16] Forty-nine percent of the FDC group were meth users, only 3 percent heroin, 12 percent some form of cocaine. Eighty-six percent had been in treatment before (versus 53 percent for the comparison group). A higher percentage of FDC parents submitted themselves to treatment. Fifty-five percent of FDC parents entered a residential program, whereas only thirty-nine percent of the comparison group did. Rates of completion among those who started were the same for both groups. At 24 months, 42 percent of the FDC children had reunified versus 27.2 percent of the comparison children. With the exception of heroin, there were no differences in treatment completion or child reunification rates by parent's primary drug problem. "Except for heroin, the rate of treatment completion was 63.9%. Parents with heroin as their primary drug problem ... 46.7% ..."

Parents who used heroin (33.3%) had the lowest rates of reunification with their children at 24 months and marijuana users had the highest rates of reunification (45.4%). Parents who used alcohol, methamphetamine, and cocaine/crack had reunification rates between 36.9% and 42.4%.[17]

For those in both groups who had reunified by 24 months, the average time to reunification was around 285 days. The picture after reunification does not favor the FDC: "Eighty-three (22.9%) of the 362 DDC children who reunified within 24 months experienced reentry into care compared to 10.6% of the comparison group children (5 of the 47 children who reunified experienced reentry)."[18] Thus, less than a third of DDC children were with their parents 30 months after the parents entered the program. Almost all who re-entered care did so because of parents' alcohol or drug use. The follow up study by Boles' team found 17 percent of FDC parents had one or more new substantiated reports of maltreatment, compared with 23 percent for the comparison group.[19]

North Carolina

A study published in 2014 was unusual in examining state-held, publicly-available retrospective data rather than working with a local court that has agreed to be studied, thus eliminating the problem of bias in selection of study sites. Unfortunately, the study was riddled with selection bias in its construction of study sample and control group. The control group consisted of parents in the state who, during a two-year period, had been offered participation in an FDC and refused. The studied treatment group consisted of parents who agreed to participate in an FDC, but then excluded any of those parents whose child was not born in North Carolina (i.e., the more transient members of the groups) as well as a significant group of parents who should have been deemed failures—namely, any whose child went into foster care after they completed the FDC and any whose child ran away, became emancipated, aged out of foster care, or died. There was no comparison with parents who were not invited to participate in the FDC. From the pool of 1862 parents who entered the FDC program, these exclusions left only 387 parents.[20] Among those, parents who entered treatment but did not complete had reunification rates similar to those of parents who declined to participate in the FDC, and both those groups had a somewhat lower rate of reunification than parents who opted in to the FDC and completed treatment.[21] The study did not examine rates at which those reunified later re-entered foster care or suffered further maltreatment.

"Large Western City"

A 2012 report described the results of a study of an FDC in an unnamed city in the west with a predominantly white, but also substantial native American, population.[22] The court allowed parents to participate if they admitted their child was maltreated, expressed desire for treatment, and had no felony child abuse or sexual abuse guilty finding.[23] Parents would have to agree to all the programs' requirements, and they were free to decline and go the traditional route for maltreatment cases. As with most programs, CPS social workers assigned to the FDC parents had reduced caseloads (15 rather than the usual 25), in recognition of the more intensive work they would do with each participating parent.[24] The parents who entered the FDC program during the study period were compared with a subset of those parents who did not enter for one of a variety of reasons—non-responsive to FDC inquiries (42 percent), the regular dependency court did not refer them (18 percent), refused to participate (8 percent), couldn't be contacted (7 percent), other issues (8 percent), and unknown reason (17 percent). To try to counteract the obvious selection bias problem, the researchers did propensity-score matching. As is uniformly true, that attempt at matching could not include the crucial variable of "motivation to enter treatment."[25] It also did not include "peer group characteristics, employment, and housing" nor concentration of poverty in neighborhood of residence. As a side note, one interesting fact the researchers discovered was that three-quarters of FDC parents had been subjected to a child protection investigation prior to the petition that led to their current court involvement—in other words, the great majority are repeat players.

The researchers found only 34 percent of FDC parents "graduated."[26] For 27 percent of FDC parents, the court dismissed the maltreatment petition against them (presumably as a reward for their efforts) and their child was returned home, another 13 percent were reunified as part of the permanency planning, and another 15 percent had "trial home visits" while their child remained in the state's legal custody.[27] However, 38 percent of children returned to their parents' home were subsequently again the subject of a CPS maltreatment investigation, and that was within a fairly short period of post-return evaluation.[28] So only about one quarter of FDC parents regained legal custody of their children and avoided another CPS investigation. For the comparison group, it seems to have been less than a tenth who had that "success" story (11 percent had petition dismissed, 7 percent had reunification, and 54 percent of the children returned again were subjects of a maltreatment investigation). For both groups, the average time from child removal to reunification, when that occurred, was over two years, so from the child's standpoint the success rate might be close to zero.

Hillsborough County, FL

The FDC in this county admits only parents who are referred by the regular dependency judge, drug court case manager, or state attorney and who have "no serious and unstable mental illness" and "no prior convictions for violent or sexual offense" or any other type of "serious offenses resulting in incarceration."[29] A study looked at outcomes for the subset of those parents who "received 9–12 months of intensive outpatient services from a local substance abuse treatment agency."[30] So parents who dropped out of treatment after less than 9 months were excluded. Those parents were compared with parents in another county that has no FDC, deemed similar by propensity-score matching, except there was no attempt to match by ability or willingness to enter and stay in treatment or attractiveness as candidates for selection by a judge; the bases for matching were simply the basic eligibility criteria of the FDC. Thus, there was significant selection bias.

This study found a 53 percent reunification rate for children of FDC parents, after an average of 16 months in foster care, and only 2 percent re-entered foster care within the year following return home. The comparison group had a 42 percent reunification rate and 12 percent re-entry rate.[31] The authors noted that although the 12-month rate of re-entry for all reunified children (i.e., not just children of substance abusers) in some other states ranged from 21 percent to 38 percent, a study had shown that between 2005 and 2007 only 11 percent of children in Florida re-enter foster care within 12 months after return home. They also noted that "FDTC participants [had taken] 27–29% longer to achieve permanency than non-FDTC participants,"[32] suggesting this FDC had such low re-entry rates because it adopted a practice of not reunifying until parents had demonstrated sobriety for a much longer period of time, leaving children longer in foster care as a result.

Rhode Island

This study appeared in one of the most poorly-regarded journals in the field, but I include it because it focused just on substance-exposed newborns.[33] Apparently there is a "specialty court" in Rhode Island for "perinatal substance users." The researchers followed participants until their children were 30 months old. Most were white, so this was probably not serving Providence. Only six mothers were married, and none had a college degree. A third had annual household income below $10,000. Twenty-nine percent used cocaine and 38 percent were polysubstance users. A quarter of babies were born prematurely. Not all mothers with a substance-abused newborn are offered participation; the Vulnerable Infants Program of RI has to refer them, on what basis the authors don't say. The sample size was small (52 mothers), and there was no control group. The researchers found a decline in mothers' functioning over time, with substantial increases in the percentage with a high probability of substance dependence, positive BSI diagnosis, psychological symptoms, poor parenting, stress, and elevated risk of child abuse.[34] Nevertheless, 81 percent graduated, and among those only 7 percent had relapsed and separated from their children at the 30-month mark. For the children, nearly 80 percent were living with their mothers at the 30-month mark, but only 41 percent of all the children displayed secure attachment.[35] On the DIAL-R test for motor, conceptual, and language skills, although "[o]f the general populations, 16% would be expected to score with potential problems," "[i]n this sample, approximately 60% of children show potential problems in at least one area of functioning."[36]

Miami

Miami's FDC, like others, excludes those deemed least likely to reunify; "parents with severe cognitive, emotional or physical disorders, or who have had their parental right terminated previously were considered ineligible."[37] In addition, of course, participants must express commitment to all the treatment and services the program entails.

> To graduate from DDCs, participants must have successfully completed substance abuse treatment, have a specified period of continuous abstinence, show evidence of a safe and stable living situation, spend a substantial period adequately performing the parent role, and have a life plan initiated and in place (e.g., employment, education, vocational training).[38]

In a study published in 2010, researchers tried to assess the impact of adding an "Engaging Moms Program (EMP)" to the FDC package. There was no non-FDC control group. The researchers included the long-time lead FDC judge in Miami, which is ethically inappropriate given her self-interest in showing good results and the non-consensual nature of the children's involvement. (Parental waiver of conflict cannot suffice for research on children as to which parents themselves have a potential conflict of interest with the children.)

EMP seems to add counselor-led group therapy sessions with members of the mother's family other than the child at issue. The researchers periodically, over an 18-month period after initiation, assessed a small group of mothers, some in the FDC and some in the FDC who also received EMP, using several predictive assessment tools they deemed to have at least adequate reliability and validity. The study population was older (30, on average) than typical FDC clientele and 29 percent were employed (which is also higher than typical). Fifty-five percent had a history of being physically abused themselves as children and 36 percent a history of being sexually abused.[39]

Under the heading of "Child Welfare Status," the researchers reported: "Sixty-six percent of mothers had positive permanency outcomes...," which meant any outcome other than TPR, including placement of the child with relatives in a guardianship.[40] (Ordinarily in this field we speak of permanency for children, not parents...) That was the extent of the researchers' discussion of "child welfare." They did not find significant difference in effects as between regular FDC and FDC+EMP. Among the 62 mothers as a whole, 37 graduated, and the state returned a child to 28 of them solely and to another four of them in a joint custody arrangement, so about half reunified.[41] The study had a short time frame and did not report on re-entry rates following reunification.

Western cities

A study with a relatively large sample (245 treatment, 559 control) looked at FDCs in three sites in the west, serving mostly white women addicted to meth or alcohol. The courts excluded child fatalities, parents who committed sexual abuse, parents with serious mental illness, incarcerated parents, and cases moving immediately to TPR. The comparison groups consisted of mothers who had not received a referral to FDC or who had refused drug court services. The authors acknowledged: "It may be that more difficult families are either never offered the opportunity to participate in FTDCs, or are more likely to decline participation."[42] Roughly a quarter of both groups were married, and about one-fifth were employed, both factors that predict reunification.[43] Nearly all had been charged with neglect; only 3 percent of the treatment group and 11 percent of the control group had been charged with physical abuse.[44] Mothers were tracked for two years after the initial child welfare petition, and any who did not achieve permanency by that point were simply excluded from the study, which is bizarre. The FDC in these locations, as in others that have been studied, got mothers enrolled in substance-abuse treatment faster—84 days on average for the treatment group, 122 days for the control group. Almost 70 percent of the treatment group mothers regained custody of their children, compared with less than 40 percent for the control group.[45] The researchers noted that most of the difference between the groups disappeared when variables other than type of intervention were controlled for, and that there was substantial variation in the gap between FDC and comparison across the three study sites.[46] Also noteworthy was that children of FDC mothers spend two months longer (288 days versus 228 days) in foster care.[47] The authors noted that "within the family drug court context, these families may be accorded more time to comply with court-ordered treatment, thus delaying the permanency decision."[48] But even 288 days is far shorter than in most other FDCs.

Pima County, AZ

This study differs from others in analyzing an FDC that appears to have had no exclu-sionary criteria at the time, so the only difference between FDC parents and those who received the traditional process is that the former chose to participate and the latter declined. A study published in 2004 found that although nearly every FDC parent entered treatment, only half finished, and so only half were reunified with their chil-dren. There was actually a higher treatment-completion rate among those who refused to participate in the FDC.[49] Moreover, half of the children reunified were again later removed and placed in foster care. Thus, even if one overestimates "success" by calling a success any case in which a parent recovers possession of her child and the child does not later return to foster care (thus ignoring cases in which subsequent maltreatment was undetected, cases in which parents later were arrested and went to jail or prison, or abandoned or killed the child, and other cases in which reunification was not in the child's best interests in the long run—e.g., because it involved traumatic separation from foster-care attachment figures), the success rate of this program was only 25 percent.

Notes

1 See, for example, Cosden and Koch (2015, 103) ("the FTDC in this study served families viewed by the courts as having the possibility of reunification within a relatively short window of time (i.e., six months)").
2 See Cosden and Koch (2015, 92).
3 See Vaughan-Eden and Vandervort (2013, 551) (noting the indifference and unwillingness to change among a large portion of parents in child protection cases).
4 Cf. Choi (2012, 458) ("the needs of parents with multiple, chronic, substance abusing prob-lems are less likely met by short-term and time-limited interventions").
5 Either you offer the FDC to everyone and limit the overall pool to those who accept, in which case the ultimate comparison group is likely to resent having the FDC rug pulled out from under them. Or you only offer the FDC to the persons in the FDC group after random assignment, and exclude those who refuse, but then you have no idea which persons in the comparison group would also have declined.
6 Johnson and Candinsky (2014).
7 van Wormer and Hsieh (2016, 55).
8 That three times the percentage of comparison-group parents ended up with a TPR might explain all or most of the huge difference in length of dependency; guardianship with relat-ives is likely to happen quickly, with parental consent and without appeal, because parents deem it far preferable to TPR, whereas TPRs involve a lot of process and are often appealed, and the child will technically be in foster care with a plan of adoption until the TPR is ulti-mately finalized and the court is free to approve the adoption.
9 Brook et al. (2015, 40).
10 Brook et al. (2015, 42).
11 Brook et al. (2015, 44–5).
12 Brook et al. (2015).
13 Brook et al. (2015).
14 Brook et al. (2015, 49) ("These findings add to a growing body of literature, suggesting that FDCs may be better suited for adjudicating child welfare cases involving parental substance abuse").
15 Child and McIntyre (2015, 67–87).
16 Boles et al. (2007, 161–71).
17 Boles et al. (2007, 170).
18 Boles et al. (2007, 169).
19 Boles and Young (2011).

20 Gifford *et al.* (2014, 1663–5).
21 Gifford *et al.* (2014, 1668).
22 Burns *et al.* (2012, 218–30).
23 Burns *et al.* (2012, 220).
24 Burns *et al.* (2012, 221).
25 Burns *et al.* (2012, 222).
26 Burns *et al.* (2012, 223).
27 Burns *et al.* (2012, 225).
28 Burns *et al.* (2012, 226).
29 Chuang *et al.* (2012, 1897).
30 Chuang *et al.* (2012, 1898).
31 Chuang *et al.* (2012, 1899).
32 Chuang *et al.* (2012, 1900).
33 Twomey *et al.* (2010, 23–41).
34 Twomey *et al.* (2010, 31–3).
35 Twomey *et al.* (2010, 34).
36 Twomey *et al.* (2010, 36).
37 Dakof *et al.* (2010, 263–74, 265).
38 Dakof *et al.* (2010, 264).
39 Dakof *et al.* (2010, 269).
40 Dakof *et al.* (2010).
41 Dakof *et al.* (2010, 270).
42 Worcel *et al.* (2008, 427–43, 442).
43 Worcel *et al.* (2008, 434).
44 Worcel *et al.* (2008, 435).
45 Worcel *et al.* (2008, 436).
46 Worcel *et al.* (2008, 439).
47 Worcel *et al.* (2008, 436).
48 Worcel *et al.* (2008, 440).
49 Ashford (2004), 34.

Bibliography

Ashford, José B. "Treating Substance-Abusing Parents: A Study of the Pima County Family Drug Court Approach," *Juvenile and Family Court Journal* 55(4) (2004): 27–37.

Boles, S. and N.K. Young. *Sacramento County Dependency Drug Court Year Eight Outcome and Process Evaluation Findings.* Irvine, CA: Children and Family Futures, 2011.

Boles, S., N. Young, T. Moore, and S. DiPirro-Beard. "The Sacramento Dependency Drug Court: Development and Outcomes," *Child Maltreatment* 12(2) (2007): 161–71.

Brook, Jody, Becci A. Akin, Margaret H. Lloyd, and Yueqi Yan. "Family Drug Court, Targeted Parent Training and Family Reunification: Did this Enhanced Service Strategy Make a Difference?" *Juvenile and Family Court Journal* 66(2) (2015): 35–52.

Burns, Eric J., Michael D. Pullmann, Ericka S. Weathers, Mark L. Wirschem, and Jill K. Murphy. "Effects of a Multidisciplinary Family Treatment Drug Court on Child and Family Outcomes: Results of a Quasi-Experimental Study," *Child Maltreatment* 17(3) (2012): 218–30.

Child, Holly and Dara McIntyre. "Examining the Relationships between Family Drug Court Program Compliance and Child Welfare Outcomes," *Child Welfare* 94(5) (2015): 67–87.

Choi, Sam. "Family Drug Courts in Child Welfare," *Child and Adolescent Social Work Journal* 29(6) (2012): 447–61.

Chuang, Emmeline, Kathleen Moore, Blake Barrett, and M. Scott Young. "Effect of an Integrated Family Dependency Treatment Court on Child Welfare Reunification, Time to Permanency and Re-Entry Rates" *Children and Youth Services Review* 34(9) (2012): 1896–902.

Cosden, Merith and Lauren M. Koch "Changes in Adult, Child, and Family Functioning among Participants in a Family Treatment Drug Court," *Child Welfare* 94(5) (2015): 89–106.

Dakof, Gayle A., Jeri B. Cohen, Craig E. Henderson, Eliette Duarte, Maya Boustani, Audra Blackburn, Ellen Venzer, and Sam Hawes. "A Randomized Pilot Study of the Engaging Moms Program for Family Drug Court," *Journal of Substance Abuse Treatment* 38(3) (2010): 263–74.

Gifford, Elizabeth J., Lindsey Morgan Eldred, Allison Vernerey, and Frank Allen Sloan. "How Does Family Drug Treatment Court Participation Affect Child Welfare Outcomes?" *Child Abuse & Neglect* 38(10) (2014): 1659–70.

Johnson, Alan and Cathy Candinsky. "When Parents Chase Drugs." *The Columbus Dispatch* (June 30, 2014).

Twomey, Jean E., Cynthia Miller-Loncar, Matthew Hinckley, and Barry M. Lester. "After Family Treatment Drug Court: Maternal, Infant, and Permanency Outcomes," *Child Welfare* 89(6) (2010): 23–41.

Van Warmer, Jaqueline and Ming-Li Hsieh. "Healing Families: Outcomes from a Family Drug Treatment Court," *Juvenile and Family Court Journal* 67(2) (2016): 49–65.

Vaughan-Eden, Viola and Frank E. Vandervort. "Invited Commentary on 'Issues in Differential Response'," *Research on Social Work Practice* 23(5) (2013): 550–3.

Worcel, Sonia D., Carrie J. Furrer, Beth L. Green, Scott W.M. Burrus, and Michael W. Finigan. "Effects of Family Treatment Drug Courts on Substance Abuse and Child Welfare Outcomes," *Child Abuse Review* 17 (2008): 427–43.

Index